T0100614

Second Edition

Risk Analysis and Security Countermeasure Selection

Second Edition

Risk Analysis and Security Countermeasure Selection

Thomas L. Norman
CPP/PSP/CSC

CRC Press
Taylor & Francis Group
Boca Raton London New York

CRC Press is an imprint of the
Taylor & Francis Group, an **informa** business

CRC Press
Taylor & Francis Group
6000 Broken Sound Parkway NW, Suite 300
Boca Raton, FL 33487-2742

Printed on acid-free paper
Version Date: 20151204

International Standard Book Number-13: 978-1-4822-4419-9 (Hardback)

Library of Congress Cataloging-in-Publication Data

Norman, Thomas L.
  Risk analysis and security countermeasure selection / Thomas L. Norman. -- Second edition.
    pages cm
  Includes bibliographical references and index.
  ISBN 978-1-4822-4419-9 (hardcover : alk. paper) 1. Security systems. 2. Business
enterprises--Security measures. 3. Office buildings--Security measures. 4. Computer security. 5.
Risk assessment. I. Title.

HV8290.N67 2015
658.4'7--dc23
                                                                                           2015025606

Visit the Taylor & Francis Web site at
http://www.taylorandfrancis.com

and the CRC Press Web site at
http://www.crcpress.com

Dedication

This book is dedicated to the more than 179 people who lost their lives and over 350 who were injured by 10 terrorists in Mumbai, India. The attack began on November 26, 2008, from land and sea and was finally put down on November 29, 2008. Included in the list of those killed was the chief of Mumbai's Anti-Terror Squad, Hemant Karkare. The attacks were a series of coordinated terrorist attacks carried out across Mumbai, India's largest city. Attack sites included Chhatrapati Shivaji Terminus, the Oberoi Trident Hotel, the Taj Mahal Palace and Tower, the Leopold Café, the Cama Hospital, the Orthodox Jewish-owned Nariman House, the Metro Cinema, and areas outside the Times of India Building at St. Xavier's College. There was also a taxi blast at Vile Parle and an explosion at the Mazagaon Docks in Mumbai's port area.

The ten attackers used simple methods, tactics, and weapons (a moving shooter attack) to kill and injure many people. The attack had been predicted for days. The attack took place during the run-up to the Indian parliamentary election cycle.

Although the attack exposed many shortcomings in the Mumbai public security apparatus, there were also great examples of heroism from these fine people.

This was particularly painful for the community, because it shook the Indian psyche and destroyed the feeling of safety and security that had been painstakingly built over several years since several previous major attacks in Mumbai in 2003.

Based on statements by Ajmal Amir, the only terrorist who was captured alive, this horrible crime was spawned by Lashkar-e-Taiba, a foreign terrorist organization operating from within Pakistan, with training and planning help from Al-Qaeda. Some of the attackers came from Pakistan and hijacked an Indian fishing vessel to avoid waterway security.

The immediate goals of the attack were to destroy the Indian community's faith in their security apparatus; to undermine the existing Indian regime; to destabilize relations between India and Pakistan; to encourage the election of more militant Indian parliamentarians with an eye toward further destabilizing Indo-Pakistan relations; to cause India to put pressure on the moderate Pakistani regime, thus undermining their popularity within Pakistan and leading toward regime change there; and to get Pakistan to move its troops from the western borders, where they had been fighting against the Taliban and Al-Qaeda, to strengthen its eastern border with India in anticipation of clashes there, thus relieving the pressure that both Pakistan and the United States had put on the Taliban and Al-Qaeda. The long-term strategic goals appear to be to create chaos and possibly anarchy inside Pakistan in order to effect regime change and thus pave the way for a Taliban-like regime that would gain access to nuclear weapons for the terrorist organizations for use against India and the West.

(Note: Subsequent to writing this Dedication, the Taliban has indeed commenced a strategic push against the Pakistani regime, which, as I write, is being opposed by a major operation by the Pakistani military, displacing tens of thousands in the Federally Administered Tribal Areas, the Swat Valley, and Waziristan.)

I had completed a risk assessment for a major Indian firm only 2 months earlier, which predicted that exactly this kind of attack could take place, as my number one concern.

Effective countermeasures exist for this and numerous other types of terrorist attacks. In the case of moving shooter attacks, the countermeasures are focused on deterrence and active intervention using reactive electronic automated protection systems (REAPSs) to contain the attack and the attackers, thus reducing the possible number of victims and rendering the attackers immobile, making them easy targets for rapid action forces. These should be coupled with off-site command and control capabilities for any Tier 1 terrorist target; these move control of the security system away from the terrorists and give it instead to Special Operations Police Units. (REAPSs are described in detail in my second book, *Integrated Security Systems Design*, Butterworth-Heinemann, 2007). REAPS elements should be accompanied by a commissioning regime of the security system that denies the attackers access to it (which they used effectively to counter police and military responders) and provides that resource remotely to the responders and not the attackers.

There are lessons to be learned from every terrorist attack. The chief lesson from the November 2008 Mumbai attacks is that it is of paramount importance to leave physical, electronic, and operations security to knowledgeable antiterrorism professionals and not to technical firms that may understand electronics but which have no expertise in planning antiterrorism measures. This is especially true when many lives depend on the quality of their ill-conceived and hopelessly inadequate recommendations based solely on their modest knowledge. Having a risk analysis performed and countermeasures developed by unqualified firms is a risky affair with dreadful consequences.

We can do better than this.

Contents

Preface   xxvii

Acknowledgments   xxxi

Author   xxxiii

SECTION I   RISK ANALYSIS

Chapter 1   Risk Analysis: The Basis for Appropriate and Economical Countermeasures   3

For Students Using This Book in an Academic Environment   3

Introduction   3

Critical Thinking   5

Qualitative versus Quantitative Analysis   5

     Required Skills   6

     Tools   8

Theory, Practice, and Tools   8

     Theory   12

     Practice   13

     Tools   15

Organization   16

Summary   17

References   18

Q&A   18

     Questions   18

     Answers   20

Chapter 2   Risk Analysis Basics and DHS-Approved Risk Analysis Methods   21

Introduction   21

U.S. Department of Homeland Security Concerns   21

Risk Analysis for Facilities and Structures   22

Many Interested Stakeholders and Agendas   23

Contents

Commercially Available Software Tools   26
Risk Analysis Basics   26
Risk Assessment Steps   28
   DHS-Approved Risk Assessment Methodologies   30
Which Methodology to Use?   32
   Community versus Facility Methodologies   32
   Strengths and Weaknesses of Major Methodologies   32
   CFATS Information   34
     CSAT Top Screen   34
     CSAT Security Vulnerability Assessment (SVA) 35
Summary   35
   Introduction   35
   Risk Analysis for Facilities and Structures   35
   Many Interested Stakeholders and Agendas   36
   Commercially Available Software Tools   36
   Risk Analysis Basics   36
   Risk Assessment Steps   37
   Which Methodology to Use?   37
   Strengths and Weaknesses of Major Methodologies   37
References   38
Q&A   39
   Questions   39
   Answers   40

Chapter 3   **Risk Analysis Skills and Tools**   41
Introduction   41
Security Risk Analysis Skills   43
Security Risk Analysis Tools   44
   Skill #1: Gathering Data   44
     Interviews   45
     Types of Data Required   45
     Get the Organization's Mission Statement   45
     Understand the Organization's Programs (Business Units) 46
     Assets by Classification   46
     Existing Countermeasures   48
   Skill #2: Research and Evidence Gathering   48
     Interviews   48

Internet Research		51
Telephone Research		53
Records Research		53
Surveys		53
Asset Classifications		54
Historical Data Relating to Security Events		54
Criticalities and Consequences Assessment		55
Bibliography Building		56
Countermeasures Research		56
Skill #3: Critical Thinking in the Risk Analysis Process		57
Skill #4: Quantitative Analysis		57
Skill #5: Qualitative Analysis		58
Converting Quantitative Data into Qualitative Data		59
Skill #6: Countermeasure Selection		59
Countermeasure Selection		59
Cost-Benefit Analysis		60
Skill #7: Report Writing		60
Tools		61
Commercially Available Software Tools		61
Lesser Software Tools		62
Affordable Tools Examples		62
Summary		67
Introduction		67
Tools		68
References		69
Q&A		69
Questions		69
Answers		70
Chapter 4	Critical Thinking and the Risk Analysis Process	71
Introduction		71
Overview of Critical Thinking		71
Importance of Critical Thinking		71
Analysis Requires Critical Thinking		73
The Eight Elements That Make Up the Thinking Process		75
The Concepts, Goals, Principles, and Elements of Critical Thinking		76
Critical Thinking Concepts and Goals		76

Principles   76

Elements of Critical Thinking   77

Purpose   77

The Question at Issue: Most Thinking Is about Problem Solving   78

Understand Our Own and Others' Points of View   78

Gather Assumptions   79

Gather Information   79

Examine the Implications and Possible Consequences Related
to the Issue   80

Determine What Concepts, Theories, Definitions, Axioms, Laws,
Principles and/or Models Are Applicable to the Issue   81

Draw Interpretations, Inferences, and Conclusions from the Data;
Validate the Data; and Formulate Recommendations Based on the
Results   81

Pseudocritical Thinking   82

Intellectual Traits   82

Importance of Integrating Critical Thinking into Everyday Thinking   82

Applying Critical Thinking to Risk Analysis   83

Inductive versus Deductive Reasoning   84

The Analysis Process   85

More about Critical Thinking   85

The Root of Problems   85

Summary   86

References   88

Q&A   88

Questions   88

Answers   90

Chapter 5   Asset Characterization and Identification   91

Introduction   91

Theory   91

Practice   91

Asset List   91

Asset Categorization   92

People   92

Property   92

Proprietary Information   93

Business Reputation   93

Interviews   93

	Facility and Asset List	95
	Research	97
	Surveys	97
Tools		103
Summary		105
	Theory	105
	Practice	105
	Facility and Asset List	106
	Tools	106
Reference		106
Q&A		107
	Questions	107
	Answers	108

Chapter 6   **Criticality and Consequence Analysis**   109

Introduction	109
Twofold Approach	109
Criticality versus Consequence	109
Criticality	110
Visualization	111
Consequence Analysis	112
Building Your Own Criticality/Consequences Matrix	113
Criticality/Consequence Matrix Instructions	113
Summary	117
Criticality	118
Consequence Analysis	118
Q&A	118
Questions	118
Answers	120

Chapter 7   **Threat Analysis**   121

Introduction	121
Theory	121
Threats versus Hazards	121
All-Hazards Risk Analysis	124
Terrorists	126
Economic Criminals	128
Nonterrorist Violent Workplace Criminals	129

Subversives	131
Petty Criminals	132
Design Basis Threat	132
Practice	133
Tools	136
Adversary/Means Matrix	137
Purpose	137
Functions	137
Attributes	137
Example	138
Predictive Threat Assessment	145
Inductive versus Deductive Reasoning	147
Deductive Reasoning	147
Inductive Reasoning	147
Inductive Context	148
Predictive Threat Analysis	148
Predictive Risk Example	148
Summary	149
Threats versus Hazards	149
Design Basis Threat	150
Practice	150
Tools	151
Predictive Threat Assessment	151
References	151
Q&A	153
Questions	153
Answers	154

Chapter 8	Assessing Vulnerability	155
	Introduction	155
	Review of Vulnerability Assessment Model	156
	Define Scenarios and Evaluate Specific Consequences	156
	Asset/Attack Matrix	159
	Threat/Target Nexus Matrix	159
	Weapons/Target Nexus Matrix	162
	Adversary Sequence Diagrams (ASD) and Path Analysis	164
	Surveillance Opportunities Matrix	164

Evaluate Vulnerability 167
    Survey Points 168
    Quantitative Analysis Matrixes 168
    Determine Accessibility 169
    Identify Intrinsic Vulnerabilities 169
    Natural Countermeasures 169
    Evaluate Effectiveness of Existing Security Measures 170
        Physical Countermeasures 170
        Electronic Countermeasures 170
        Operational Countermeasures 171
    Vulnerability Calculation Spreadsheet 171
    Qualitative Analysis Section 171
    Vulnerability Detail Spreadsheet 173
    Vulnerability Detail Matrix 173
Summary 173
    Introduction: Review of Vulnerability Assessment Model 173
    Define Scenarios and Evaluate Specific Consequences 175
    Evaluate Vulnerability 175
    Vulnerability Calculation 176
    Qualitative Analysis Section 176
    Vulnerability Listing 176
References 177
Q&A 177
    Questions 177
    Answers 178

Chapter 9   **Estimating Probability** 179
Introduction 179
    Basic Risk Formula 179
    Likelihood 179
    Terrorism Probability Estimates and Surrogates 181
Resources for Likelihood 181
    Viewing the Range of Possible Threat Actors 181
        Terrorist Threat Actors 181
        Criminal Threat Actors 183
Criminal versus Terrorism Likelihood Resources 184
    General Comparison for Resources 184

Terrorism Asset Target Value Estimates   184
    CARVER+Shock   184
    KSM Asset Target Value Model   185
Criminal Incident Likelihood Estimates   186
    Criminal Statistics   186
    Economic Crime Asset Target Value Estimate   187
    Nonterrorism Violent Crime Asset Target Value Estimate   187
    Petty Crimes Asset Target Value Estimate   188
Summary   189
    Likelihood   189
    Terrorism Asset Target Value Estimates   190
    Criminal Incident Likelihood Estimates   190
        Criminal Statistics   190
        Economic Crime Asset Target Value Estimate   191
        Nonterrorism Violent Crime Asset Target Value Estimate   191
        Petty Crimes Asset Target Value Estimate   191
References   191
Q&A   192
    Questions   192
    Answers   193

Chapter 10   Risk Analysis Process   195
Introduction   195
Objective   195
    Examples   196
    Displaying Risk Formula Results   196
Complete Risk Analysis Process   199
    Probability (Likelihood) Factors   199
    Vulnerability Factors   200
    Consequence Factors   200
Risk Analysis Process   200
    Probability Factors   201
        AO Information   201
        Targeteering Information   201
        Terrorist Group Attack Scenarios   202
Diagram Analysis   203
Asset Target Value Matrixes   203

Probability Summary Matrix 205

Vulnerability Components 205

    Vulnerability Tools 207

    Consequence Components 208

    Risk Formulas 208

    Risk Results (Unranked) 209

Summary 209

    Introduction 209

    Displaying Risk Formula Results 210

    Complete Risk Analysis Process 210

    Probability Factors 211

    Vulnerability Factors 211

    Consequence Factors 211

    Risk Formulas 211

    Risk Results (Unranked) 212

Q&A 212

    Questions 212

    Answers 214

Chapter 11   Prioritizing Risk 215

Introduction 215

Prioritization Criteria 215

Natural Prioritization (Prioritizing by Formula) 216

Prioritization of Risk 216

    Prioritizing by Probability 217

    Prioritizing by Consequences 217

    Prioritizing by Criticality 217

    Prioritizing by Cost 217

        Simple Cost Prioritization 217

        Process-Driven Cost Prioritization 218

Communicating Priorities Effectively 218

    Making the Case 218

    Developing the Arguments 218

Best Practices: Ranking Risk Results 219

    Displaying the Ranked Results as a Visual Graphic 220

Summary 222

    Prioritization Criteria 222

Natural Prioritization (Prioritizing by Formula)   222

Prioritization of Risk   222

Communicating Priorities Effectively   223

    Making the Case   223

Best Practices: Ranking Risk Results   223

Displaying the Ranked Results as a Visual Graphic   223

Q&A   224

    Questions   224

    Answers   225

SECTION II   POLICY DEVELOPMENT BEFORE COUNTERMEASURES

Chapter 12   Security Policy Introduction   229

Introduction   229

Hierarchy of Security Program Development   229

What are Policies, Standards, Guidelines, and Procedures?   230

    Other Key Documents   231

        Standards   231

        Guidelines   231

        Procedures   231

        Position Paper   232

        Guiding Principles   232

    The Key Role of Policies in the Overall Security Program   232

        Policies Define All Other Countermeasures   232

        Legal Challenges   233

        Challenges by Users   233

    Benefits of Having Proper Policies   234

        Control Factors   235

Summary   236

    Hierarchy of Security Program Development   236

    Policies, Standards, Guidelines, and Procedures   236

        Other Key Documents   237

    The Key Role of Policies in the Overall Security Program   237

    Benefits of Having Proper Policies   237

        Control Factors   237

Q&A   238

	Questions	238
	Answers	239
Chapter 13	**Security Policy and Countermeasure Goals**	**241**
	Introduction	241
	Theory	241
	Role of Policies in the Security Program	243
	Role of Countermeasures in the Security Program	244
	Why Should Policies Precede Countermeasures?	247
	Security Policy Goals	248
	Security Countermeasure Goals	249
	Policy Support for Countermeasures	250
	Key Policies	250
	Authorities and Responsibilities	250
	Protection of Life	251
	Special Countermeasures Example	251
	Crime Prevention	252
	Access Control Program	253
	Asset and Property Protection	254
	Individual Responsibilities for Security	255
	Guards	255
	VIP Protection Program	256
	Emergency Security Plans	256
	Summary	257
	Introduction	257
	Questions That Policies Answer	257
	Role of Policies in the Security Program	257
	Role of Countermeasures in the Security Program	258
	Q&A	260
	Questions	260
	Answers	261
Chapter 14	**Developing Effective Security Policies**	**263**
	Introduction	263
	Process for Developing and Introducing Security Policies	263
	Triggers for Policy Changes	263
	Policy Request Review	264
	Policy Impact Statement	264

	Subject Matter Expert and Management Review Process	265
	Policy Requirements	266
	Basic Security Policies	266
	Security Policy Implementation Guidelines	267
	Regulation-Driven Policies	268
	Non-Regulation-Driven Policies	270
	Summary	272
	Process for Developing and Introducing Security Policies	272
	Policy Requirements	273
	Basic Security Policies	273
	Security Policy Implementation Guidelines	273
	Q&A	274
	Questions	274
	Answers	275

SECTION III   COUNTERMEASURE SELECTION AND BUDGETING

Chapter 15	Countermeasure Goals and Strategies	279
	Introduction	279
	Countermeasure Objectives, Goals, and Strategies	280
	Access Control	280
	Goals	280
	Modes	282
	Deterrence	282
	Goals	282
	Strategies	283
	Detection	284
	Goals	284
	Strategies	285
	Surveillance Detection	285
	Attack Detection	285
	Assessment	286
	Goals	286
	Is the Detection Itself Real, False, or a Nuisance Detection?	286
	If the Detection Is Real, What Is the Level and Nature of the Threat Actors?	286
	What Is Their Goal?	286

What Weapons Are They Carrying? 287

What Are Their Tactics? 287

Could Their Intentions Include Violence? 287

Are They Employing Countersurveillance Methods? 287

How Are They Dressed? How Can Law Enforcement Distinguish the Threat Actors from Ordinary Employees or Customers? 287

What Is Their Apparent Exit Strategy? 287

Strategies 287

Response 288

Goals 288

Strategies 288

Evidence Gathering 289

Goals 289

Strategies 289

Comply with The Business Culture of the Organization 290

Goal 290

Strategies 291

Minimize Impediments to Normal Business Operations 291

Goals 291

Strategies 291

Safe and Secure Environment 292

Goals 292

Strategies 292

Design Programs to Mitigate Possible Harm from Hazards and Threat Actors 292

Summary 292

Introduction 292

Access Control 293

Goals 293

Strategies 293

Deterrence 294

Goals 294

Strategies 294

Detection 294

Goals 294

Strategies 294

Assessment 295

	Goals	295
	Strategies	295
	Response	295
	Goals	295
	Strategies	295
	Evidence Gathering	296
	Goals	296
	Strategies	296
	Comply with the Business Culture of the Organization	296
	Goal	296
	Strategies	296
	Minimize Impediments to Normal Business Operations	297
	Goals	297
	Strategies	297
	Safe and Secure Environment	297
	Goals	297
	Strategies	297
	Design Programs to Mitigate Possible Harm from Hazards and Threat Actors	297
	Reference	297
	Q&A	298
	Questions	298
	Answers	299
Chapter 16	**Types of Countermeasures**	301
	Introduction	301
	Baseline Security Program	301
	Typical Baseline Security Program Elements and Implementation	302
	Designing Baseline Countermeasures (and Qualifications)	303
	Qualifications	303
	Design Process	303
	Specific Countermeasures	304
	Countermeasure Selection Basics	305
	High-Tech Elements	305
	Access Control Systems	305
	Detection Systems	311
	Consoles and Management Offices	322
	Security System Archiving Technologies	323

Security System Archiving Schemes		325
Security System Infrastructures		326
Low-Tech Elements		328
Locks		328
Revolving Doors		329
Mechanical and Electronic Turnstiles		329
Vehicle Gates		330
Deployable Barriers		330
Lighting		330
Signage		331
No-Tech Elements		332
Define the Deterrence Program		332
Define the Response Program		336
Define the Evidence Gathering Program		338
Summary		338
Introduction		338
Baseline Security Program (BSP)		339
Specific Countermeasures		339
Countermeasure Selection Basics		339
References		340
Q&A		340
Questions		340
Answers		342
Chapter 17	Countermeasure Selection and Budgeting Tools	343
Introduction		343
The Challenge		343
Countermeasure Effectiveness		344
Functions of Countermeasures		344
Examples		344
Infiltration Scenarios		346
Attack Scenarios		346
Attack Objective Parameters		348
Specific Targeting Objectives		349
Criminal Violent Offender Types		349
Mentally Unstable Offenders		349
Economic Criminal Types		350

Economic Criminal Objectives   350

Criminal Offender Countermeasures   351

Countermeasure Effectiveness Metrics: Functional Effectiveness   352

Helping Decision Makers Reach Consensus on Countermeasure
Alternatives   353

Summary   354

Introduction   354

Countermeasure Effectiveness   354

Functions of Countermeasures   354

Infiltration Scenarios   354

Attack Scenarios   355

Attack Objective Parameters   355

General Objectives of Terrorism   355

Specific Targeting Objectives   355

Offender Types   356

Criminal Violent Offender Types   356

Economic Criminal Types   356

Economic Criminal Objectives   356

Criminal Offender Countermeasures   356

Countermeasure Effectiveness Metrics   356

Functional Effectiveness   356

Helping Decision Makers Reach Consensus on Countermeasure
Alternatives   357

Q&A   357

Questions   357

Answers   358

Chapter 18   Security Effectiveness Metrics   359

Introduction   359

Theory   359

Sandia Model   359

A Useful Commercial Model   361

What Kind of Information Do We Need to Evaluate to Determine
Security Program Effectiveness?   366

What Kind of Metrics Can Help Us Analyze Security Program
Effectiveness?   367

Adversary Sequence Diagrams   368

Vulnerability/Countermeasure Matrix   369

Security Event Logs 374

Patrol Logs (Vulnerabilities Spotting/Violations Spotting) 374

Annual Risk Analysis 375

Summary 375

Introduction 375

Sandia Model 375

A Useful Commercial Model 376

What Kind of Metrics Can Help Us Analyze Security Program
Effectiveness? 377

Security Event Logs 377

Patrol Logs (Vulnerabilities Spotting/Violations Spotting) 377

Annual Risk Analysis 378

References 378

Q&A 378

Questions 378

Answers 379

Chapter 19   Cost-Effectiveness Metrics   381

Introduction 381

What Are the Limitations of Cost-Effectiveness Metrics? 382

What Metrics Can Be Used to Determine Cost-Effectiveness? 386

Communicating Priorities Effectively 389

Making the Case 389

Developing the Arguments 390

Presenting the Case 391

Basis of Argument 391

Countering Arguments 392

Complete Cost-Effectiveness Matrix 393

Complete Cost-Effectiveness Matrix Elements 393

Security Program Recommendations Summary Board 396

Vertical and Horizontal Elements 396

Vertical Elements 396

Horizontal Elements 396

Risk Descriptions 398

Countermeasure Options and Cost Elements 398

Countermeasure Mitigation Values 398

Risk Rankings and Budgets 398

Phase Recommendations and Phasing Budgets   398

Budget Breakdowns by Phases and Risks   403

Summary   406

Introduction   406

What Are the Limitations of Cost-Effectiveness Metrics?   406

What Metrics Can Be Used to Determine Cost-Effectiveness?   406

Communicating Priorities Effectively   407

Making the Case   407

Q&A   408

Questions   408

Answers   409

Chapter 20   Writing Effective Reports   411

Introduction   411

Presentation   412

Graphics   412

Preparation for a Successful Presentation   412

Comprehensive Risk Analysis Report   415

Executive Summary   415

Introduction   416

Assessment Process   416

Facility Characterization   416

Threat Assessment   417

Vulnerability Assessment   418

Asset/Attack Matrix   419

Threat/Target Nexus Matrix   419

Weapon/Target Nexus Matrix   419

Surveillance Opportunities   420

Likelihood (Probability) Calculation   420

Risk Calculation   420

Countermeasures   421

Baseline Security Program   421

Identifying Key Assets for Special Consideration   422

Develop Countermeasure Budgets   423

Countermeasure Implementation Recommendations   423

Report Supplements   424

Risk Register   424

Footnotes   424

Tables   424

Index and Glossary   426

Attachments   426

Countermeasure Budget Presentation   426

Microsoft PowerPoint Presentation   426

Handouts for the Presentation   427

Summary   427

Comprehensive Report   427

Countermeasure Budgets   427

PowerPoint Presentation   427

Handouts for Presentation   428

Presentation   428

Graphics   428

Preparation for a Successful Presentation   428

Comprehensive Risk Analysis Report   429

Executive Summary   429

Introduction   429

Assessment Process   429

Facility Characterization   429

Threat Assessment   430

Vulnerability Assessment   430

Risk Calculation   430

Countermeasures   430

Countermeasure Budgets   431

Countermeasure Implementation Recommendations   431

Report Supplements   431

Q&A   432

Questions   432

Answers   433

Index   435

Preface

When people ask me how long I have been in security consulting, I usually tell them that I have been working in the security industry since before electricity. It has been over 35 years now and as an old guy, I have seen a lot of things. The security industry is simply fascinating. There are few human endeavors that bring together sociology, economics, psychology, technology, architecture, landscaping, project management, engineering, critical thinking game theory, and logic into one big bowl of soup. I love this industry.

I have watched the industry grow and mature from a general lack of awareness of security, on the part of most of the public and corporate management, to a current state where there is a heightened sense of security among many public and private sectors. Governments have always been aware of security, as they are prone to trying to protect themselves against all kinds of threats. Since September 11, 2001, I have seen a fundamental shift in security awareness that is refreshing, startling, and concerning all at the same time.

I see a desire to look at security as more of a business unit, in a more professional and methodical way (that is good). There is also a tendency to treat every facility as a potential terrorist target, often wasting the organization's resources on facilities that terrorists have no history of targeting and which do not fit the strategic objectives of any known terrorist organization (not so good). My kudos go to the New York City Police Department for their important work in this area.

Most organizations today want a risk analysis before committing resources to solutions (also good). However, the industry is now fraught with "consultants" who have little if any formal training or education and who often propose their company's products or services as the obvious solution. Oddly, a single organization can go to several different security vendors (dogs, guards, systems, investigators) and get answers from each vendor—which is that it is the specific vendor's products or services that the organization needs the most. This is not consulting. This is predatory behavior by self-interested vendors, which is above the interests of their clients. This is also not a display of any functioning concern for the lives of the people who dwell in the organization's buildings. Uniquely, these firms who employ "consultants" with little or no real knowledge about risk almost always charge little or nothing for their consulting efforts, and it is easily worth the cost (little or nothing).

This is sad and unfortunate and I think almost criminal, as people's lives and livelihoods are at great risk when poor risk analysis is employed. These organizations would not hire a physician, accountant, structural engineer, or architect without credentials, yet they will often hire anyone who has the word "consultant" on his or her business card, with no check of qualifications whatsoever.

Risk analysis is heady stuff. A good risk analysis is a marvelous thing. It enlightens, it informs, it educates, and it illuminates the vague into the clear. It helps management organize its thinking into clear and obvious action, properly prioritized, with precious organizational resources spent on the least-cost, most-effective solutions. Poor risk analysis results in vague programs with no clear direction or purpose and no metrics for measurement. What other business unit could operate in such darkness?

I have read many books on risk analysis, but I have never read one "risk analysis" book that teaches the process of analysis.* All these books talk about security principles. Most discuss methodologies. Some teach how to conduct interviews and surveys and write reports. I have not read one that teaches analytical skills. Perhaps there is one, but I have not seen it. I think a book on risk analysis should leave the reader understanding what analysis is and what it is not, and teach the ideas, principles, elements, and process.

There are many software tools to assist in risk analysis, but only a few are analytical in nature. Most are checklists that leave a sense of protection while actually offering little insight into risk. Some of the software tools create vast lists that are impressive in weight but do not categorize, sort, or present the data in any meaningful way. Others are so scant that they can hardly be called tools at all. Still, they present themselves in the market as useful tools.

There are also a number of approved risk analysis methodologies. I have used many models (including the Central Intelligence Agency model) promoted by the U.S. Armed Forces, the U.S. Department of State, the Department of Justice, the Federal Emergency Management Agency, and the Department of Homeland Security (DHS), and models created by Sandia National Laboratories, along with others. There are methodologies that are particular to specific industries—water departments, high-rise office buildings, oil/gas/chemical facilities, pipelines, railroads, bridges, government buildings, prisons, and so forth. The DHS has an evolving list of approved methodologies that apply to various types of facilities and industries, all of which are valuable.

It can be confusing for an aspiring security practitioner to try and understand all of these ideas and to master even some of all the software tools and methodologies. So how is one to wade through all this and find the way? I have used both the great and small in my long career. I have read hundreds of security books, used software tools that cost thousands of dollars, and used tools that were free. I have found all somewhat useful and have learned much from each experience.

Years ago, when I first began consulting, I was confronted by various client accounting departments demanding that specific information be presented with my invoices. I found this time-consuming, confounding, and downright unproductive to collect all these data and present them to each client according to their specific procedures. In many ways, the DHS-approved list of methodologies is much like that. All methodologies require much of the same information, presented in much the same way, but with slight variations in data collection, processing, and presentation.

I solved my accounting dilemma by looking at the worst case of what every client was asking for (including my most demanding client, an agency of the U.S. government), and then I developed a time-keeping and accounting system that presented all the information they asked for, every time, for every invoice. I never received one complaint from any of my clients after that. As a result, my efficiency immediately increased, because I no longer had to keep different time and expense records for each client. I spent less time doing more. It was an important lesson that has served me well in my career. Do the best for everyone, and one can do more for everyone with much less effort than creating a unique

---

* There is one book on "vulnerability" that does teach analysis: *Vulnerability Assessment of Physical Protection Systems* by Mary Lynn Garcia[1]. Mary Lynn Garcia is a light in the wilderness.

program for each. It is the commoditization of data services to the best advantage for stakeholders and clients, as well as the consultant.

Over the years, I have developed a process of risk analysis (not itself an actual methodology) that is scientific, methodical, extensively thorough, and one that I believe fits the requirements of every methodology approved by the DHS. Where most analysts consider perhaps a hundred points of analysis, this process considers many thousands. This process takes into account every requirement of every major risk analysis methodology and pretty much fulfills the requirements of them all. Thus, in one single approach, one can easily move from reviewing water facilities to liquefied natural gas terminals, to retail malls, to airports, to hotels, to office towers, and to entire cities. Over the years, I have developed a reputation as a consultant who produces astonishingly complete reports at highly competitive rates. I have been asked to teach this approach by other colleagues and have been pleased to do so. Even though most consultants diligently try to conceal their methods, I have always believed in teaching. After my second book, *Integrated Security Systems Design* (Butterworth-Heinemann, 2007), which taught security-system design in a new, thorough, and comprehensible way, I received many requests from colleagues to write another book to present risk analysis in the same way.

This approach is both thorough and fast and can produce results that can usually fit the requirements of almost every major risk analysis methodology. In the same amount of time that others take to create mediocre work, you can easily produce a risk analysis that is unbelievably comprehensive. This methodology also produces the holy grail of budgeting. That is, it creates budgets that are prioritized by relative effectiveness and relative risk. It creates budgets that allow management to clearly see what and how to prioritize the organization's assets in the most effective way. You can also do this. By reading this book, you will learn what many security practitioners for many years thought was impossible—to produce a risk analysis that accurately estimates and presents the risks of all threats and budgets that are supported by both effectiveness and cost-effectiveness calculations.

This book provides insight into threat actors of all types that is unavailable from any other single source. It is organized in a way that conveys meaning, not just information. You will learn more from this book than from any other book on the subject of risk analysis, including, and most importantly, how to actually perform risk analysis, a subject that one would think would be the keystone of every book on the subject but which for a number of reasons is simply missing from virtually every other risk analysis book.

This book will open your eyes not only to risk analysis, but most likely to a whole new way of thinking.

Now, begin reading. Begin learning the amazing art of critical thinking and how to apply it to the very important task of risk analysis. Then, get ready to create the most comprehensive and easy-to-understand risk assessments you ever thought possible.

REFERENCE

1. Garcia, M. L. 2005. *Vulnerability Assessment of Physical Protection Systems.* Butterworth-Heinemann, Oxford.

Acknowledgments

I am deeply thankful to my very lovely wife, Dr. Nadia Norman, who has retired from a lifelong career in medicine, and who endured endless hours of my absence while I completed the second edition of this book.

I am thankful to my adopted home of Beirut, Lebanon, and my wonderful business associates, Cheikh Nabil el Khazen and Mr. Adel Mardelli, for 15 years of constant encouragement and support, especially for their support for my efforts toward perfection in the craft of risk analysis and security systems design.

I am also grateful to my business associates Mr. Benjamin Butchko, CPP; Mr. Charles Goslin, CPP, CISSP; Ms. Megan Bradley; and Mr. Michael Newsome (Butchko, Inc.), who I work with enjoyably every day in Houston, Texas.

Both teams, in Beirut and Houston, are dream teams in terms of qualifications, consideration, professionalism, and kindness.

I am grateful for the review and guiding comments on the manuscript by Ben Butchko and Charles Goslin. Additional thanks to Mr. Malcom Nance, Mr. David Moore, CPP (Acutech Consulting Group); Mr. Ross Johnson, CPP (ASIS International); and Ms. Mary Lynn Garcia (Sandia National Labs) for their excellent and groundbreaking work in this subject field.

I am grateful to Mr. Mark Listewnick and Ms. Jennifer Abbott, from Taylor & Francis Group (CRC Press), for their constant encouragement and patience. Thanks to Mark for seeking me out to write the first edition and to Jennifer who guided me flawlessly through the second edition.

I am endlessly grateful to ASIS International, the Petroleum, Chemical and Extraction Technologies (PCE) Council, and Mr. Ross Johnson, CPP (who chairs that council), for their important support of the entire security industry and whose encouragement to aspiring industry professionals helps them to grow and culture their skills.

I am grateful to the many consultants and security practitioners who have picked my brain and encouraged me to write this book about risk analysis, and to the many readers of my articles and books who send e-mails and letters encouraging me to write more and asking for expansions on what I have written. It is for you that I write.

I am thankful to the security industry for tempting a poor wayward young audio designer to forsake his career in commercial audio systems and move over to a far more rewarding career in security.

For each of those above, I am humbled by their encouragement and kindness, without whom this book would never have been written.

Author

Thomas L. Norman, CPP/PSP/CSC, is an internationally acclaimed security risk management consultant with experience in the United States, the Middle East, Europe, Africa, and Asia. As the author of the industry reference manual on integrated security system design, and with more than 35 years of experience in design, construction management, and commissioning, Mr. Norman is one of the industry's leading design consultants, worldwide. Mr. Norman has developed formulas and detailed processes that are used by the entire security industry to calculate the effectiveness of security programs and security program elements and also overall security program cost-effectiveness. Mr. Norman has authored five books and coauthored two others (for the American Institute of Architects; *Security Planning and Design: A Guide for Architects and Building Owners*; *Integrated Security Systems Design*, first and second editions; *Risk Analysis and Security Countermeasures Selection*, first and second editions; the latest ASIS International Physical Security Professional (PSP) certification study materials; and *Electronic Access Control*. Mr. Norman's works have been quoted and referenced by organizations such as the Cato Institute, National Broadcasting Company (NBC), and Security Management.

Risk Analysis

CHAPTER 1

Risk Analysis
The Basis for Appropriate and Economical Countermeasures

FOR STUDENTS USING THIS BOOK IN AN
ACADEMIC ENVIRONMENT

Although many colleges and universities around the world have used this book to teach risk analysis, this book was originally written as a reference manual for professional security practitioners. The book is written in an engaging, first-person approach, rather than in normal dry textbook style. The book employs stories from my experience and offers insight and opinions. As such, it will be a different and hopefully more interesting reading experience than other textbooks you may have encountered.

INTRODUCTION

With the exception of militaries and nongovernmental organizations (NGOs), such as peacekeeping organizations, most organizations seek to fulfill their mission by positioning themselves in an area of need for which they have expertise to offer, and otherwise seek to avoid risk and to benefit from positive political, business, social, and economic trends. The most successful organizations do this not intuitively but analytically, annually reviewing their situation with respect to industry and market trends, to economic trends, and to business, political, and security risks.

As the world becomes increasingly volatile in all of these areas, the skillful analysis and reporting of these issues becomes increasingly critical to the success of organizations of all types.

But sadly, my experience indicates that many organizations employ vaguely defined security programs that often attempt to protect unknown vulnerabilities from unknown threats. Still, today, many organizations do not employ reliable risk assessment methods to establish their security programs. We often see countermeasure programs employed with no security policies whatsoever to support the programs. This results in uncoordinated, often purposeless countermeasures that are a waste of money. This is the result of tactical rather than strategic thinking, solving a problem while often creating others; it is similar to constructing a building with only a cursory understanding of its purpose.

Often, countermeasures are poorly conceived, protecting the organization against risks that are only assumed and for which no empirical data exist. This blundering approach would not be tolerated in any other business unit of the organization. But because management may often base their decisions on hastily and poorly prepared risk assessments (or also commonly base them simply on a vague description of a specific threat that must be addressed), such decisions are based on assumptions rather than facts and clearly drawn analysis-based conclusions.

Many organizations believe that they cannot afford any risk assessment and base their security programs entirely on the ill-advised judgments of single (often totally unqualified) individuals. I often hear that management does not wish to spend funds to study risk. But the same management is willing to spend far larger amounts to protect the organization against some unknown risk. This would not happen in any other business unit. Just as bad are organizations that utilize a risk assessment offered by a contractor or vendor, which (quite unsurprisingly) usually finds a compelling need for large expenditures on that vendor's own products or services.

There are many reasons for this, but most derive from the fact that security risk assessment is still a black art to some, less science than voodoo. Many methodologies are applied using a series of assumptions instead of analysis, and many security managers are not truly well grounded in the science of risk assessment. As in any discipline, one can only be effective in one's job if one is very well grounded in the basic principles of the discipline.

Let me make the case here that any security professional who is not extremely well grounded in risk analysis is handicapped in every other portion of the security profession. Risk assessment is the foundational skill of all other security skills. It is like basic math to accounting, finance, or science. It is like grammar and vocabulary to a historian, author, or journalist. It is like critical thinking and debate to policy makers. Any security professional who is not extremely well grounded in risk assessment can simply not succeed well in his or her own career or well serve the organization he/she works for in any security role.

This is because everything else in a security program derives from the risk analysis process. The countermeasure selection process, operational decisions, staff deployment, the use of electronic solutions, the development of policies and procedures, training, liaison with local authorities, emergency preparedness, and indeed everything else is founded on security risk analysis. So the quality of every downline decision is affected by the quality of that person's skills in risk analysis.

Without the insight into risk that that skill gives, every other decision is based on assumptions founded on ignorance instead of qualitative insight. A decision that may appear to be tactically correct to a security supervisor may in fact be strategically inept. The supervisor may not possess the risk analysis skills to understand the threat environment or to see vulnerabilities that would be immediately apparent to a skilled risk analyst. So he orders a guard to ignore his patrol in order to make an appearance when the chairman will be passing by in order to give an appearance of better security. Skilled threat actors will see this habit and plan their operation to exploit this vulnerability.

Any risk assessment done by anyone who is not well grounded in the fundamentals of risk assessment will by definition be an incompetent risk assessment and may instead actually insert additional risk into the countermeasures program through ill-advised recommendations.

Any risk assessment done by a contractor or vendor whose recommendations include needs for their services or products is, by nature, inherently full of conflicts of interest and cannot be trusted. This is especially true in cases where the cost of the risk assessment is nil or substantially less than one performed by a competent risk analyst. In almost every case where I have seen a risk assessment performed by a contractor or vendor, the "analyst" had few qualifications, or none whatsoever. Many are done by individuals who have attended many seminars on sales techniques but few, if any, seminars on risk analysis. During one vendor risk analysis presentation a client invited me to attend, I asked the vendor what risk analysis methodology they used to reach these conclusions. The vendor asked what I meant by the term "risk analysis methodology"! These contractors and vendors do a terrible disservice to their clients and may be exposing themselves to very high legal liability.

Now the good news. When you finish reading this book, you *will* be well grounded in the foundations of the process of risk analysis conforming to common U.S. Department of Homeland Security (DHS) requirements. You will be able to provide a quality report with convincing arguments and findings, with countermeasure selections that are reasonable and cost effective, and with the evidence to back up your claims.

This is the book for organizations that need a world-class risk assessment but cannot budget the $100,000+ that some consultants charge or even the $10,000+ that some better risk assessment software costs. This is the book that teaches how to equal or better those results with only your time and basic spreadsheet and word-processing software. You will do that because you will learn the analysis skills necessary to accomplish the task, develop the tools to analyze and develop a report at a level of depth that few others can equal at any price, and learn how to present those data in a form that anyone can understand.

This book discusses the various risk analysis methodologies currently used by the DHS and helps the reader to understand which of these is the best to use for a particular type of facility.

CRITICAL THINKING

No other risk assessment book that I have read teaches the process of critical thinking, which is a *required skill* for correct analysis of any kind. Critical thinking is not taught in most high schools, colleges, and universities, except at the most cursory level. A California study on the role of critical thinking in the curricula of 38 public and 28 private universities concluded that the skill of critical thinking is "clearly an honorific phrase in the minds of most educators."[1] The study concluded that university faculty members "feel obliged to claim both familiarity with it and commitment to it in their teaching, despite the fact that … most have only a vague understanding of what it is and what is involved in bringing it successfully into instruction." Indeed, the authors of the study found that while 89% of the faculty interviewed "claimed critical thinking was the primary objective of their instruction," only 19% could define the term and only 9% were evidently using it on a daily basis in their instruction.[2] Critical thinking is a required skill for risk analysis, despite the fact that most security industry books do not teach the skill and very, very few security consultants seem to understand or use the practice in the development of their risk assessments. You will learn the fundamentals of critical thinking in this book.

QUALITATIVE VERSUS QUANTITATIVE ANALYSIS

There are two main schools of risk analysis report writing: quantitative and qualitative. Qualitative analysis involves interpreting interviews, words, and images; and quantitative analysis involves interpreting numbers from data and estimates. In simple terms, qualitative analysis is intuitive, and quantitative analysis is mathematical. Qualitative reports tend to be wordy and require extensive reading, while quantitative reports tend to be full of charts, graphs, and tables and can be equally laborious to digest. In the hands of highly skilled analysts, qualitative reports can be a thing of beauty, and it is very obvious whether a qualitative report was written by an experienced analyst because the skill of the analyst emerges obviously through his/her reports as, equally, the lack of skill emerges from unskilled and inexperienced analysts. It is often more difficult to see the experience level in quantitative reports, and it can be difficult to judge the quality of the analysis in these reports. It is entirely possible to generate a quantitative report that is of poor quality if simple data crunching takes place in the absence of good analytical skills. Which method is better? I say, both. By that, I do not mean that they are equally valuable; I mean that a thorough analysis should use both qualitative and quantitative analysis. This book teaches a process that combines both into a very thorough analysis process that guides the analyst to the correct results. To the best of my knowledge, this process complies with all of the DHS-approved methodologies.

This book will provide you with the skills and the tools to perform risk analysis and to create reports using a superset of one of the most powerful risk assessment methodologies available. Your analysis will be more complete, with many more points of analysis than the large majority of professional security consultants, and your reports will also be more organized and easy to read and have much more depth than many security consulting firms that charge over $100,000 for their reports. You will not only learn all the fundamentals of the science of risk analysis, but you will also have learned the skills for analysis, including research and reference, analysis, and presentation. You will also learn how to build and use your own skills and tools:

Required Skills

- Skill #1: How to gather data (Figure 1.1)
  - Planning
  - Interviews
  - Research
  - Asset classifications
  - Criticalities
  - Consequences
- Skill #2: Research and evidence gathering
  - Internet research
  - Telephone research

FIGURE 1.1   Interview.

- Bibliography building
- Countermeasures research
- Skill #3: Critical thinking in the risk analysis process
  - Maintaining focus on purpose: Why examine this? What is the issue at hand?
  - Identifying key questions to be answered in the analysis
  - Observing and understanding the implications of different points of view
  - Examining evidence and its implications for the analysis
  - Drawing inferences from the evidence
  - Concepts affecting the evidence:
    - What theories, definitions, axioms, laws, and principles or models underlie the issue?
    - What is the reliability of the evidence?
    - What are the effects of personal prejudices on the reliability of inferences?
    - What are the assumptions and what is their effect on risk conclusions?
  - Drawing implications on the consequences of the risk: What might happen and what does happen?
- Skill #4: Quantitative analysis
  - Data classifications
  - Data input
  - Data crunching
  - Risk analysis results calculations
- Skill #5: Qualitative analysis
  - Survey-based qualitative comments
  - Converting quantitative data into qualitative data
  - Qualitative analysis
    - Providing context for the quantitative analysis
    - Combining qualitative data with quantitative data in order to improve the quality of the analysis
    - What to do with data that "doesn't fit"
- Skill #6: Countermeasures selection
  - Countermeasures selection
  - Cost–benefit analysis
- Skill #7: Report writing (Figure 1.2)

FIGURE 1.2 Quantitative analysis.

- Report organization
- Expanding and explaining quantitative data
- Writing qualitative sections
- Writing the recommendations
- Writing the executive summary
- Addendums

Tools

This book also presents the essential tools to produce world-class risk analysis reports. These include

- Tool #1: The elements of a high-quality risk analysis report
- Tool #2: The risk analysis tool
- Tool #3: The countermeasure options analysis tool
- Tool #4: The countermeasure decision matrix (Figure 1.3)

Furthermore, the book provides the reader with these technical tools, which are available at virtually no cost (assuming the reader already owns a word processor and spreadsheet program), and these tools rival or exceed the effectiveness of some of the most expensive risk analysis programs available in the marketplace today. Some of those software programs cost up to $6000 (including training). For the price of this book, you may be able to exceed the results of those programs.

THEORY, PRACTICE, AND TOOLS

This book will explain each element of risk analysis and countermeasure selection in terms of its theory, practice, and tools. The reader can use any good commercial risk analysis software. Additionally, for those readers who do not have the budget for such software, the book will explain in adequate detail how to assemble spreadsheets for each element. These descriptions are specific enough that they can be used with any commercial or open-source spreadsheet program. MS Excel is used as an example. Those readers who prefer to use a commercial software tool may skip the sections explaining how to build the Excel spreadsheets. For those who are interested in building and using their own world-class risk analysis software tool, the first two tabs on the spreadsheets are explained in cell-by-cell detail and after that in adequate detail to build the remaining sheets. Let me emphasize that this book is *not* about how to use spreadsheets to do risk analysis. It *is* a book that teaches comprehensive risk analysis in a variety of forms, and it provides an application example of how to do this on spreadsheets only as a courtesy for those readers who do not have the budget for a multi-thousand-dollar piece of software. Regardless of the tool used, the principles taught in this book stand alone, with or without the example.

The process fully complies with every accepted risk assessment methodology in use today and generally exceeds all of them in pure depth of analysis (the lone exception being the Sandia team process, which stands alone as the pinnacle of risk assessment, although it is completely unaffordable for almost all commercial applications). For affordable processes, those taught in this book represent the peak of the risk assessment industry.

Our Lady of Perpetual Funding—Medical Center
Security Landscaping and Fencing
Decision Matrix

Goals Description

1 To Deny Access to Nonauthorized Persons to Parking Areas
2 To Create a Pleasant and Visually Pleasing Environment
3 Cost-Effectiveness Based on Goals and Threats Mitigated or Eliminated
4 Convenience for Employees
5 Conformance to Business Culture
6 Conformance to Aesthetic Values

Risks Description

A Harmless Unvetted Visitor: No criminal intent
B Unauthorized Visitor Having No Business with BMC—Possible criminal actor based on crimes of opportunity
C Property Criminal: Nonviolent criminal intent directed at property crimes only
D Personal or Sexual Attack Criminal—Nonvictim-specific violent crime with intent to compel property or induce victim to comply with sexual attack
E Workplace Violence Visitor: Victim-specific violent crime which sometimes escalates to include violent attacks against innocent coworkers and Law Enforcement ***

Methods	Goals Achieved						Risks Mitigated					Score	Rank	Risks Accepted					Estimated Cost	Effectiveness
	1	2	3	4	5	6	A	B	C	D	E			A	B	C	D	E		
Fence Entire Property with Gates at Major Road Entrances only *	1			1	1		1	1	1	1	1	7	2					•	$400,000	High
Fence Parking Lots and Garage Only **		1	1	1	1		1					4	3		•	•	•	•	$150,000	Low
Use Landscaping Only to Create a Barrier to Unwanted Visitors			1	1	1	1	1	1				3	4		•	•	•	•	$400,000	Low
Use Landscaping and Fencing to Enclose Property and Deny Access Except at Major Road Entrances Only.*	1	1	1	1	1	1	1	1	1	1	1	10	1	•					$500,000	High

Notes:

Score is based on highest number of goals achieved and threats mitigated or eliminated.

Rank is based on highest score.

Final *Estimated Cost* numbers may be lower than estimates on revolving doors

* Assumes guard house at major road entrances.

** Assumes no guard houses at any entrance.

*** Workplace violence threat actors cannot be easily identified at the perimeter. None of these options is an effective deterrent.

(Decision Matrix is a PPI Best Practices Tool)

FIGURE 1.3   Decision matrix.

The processes discussed herein will demystify risk and move the reader from the tactical to the strategic; from being reactive to being proactive.

- Who should read this book?
  - You should. If you are reading this now, it is almost certainly because you have been asked to perform a risk analysis and are trying to make certain that the risk analysis report will be thorough and accurate and result in effective and affordable recommendations. You no doubt have a background in security manpower management or some aspect of security technology. In some cases, the reader may be an architectural professional who has been asked to take security measures into consideration. In every case, you will be a person who wants to assure the success of your project. This book will help you do that.
- Why should you read this book?
  - Part of what is confusing about risk analysis to most security professionals is that there is no unique way to analyze risk. Dozens of methodologies exist, from simple checklists to highly structured and detailed methodologies that can cost millions to fully implement for a megaorganization. The DHS alone references over a dozen different methodologies at the time of this writing. Which methodology is the correct one to use? How do we select it? How do we defend the choice?
  - Once a risk analysis methodology is selected and implemented, how do we select appropriate countermeasures? These questions often confound even veteran security professionals, who often end up advancing a tried and true method they have used for years in lieu of one possibly more appropriate. In Chapters 15 through 19, we will discuss various types of security countermeasures and how to select which one(s) to use for any particular project.
- How can I be sure that I will really learn the principles of risk analysis from this book?
  - This book uses a convention that absolutely works, which is the repetition of important principles. You will find that the book introduces a subject early in the book and then, as you progress through the book, that same principle will be illustrated again in many different ways as other principles are explained. All of the principles of risk analysis are related, like the parts of an engine. One cannot understand the role of pistons without understanding the role of the cylinders and crankshaft. The same applies to risk analysis. Probability, vulnerability, and consequences are highly interrelated, as are their constituent components. As we explore the role of vulnerability, we will revisit the role of assets and threats. As we explore assets, we will see a prelude to the discussion on criticality and consequences. You will understand these principles because they are not just visited once but are explored in many different ways as they relate to each other.

From a general standpoint, all good risk analysis methodologies have two main sections:

- Analyze risks
- Recommend countermeasures to mitigate the risks

The risk analysis portions of all good risk analysis methodologies have certain things in common:

- They begin the process of risk analysis by reviewing the organization's assets.
- Then they review threats (and probabilities).
- Then they review vulnerabilities.
- Then they calculate risks.

Certain risk analysis methodologies, notably ASME RAMCAP* and DHS CFATS,† rely on threat-assessment results from government sources.

Subsequently, all better risk analysis methodologies also delve into countermeasures selection. It is also customary to develop budgets for the countermeasures.

This is where risk mitigation programs often fall apart however. Most budgeting programs are pretty basic. The more advanced methodologies still only offer "good, better, best" options for mitigating specific risks without much detail on why one is good, another is better, and one is best. This causes two main problems: (1) The vagaries of that approach do not provide useful data on why one approach is better than another, and (2) that approach does not provide the organization's security program advocate with much useful data to support him or her in putting their case to the management or budgeting authorities from whom monies to implement the security programs will be sourced.

Any analysis should result in countermeasure recommendations that can convincingly make the case that actual risk mitigation can occur at a cost that is affordable to the operation of the organization. If not, how can an organization's budgeting committee be expected to part with funds for unknown results?

How do "good, better, best" relate to cost-effectiveness? Does "best" reduce the possibility of risks occurring by a multiple of the cost of the mitigation? Are there any metrics whatsoever? Often the answer is "No" or "I don't know," and the response from management is not surprisingly often "Hell no!" Thus, the entire risk assessment exercise gets laid aside, with only a few uncoordinated, scattered programs or applications being implemented; these are often the least cost effective, the most common being the implementation of incomplete and poorly planned electronic security systems. As a lifelong designer of electronic security systems, I am nonetheless convinced that "electronics is the high priest of false security," and that electronic measures should supplement rather than supplant operational security measures.

This book is all about risk assessment and mitigation metrics: how to develop them, how to proof them, and how to present them in a fashion that is virtually irrefutable. This book arguably presents the penultimate approach to risk assessment and shows you how to scale that up or down to meet the organization's budget and schedule. *This book also shows you how to present to the organization's management the fact that any risk not mitigated is accepted.* (This is one of the most important facts to end any risk analysis presentation.)

I have tried to make this book sufficiently thorough so that it can be used as the single industry reference guide for professional risk assessment. The first edition of this book was reviewed by one of the leading international "think tanks" specializing in

---

* ASME Innovative Technologies Institute, LLC—Risk Analysis and Management for Critical Asset Protection (RAMCAP).
† DHS Chemical Facility Anti-Terrorism Standards (CFATS).

international risk analysis, and it confirmed that this objective has been met.[3] This book is usable across a very broad range of risk analysis case studies. It is specifically designed to be useful at the highest level (global and regional security risk analysis in terrorism environments—the area where I do most of my work). The book is also useful down to the level of assessing and mitigating risk for the smallest assets, such as a single electrical substation or executive suite.

We begin the book by studying risk analysis, later moving into countermeasures selection and budgeting. The book will also teach you how to prepare a high-quality risk analysis report that will be the envy of very expensive security consulting firms. Any report prepared using the tools and methods taught in this book will compete head-to-head with the most expensive and thorough risk assessment reports in the marketplace today. In fact, arguably, using the practice and tools taught in this book, your reports will make many security consulting firms' reports look unprepared and amateur by comparison. This is not meant as a criticism of most security consulting firms, but just a statement that this important work can be done much better; after completing this book, the reader will know how to do much better.

Although the principles discussed focus on security risks, many if not most of these principles can also be applied, with minor modifications, to political, economic, social, and business risks as well. This is the only book you will ever need on risk analysis and countermeasures selection.

Theory

The difference between success and failure in risk analysis lies in the difference between knowledge and assumptions.

Let us begin with some simple questions that are often never asked. These questions are foundational. That is, understand them and their answers, and you understand what is behind risk. Most people I have met who are performing security assessments cannot answer many of these questions correctly. Most people operate at a more intuitive level, from their assumptions. *However, trying to analyze risk from a standpoint of assumptions is in its own way the very definition of risk.*

Without understanding the questions and their answers, it is not possible to mitigate risks correctly. So although these questions seem very basic, they are essential.

- What is risk?
  - Risk is the likelihood of occurrence of an unwanted event that can adversely affect the mission of the organization. It comprises four elements:
    - An asset (facility, structure, etc.).
    - The likelihood of a threat actor with intent.
    - Vulnerabilities in the protective systems of the asset.
    - Consequences of the threat action.
- What types of risk do organizations face?
  - Risks exist in two forms: natural and man-made.
- What are the five types of threat actors?
  - Terrorists.
  - Economic criminals (from your friendly local mugger ["Hello, my name is Phil, and I'll be your mugger this evening"] to transnational criminal organizations).

- Violent criminals (other than terrorists who use violence as a means to achieving their goals).
- Subversives (protest organizations, etc.).
- Petty criminals (involved in vandalism, prostitution, invasion of privacy, etc.).
- Why do organizations face risks?
  - Most risks are those that organizations face because they do not plan for them.
  - Most risks can be mitigated to a greater or lesser extent.
- Why do organizations care about risk?
  - Every organization begins with a mission.
  - The organization acquires assets in order to support the carrying out of its mission.
  - Those assets range from miscellaneous (paper clips) to critical (its information technology department).
  - The loss of one or more critical assets could prevent the organization from carrying out its mission.
- How does one analyze risk?
  - Risk is the combination of a possibility of an unwanted event, times the severity of that event on the most critical assets of the organization, times the probability of such an event actually occurring.
  - For terrorism, probability is replaced by gauging the value of the assets in question as a potential target to the aggressor (asset target value).
  - For natural risks, tables of probability exist.
  - Man-made events fall into five categories: terrorism, economic crimes, violent crimes, subversive crimes, and petty crimes.
  - Risks can only occur where there are assets and vulnerabilities.
- What can one do to mitigate risk? Risks can be mitigated by
  - Shedding assets.
  - Duplicating assets.
  - Protecting assets (reducing vulnerabilities: reducing the probability of success of a threat action).
  - Transferring the risk to others (e.g., by insuring the assets).
- Can one eliminate all risk?
  - No.
  - Every organization must accept some risk because the cost of mitigating against all risk would be more than the probable damage caused by letting the risk occur (for economic risks and unforeseen violent crimes).
  - For terrorism, the cost of mitigating some risks could itself prevent the organization from carrying out its mission.
  - Subversive risk often requires high levels of cooperation with sometimes reticent law enforcement.
  - Some levels of petty crime will always exist.

Practice

All better risk assessment methodologies include the following elements. Different risk assessment methodologies express these attributes in different ways and may use different terminologies to describe them.

- Asset characterization: Understand and describe the organization's assets.
- Threat identification: Understand and describe what threats there are to the organization's assets.
- Consequence analysis: Understand and describe the criticalities of the listed assets to the organization's mission and the consequences for the organization of a successful threat action.
- Vulnerability analysis: Understand and express the vulnerabilities of the organization's assets.
- Threat assessment: Understand how threat actors view the organization's assets and which assets the threat actors would find most interesting.
- Risk assessment: Express risk in the form of a calculation (this should be scalable, so that risk can be calculated for any single asset or for the entire organization).
- Risk prioritization: Prioritize the risks, so that the most important risks can be mitigated first and the least important risks will be mitigated last.
- Risk management: Provide recommendations for countermeasures to mitigate the risks.

Additionally, any risk analysis report ideally should include

- A statement of the organization's mission
- A statement describing the organization's business programs and the business processes that are critical to the success of carrying out those programs
- A statement of how the organization's assets support the business programs (including ranking of asset criticalities)
- A list of the users of those assets and a definition of those categories from which the threat actors may arise
- Prioritized budgets for the proposed countermeasures
- Space planning information
- Blast calculation resource information
- The qualifications of the risk analyst (including the analyst and his/her organization)
- A bibliography of references
- A table of contents
- A table of figures
- An index
- Optionally, a risk register may be required by the client. This is discussed in Chapter 20.

Of the dozens of popular risk analysis methodologies, there are great and small. Many are specifically designed to address risk at a specific type of organization (pipelines, water supply facilities, chemical facilities, marine facilities, etc.). These will be covered in some detail in later chapters. But it is important to be well grounded in the fundamentals of risk analysis in order to be able to traverse the broad terrain of the many different types of facilities to which your skills will be applied.

There are also dozens of popular risk assessment methodologies that do a very poor job of serving the client's needs. Look carefully at the list of basic risk analysis elements above. I will say definitively that any methodology that does not include *all* of these elements is inadequate to the task and *cannot* result in a successful mitigation of risk. This is especially true of so-called risk assessment checklists, of which dozens exist in the commercial sector. Most of these focus on vulnerabilities rather than on a total risk equation. And most of these do not use any systematic approach even to evaluating vulnerability. These all do a terrible disservice to their clients by giving a feeling that risk has been studied when this is not the case. Worse, those checklists are often used by people who have little understanding of who the potential threat actors are and what tactics they use to carry out their terrorism and criminal attacks. In short, such inadequate checklists in the hands of incompetent "security providers" can actually increase a facility's risks by ending the process of risk analysis with one effort, which results in totally inadequate security planning.

Any methodology that does not address a list of the organization's assets is assuming facts not in evidence. Any methodology that does not analyze threat actors assumes facts not in evidence. Any methodology that checklists vulnerabilities is certain to miss other vulnerabilities that are not on the checklist.

Many security professionals assume that it is acceptable to insert gross assumptions into the risk analysis equation. For example, most risk assessment methodologies determine the vulnerability level of listed assets, but they do not identify what vulnerability means or evaluate the component variables of the vulnerabilities. Let me say again: *The difference between success and failure in risk analysis lies in the difference between knowledge and assumptions.*

I am not saying that there are not times when expediency or budget demands a quick, intuitive risk estimate, but let's not call it an analysis. Let's call it what it is: it is a risk estimate.

Tools

This book is about the process of understanding, analyzing, and mitigating security risks and then developing workable, cost-effective solutions to mitigate the risks.

It is also about empowering any professional security manager, analyst, or consultant to do the very best work in the industry without expending thousands of dollars for conventional risk analysis software.

The first and most important point of success for a quality risk analysis is the analysis skill itself. So the first set of skills taught in this book involves research, analysis, and critical thinking and how to select and use the proper tools of analysis.

I am repeating the following for emphasis as this is the core of the book, which must be fully and intuitively understood. This book also presents four software word-processing and spreadsheet examples, which show you how to make convincing and nearly irrefutable arguments to support the risk conclusions and countermeasure recommendations and which help drive consensus when there are multiple options on the table to choose from. These last points are most important and are widely disregarded by most risk analysis methodologies.

Tool #1: The book presents the elements of a high-quality risk analysis report so that the reader can generate very complete and convincing reports.

Tool #2: The risk analysis tool: One of the most frustrating things for veteran security analysts is the virtual requirement to purchase (and continue investing in annual updates of) very expensive risk analysis programs. Some of the best of these programs cost thousands of dollars each year to buy and keep current. Failing to pay for updates on some will result in not being able to access the data of assessments conducted in previous years. Data that represent between dozens and hundreds of hours of your efforts. Data that you own. I understand prohibiting the creation of new assessments, but to prohibit access to data that you created during a time when you had paid the license, data that you own, seems outrageous. This book presents examples of data creation using a spreadsheet as a risk analysis tool, that will result in deep and convincing risk analysis results, comparable to (and quite arguably superior to) the programs that cost thousands of dollars a year to buy and maintain. The tool results are color coded to help assure that organization leadership, who may be unfamiliar with risk analysis methodologies, can digest massive amounts of data in seconds. Remember please that I am not advocating one kind of assessment tool over another. I'm just giving examples using an option that anyone can afford.

Tool #3: The countermeasure options analysis tool: This tool does something amazing that to my knowledge has never been done before and most security professionals think cannot be done at all. That is, it allows the security analyst to determine the best countermeasure based upon effectiveness and cost-effectiveness. The latter is a function of cost versus the countermeasure's effectiveness elements, including the countermeasure's ability to:

- Control access
- Deter attacks
- Detect attacks
- Assess the event
- Respond to the event
- Collect evidence
- Mitigate multiple vulnerabilities
- Sort the countermeasures into a three-dimensional color-coded spreadsheet:
  - From
    - Most critical vulnerabilities and
    - Most cost-effective solutions
  - To
    - Least critical vulnerabilities and
    - Least cost-effective solutions

Tool #4: The countermeasure decision matrix: The book presents a decision matrix tool that helps achieve consensus as to the correct countermeasure solution when there are several popular options, or when options are contentious, or when ideas are few. This tool (the countermeasure decision matrix) has on many occasions achieved total unanimous consensus among a large group of managers who were each highly committed to widely differing options.

ORGANIZATION

This book is presented in three sections:

- Section I: Risk Analysis
  1. Risk Analysis: The Basis for Appropriate and Economical Countermeasures
  2. Risk Analysis Basics and DHS-Approved Risk Analysis Methods
  3. Risk Analysis Skills and Tools
  4. Critical Thinking and the Risk Analysis Process
  5. Asset Characterization and Identification
  6. Criticality and Consequence Analysis
  7. Threat Analysis
  8. Assessing Vulnerability

9. Estimating Probability
10. Risk Analysis Process
11. Prioritizing Risk
- Section II: Policy Development before Countermeasures
12. Security Policy Introduction
13. Security Policy and Countermeasure Goals
14. Developing Effective Security Policies
- Section III: Countermeasure Selection and Budgeting
15. Countermeasure Goals and Strategies
16. Types of Countermeasures
17. Countermeasure Selection and Budgeting Tools
18. Security Effectiveness Metrics
19. Cost-Effectiveness Metrics
20. Writing Effective Reports

SUMMARY

A security risk analysis should be performed before any countermeasures are selected or implemented.

- Qualitative reports mainly focus on interviews, words, and images, while quantitative reports mainly focus on the analysis of numbers. The use of both is better than the use of either one alone.
- All better risk assessment methodologies include the following elements:
  - Asset characterization: Understand and describe the organization's assets.
  - Threat identification: Understand and describe what threats there are against the organization's assets.
  - Consequence analysis: Understand and describe the criticalities of the listed assets to the organization's mission.
  - Vulnerability analysis: Understand and express the vulnerabilities of the organization's assets.
  - Threat assessment: Understand how threat actors view the organization's assets and which assets the threat actors would find most interesting.
  - Risk assessment: Express risk in the form of a calculation (this should be scalable, so that risk can be calculated for any single asset, or for the entire organization).
  - Risk prioritization: Prioritize the risks, so that the most important risks can be mitigated first and the least important risks will be mitigated last.
  - Risk management: Provide recommendations for countermeasures to mitigate the risks.
- Additionally, any risk analysis report ideally should include the following:
  - A statement of the organization's mission
  - A statement describing the organization's business programs and the business processes that are critical to the success of carrying out those programs
  - A statement of how the organization's assets support the business programs (including ranking of asset criticalities)
  - A list of the users of those assets and a definition of the categories from which the threat actors may arise

- Prioritized budgets for the proposed countermeasures
- Space planning information
- Blast calculation resource information
- The qualifications of the risk analyst (including the analyst and his/her organization)
- A bibliography of references
- A table of Contents
- A table of Figures
- An index
- Skills taught in this book:
  - Skill #1: How to gather data including:
  - Skill #2: Research and evidence gathering
  - Skill #3: Critical thinking in the risk analysis process
  - Skill #4: Quantitative analysis
  - Skill #5: Qualitative analysis
  - Skill #6: Countermeasures selection
  - Skill #7: Report writing
- Tools presented in this book:
  - Tool #1: The elements of a high-quality risk analysis report format, so that the reader can generate very complete and convincing reports.
  - Tool #2: The risk analysis tool.
  - Tool #3: The countermeasure options analysis tool.
  - Tool #4: The countermeasure decision matrix.

REFERENCES

1. Paul, R. W., Elder, L., and Bartell, T. 1997. Executive summary: Study of 38 public universities and 28 private universities to determine faculty emphasis on critical thinking in instruction. In *California Teacher Preparation for Instruction in Critical Thinking: Research Findings and Policy Recommendations*, California Commission on Teacher Credentialing, Sacramento, CA; Foundation for Critical Thinking, Dillon, CA.
2. Moore, D. T. 2010. *Critical Thinking and Intelligence Analysis*, 2nd edn, p. 62. Government Printing Office, Washington, DC.
3. Harper, J. 2010. U.S. counter-terrorism strategy and Al-Qaeda (review of Thomas L. Norman's/CPP/PSP/CSC's book "Risk Analysis and Security Countermeasure Selection"). Cato Institute, Washington, DC, June 30.

Q&A

Questions

Q1: Often, countermeasures are
  A. Poorly conceived to protect the organization against risks that are only assumed and for which no empirical data exist.
  B. Well conceived because they are designed by security installers.

C. Well conceived and protect the organization against all risks.

D. Able to accommodate any contingency, no matter how high the threat.

Q2: Many organizations believe that they cannot afford any risk assessment and base their security programs

A. On insurance actuaries.

B. Entirely on American National Standards Institute (ANSI) standards.

C. Entirely on the ill-advised judgments of single (often totally unqualified) individuals.

D. Entirely on National Institute of Standards and Technology (NIST) standards.

Q3: Everything in a security program

A. Is a result of good electronics technology skills.

B. Needs guards, dogs, lighting, signage, and computers.

C. Is based on good guard scheduling.

D. Derives from the risk analysis process.

Q4: By definition, any risk assessment done by anyone who is not well grounded in the fundamentals of risk assessment

A. Can be used for simple risk assessments.

B. Will be an incompetent risk assessment and may instead actually insert additional risk into the countermeasures program through ill-advised recommendations.

C. May be done if the project is small enough.

D. Can result in complex studies by university professors.

Q5: There are two main schools of risk analysis report writing:

A. Exotative and intotative

B. Qualified and quantified

C. Quantitative and qualified

D. Quantitative and qualitative

Q6: Required risk analysis skills include

A. Data gathering, research and evidence gathering, critical thinking, quantitative analysis, qualitative analysis, countermeasure selection, and report writing and presentation.

B. Data gathering, critical thinking, analysis, security system design, and report writing.

C. Sales and marketing, guard management, and report writing.

D. Sales and management and presentation.

Q7: All good risk analysis methodologies have two main sections:

A. Analyze risks, write reports

B. Analyze risks, recommend countermeasures to mitigate the risks

C. Analyze risks, create security programs

D. Analyze risks and fully eliminate them

Q8: It is customary to develop

A. Large spreadsheets.

B. Long reports.

C. Budgets for the countermeasures.
D. Detailed drawings to support the risk analysis.

Q9: Any risk that is not mitigated
A. Can be ignored.
B. Will not likely occur.
C. May require an immediate response when it occurs.
D. Is accepted.

Q10: The difference between success and failure in risk analysis
A. Lies in the difference between knowledge and assumptions.
B. Lies in the amount of hours in the analysis.
C. Lies in the length of the report.
D. Can be demonstrated in the budget.

Answers

Q1 – A, Q2 – C, Q3 – D, Q4 – B, Q5 – D, Q6 – A, Q7 – B, Q8 – C, Q9 – D, Q10 – A

CHAPTER 2

Risk Analysis Basics and DHS-Approved Risk Analysis Methods

INTRODUCTION

Risk analysis is the process by which organizations determine how best to protect their assets. The risk analysis process includes developing a comprehensive understanding of the organization's critical assets, the criticality of those assets, the consequences of the potential loss of those assets, and the potential risks faced by those assets. Risks are comprised of a threat actor with the intent to harm, the capabilities to carry out that intent (a threat), and vulnerabilites. Risks vary in seriousness by the degree of likelihood that the threat may be carried out and the consequences to the organization of the loss of the asset. Likelihood is determined by the determination and capabilities of the threat actor and the vulnerabilities in the assets that could be exploited by the threat actor. Risk therefore includes threat, likelihood, vulnerability, and consequences. Many risk formulas combine threat and likelihood into a single variable (threat). Many risk formulas view threat (including likelihood) and vulnerabilites and then prioritize the risk results by the consequences of the event.

U.S. DEPARTMENT OF HOMELAND SECURITY CONCERNS

At the end of this chapter, you will understand the approaches that the U.S. Department of Homeland Security (DHS) has embraced over time to study risk, the elements of risk analysis, typical interested stakeholders and agendas for a risk analysis study, commercially available risk analysis software tools, risk analysis basics, risk assessment steps, some information on how to select the right methodology for a particular kind of project, and why the DHS is unconcerned for most facilities about the specific risk assessment methodology used to study risk.

"Over the years, there have been numerous criticisms from various groups over how risk is assessed and, as a result, DHS grants are allocated."[1] The DHS itself has evolved in its understanding of risk and its application of formulas to measure it. From a "macro-risk" standpoint (risk to communities vs. risk to facilities or structures), the DHS risk approach has evolved as follows:

Stage I: R = P. from Fiscal Year (FY) 2001, when the Department of justice (DOJ) had primary responsibility for assessing risk, to FY 2002–2003, when this responsibility was transferred to DHS. This first stage of risk assessment could be characterized as early stage developmental. During this period, risk was generally assessed and measured according to population numbers. In short, risk (R) was equated to population (P).

Stage II: $R = T + CI + PD$. This period covers from FY2004 to FY2005. During this period, the importance of critical infrastructure, population density and a number of other variables was included in the assessment of risk. However, the formula for risk remained additive and "risk-like," as probabilities were not an essential element of the risk assessment process. Risk was assessed as the sum or threat (T), critical infrastructure (CI), and population density (PD).

Stage III: $R - T * V * C = T * (V\&C)$. This period covers from FY2006 to today [author's notes: 2009], a time when probability of particular events was systematically introduced into the formula.

The U.S. Department of Homeland Security (DHS) has overtly or tacitly approved a number of different risk assessment methodologies for use on critical infrastructure facilities. ... This new approach to allocating the remaining funds required an assessment of risk using a formula that considers the threat to a target/area, multiplied by vulnerability (V) of the target/area, multiplied by consequence (C) of an attack on that target/area. As a result, the risk assessment formula became $R = T * V * C$. Variables were no longer additive but were multiplied, implying weighting of variables and some assessment of the likelihood that certain events would occur.

The Current Process

FY2007. ... Risk will be evaluated at the Federal level using a risk analysis model developed by DHS in conjunction with other Federal entities. Risk is defined as the product of three principal variables:

- Threat (T): the likelihood of an attack occurring
- Vulnerability and Consequence (V&C): the relative exposure and expected impact of an attack

Although DHS continues to discuss its risk methodology in terms of the $R = T * V * C$ formula, it appears as if the department is treating vulnerability (V) and consequence (C) as an amalgamated, single variable.[2]

In the discussion above, it can be seen that the DHS view relates to communities more than to individual facilities and structures. And this explains much about why the DHS has taken the relaxed attitude that it has toward establishing definitions for risk assessment methodologies for individual facilities and structures. Those have been left up to the interpretation of DHS departments (e.g., U.S. Coast Guard for maritime facilities, waterways, and terminals), and the DHS has been open to industry input vis-à-vis individual industries and special interest groups.

RISK ANALYSIS FOR FACILITIES AND STRUCTURES

The object of risk analysis is to understand the risks, threats, vulnerabilities, criticalities, and consequences well enough to develop or improve security countermeasures that can effectively deter, detect, assess, delay, respond to, and gather evidence of serious threat actions against the facility in question.

Through the years, various risk analysis formulas have been developed with greater or lesser compliance with this goal. All good risk assessment methodologies include four things:

- Consideration of threat
- Consideration of probability

- Consideration of vulnerability
- Consideration of consequences

Better risk assessment methodologies also include methods to guide the analyst toward appropriate countermeasures.

The best risk assessment methodologies also include metrics for assessing the best choice of countermeasures as measured by their effectiveness in countering potential threats.

The very best methodologies also include metrics for assessing the best choice of countermeasures not only from an effectiveness point of view, but also from a cost-effectiveness point of view.

Critical infrastructure and key resources (CIKR) sectors include[3]

- Agriculture and food.
- Commercial facilities.
- Dams.
- Energy.
- Information technology.
- Postal and shipping.
- Banking and finance.
- Communications.
- Defense industrial base.
- National monuments and icons.
- Transportation systems.
- Chemical.
- Critical manufacturing.
- Emergency services.
- Healthcare and public health.
- Nuclear reactors, materials, and waste.
- Water.
- Military sites are under the purview of the U.S. Department of Defense, not the DHS.
- Government facilities, including the educational facilities subsector.

Guidelines for the protection of such facilities include the Homeland Security Act of 2002 and the National Infrastructure Protection Plan (NIPP). These guidelines are useful for determining the criticality and protection measures appropriate for similar facilities in any country in the world and thus serve as a benchmark for the protection of such facilities. The balance of this book is about risk analysis for CIKR facilities worldwide. However, the methods may also be used on facilities that do not fit these criteria.

The NIPP is comprehensive and can be reviewed in detail at www.dhs.gov. In the search field, enter NIPP.

MANY INTERESTED STAKEHOLDERS AND AGENDAS

As with any important issue, many individuals and organizations can be expected to provide input on how to achieve the objectives of the program. In the case of the NIPP, this includes interests from various branches of the government, such as the U.S. Coast Guard, who are responsible for enforcement or standards and guidelines, and also industry and special interest groups. Resulting from this, as one might expect, there is no single standard for risk assessment for critical infrastructure facilities. So for any particular type of facility, there may be competing risk assessment methodologies forwarded by government agencies, national laboratories, branches of the military, industries, and industry interest groups. All of these have put forward risk assessment methodologies for use on CIKR facilities, and the DHS has either directly or tacitly approved a wide variety of risk assessment methodologies for use.

Certain of these methodologies are industry specific, and a few are intentionally widely applicable. Some of these methodologies are highly detailed and scientific, while others are generic and vague. Some of the methodologies place a high degree of control in the hands of the analyst, while others remove important segments such as threat and asset target analysis and place them in the hands of the reviewing agency.* This is most confusing for the management of these facilities and for risk analysts, making it difficult to know which methodology to use for a specific facility. Should the analyst use a methodology that was developed for that specific industry or a more generic model that is suitable for all? Would the generic model work on every type of facility? Would it be accepted by everyone, including the DHS? Can the analyst use an industry-specific model on a facility that is not part of that industry? Would that be accepted by the DHS or by stakeholders? How many risk assessment methodologies should an analyst be competent in? How many types of risk assessment software should he or she buy and maintain?

Obviously, the direct and indirect costs of buying and training in a variety of methodologies are a consideration. Lost time, lost productivity, and sorting through the vagaries of many different programs can all become confusing to the analyst and can actually reduce his/her effectiveness.

The cost of some of the risk assessment programs runs into tens of thousands of dollars, and training costs can add many more thousands to the cost of the programs. As many of these methodologies and programs utilize different formulas and interpretations of the same basic data, one can easily become lost in the sheer size of the forest of methodologies. It would be useful if there was one methodology that could be relied on to do the job in every type of facility and that would be unquestioned as to completeness and authenticity. The good news is that there are two that easily fit this bill.

Sandia National Laboratories has developed a set of methodologies called RAM (Risk Assessment Methodology), for which many subsectors have been developed. All of the subsector methodologies rely on the same basic risk analysis formula. The main differences involve vulnerability assessment aspects that are unique to the facility types.

Another such methodology has been developed for the oil/gas/chemical sector, called NIST 780. This is derived from a previous methodology called the NIST 780 SVA method (American Petroleum Institute/National Petrochemical & Refiners Association Security Vulnerability Assessment method). The NIST 780 methodology, which was crafted to a NIST standard, enhances the best attributes of the API/NPRA SVA methodology. Both of these methods (Sandia and NIST 780) are so thorough

---

* For example, RAMCAP. Chemical Facility Antiterrorism Standards (CFATS) also places threat and asset target value definitions in the hands of the reviewing agency.

and complete that they are widely accepted as being at the pinnacle of risk assessment methodologies.

Both the Sandia RAM and the NIST 780 models are scalable. That is, they can both be applied to relatively simple sites with minimal analytical requirements or to complex organizations with many campuses, many facility types, and many departments and services.

The Sandia models are scalable to the point of being virtually certain with respect to the efficacy of existing countermeasures, as details such as the mixture of concrete and spacing of rebar in defensive walls can be considered in the delay formula.

The third major risk assessment methodology is ISO 31000. ISO 31000 is an international risk assessment standard that also outlines the framework for the implementation of an enterprise risk management program. ISO 31000 is especially well suited to large enterprise organizations. ISO 31000 is entirely consistent in its findings with both the Sandia model and NIST 780.

Such levels of detail, while completely appropriate for facilities such as nuclear power plants, nuclear stockpiles, and weapons facilities, can be far too much for most commercial facilities such as airports and hotels, where serious threats of terrorism exist. In such cases, the cost of analyzing to Sandia's level of detail, while laudable, can make not only the cost of countermeasures, but also the cost of the analysis itself, completely unaffordable. In Sandia's model, for example, the analysis team for the vulnerability portion alone may include[4]

- A vulnerability assessment project leader
- A systems engineer
- A security systems engineer
- An intrusion sensing subsystem subject matter expert (SME)
- An alarm assessment subsystem SME
- An alarm communication & display (AC&D) subsystem SME
- An entry control subsystem SME
- A delay subsystem SME
- A response system SME
- A communications subsystem SME
- An SME analyst

Such a team, when evaluating a hotel that caters to Western guests in Pakistan, for example, will produce a risk analysis that is itself cost prohibitive and findings and recommendations that do not support the function of running a hotel. So, despite Mae West's assertion that "Too much of a good thing—is wonderful!", in risk analysis, one must strike a balance between affordability and results. Despite my very high regard for Sandia reaching the practical pinnacle of risk analysis methodologies (and that *is* my opinion), in some cases too much of a good thing is too much to use in practicality. The Sandia model can be scaled back to the minimum, and the methods taught in this book can be applied to the minimum to medium application of Sandia's model. It is also notable that the Sandia model focuses primarily on terrorist threats rather than economic crimes or petty criminal threats. The Sandia model offers little focus on internal economic threats, for example. As such, the Sandia model is extraordinarily well suited to facilities such as nuclear storage facilities and nuclear power plants, while in the opinion of some, it is not as well suited to conventional commercial facilities such as hotels, shopping malls, and stock exchanges.

COMMERCIALLY AVAILABLE SOFTWARE TOOLS

Commercial software programs have been developed to support these and other DHS-approved methodologies. Many of these programs cost thousands of dollars and require thousands more in costs for training courses in the methodologies and software tools. Thus, a cottage business has grown around the complexities of implementation of the various methods. This is a common response to regulation. That is, regulation spawns implementation tools and training, on which businesses are built to service these perceived needs, and those businesses have a vested interest in building and maintaining a perception of complexity, thus driving the need for the training and software programs. Some of these programs produce volumes of information with little if any useful summary.

At this point it should be noted that the DHS does not require the use of any specific software program to perform the analysis.

The risk analysis methods discussed in this book can be used to support all DHS-approved methodologies equally well. Variations between the methodologies are in four main areas:

- Scaling of estimates (0–1, 1–5, or 1–10)
- Order of valuation (e.g., some view asset target value as part of vulnerability while others view it as part of threat analysis)
- Formulas (although there are marked differences in formulas and some like Sandia are more scientific than others, most reach conclusions that are in the same order of magnitude)
- Qualitative versus quantitative analysis (most adapt well to qualitative analysis, while some like NIST 780 and Sandia rely more on quantitative approaches, though qualitative analysis summaries can be added)

The methods taught in this book are extremely thorough and can be applied to all DHS-approved methodologies in all of their interpretations.

RISK ANALYSIS BASICS

Risk formulas are usually quite simple. Most typically involve risk = a threat actor with intent (probability) * an exploitable vulnerability, prioritized by criticality and consequences.

Numerous variations exist, but all formulas result in a ranking of risk by some combination of probability, vulnerabilities, and consequences.

A variation on the risk formula is risk = (a threat actor with intent + probability + an exploitable vulnerability)/3, prioritized by criticality and consequences.

Threat = an active threat actor with the capabilities and intent to do harm to the organization.

Probability = the likelihood that a target has been or will be selected by a threat actor (any asset of the organization that can be attacked in fulfillment of the mission of the threat actor).

Vulnerability = any condition or factor associated with the selected target that can be exploited to carry out an attack. Vulnerabilities may be individual or systemic (e.g., a door left unlocked or poor training of guards).

Different methodologies sort these elements in different ways, sometimes renaming them, but the elements are really always the same.

The degree of risk varies in accordance with

- Likelihood variables
  - Threat variables
    - The existence and degree of motivation of a threat actor
    - The capabilities of the threat actor, including their training
    - The availability of resources to the threat actor
    - Types of threat actors
      - Terrorists
      - Economic criminals
      - Violent criminals
      - Subversives
      - Petty criminals
  - Target selection variables (target selection variables depend on the type of threat actor)
- Vulnerability variables
  - Accessibility
  - Surveillance opportunities
  - Intrinsic vulnerabilities
  - Natural and existing countermeasures including:
    - Physical countermeasures
    - Electronic countermeasures
    - Operational countermeasures
- Consequence variables
  - Criticality of assets to the mission of the organization
  - Difficulty in replacing assets (recuperation)
  - Consequences of loss
    - Loss of life
    - Loss of property
    - Loss of proprietary information
    - Loss of business reputation
    - Loss of business productivity

All of the many and varied risk analysis methodologies utilize these three basic elements (Figure 2.1):

- Probability (threat actors and target selection)
- Vulnerability
- Consequences

Probability is simply the likelihood that a threat actor will select and then act on a target. For certain criminal acts in certain geographic regions where accurate criminal records are kept and are available to the risk analyst, probability can be derived by historical data. That is never so for terrorism, where too few instances and evolving tactics prevent historical data from being developed. Therefore, for terrorism, target selection factors are an appropriate surrogate for probability factors.

FIGURE 2.1   Risk factors.

RISK ASSESSMENT STEPS

The steps involved in risk assessment include

- Asset characterization: understanding and describing the organization's assets (business function, environment, building and perimeter types, population, access/egress, etc.).
- Threat identification: understanding and describing what threats there are against the organization's assets and selecting a threat level that the security program will be designed to counter or otherwise mitigate effectively.
- Criticality analysis: understanding, describing, and ranking the criticalities of each of the listed assets to the organization's mission.
- Consequence analysis: understanding, describing, and ranking the consequences of loss of the listed assets to the organization's mission in terms of the severity of the loss of
  - Casualties
  - Production or business function
  - Proprietary information
  - Business reputation
- Vulnerability analysis: understanding and expressing the vulnerabilities of the organization's assets.
- Likelihood (probability) assessment: understanding how threat actors view the organization's assets and which assets the threat actors would find most attractive to exploit. This can be accomplished using statistical values or asset target value estimates.
- Risk assessment: expressing risk in the form of a calculation (this should be scalable, so that risk can be calculated for any single asset or for the entire organization).

- Risk prioritization: prioritizing the risks so that the most important risks can be mitigated first and the least important risks will be mitigated last.
- Risk management: providing recommendations for countermeasures to mitigate the risks.

In order to protect the organization's assets, the analyst must determine what those assets are. All organizations have four types of assets:

- People: including management, employees, customers, visitors, contractors, and vendors
- Property: including real property, fixtures, furnishings, and equipment (FF&E)
- Proprietary information: including proprietary business processes, strategic plans, customer lists, vital records, accounting records, and so on
- Business reputation: ask any ex-employee of Arthur Anderson, LLP*

In order to protect the organization's assets, the risk analyst must determine what those assets are, how critical they are to the organization's mission, and what the consequences could be if the vulnerabilities were exploited. It is important to understand that what we are really protecting is the mission of the organization. Let me repeat that. *It is important to understand that what we are really protecting is the mission of the organization.*

- Threat identification: understanding and describing what threats there are against the organization's assets
- Criticality analysis: understanding what assets are critical to carrying out the mission of the organization
- Consequence analysis: understanding and describing what unwanted consequences could occur if a threat actor exploits a vulnerability in the critical assets of the organization's mission

Now, let us talk about the root of the problem. All risk derives from threat actors who are interested in the organization's assets. No threat actor = no risk. No assets = no risk. Now, this may seem obvious, but it is illuminating to remember that security organizations do not attempt to protect *all* of the organization's assets equally. Therefore, all assets are not equal. That is, all assets are not of equal value to the client. Some assets are more critical than others. And due to the varying degrees of criticality and consequences, not all vulnerabilities are equal in the eyes of threat actors.

- Vulnerability analysis: understanding and expressing the vulnerabilities of the organization's assets
- Threat assessment: understanding how threat actors view the organization's assets and which assets the threat actors would find most interesting
- Risk assessment: expressing risk in the form of a calculation (this should be scalable, so that risk can be calculated for any single asset or for the entire organization)
- Risk prioritization: prioritizing the risks, so that the most important risks can be mitigated first and the least important risks will be mitigated last
- Risk management: providing recommendations for countermeasures to mitigate the risks

---

* Arthur Anderson, LLP, was once one of the "Big Five" accounting firms along with PricewaterhouseCoopers, Deloitte & Touche, Ernst & Young, and Tomatsu. Now there are four.

Formulas that include consequence as part of the basic analysis include all of the Sandia National Laboratories formulas. Sandia uses a model called RAM.

In the Sandia formula,

$$Risk = P_A * (1 - P_E) * C$$

where:

P_A is the likelihood of adversary attack
P_E is the security system effectiveness
$1 - P_E$ is adversary success
C   is the consequence of loss of the asset

For simplicity, in the Sandia model, Risk = Likelihood * Vulnerability * Consequence. Note that the elements are the same and that the net result is virtually identical. All three formulas result in virtually the same result. Sandia has versions of RAM for biological facilities (Bio-RAM), communities (RAM-C), chemical facilities (RAM-CF), dams (RAM-D), energy infrastructures (RAM-E), prisons (RAM-P), power transmission systems (RAM-T), and water utilities (RAM-W).

While Sandia National Laboratories is highly respected and has created numerous effective tools, not all industries have widely adopted the Sandia RAM.

DHS-Approved Risk Assessment Methodologies

Now, let us look at relevant codes and standards and the risk analysis methodologies that are accepted for use by the DHS.

- ASME-ITI tools
  - RAMCAP™: ASME Innovative Technologies Institute, LLC is used by the DHS to assess critical infrastructure facilities. RAMCAP is a relatively complete methodology that is designed for a facility's own staff to use.
- Sandia tools
  - Bio-RAM
  - RAF-D
  - RAM-C
  - RAM-CF
  - RAM-E
  - RAM-P
  - RAM-W
- DHS tools
  - CARVER+Shock
  - ISPS
  - NVIC-05-05: LNG risk assessment
- FEMA tools
  - FEMA-452
- Relevant codes and standards
  - FEMA 386-7: Integrating Human-Caused Hazards into Mitigation Planning
  - FEMA-426: Plan of Instruction for Building Design for Homeland Security

- FEMA-452: Risk Assessment—A How-To Guide to Mitigate Potential Terrorist Attacks against Buildings
- DHS: OIG-07-33—Department of Homeland Security—Office of Inspector General—The Department of Homeland Security's Role in Food Defense and Critical Infrastructure Protection—February 2007—CARVER+Shock Method
- DOD: Unified Facilities Criteria (UFC)—UFC4-010-01DoDMinimumAnti-TerrorismStandardsforBuildings
- DOD-5200.08-R and Army Regulation 190-13: Physical Security Program
- Department of Justice: minimum security standards for federal buildings
- General Services Administration: The Facilities Standards for the Public Buildings Service
- Occupational Safety and Health Act (OSHA) Section 1910: General industry standards
- Military standards
  - (MIL-HDBK) 1013/1, Design Guidelines for Physical Security of Facilities
  - FM 3-19.30: Physical security
- Federal specifications
  - RR-F-191 Chain-link fence specifications
  - RR-F-191K_Gen: Fencing general specification
- DHS-approved methodologies for specific industries
  - Chemical: RAMCAP—ASME
  - Critical infrastructure: RAMCAP—ASME
  - Gas/oil/chemical: NIST 780
  - Nuclear: ASME RA-S Probabilistic risk assessment for nuclear power plants
  - Food: CARVER+Shock
  - Sandia Methodologies:
    - Bio-RAM: Biological facilities
    - RAM-C: Communities
    - RAM-CF: Chemical facilities
    - RAM-CI: Critical infrastructures
    - RAM-D: Dams
    - RAM-E: Energy infrastructures
    - RAM-P: Prisons
    - RAM-T: Electrical transmission systems
    - RAM-W: Water facilities
- Commercially available software tools supporting these methodologies:
  - Chemical: RAMCAP Plus—ASME software tool for evaluating RAMCAP projects
  - Critical infrastructure: RAMCAP Plus—ASME tool (as above)
  - Gas/oil/chemical: NIST 780—SVA-Pro (Dyadem)
  - Nuclear: ASME RA-S Probabilistic risk assessment for nuclear power plants
  - Food: CARVER+Shock
  - Sandia software tools:
    - Adversary sequence diagram (ASD): graphical representation of physical protection system elements along paths that adversaries can follow to accomplish their objective
    - Systematic analysis of vulnerability to intrusion (SAVI): Determines the most vulnerable path to a specific asset

- Analytic system and software for evaluating safeguards and security (ASSESS): Determines the most vulnerable path to a specific asset
- Joint combat and tactical simulation (JCATS): Estimates response force effectiveness

Many of these software tools can be applied to methodologies for which they were not originally written. (See the list of methodologies that each software tool can support on the website for that software tool. As this list changes often, the author is not providing it, so as not to be obsolete.)

WHICH METHODOLOGY TO USE?

Community versus Facility Methodologies

The DHS community methodology R = T * (VC) is not usable for individual facilities due to the fact that the DHS is using that formula for allocation of funds to communities, and it is not granular enough to apply to individual facilities.

For most types of individual facilities, the DHS continues to allow latitude in methodologies as long as the methodology submitted considers threat likelihood, vulnerability, and consequences. Arguments rage over whether threat and probability should be calculated by the DHS or by the submitting risk analyst. There are compelling arguments in both camps. The DHS in fact requires that the threat component be supplied only by the DHS itself for certain specific fields (RAMCAP, CFATS, etc.). And for facilities that are clearly outside the purview of the DHS, such as hotels and sports arenas, the argument is absolutely in favor of the individual analyst, as the DHS is not an option.

Further, for any facility for which the risk analysis is *not* being submitted to the DHS or one of its departments for review, the risk analyst must conduct the threat/probability analysis (Figure 2.2).

Strengths and Weaknesses of Major Methodologies

- Full-scale Sandia process: Extremely robust analysis method; very scalable; completely scientifically supportable; may be used qualitatively, quantitatively, or a

FIGURE 2.2 NIST 780 Cover.

combination of both; ideal for facilities where a very robust analysis is required necessitating very deep analysis of vulnerabilities, though can be used in a less robust fashion. The full-scale Sandia process utilizes deeply researched calculations for every quantitative date entry point, which makes it both highly precise and simultaneously very costly to perform. The full-scale Sandia process is usually performed only by Sandia National Laboratories, due to the expertise required to accommodate its stringent requirements successfully. It is outside the abilities of all but the most capable and well-equipped risk laboratory teams. This approach is highly recommended for high-consequence critical infrastructure facilities.

In my opinion, it is unwise to use any other risk analysis process than the full-scale Sandia process for any facility where the consequences of loss could affect the health or lives of an entire community (such as for facilities dealing with certain high-consequence chemicals, i.e., phosgene, ammonium nitrate, methyl isocyanate, etc.). (On December 3, 1984, an estimated 30 tons of methyl isocyanate and other poisonous chemicals were released from a Union Carbide plant in the city of Bhopal, India, exposing the nearby community of Bhopal, India, mostly those living in nearby shanty towns, to the fumes. According to government estimates, more than 15,000 people have since died from gas-related diseases.[5])

- ASME RA-S: Limited to heavy nuclear facilities.
- NIST 780: A very good analysis methodology; extremely thorough; originally developed for oil/gas/chemical facilities, but works equally well on any facility; fully scalable; ideal for any type of facility for government, industry, or commercial sectors; may be used as a qualitative or quantitative analysis tool or a combination of both. Can be used on almost any facility, except where the DHS stipulates RAMCAP or CFATS.

  NIST 780 is the next best thing to the full-scale Sandia process in my opinion. It uses essentially the same elements but relies on the expertise and experience of the risk analyst for *estimating* the factors rather than precise scientific tests to *scientifically determine* the factors. In the hands of a highly skilled risk analyst, NIST 780 can produce very similar results to the full-scale Sandia process. (RAMCAP Plus would be third in my opinion—see following section.)
- CARVER+Shock: A very weak analysis tool, originally intended for target selection for special forces; makes only the vaguest definition of criticality, consequence, and vulnerability; almost useless for most facilities as a complete analysis tool but may be used as part of NIST 780 for a portion only of asset target value analysis. Not recommended as a stand-alone risk analysis methodology.
- RAMCAP Framework: A good analysis tool, but in certain uses it relies on a top-screen process so that the DHS can provide a threat assessment for use in the RAMCAP framework.* While having the DHS provide the threat assessment helps to assure that such data are up to date, it arguably is less transparent to the client and the analyst. RAMCAP Plus (the ASME RAMCAP software tool) does provide the ability to analyze threats independently to some extent.
- CFATS is a DHS process that is specific to chemical facilities. Like RAMCAP, threat analysis is in the hands of the DHS.

---

* RAMCAP Framework Version 2.0, p. 25.

Now there are two important things to note:

First: Neither the DHS nor any of the methodologies themselves actually require the use of any specific software tool. That is, any software tool, whether commercially available, manually assembled, or simply comprising paper-and-pencil calculations, is acceptable to the methodologies and to the DHS, as long as the calculations are submitted and supported. That means that if a risk analyst settles on a particular software tool that can support any methodology, the DHS will accept the use of that tool for analysis.

Second: In most cases, the DHS does not actually require any particular methodology to be applied to any particular type of facility. (Notable exceptions are CFATS, which are required for the chemical industry, and the Sandia or ASME RA-S methods, which are required for nuclear facilities.) That is, the Sandia model or NIST 780 models, which are extremely thorough, can be and have been applied to many facility types for which they were not originally intended. As both Sandia and NIST 780 are both recognized as being at the pinnacle of analysis in terms of being thorough, both are ideal candidates for use on all types of facilities. Both are scalable and can be applied simply or to the extreme. RAMCAP is also worthy of consideration.

CFATS Information*

CFATS is a DHS process that is specific to facilities involved with specific chemicals. Facilities that use, produce, or store any of the chemicals of interest (COIs) in quantities above a screening threshold quantity (STQ) as determined by the DHS are subject to the regulation. The COIs and thresholds are listed in Appendix A of the CFATS legislation and are available on the DHS website.

The regulation is published at 6 CFR § 27 and requires "high-risk" chemical facilities to enhance security and establish procedures for protecting chemical facility security information. The DHS determines the level of risk on a facility-specific basis and determines if and to what extent the facility is a "covered facility" subject to regulation.

The CFATS process involves six phases: submission of a top screen, notification of a preliminary risk tier, submission of a security vulnerability assessment (SVA), DHS notification of its final tier determination, submission of a site security plan (SSP), and ongoing compliance.

The process involves the use of the DHS-developed chemical security assessment tool (CSAT) through a secure DHS web link to proceed through the process. Tool users provide characterization information on the site, chemicals and processes, and protection measures present at a facility. From this information, the DHS performs a threat assessment and determines the level of risk for the facility. This risk level allows the DHS to apply a rating for each facility: exempt from further regulation.

CSAT Top Screen

The CSAT top screen follows a logical, two-step data collection process:[6]

- Step 1 involves collecting basic facility identification information.

---

* CFATS Information was graciously provided by Mr. Benjamin Butchko (Butchko Inc., Tomball, TX, +1-832-460-6942, info@butchkoinc.com).

- Step 2 involves collecting information about the chemicals a facility possesses, manufactures, processes, uses, stores, and/or distributes. Questions cover the following security issues:
- Release-toxic, release-flammable, and release-explosive chemicals with the potential for impacts within and beyond a facility.
- Theft of explosive/improvised explosive device–precursor (Theft/Diversion-EXP/IEDP) chemicals, theft of weapon-of-mass-effect (Theft/Diversion-WME) chemicals, and theft of chemical weapon/chemical weapon–precursor (Theft/Diversion-CW/CWP) chemicals.
- Sabotage/contamination chemicals.
  - Chemicals that are critical to the government's mission and the national economy. The top screen also provides additional questions for each of the following facility types:
    - Petroleum refining
    - Liquefied natural gas (LNG) storage (e.g., peak shaving facilities)
    - Agricultural faculties

CSAT Security Vulnerability Assessment (SVA)

Based on top-screen results, if the DHS determines the facility is subject to regulation, the DHS assigns one of four risk tiers that require increasingly stringent levels of security: Tier 1 represents greatest risk and requires the most stringent security, continuing to Tier 4, which represents the smallest risk and requires less stringent security.

All tiered facilities are required to complete an SVA. Tier 4 facilities are permitted to submit either the CSAT SVA or an alternative security program SVA. The DHS has provided SVA instructions to assist with completion of the required SVA questions.

Following a facility's submission of the SVA, the DHS will analyze the submission and may adjust or remove a tier designation. The DHS will provide a final tier designation or remove the site from regulatory mandate. All tiered facilities are required to submit an SSP that satisfies the DHS Risk-Based Performance Standards (RBPS) enumerated in 6 CFR § 27.230.

SUMMARY

Introduction

It can be seen that the DHS view relates to communities more than to individual facilities and structures. And this explains much about why the DHS has taken the relaxed attitude that it has toward establishing definitions for risk assessment methodologies for individual facilities and structures. Those have been left up to interpretation of the DHS departments (e.g., U.S. Coast Guard for maritime facilities, waterways, and terminals), and the DHS has been open to industry input vis-à-vis individual industries and special interest groups.

Risk Analysis for Facilities and Structures

The object of risk analysis is to understand the risks, vulnerabilities, criticalities, and consequences well enough to develop or improve security countermeasures that can effectively deter, detect, assess, delay, respond, and gather evidence of serious threat actions against the facility in question.

Through the years, various risk analysis formulas have been developed with greater or lesser compliance to this goal. All good risk assessment methodologies include four things:

- Consideration of threat
- Consideration of probability
- Consideration of vulnerability
- Consideration of consequences

Better risk assessment methodologies also include methods to guide the analyst toward appropriate countermeasures. The best risk assessment methodologies also include metrics for assessing the best choice of countermeasures as measured by their effectiveness in countering potential threats. The very best methodologies also include metrics for assessing the best choice of countermeasures not only from an effectiveness point of view, but also from a cost-effectiveness point of view.

Guidelines for the protection of such facilities include the Homeland Security Act of 2002 and the NIPP. These guidelines are useful for determining the criticality and protection measures appropriate for similar facilities in any country in the world and thus serve as a benchmark for protection of such facilities.

Many Interested Stakeholders and Agendas

As with any important issue, many individuals and organizations can be expected to express input on how to achieve the objectives of the program. In the case of the NIPP, this includes interests from various branches of the government, such as the U.S. Coast Guard, who are responsible for enforcement or standards and guidelines, and also industry and special interest groups. Resulting from this, as one might expect, there is no single standard for risk assessment for critical infrastructure facilities. So for any particular type of facility, there may be competing risk assessment methodologies that are forwarded by government agencies, national laboratories, branches of the military, industries, and industry interest groups. All of these have put forward risk assessment methodologies for use on CIKR facilities, and the DHS has either directly or tacitly approved a wide variety of risk assessment methodologies for use.

Commercially Available Software Tools

Commercial software programs have been developed to support a number of DHS-approved methodologies. It should be noted that the DHS does not require the use of any specific software program to perform the analysis.

Risk Analysis Basics

Risk formulas are usually quite simple. Most typically involve risk=a threat actor with intent (probability) * an exploitable vulnerability, prioritized by criticality and consequences.

Numerous variations exist, but all formulas result in a ranking of risk by some combination of probability, vulnerabilities, and consequences.

A variation on the risk formula is risk = (a threat actor with intent + probability + an exploitable vulnerability)/3, prioritized by criticality and consequences.

Threat = an active threat actor with the capabilities and intent to do harm to the organization.

Probability = the likelihood that a target has been or will be selected by a threat actor (a target being any asset of the organization that can be attacked in fulfillment of the mission of the threat actor).

Vulnerability = any condition or factor associated with the selected target that can be exploited to carry out an attack—vulnerabilities may be individual or systemic (e.g., a door left unlocked or poor training of guards).

Different methodologies sort these elements in different ways, sometimes renaming them, but the elements are really always the same.

The advent of ISO 31000 actually simplified the above formula by including vulnerability within the probability calculation. This makes perfect sense in that any threat actor will calculate a facility's vulnerability into his decision on whether or not to target the facility. According to ISO 31000, risk = likelihood * consequences $(R = L * C)$. I personally prefer this formula, and I think it best represents the variables of risk.

Risk Assessment Steps

The steps involved in risk assessment include

- Asset characterization
- Threat identification
- Criticality analysis
- Consequence analysis
- Understanding and expressing the vulnerabilities of the organization's assets
- Likelihood (probability) assessment
- Risk assessment
- Risk prioritization
- Risk management recommendations

Which Methodology to Use?

Strengths and Weaknesses of Major Methodologies

- RAMCAP: Good analysis tool, but relies on the DHS to add threat and asset target value to the client analyst's RAMCAP calculations. While this assures that such data are up to date, it is not transparent to the client or the analyst.
- NIST 780: Very good analysis method; extremely thorough; intended for oil/gas/chemical facilities, but works equally well on any facility; fully scalable; ideal for any type of facility for government, industry, or commercial sectors; may be used

as qualitative or quantitative analysis tool or a combination of both. Can be used on almost any facility, except where the DHS stipulates RAMCAP.

- ISO 31000: One of the best all-around methodologies and one of the most complete. ISO 31000 takes into account the time continuum of operations better than any other methodology, and although it includes all of the same constituent components of other leading methodologies (perhaps not with the depth of the Sandia model), it is one of the easiest to condense into a simplified yet complete risk analysis process.
- ASME RA-S: Limited to nuclear facilities.
- CARVER+Shock: Very weak analysis tool; originally intended for target selection for special forces; makes only the vaguest definition of criticality, consequence, and vulnerability; almost useless for most facilities as a complete analysis tool, but may be used as part of NIST 780 for a portion only of asset target value analysis. Not recommended as a stand-alone risk analysis methodology.
- Sandia methodologies: Extremely robust analysis method; very scalable; completely scientifically supportable; may be used qualitatively, quantitatively, or a combination of both; ideal for facilities where a very robust analysis is required, necessitating very deep analysis of vulnerabilities, though can be used in a less robust fashion. Recommended for high-consequence critical infrastructure facilities.

In many cases, neither the DHS nor any of the methodologies themselves actually require the use of any specific software tool. In most cases, the DHS does not actually require any particular methodology to be applied to any particular type of facility. (The main exception to this rule is the CFATS methodology, which is required for the chemical industry.)

REFERENCES

1. CRS. 2007. CRS report for Congress. The Department of Homeland Security's risk assessment methodology: Evolution, issues, and options for Congress, February 2. Congressional Research Service. Prepared for members and committees of Congress. Order Code RL33858, p. CRS-4.
2. CRS. 2007. CRS report for Congress. The Department of Homeland Security's risk assessment methodology: Evolution, issues, and options for Congress, February 2. Congressional Research Service. Prepared for members and committees of Congress. Order Code RL33858, pp. CRS-6–8.
3. U.S. Department of Homeland Security. 2008. Critical infrastructure and key resources support annex, Appendix A, Table A-1. DHS. http://www.fema.gov/pdf/ emergency/nrf/nrf-support-cikr.pdf.
4. Garcia, M. L. 2006. *Vulnerability Assessment of Physical Protection Systems*. Elsevier Butterworth–Heinemann, Burlington, MA, p. 55.
5. Taylor, A. 2014. Bhopal: The world's worst industrial disaster, 30 years later. *Atlantic*, December 2.
6. U.S. Department of Homeland Security. 2010. CSAT Top-Screen Survey Application User Guide, Version 1.99, September. U.S. Department of Homeland Security.

Q&A

Questions

Q1: DHS has overtly or tacitly approved
  A. Only one risk assessment methodology for use on critical infrastructure facilities.
  B. Exactly four risk assessment methodologies for use on critical infrastructure facilities.
  C. A number of different risk assessment methodologies for use on critical infrastructure facilities.
  D. The use of any risk assessment methodology for use on critical infrastructure facilities, including simple risk estimates prepared by the facility itself.

Q2: The object of risk analysis is to understand the _____ well enough to develop or improve security countermeasures that can effectively deter, detect, assess, delay, respond, and gather evidence of serious threat actions against the facility in question.
  A. Vulnerabilities, threats, and consequences
  B. Risks, threats, vulnerabilities, criticalities, and consequences
  C. Risks
  D. Criticalities and consequences

Q3: All good risk assessment methodologies include four things:
  A. Consideration of threat, probability, vulnerability, and consequences
  B. Consideration of risks, countermeasures, budgets, and schedules
  C. Consideration of business culture, regional culture, economics, and political correctness
  D. Consideration of politics, feelings of management, how things appear (the optics), and effectively hiding anything that does not look good for management

Q4: Better risk assessment methodologies also include
  A. Methods to guide the analyst toward appropriate countermeasures.
  B. Methods to hide vulnerabilities from the press, employees, and visitors.
  C. Methods to improve the health of workers.
  D. Methods to keep guns out of the workplace.

Q5: The best risk assessment methodologies
  A. Also include metrics for assessing the best choice of countermeasures as measured by their effectiveness in countering potential threats.
  B. Also include methods to improve the organization's public image.
  C. Also include methods to keep guns out of the workplace.
  D. Also include methods to protect daycare centers.

Q6: The very best methodologies also include
  A. Metrics for assessing the best choice of countermeasures not only from an effectiveness point of view, but also from a cost-effectiveness point of view.

B. Methods to improve the organization's public image.

C. Methods to keep guns out of the workplace.

D. Methods to protect daycare centers.

Q7: Risk formulas are usually quite simple. Most typically involve

A. Risk=a threat actor with intent (probability)* an exploitable vulnerability, prioritized by criticality and consequences.

B. Risk=probability * threat+vulnerability * criticality/consequences.

C. Risk=probability/threat * vulnerability * criticality/consequences.

D. Risk=probability * threat/vulnerability * criticality+consequences.

Q8: In order to protect the organization's assets, the analyst must determine what those assets are. All organizations have four types of assets:

A. People, real estate, data processing systems, and hurricanes

B. People, personal property, and public information

C. Employees, contractors, vendors, and visitors

D. People, property, proprietary information, and the organization's reputation

Q9: Neither the DHS nor any of the methodologies themselves actually require

A. The use of paper and pencil.

B. Analysts with any qualifications at all.

C. The use of any specific software tool.

D. Any of the above.

Q10: The steps involved in risk assessment include

A. Asset characterization, threat identification, criticality analysis, consequence analysis, vulnerability analysis, likelihood assessment, risk assessment, risk prioritization, and risk management.

B. Budgeting, determining the right kind of video cameras, dogs, guard force scheduling, signage, and lighting.

C. Economics, political risk studies, military preparation, a good supply of ammunition and rifles, fire-fighting equipment, and first aid kits.

D. Countermeasures selected by qualified technicians who have installed at least one previous system.

Answers

Q1 – C, Q2 – B, Q3 – B, Q4 – A, Q5 – A, Q6 – A, Q7 – A, Q8 – D, Q9 – C, Q10 – A

CHAPTER 3

Risk Analysis Skills and Tools

INTRODUCTION

On completion of this chapter, you will understand all of the skills necessary to perform a comprehensive world-class risk analysis as well the tools available to help you do it. You will be introduced to both commercial and self-developed tools, both of which can result in risk assessments that are well beyond the quality of the average assessment in the commercial security consulting marketplace. But they are not beyond your reach.

The information in this book is useful regardless of what type of tool the analyst uses to analyze risk, whether that is a commercially available program, manual sheets, or any other way. For those readers who might be interested in developing their own risk analysis templates rather than using a commercially available program, *please understand that the spreadsheet templates are not the primary purpose of the book but are provided only to help readers who have requested information about developing their own in-house tool and have limited funds to do so.* Using this approach, these people can achieve similar results to those who have many thousands of dollars to spend on software programs. This implies no personal preference on the author's part for any tool.

- In addition to teaching risk analysis, this book also presents a variety of Microsoft Excel® templates that generally conform to all of the U.S. Department of Homeland Security (DHS)-approved methodologies listed in Chapter 2. These will help users who may not be able to afford a world-class risk assessment software program to equal the results of those programs. Any good spreadsheet program can be used to develop the templates. Taken together, they comprise a complete quantitative risk analysis approach to fulfill the requirements of any better risk assessment methodology. Each of these templates breaks down the components of threat, vulnerability, probability, and risk in detail, allowing for a very complete assessment. Coupled with qualitative text developed from the quantitative data of these templates, a very comprehensive risk analysis report can be developed at virtually no software cost (assuming the analyst already has access to Microsoft [MS] Excel or similar spreadsheet software). Once the templates are developed, they can be used again and again on project after project, with equally excellent results.
- These templates help the analyst through the various steps to analyze risk quantitatively, culminating in a set of charts displaying risk by facility and area that anyone can easily understand. The ultimate charts display the organization's assets arrayed in a prioritized fashion, so that anyone can easily see what assets are most at risk and which of those are most critical to the organization. Some tools are useful to help the analyst understand various areas of analysis. For

example, the Sandia adversary sequence diagram concept is useful for helping the analyst understand vulnerabilities and probabilities and select appropriate countermeasures.

- These templates will each be explained throughout this book in enough detail so that people with a basic understanding of how to use a spreadsheet program from any major software vendor can build their own set of templates, which can be adapted for all future risk analysis projects throughout their long careers. The matrixes relating to a risk analysis topic are explained within the chapter describing that topic.
- Those readers who are not interested in developing a set of templates as described herein can skip the sections that explain how to build the templates. These are usually contained at the end of each chapter relating to a specific matrix. The balance of the chapter will teach the principles that are useful with any software tool and provide a deeper understanding of the process than is usually available.
- Those readers who are interested in developing a set of templates should read these sections carefully and then develop the matrixes one at a time until the entire set is developed. These can be developed all in one single workbook with a separate tab at the bottom for each individual matrix, so that a given project comprises only a single spreadsheet file with all matrixes contained within that one file.
- This book will explain each element of risk analysis and countermeasure selection in terms of its theory, practice, and tools. It will also explain in adequate detail how to assemble MS Excel spreadsheets for each element. Those readers who prefer to use a commercial software tool may skip the sections explaining how to build the Excel spreadsheets. For those who are interested in building and using their own world-class risk analysis software tool, the first two tabs on the Excel workbooks are explained in cell-by-cell detail and after that, in adequate detail to build the remaining sheets.
- It is typical for security practitioners to present a proposal to conduct a risk assessment in several phases of work. These often correspond to the skills needed to perform the work and also to deliverables (reports) that are presented to the client at the end of each phase of work.
- I am not advocating the use of Excel spreadsheets, any commercially available tool, or any other self-developed tool in particular. The objective is to utilize any tool that helps the analyst conduct a comprehensive risk analysis.

Risk assessment phases often include

- Survey and research phase
- Analysis phase
- Countermeasures selection and budgeting phase
- Report phase

Deliverables corresponding to these phases often include

- Survey phase
  - Report: survey findings and immediate action items
- Analysis phase
  - Report or notice of completion including general findings
- Countermeasures selection and budgeting phase

- Notice of completion and sometimes a rough-order magnitude budget
- Report phase
  - Comprehensive report, usually in two phases
    - 75% report: for presentation and review by the client
    - 100% report: including responses to client comments from the 75% report

SECURITY RISK ANALYSIS SKILLS

Risk analysis requires seven basic skills. These are

- Skill #1: How to gather data, including
  - Interviews
  - Research
    - Threat actor research
    - Bibliography
      - Unique for each project
      - Master database
  - Surveys
  - Asset classifications
  - Criticalities
  - Consequences
- Skill #2: Research and evidence gathering
  - Internet research
  - Telephone research
  - Bibliography building
  - Countermeasures research
- Skill #3: Critical thinking in the risk analysis process
  - Maintaining focus on purpose: Why examine this, and what is the issue at hand?
  - Identifying key questions to be answered in the analysis
  - Observing and understanding the implications of different points of view
  - Examining evidence and its implications for the analysis
  - Drawing inferences from the evidence
  - Concepts affecting the evidence
    - What theories, definitions, axioms, laws, and principles or models underlie the issue?
    - What is the reliability of the evidence?
    - What are the effects of personal prejudices on the reliability of inferences?
    - What are the assumptions and what is their effect on risk conclusions?
  - Drawing implications on the consequences of the risk: What might happen and what does happen?
- Skill #4: Quantitative analysis
  - Data classifications
  - Data input
  - Data crunching
  - Risk analysis results calculations
- Skill #5: Qualitative analysis

- Converting quantitative data into qualitative data
- Skill #6: Countermeasures selection
  - Countermeasures selection
  - Cost-benefit analysis
- Skill #7: Report writing
  - Report organization
  - Expanding and explaining quantitative data
  - Writing qualitative sections
  - Writing the recommendations
  - Writing the executive summary
  - Addendums

SECURITY RISK ANALYSIS TOOLS

- Tool set A: asset identification tools (including consequences analysis)
- Tool set B: probability assessment tools (threats and asset target value)
- Tool set C: vulnerability assessment tools
- Tool set D: risk analysis tools

Now let us examine each one of these skills in order.

Skill #1: Gathering Data

All risk analysis is based on the data gathered at the beginning of the risk analysis process. Typically, the analyst includes a survey phase for the purpose of containing the data-gathering tasks together.

All the data to be gathered are related, so it is often an iterative process; that is, we may interview key stakeholders and conduct surveys of properties and during the survey find items or issues that we want to bring back to the stakeholders in order to get clarification.

The primary data needed for a risk assessment should include the organization's mission statement, a list of programs they have developed in support of that mission, a list of assets by classification that support the programs, the organization's functional organization chart, the relationship between the organization's business functions and the physical property, the existing countermeasures used to protect those assets, and any historical data relating to past security events.

I cannot stress enough the importance of getting data gathering right: complete and right! Any failures in data gathering will result in incomplete, insufficient, or incorrect data sources for analysis. Therefore, the analysis could be missing vital information that could point to major risk. I will give you two examples.

On one project, we noticed that the truck tunnel to the loading dock of a project on an island also contained a chase housing all of the utility services to the entire island. Thus, any major truck bomb would not only result in a massive crater but would also destroy all the utilities to the island, rendering the island and all the buildings on it uninhabitable and leaving no vehicular access to the island.

On another project, we were considering options for controlling access to a property that had a very leaky perimeter with many entrances for vehicles and for pedestrians of all types. We had finally developed what we thought was a workable scheme to screen visitors and employees when we were informed that there was an off-site employee parking lot that would create a traffic flow of hundreds of employees every day into and out of one of the screening points that we had not accounted for. This threw off our entire throughput calculation and made our scheme unworkable. The truth is in the details.

Interviews

Most basic data can be gathered in initial interviews. Follow-up interviews may also be required as new information comes to light in the survey and research process.

Types of Data Required

Let us examine the type of data we need and review the skills and work processes needed to accumulate all the data. Remember, it will be from this data and this data alone that all of our analysis, risk conclusions, and recommendations will derive, so completeness is essential.

Get the Organization's Mission Statement

Few security consultants bother with the organization's mission statement, but it is foundational to understanding everything else about the organization. The organization grows entirely out of its mission statement; that is, every program, every asset, every business process, every customer served, and every action taken by the organization is in support of its mission statement. Every function of every asset and employee, contractor, and vendor is in support of the mission statement. The organization's mission statement relates to asset target value calculations; that is, how attractive is this organization to various types of attackers? Different threat actors select their targets primarily based on the organization's mission statement. For example, nongovernmental organizations (NGOs) working in high-threat zones may all be subject to attack by insurgents, but those whose mission statement includes the goal of proselytizing for a religion different than that of the insurgents may be most at risk (and in my opinion should not be there as they arrogantly disrespect the sensitivities of the local culture and in so doing put many other lives than their own at risk, including those who are working to help the local populace in a much more respectful manner). So, get the mission statement!

Understand the implications of the mission statement. Mission statements can be either lofty or humble, convoluted or direct. One organization I knew joked that their mission statement was "piles and piles of cash!" Another had a heartfelt goal of bettering the community through its services. So each mission statement contains clues about management attitudes and goals. By comparing these attitudes and goals with the reality of the workplace one can also judge the sincerity of the mission statement. The organization that joked about "piles and piles of cash" ended up abandoning its initial business plan of security consulting and became a security integrator when the first multimillion-dollar opportunity presented itself. By abandoning its original mission statement, the organization became unfocused and transitioned to a business model it did not understand, ultimately not serving its customers and (arguably) its reputation well in the local marketplace. As in the marketplace, organizations that do not act in concert with their mission statement often develop competing programs that make the job of security much harder.

Competing programs and business agendas also often result in unfocused applications of other supporting programs, including security programs. Those organizations may pay lip service to security while actually doing little that supports a secure environment.

The consultant who does not fully understand and appreciate the organization's mission statement and does not compare it to the reality on the ground will surely miss the point when analyzing risk.

Understand the Organization's Programs (Business Units)

Deriving from the organization's mission statement, the first agenda of any organization is to develop programs in support of that mission. All assets of all types as well as all of the organization's business processes are derived from the programs.

The role of security in an organization is to assist in protecting these assets and business processes from potential threat actors and hazards. The key to understanding the programs and business processes is in the organization's functional organization chart.

Now, let me pause a moment to advise the reader that functional organization charts do not always tell a true story, so I recommend highly that the security risk analyst should ask first what programs the organization has established to support its mission statement. If you rely solely on the functional organization chart or if you ask for and receive the functional organization chart before asking what programs the organization has put in place in support of its mission, it is very likely that the client's respondent will simply point you to the functional organization chart, which may have errors, flaws, missing elements, and deviations from the real set of programs. For example, I am always surprised to find that the security organization is not listed on the organization chart. This is because it is not a program in direct support of the mission but is one of the several programs in "dotted-line" support of the mission; that is, it is a program that supports programs that directly support the mission.

This is also a critical example of how the organization's management thinks and approaches the organization, program development, and problem solving in general. The degree to which the functional organization chart accurately reflects all of the actual programs is a good indication of how the organization approaches its program development and problem solving in general. You will likely see this reflected in how the organization approaches the recommendations of the risk assessment report later on.

Assets by Classification

There are four major classes of assets (Figure 3.1). These include

- People
- Property
- Proprietary information
- Business reputation

People Itemize each type of user in the building. Users will typically include

- Key senior management
- Management and employees
- Contractors
- Vendors
- Visitors
- Customers

FIGURE 3.1   Asset classes.

You will need to note the occupancies (where they work and interact), the hours of occupancy, tasks, uses of hazardous materials or equipment, their needs for access, and their frequency of access. It is also important to note any classic or specific threats against these people.

Property   Classify the organization's property in the following ways:

- Real property: Real property (land and buildings) should be classified by its location and purpose (what business units serves), and what type of property it is (office building, office suite, bridge, airport hangar or terminal, warehouse, maintenance yard, vehicle storage yard, etc.). Larger organizations will have many locations and types of buildings. These should be categorized by type and size of facility in a spreadsheet and mapped.
- Vehicles: Company owned, or leased and privately owned vehicles on company or company leasehold property (office building parking lot).
- Equipment: Equipment can include information technology systems (file servers, etc.) and other office equipment such as copiers, printers, furniture, cash registers, and so on. For most projects, a detailed list is not necessary, just a set of categories and their general locations.

Proprietary Information   Proprietary information is information that is unique to a particular organization, facilitates the conduct of business and should not be available freely to the public or competitors. Classify the organization's proprietary information as follows:

- Information technology system
- Security system
- Voice communications system
- Paper files (also including vital records)

The location, quantity, and type of information should be noted, as well as its sensitivity and criticality.

Business Reputation The organization's business reputation should be characterized from several points of view, including

- Senior management's characterization
- Management and employees' characterization
- Contractor/vendor's characterization
- Several customers' characterization

Gather the good and the bad. Categorize by the sources above and by characterization into a small spreadsheet.

Existing Countermeasures

In interviews, try to determine the organization's security program. This will include

- Mission statement and goals of the program
- Security management, including their qualifications, skills, and training
- High-tech elements: electronic security program (alarm/access control system, photo ID system, security video system, security communications systems including radios and intercoms, etc.)
- Low-tech elements: access-controlled and non-access-controlled gates, doors, and barriers; lighting; signage; property marking system; key control system; and so on
- No-tech elements: policies and procedures, guard patrol and posts, trained dogs, investigations programs, law enforcement liaison program, security awareness program, emergency preparedness program, disaster recovery program
- Future plans

Skill #2: Research and Evidence Gathering

All analysis is based on information and evidence. Information and evidence can be gathered in numerous ways, including

- Interviews
- Internet research
- Telephone research
- Surveys
- Asset classifications
- Historical data relating to security events
- Criticalities and consequences assessment
- Bibliography building
- Countermeasures research

Interviews

- Conducting interviews is more than just making a list and checking it twice. Interviews are a skill, science, and art. The following are key elements*:

---

* Interviewing techniques here are adapted from McNamara.[1]

- Preparation for the interview: Choose a setting with few distractions. Avoid settings with loud noises. (I once had to conduct interviews next door to a construction site where piles were being driven into the earth. It was nearly impossible for anyone in the room to stay on point.) Additionally, try to avoid interviewing people in their offices, as it is a sure bet they will be distracted by phone calls and people walking in.
- Explain the purpose of the interview.
- Cover any terms of confidentiality.
- Explain the format for the interview.
- Indicate how long you expect the interview to take.
- Invite them to contact you later if they remember anything relevant that was missed in the interview.
- Ask them if they have any questions.
- Record the interview by notes or tape. It is best to have someone dedicated to taking notes.
- Types of interviews
  - Informal, conversational interview: Some interviews are best held as informal discussions. This is generally true of interviews with any top management, as they usually do not have time for extended structured interviews. These will be held with other management and staff.
  - Closed, structured response interview: Some practitioners prefer to use a series of structured questions. These are useful as they can be on hand-outs that the interviewee can easily follow. Looking ahead, he or she can also have time to formulate more meaningful responses to upcoming questions.
  - Guided interview: Most of my interviews are guided interviews. These are characterized by a series of topics rather than specific questions. This allows straying from a topic in order to expand on a point or go to something noteworthy but not exactly on topic.
  - Open-ended interview: Open-ended interviews can be held with management and incidental employees. For example, I often stop during a survey and ask questions of employees who seem willing to facilitate. While asking questions about the facility and its use, I may also interject questions about the company's mission, security habits, and so on. These can be most illuminating as one can often get "the unvarnished truth" from such interviewees.
- Types of Questions
  - Background: It is good to begin an interview with a few background questions. I usually focus on how that person came to be in their position (early training, education, choice of career, choice of company, progress within the firm, challenges, working conditions, etc.).
  - Knowledge: This is the heart of the interview. What does the person know to be true about the topics or questions? Knowledge is provable and confirmable. No opinions should be entered into here.
  - Opinions or values: Any opinions should be noted as such, differentiating them from provable knowledge. Opinions have value. Opinions focus on what should change, not just what is.
  - Feelings: how the person feels about a condition, a topic, and so on.

- Sequence of Questions
  - Get the interviewee involved and focused on the topics as soon as possible.
  - Gather facts before asking about any opinions or conclusions.
  - Ask questions about the present before asking questions about the past or future. This gives context, and it is usually easier for someone to talk about the present.
  - Get the person's point of view about the topics.
  - Allow and encourage the interviewee to provide additional information of their own preference and to expand on their opinions about the problems that need to be addressed and what should be done.
- Wording of questions
  - Generally, questions should be open ended.
  - Questions should be as neutral as possible, avoiding any questions that might influence their answers. For example, never ask something like: "I don't think these people should be allowed to ..., do you?"
  - Ask questions one at a time, not compounded together.
  - Word questions clearly, using simple sentences. Define any special terms involved in the question.
  - Watch out for "why" questions. These imply a cause and effect that may not actually exist. Such questions may also cause the interviewee to become defensive, in that they may feel it necessary to justify their response. This can inhibit their response to future questions.
- Conducting the interview
  - Be professional but engaging. Everyone likes to open up to a person who makes them feel welcome, and conversely few open up to interviewers that are "stuffed shirts."
  - Occasionally verify that notes are up to date or that the tape recorder is working.
  - Ask one question at a time.
  - Remain as neutral as possible. It should not be possible for the interviewee to sense any agenda on your part. Act as if you have heard it all before.
  - Encourage responses with occasional nods and confirmations.
  - Using recorders or note takers is better than taking notes yourself. Whenever you take a note, the interviewee also notes that that answer is of interest to you. This can affect their future responses.
  - Provide a transition between major topics; for example, "Let's move on to..."
  - Keep the interview on topic. Do not lose control of the interview. For example, do not let the interviewee stray off topic, take so long to answer questions that time runs out, or begin asking leading questions of you. Their questions can come at the end of the interview if you are willing.
- Follow-up
  - Verify the tape recording or notes are complete.
  - Clarify any vague notes.
  - Write down any observations made during the interview, such as whether there were any surprises in the interview, where the interview took place

and at what time, whether you noticed any deception or unwillingness to cover any topics, and so on.

Internet Research

Research is the key to credibility in reports. Every source of data, especially controversial data, and every inference, implication, or conclusion should have solid reference to concepts, theories, definitions, axioms, laws, principles, models, and credible sources. Research is also the key to good conclusions. Research ferrets out valid and invalid points of view and relevant and irrelevant issues. Research helps the analyst understand the data at a level of depth and breadth not possible with only interviews and surveys.

When you are creating a risk analysis, research should be conducted into the organization's mission, history, key stakeholders, and its industry and criminal history vis-à-vis attacks against its assets.

Research on the assets can be conducted through the Internet using such online tools as Lexis/Nexis (www.lexis-nexis.com), Highbeam Research (www.highbeam. com), Bedford/St. Martin's (www.dianahacker.com/resdoc/), Questia (www.questia. com/Index.jsp), Purdue University's CORE (Comprehensive Online Research Education), Rand Research (www.rand.org), University of California, Irvine: Criminology, Law and Society, McAfee®, Google (www.Google.com), and Amazon (www.amazon.com).

Anyone who has ever used Google has a pretty good sense of how to conduct online research. The methods are usually simple and straightforward. Most online research tools search periodicals, books, and professional and academic papers. Google also searches for web pages, images, news, and shopping. Google is also a good source of information for road and satellite maps relating to organizations worldwide.

Most of these tools permit searches one of two ways: basic or advanced. To perform a basic search, one simply enters the search criteria in the search field. Simple searches can be conducted by entering all of the search criteria. In response, most search engines produce a results page, which is a list of references related to the search terms, generally with the most relevant searches nested near the top of the search (Figure 3.2).

FIGURE 3.2 Internet research.

More advanced searches can be conducted in several other ways:

Choosing search terms: Choosing the correct search terms is a primary key to finding the information you need. Start with the obvious; for example, the industry *oil*. Then add a more specific term; for example, *pipeline attacks*.

Framing: You can also look for exact finds by *framing* the search; placing an exact phrase within quotes, such as *"oil pipeline attacks"* will assure that everything will be excluded except those results that contain that exact phrase.

Exclude words: You can exclude certain terms by adding a minus sign in front of a word you do *not* want the search engine to find results for; for example, *oil pipeline attack -gas*.

Site-specific search: Even if a website does not support searches for content that matches a certain phrase, Google can search the entire site for you. Enter *"site:something.com"* after the search string. For example, *"oil pipeline attack" site: www.something.com*

Similar words and synonyms: Enter the tilde sign "~" before the word you want to find similar words or synonyms for. For example, *"Oil pipeline" ~attack*

Specific document types: If you want to find a particular document type, say portable document format (PDF) or PowerPoint (PPT) files, enter *"Oil pipeline" ~attack filetype:ppt*

This *or* that: By default, Google searches for websites that contain all words. If you want to find just this or that, enter *"oil pipeline disaster"* OR *"oil pipeline attack"*. The word *or* should be upper case.

Phone listing: You can find a person or organization's phone number or find out who owns a phone number. To find an organization's phone number enter *contact "organization name"* or *phone "organization name"*. To find who owns a phone number, enter *phonebook: 617-555-1212* (note that this number does not work; use a real phone number).

Area code lookup: To find the area corresponding to a telephone's area code, enter the area code, for example *"617"*.

Answer to life, the universe, and everything: You can also look this up on Google, but I will just give you this answer: 42.

Advanced searches:

- Google also has an advanced search function, which is to the right of the Google search field under www.Google.com and www.google.com/ig (which is a wonderful website that consolidates Google Calendar®, Gmail®, date/time/news/ weather, and other useful tools altogether). The advanced search fields include many variations and exclusions that are useful.
- Certain research websites facilitate highly detailed searches. One of the best of these is Highbeam Research® (Figure 3.3). Each research website has its own protocols but generally includes most of the categories below:
  - General search terms
  - Exclusions
  - And/or functions
  - Synonyms
  - Sources from which to search
  - Specific sources (e.g., individual magazines)

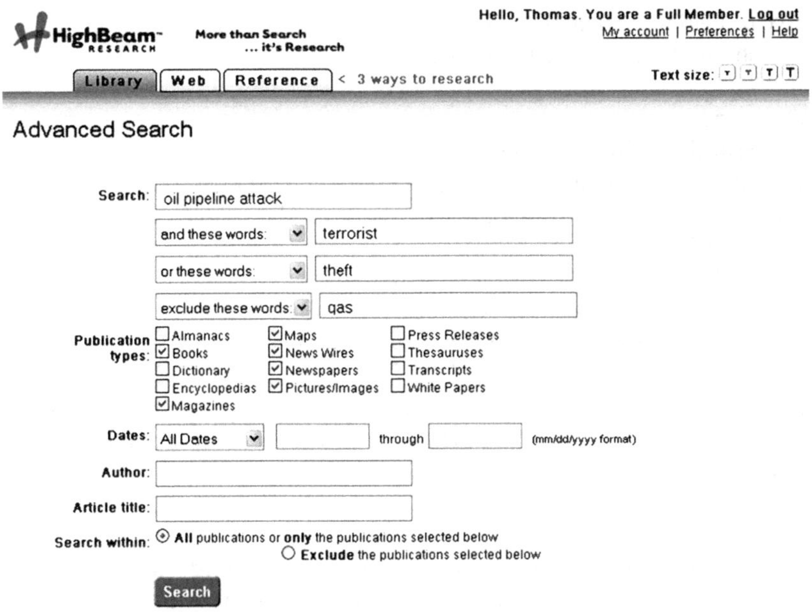

FIGURE 3.3   Advanced search example: Highbeam Research.

Telephone Research

Much research can also be conducted by telephone. You can find additional sources for information by asking key stakeholders who they think might have this information, and often they will have the contact and phone number handy and may be willing to make an introduction for you. Telephone research is particularly valuable when you have to confirm or expand on knowledge about a contractor's contribution to the organization; for example, to get information from a shipping company, information technology consultant, support vendor, and so on.

Records Research

Certain information can only be obtained through records research. Examples may include police records of crime statistics for a given facility and questions of ownership or lease terms. For some sites, the applications of certain countermeasures are constrained by lease terms. For example, if a 4-floor tenant of a 12-story building wants to place electronic turnstiles in the main lobby, this affects other tenants and so it will be necessary to clarify leasing terms and management willingness.

Surveys

Like interviews, surveys are the backbone of information gathering. Unlike interviews, however, surveys rely mostly on your own observations and expertise. Surveys can also be combined with interviews where a risk assessment of many facilities is involved, thus saving numerous repeat trips. Surveys deserve a checklist, but do not feel constrained to stay on point; just be certain to cover all the points. During surveys, you will likely find many unexpected things.

Notes: Notes help us not only to remember what we saw but also to add context to the notes themselves, thus helping us remember things that were not noted. This is an important principle. The very act of taking down a note helps us to remember things we saw, heard, or concluded that occurred in the general time frame of the note. Thus, a single note can help us remember a dozen things or more that are not related to the note itself. Notes should be taken for the following:

- Key concepts
- Architectural, landscaping observances
- System observances (condition, age, technology, brands, models, etc.)
- Operational observances (the operations of both the security group and the overall organization itself)
- Cultural observances (the business or regional culture has a profound effect on what sorts of countermeasures will be accepted)
- Points of view expressed by stakeholders, including users (these should be sought out)
- Detailed notes on existing console rooms, including all security system equipment and the nature and equipment in the room itself, including noise level, activity, other equipment available, and so on.

Photos Take many photos or videos. Invariably, the one thing I need a picture of most is the thing I thought was too unimportant to shoot during the survey. Shoot everything whether it seems relevant or not. Video can be most helpful as you may capture a fleeting image of that thing you did not think you would need as you pan across from one thing to another. I use a 12-megapixel camera with a 150° field of view lens for all indoor and much outdoor work. This allows me to zoom in digitally to see details that I thought were irrelevant at the time of shooting.

Files Save photos and notes in a file. Digital files are better as they can be edited and inserted into reports more easily.

Day and night Conduct the survey during both the day and the night. Everything changes at night, including the lighting, the character of the workforce, the quantity and quality of employees, the way they work and interact with each other, the public, and access points, and so on. Take lighting levels using a quality light meter. My personal favorite is the pocket digital light meter type, which typically ranges down to 0.1 Fc (foot-candles) and up to 2000 Fc. The accuracy is acceptable and cost is low. Additionally, these light meters have a separate sensor and display, separated by a 1 m or so cable, so readings can be taken accurately and seen readily without affecting the sensor. Any good meter will do (Figure 3.4).

Asset Classifications

The risk analysis is measured as the risk of an unwanted event happening to any of the organization's assets. See Chapter 5 on Assets for a detailed description.

Historical Data Relating to Security Events

For criminal threats history, it is useful to research the history of crimes at the location, for the client's industry or for the client's other similar facilities. Location criminal history can be obtained from the local police database or from a commercial source such as CAP Index®. A history of crimes against the client's industry or against the client's other properties may be obtainable from Internet research or from the client's own security department.

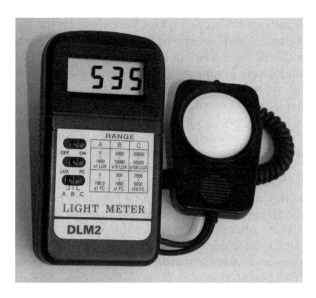

FIGURE 3.4 Pocket digital light meter.

Criticalities and Consequences Assessment

Each asset has two criticality factors. The first factor is the asset's criticality to the mission of the organization and the second is the lost time and productivity and the cost of recuperating the asset if it is damaged or lost. Actually, the first element is criticality and the second is the consequence. Only the client can determine criticality, although the security analyst may estimate criticality in the absence of client input on the subject.

An asset's criticality to the mission of the organization is gauged by how severe the damage to an organization's operations would be if the asset was lost or severely damaged. Certain assets are critical to the mission of an organization. For example, in small organizations, the key management may be critical. The loss of their expertise, strategic insight, and so on could spell disaster for a small organization. For larger organizations, the critical asset could be a key facility, business process, or formula. For example, a software manufacturer's business would be severely disrupted if the source code to their operating system or software suite was openly available. Likewise, military or marketing strategy could be a critical asset and its compromise could spell military or market defeat at the hands of enemies or competitors. In 2008, during the credit crisis, automakers found it nearly impossible to finance cars and trucks as their credit sources dried up. As few customers can pay cash for a new vehicle, this had an immediate and severe impact on auto and truck sales. To determine critical assets, one must be open-minded and look at the whole business process, including all kinds of suppliers. This is an example of where critical thinking (see Chapter 4) is important because it places a focus on assumptions. Few automakers were prepared for the credit crunch because they had assumed that credit availability was a given. Nothing in the business process is a given.

Certain assets may not be critical to the mission of the organization in its initial loss, (i.e., the organization could continue to operate for a while by working around the asset's loss by depending more on other assets), but the loss of the asset could compel the organization to replace the asset at a cost so great or a time cycle so long as to make continued normal operations impractical. For example, during the San Francisco earthquake of October 17, 1989, many businesses were disrupted when transportation bridges and elevated motorways collapsed. This had a knock-on effect on the transit time for workers living across the water and those who had always depended on those motorways. As employees were not able to get to work in a timely manner and the length of time necessary to repair the motorways became more apparent, the critical employees looked for other employment nearer to home rather than looking for new homes nearer their work. Many businesses that depended on employees with special skills were severely disrupted, as it was often those very employees who commuted the farthest across those bridges and motorways. Those businesses and employees had always assumed that the transportation corridors were a given. Nothing in the business process is a given.

Bibliography Building

As research accumulates, it is helpful to build a bibliography of books and articles. I find it helpful as I am conducting Internet research, for example, to print the reference web page or article to a PDF* file and save it under the project directory in a subdirectory named "bibliography." I codename the file itself for a keyword lookup. This is particularly helpful for references to websites, articles, and papers, which can vanish from the Internet over time. This assures that, if challenged, the reference is available and provable.

Countermeasures Research

Research on appropriate countermeasures is a science and an art, requiring significant skills to find correct products for unique applications. The following list is by no means comprehensive, but includes the key elements:

- Determine an available range of possible countermeasures, including high-tech, low-tech, and no-tech options.
- One way to do this is to use Google® and enter the vulnerability and the word countermeasures; for example, if one enters the phrase "B&E† door vulnerability countermeasures," many references are given. One is http://www.spymall.com/catalog/library-lock.htm, which is a library of locksmithing, including a reference to many books on techniques of breaking and entering and a range of effective countermeasures to those methods and tactics.
- If research is needed on a specific type or manufacturer of a specific countermeasure, this can be found by searching Google for variants on the name of the countermeasure or its possible product name or on the vulnerability the countermeasure is designed to address, or by searching ASIS International's Seminar and Exhibits Final Program and Exhibits Guide (for a comprehensive list of security industry manufacturers and service providers) and ASIS International's Security Industry Buyers Guide®, both of which are briefs of offerings of the entire security industry. The Security Industry Buyer's Guide can also be found at the following website, which is worth bookmarking: http://www.securitymanagementbuyersguide.com/BrowseDirectory.aspx.
- Regarding bookmarking, I recommend organizing browser bookmarks into categories using the "organize bookmarks" function of Firefox® or the "organize favorites" function of Microsoft Internet Explorer®. Firefox's Foxmarks function also synchronizes home, work, and laptop computer browsers so that the same bookmarks are available on all and are continuously updated.

---

* PDF = portable document format, invented by Adobe Systems® in 1993 for universal document exchanges in a manner that is completely independent of any hardware, software, or operating system and not requiring any costly application software to view. PDF is an open standard and conforms to ISO 32000-1:2008.
† B&E = breaking and entering.

- It is most helpful to build a library of useful manufacturers' websites, and I routinely copy *all* product data sheets I find on the Internet into a directory of reference products, services, and security solutions. To do this, one needs a PDF printer or writer (many are available online, including some that are free downloads; look for PDF printer or writer under Google). The extra time it takes to print the data sheet and file it away is time well spent and will pay off the next time you are looking for that unique wall-mounted duress button, automatic security electronic turnstile, or DHS-rated vehicle crash barrier and you just cannot remember the name of the product or manufacturer.
- I highly recommend having a copy of and subscribing to ASIS International's Protection of Assets Manual® (POA manual), which is itself a basic library of security strategies and solutions. The hard copy is valuable as a quick reference and the online copy is searchable. One cannot get the whole story of the POA manual in the online version. The hard copy is good to have.
- Additionally, a good library is critical to a security practitioner's professional development and acts as a powerful research tool. One should buy books voraciously. Your spouse will complain about the budget, but it is money well spent and will save countless hours searching for that one thing you remember seeing on the news or the Internet but cannot find. Usually, it has been written about in a book. There are many excellent books in the footnotes of each chapter of this book that together form the foundation of an excellent security library.

Skill #3: Critical Thinking in the Risk Analysis Process

- See Chapter 4 for a detailed discussion on critical thinking and its application to the risk analysis process. The essentials of critical thinking as it applies to risk analysis are covered in detail. These include
- Maintaining focus on purpose: Why examine this, and what is the issue at hand?
- Identifying key questions to be answered in the analysis
- Observing and understanding the implications of different points of view
- Examining evidence and its implications on the analysis
- Drawing inferences from the evidence
- Concepts affecting the evidence
    - What theories, definitions, axioms, laws, and principles or models underlie the issue?
    - What is the reliability of the evidence?
    - What are the effects of personal prejudices on the reliability of inferences?
    - What are the assumptions and what is their effect on risk conclusions?
- Drawing implications on the consequences of the risk: What might happen and what does happen?

Skill #4: Quantitative Analysis

There are two forms of risk analysis: quantitative and qualitative. In the simplest form, quantitative analysis has to do with the measurement or estimation of a thing, and qualitative analysis has to do with the description of its characteristics, attributes, features, or value.

A debate has raged for decades over the merits of one versus the other. The debate originated in the science of sociology and has expanded into many other sciences, including risk analysis. The debate rose to prominence in the 1970s through a backlash against the priority attached to scientific or positivist methodology in sociological textbooks. And attempts to reconcile the two points of view date back to Michael Mann (in the journal *Sociology*, 1981).[3]

Quantitative analysis is based upon quantitative (numeric) data. The terms *data crunching*[4] and *data mining** both relate to quantitative analysis. The idea of quantitative analysis is that if one can examine a problem from enough points of view and measure or estimate each of those elements, one can understand enough about it to make valid conclusions. For example, nearly every university that teaches geology begins by teaching students how to classify rocks into their shapes, textures, colors, density, mass, hardness, and so on. All other aspects of geology are built on this fundamental understanding of the subject. Quantitative analysis is built on classification and measurement or estimation.

- Data classifications: Data must be classified into their constituent components. In risk analysis, one classifies assets, threats, vulnerabilities, and probabilities, and then risk can be estimated.
- Data input: Once classified, data about the assets, threats, vulnerabilities, and probabilities must be gathered or estimated and inputted. Data estimates are in the form of numbers or estimates, usually along a range of least to worst. Each data entry cell is a point of analysis as it represents consideration of a factor of an asset, threat, vulnerability, or probability.
- Data crunching: Raw data (the input) must be crunched (calculated) in some meaningful way to reach conclusions. This is often a two-step process, with step one being sums, multiples, averages, and so on of the data inputted; and step two being the setting up and running of structured query language (SQL) algorithms, which bring meaning to the data.
- Risk analysis results calculations: Meaningful calculations can be concluded from this by ranking the results of the data crunching.
- DHS-approved risk analysis methods all use some measure of quantitative analysis.

Quantitative analysis is always a component of qualitative analysis, even when the quantitative analysis is not forthright (not calculated). The analyst must perform some quantitative analysis in order to reach any meaningful conclusions about the assets, threats, vulnerabilities, and probabilities.

Skill #5: Qualitative Analysis

Qualitative analysis involves the description of the data's characteristics, attributes, features, or value and the estimating of those values in general terms (low, medium, high, etc.). In the end, data only have meaning qualitatively. Most commonly, qualitative analysis is based on observer impressions of relatively small (presumably representative) samples. Thus, qualitative data are often subjective as they represent the analyst's interpretation of the research and

---

* Data mining is the process of sorting through large amounts of information to find patterns or symbolic clusters of information.

analysis. But that, in fact, is the point of analysis: to come to a conclusion about what to do about the issue. Every risk assessment uses qualitative analysis, as the act of writing the report itself and its conclusions and recommendations is an act of qualitative analysis.

Presumably, the analyst should know enough about the subject to reach valid conclusions. Unfortunately, most analysts are not trained or skilled in critical thinking, and without that, any analysis will almost certainly be based upon assumptions, biases, and preconceptions. The data are too often used to support an original conclusion that was reached before gathering the data. Qualitative analysis can be prone to significant flaws unless the analysis is based on critical thinking processes. In such cases, qualitative analysis is often conducted from a basis of quantitative data. I believe that the best reports are the result of both quantitative and qualitative approaches. Quantitative data can sample very large quantities of data, while qualitative analysis usually focuses on a small (hopefully representative) data field. The use of quantitative data helps assure that the small data sampled for the qualitative analysis are truly representative, relevant to the issues, and less biased by personal prejudices.

Converting Quantitative Data into Qualitative Data

Data versus Information: For analysts who use the dual analysis approach, one must collect and process quantitative data and then process them into meaningful information. Data are only plain facts, but information is actionable. Data are abstract, while information has focus. Information is a collection of data that are interpreted and processed to determine their meaning; then they are useful and become information.

I suggest that quantitative analysis should be conducted in a way that computes averages, sums, or multiples of the raw input points and then ranks that data from highest to lowest. This provides the analyst with a comparison of the data that is useful to determine which data are most relevant and important.

Skill #6: Countermeasure Selection

Chapters 15, 16, and 19 all deal with countermeasures selection from three distinct points of view. Chapter 15 focuses on the goals of countermeasures. Chapter 16 explains the three types of countermeasures and gives examples of many, including their applications, capabilities, and exploits; and Chapter 19 introduces a countermeasure selection tool, which helps focus the analyst and client on the best type of countermeasure for a particular vulnerability.

Countermeasure Selection

The whole idea of security is to understand risks that could be exploited by potential threat actors and to create measures to counter the potential threats (i.e., countermeasures). There are three broad types of countermeasures: high-tech, low-tech, and no-tech. High-tech (electronic) countermeasures employ electronic systems to deter, detect, and assess threats; to assist in the response; and to collect evidence. Low-tech solutions include locks, barriers, lighting, and architectural and crime prevention through environmental design (CPTED)* solutions. No-tech solutions include policies and procedures, security staffing, training, awareness programs, investigations, security dogs, and so on.

---

* "CPTED is the proper design and effective use of the built environment which may lead to a reduction in the fear and incidence of crime, and an improvement of the quality of life."[5]

These three types of solutions should be used in combination to address vulnerabilities and to achieve multiple layers of protection. The most valuable assets should be protected by multiple layers, from the outer perimeter inward.

The key elements of protection include

- Access Control: Limiting access to vulnerable assets to only those who have a legitimate need to access them.
- Deterrence: Creating a psychological impression that the risk of acting as a threat actor could be greater than the reward, either through creating the possibility that the threat action may not succeed or that the threat actor may be caught and penalized.
- Detection: Creating detection technologies that can alert a security staff of any unwanted or inappropriate activity within their purview.
- Assessment: Technologies that can help the security staff assess what has been detected to determine if it is a real threat or just a false alarm.
- Response, including delaying technologies: A variety of responses can be mounted to legitimate threat actions, including the response of security staff, voice communications from a console to a threat actor to warn them away, delaying technologies such as deployable barriers, and aggressive responses to aggressive threats (automated weapons, etc.).
- Gathering evidence: CCTV systems and audio systems can gather evidence for prosecution and training.

Cost-Benefit Analysis

- It is not enough just to determine a range of possible countermeasures; one must also select the ones that are most appropriate. Appropriateness can be measured in two dimensions: effectiveness and cost.
- Effectiveness can be assessed by the potential countermeasure's ability to perform the six roles above (I break the assessment down into seven, including the countermeasure's ability to delay an intruder). Each countermeasure can be estimated to be able to perform one of these six functions more or less effectively.
- Cost is the second factor. The two factors together create the function of cost-effectiveness. Thus, in the comparison of any two countermeasures that are equally effective, the one with the lower cost is more cost effective.

Skill #7: Report Writing

Report writing is one of the most critical skills of a good risk analyst. Analysts that cannot write well cannot communicate their analysis effectively and thus are less effective analysts.

Chapter 20 focuses entirely on effective report writing. The keys to effective report writing include

- Report organization
- Expanding and explaining quantitative data
- Writing qualitative sections
- Writing the recommendations
- Writing the executive summary
- Addendums

Tools

In order to perform analysis, a risk analyst must have tools to collect and analyze the pertinent data. This can be done using a simple notepad and pencil or a software tool. Many commercially available software tools have been developed, both great and small, ranging from the economical to the very expensive. Additionally, I and many other analysts who perform analysis frequently have developed individual software tools to perform the analysis that are as effective as commercially available tools. I do not wish to say that either commercial software or custom software templates are better or worse than the other. You can judge for yourself. However, so many other analysts have asked me to explain my approach that I am presenting it for open copy by anyone. It is based upon a Microsoft Excel template that I developed and is among the most thorough quantitative analysis tools that I have ever seen, exceeded only by a deep Sandia team analysis, costing many times more. Arguably, a couple of commercially available tools are as effective, but they cost thousands of dollars. The Excel template tools that are illustrated in this book are not meant to be *the* solution, but should be used an exemplar of what a good tool should do. Any software tool that embodies the characteristics of these template tools will do the job, including sophisticated, formally written risk assessment software costing many thousands of dollars.

Analysts that select more economical software options should assure that they perform all of the analysis illustrated in the tools that follow in this book. Most economical software tools do not and thus fall short of the objective of actual analysis, but should rather be considered risk estimating tools. While there is nothing wrong with the use of risk estimating tools for simple projects on low-risk facilities, one should not expect the results of actual analysis. That is, one should expect that undiscovered risks may exist against which no countermeasure has been programmed and that certain of those risks could be severe and could result in a catastrophic lapse of security programming, possibly costing careers and even lives.

Analysis is a process and is not inherently dependent on any specific tool. Thus, these tools have been developed to illustrate the risk analysis process and provide a cost-efficient and very effective means of accomplishing that task. The use of far more expensive software may be appropriate, depending on the budget and circumstances of your particular organization, and it is not my intent to dissuade any reader from obtaining and using more sophisticated software tools.

Commercially Available Software Tools

SVA-Pro® One of the best of the commercially available tools is SVA-Pro. SVA-Pro was developed by Dyadem International Ltd. (a Canadian firm), largely in response to the requirements of AcuTech Consulting Services®, one of the finest risk consulting firms in the world. AcuTech was founded by David A. Moore, a professional engineer (P.E.) and certified safety professional (CSP). SVA-Pro is one of a suite of software products that were developed to address a wide range of industry risks. I have used SVA-Pro and, once formatted for the specific needs of the project, it is a highly competent tool. The software requires significant customization (which is possible through paid training from Dyadem, or can be done by Dyadem in response to submitted criteria with one of their paid support packages). The software is highly difficult to customize without the direct and costly support of Dyadem, which seems to wish to compel its users to avail of both support and training in order to receive adequate support to customize the program to specific project needs. (This is the personal opinion of the author, also supported by other SVA-Pro users I have spoken with.)

SVA-Pro, once configured, creates voluminous quantitative data. SVA-Pro has industry standard templates for CCPS's SVA, NIST 780's SVA for petroleum and petrochemical industries, and risk analysis and management for critical asset production (RAMCAP). SVA-Pro is arguably one of the finest commercially available risk analysis tools.

RAMCAP Plus®   RAMCAP Plus® was developed as a software tool to support RAMCAP projects. It is generally quite thorough and presents usable reports. Opinions differ on whether SVA-Pro or RAMCAP Plus is better. RAMCAP Plus seems to require less custom configuration.

RiskWatch®   RiskWatch software (produced by RiskWatch in Annapolis, Maryland) allows the user to evaluate their risks and produces reports and graphs that specifically detail compliance within these regulations, showing where controls are needed. RiskWatch conducts automated risk analysis, physical security reviews, audits, and vulnerability assessments of facilities and personnel. Security threats include crimes against property, crimes against people, equipment of systems failure, terrorism, natural disasters, and fire and bomb threats. Question sets include entry control, perimeters, fire, facilities management, and guards.* RiskWatch software appears to comply with the requirements of most DHS risk analysis methodologies.

These two tools can be used as a benchmark comparison for others.

Lesser Software Tools

Numerous software templates are available such as the National Fire Protection Association (NFPA) risk assessment checklist. Many of these types of tools provide a simple checklist with the idea of helping the security practitioner evaluate risk. The NFPA checklist, for example, is a two-page checklist divided into two parts. Part one identifies assets or operations at risk, and part two determines facility hazards. Such checklists do little to help security practitioners assess risks (notwithstanding the document's name: "Risk Assessment Checklist"). This particular checklist (which is typical of many) completely ignores vulnerabilities and is otherwise only binary in nature (hazard is possible or is not possible, terrorism is possible or is not possible, etc.). There is no risk calculation at all. Anyone using this template would be utterly unprepared to develop a security program of any kind. Such tools are to be avoided.

Affordable Tools Examples

The next few paragraphs reiterate information at the beginning of this chapter for clarity.

- One of the objectives of this book is to help cash-strapped security managers develop a world-class risk assessment tool that is the equal of multithousand-dollar programs. To that end, this book presents a variety of Microsoft Excel templates, which I believe conform to all of the DHS-approved methodologies listed in Chapter 2. Taken together, they comprise a complete quantitative risk analysis approach to fulfill the requirements of any better risk assessment methodology. Each of these templates breaks down the components of threat, vulnerability, probability, and risk in detail, allowing for a very complete assessment. Coupled with qualitative text developed from the quantitative data of these templates, a very comprehensive risk analysis report can be developed at virtually no software

---

* Excerpted from the RiskWatch® website.

cost (assuming the analyst already has access to Microsoft Excel or similar spreadsheet software). Once the templates are developed in the first instance, they can be used again and again on project after project, with equally excellent results.

- These templates help the analyst through the various steps to analyze risk quantitatively, culminating in a set of charts displaying risk by facility and area that anyone can easily understand. The ultimate charts display the organization's assets arrayed in a prioritized fashion so that anyone can easily see what assets are most at risk and which of those are most critical to the organization. Some tools are useful to help the analyst understand several areas of analysis. For example, the Sandia adversary sequence diagram concept is useful to help the analyst understand vulnerabilities and probabilities and to help select appropriate countermeasures.

- These templates will each be explained throughout this book in enough detail so that any person who has basic understanding of how to use a spreadsheet program from any major software vendor can build his or her own set of templates that can be adapted for all future risk analysis projects throughout his or her long career. The matrixes relating to a risk analysis topic are explained within the chapter describing that topic.

- Those readers who are not interested in developing a set of templates as described herein can skip the sections that explain how to build the templates. These are usually contained at the end of each chapter relating to a specific matrix.

- Those readers who are interested in developing a set of templates should read these sections carefully and then develop the matrixes one at a time until the entire set is developed. These can be developed all in one single workbook with a separate tab at the bottom for each individual matrix, so that a given project comprises only a single spreadsheet file with all matrixes contained within that one file.

- This approach is arguably equal or superior to any of the commercially available software tools and dispenses with the need to expend thousands of dollars.

- Tool set A: assets and consequences tools
  - Asset list: The first step uses a spreadsheet to create a list of the organizations' assets in an organized fashion, broken down into the four major categories of assets: people, property, proprietary information, and business reputation. These are the categories that most following tools will use. This tool is described in Chapter 5: Asset Characterization and Identification. This will form the basis (asset target list) for most of the other matrixes.
  - Criticalities and Consequence Matrix: The Criticalities and Consequences Matrix defines the criticalities of each listed asset to the mission of the organization and the resulting consequences of its loss in terms of:
    - Loss of life
    - Loss of property
    - Loss of productivity
    - Loss of proprietary information
    - Loss of business reputation

- Tool set B: probability (likelihood) assessment tools
  - Adversary/Means Matrix: The Adversary/Means Matrix defines potential threat actors and provides an estimate of their motivation, capabilities, history, weapons used, and attack scenarios. This information helps the analyst to understand which threat actors to be most concerned about and is

essential to establishing a design basis threat (DBT). The DBT is that threat against which protective measures are designed to be effective. Threats that exceed the DBT are beyond the capabilities of the countermeasures.

- Adversary sequence diagram: The adversary sequence diagram is a tool developed by Sandia Laboratories, which comprises a drawing(s) of the facility that identifies the entry locations and pathways that a threat actor could take to reach target objectives. This helps the risk analyst understand where detection, assessment, and delay countermeasures should be placed.
- Asset Target Value Matrixes
  - Historical statistics are of no use in likelihood predictions for terrorism events because these events are too rare and there are not enough historical data. In the absence of historical data, one can use asset target value estimates. Asset Target Value Matrixes use a set of metrics that help the analyst determine what kind of targets are most likely to be subject to a terrorist event and the risk at any given facility where such attacks might take place. Asset Target Value Matrixes examine the factors that terrorists might use to select a facility to target and where in the target a successful attack would be most likely. Asset Target Value Matrixes can also be of value in estimating likely locations for various types of criminal behavior.
  - Terrorism Asset Target Value Matrixes: I use two different types of matrixes for terrorism. There is no single matrix that is widely accepted by the entire security industry. However, soon after the attacks of September 11, 2001, in New York and Washington, a model appeared from the Department of Defense that gained wide acceptance, called the CARVER+Shock model. The second model is the KSM Matrix. Each of these evaluates a facility or area of a facility for factors that designated terrorist organizations would use for targeteering (target selection).
    - CARVER+Shock Matrix: CARVER is an abbreviation for:
      - Criticality
      - Accessibility
      - Recuperability
      - Vulnerability
      - Effect
      - Recognizability

      The CARVER has long been used by special forces around the globe as a basis for targeting for military purposes. The additional attribute "Shock" was added to adapt the familiar CARVER model to terrorism. CARVER is still widely accepted, though critically flawed. I use it as one of two models because it is widely accepted. It is flawed because evidence indicates that no terrorist organization uses all these factors (or these factors alone) for targeteering.
    - KSM Matrix: The second matrix, which I use, is the KSM Matrix. KSM stands for Khalid Shaikh Mohammed, the presumed mastermind behind the 9/11 attacks and reportedly many others. When one examines the elements of the targets selected by KSM, a pattern emerges that is useful for analyzing potential targets of attacks by major terrorist organizations. The factors include
      - The target fits the strategic objectives of the organization.
      - Mass casualties are possible.

- The target will attract the media and is on "media friendly" ground (visually accessible).
- The target is of economic importance or represents an economically important sector of the economy.
- The target is of cultural importance to the constituent community of the victims and where possible is also culturally important to the terrorist organization's constituent community.
- The target is vulnerable.
- There is a high probability of success of the planned attack scenario.
- A successful attack against this target could result in increased recruiting and fund-raising for the terrorist organization.

These factors make it a useful matrix for many major terrorist organizations: not only Al-Qaeda, but especially for organizations that have close ties with Al-Qaeda. However, the actual matrix factors should be analyzed in the context of the elements of the targeting history of each terrorist organization under consideration.

- Economic Crimes Asset Target Value Matrix: Economic crimes probabilities can be derived from historical records (crime statistics, CAP Index® reports, etc.) or, if these are not available, such as in the case of a new facility, an estimate can be constructed from an Economic Crimes Asset Target Value Matrix. Factors that are useful for the latter include
  - An attack against this target could result in economic gain.
  - There is a high probability of success.
  - There is a high probability of escape.
  - There is a low probability of subsequent capture.
- Violent Crimes Asset Target Value Matrix: Similarly, violent crimes probabilities can be derived from historical records or estimated from the following factors:
  - There are available surveillance positions.
  - Access identification is not required.
  - Forcible access is possible.
  - A sneak-path is possible.
  - The target is vulnerable to physical attack.
  - The target is vulnerable to social engineering* access methods.
  - There is a high probability of success.
  - There is a high probability of escape.
- Subversives Matrix: Subversives, as it applies to nongovernmental organizations (NGOs), include any person or organization that acts in a disruptive manner, contrary to the organization's operating interests. Subversives can be acting with intent against the organization's interests or without intent, disregarding the organization's interests and in a manner that is counter to those interests. Examples: The first category of subversives may include activist organizations and individuals, and the second category could include persistently disruptive employees or

---

* Wikipedia: "Social Engineering is the art of manipulating people into performing actions or divulging confidential information." For security purposes, social engineering can also be used to assist a perpetrator in gaining access to a secure or semisecure facility.

persons who intrude on the privacy of VIP patrons. Factors for subversives could include:
- The target conforms to the strategic objectives of the activist organization or individual.
- The target is accessible.
- The target operations are easily disrupted.
- Time on premises is possible.
- If apprehended, penalties are bearable.
- Petty Crimes Matrix: Petty crimes include any misdemeanor (with punishment being less than one year in jail, no prison time). Petty crimes may include any chronic or persistent minor criminal activity that could affect the operations or reputation of the organization if left unchecked. Some petty crimes are economic in nature and some are social expressions. Examples may include
  - Pickpockets and purse snatchers
  - Prostitution-related activities
  - Trespassers
  - Vandals
  - Stalkers
- Matrix factors could include
  - Discrete criminal activity is possible in the public space.
  - Trespassing is possible or the activity will not likely be viewed as trespassing.
  - Acceptable security risk to threat actor.
  - Activity may not be discovered until later.
- Tool set C: vulnerability assessment tools
  - Asset/Attack Matrix: The Asset/Attack Matrix is used to determine what kinds of weapons and threat scenarios could be most effective against which assets. This information is valuable to the risk analyst to help determine which threat scenarios are most appropriate to design against and where they should be applied.
  - Surveillance Matrix: Surveillance is an element of vulnerability and is also essential for conducting any type of criminal or terrorist attack. The Surveillance Matrix identifies which types of surveillance can be effectively conducted regarding which assets.
  - Circulation Path/Threat Nexus: The Circulation Path/Threat Nexus identifies where along building circulation paths there are natural crossing points for high-value personnel and potential threat actors. This matrix can be used on larger projects and those with high-value personnel assets.
  - Circulation Path/Weapons Nexus: The Circulation Path/Weapons Nexus identifies where along building circulation paths there are natural crossing points for high-value personnel and where various types of weapons could be used. This is valuable for determining not only special areas of risk, but also what types of weapons are likely to be used in these locations. This matrix can be used on larger projects and those with high-value personnel assets.
  - Adversary sequence diagram: Graphically addresses the entry locations and pathways that an aggressor could take to reach possible targets.
  - Vulnerability Matrix: Vulnerability comprises accessibility, surveillance, and intrinsic vulnerability. These are mitigated by existing factors, which could

include natural countermeasures, physical measures, electronic measures, and operational measures.

- Tool set D: risk analysis tools
  - Unsorted Risk Matrix: The Unsorted Risk Matrix views the consequence, vulnerability, and various asset target value results from the various matrixes above in the worst-case scenario for each asset under consideration. The results are ranked by severity but are left unsorted (although still sorted by the list of assets). I often create two Unsorted Risk Matrixes, one for terrorism risks and a separate one for criminal risks.
  - Sorted Risk Matrix: The Sorted Risk Matrix is the same matrix as above, but is sorted by consequences.
  - V^2 Matrixes: The V^2 Matrixes present the risk factors in two dimensions (Vulnerability and Asset Target Value [equating to probability]): "V^2"; and also overlay the criticality/consequence ranking of the asset, thus providing a three-dimensional picture of the risk for each asset and category of assets. The V^2 Matrix provides a way to present the final data that is easy for anyone to interpret, regardless of their knowledge or skill regarding risk.

Certain of these tools are also useful in developing security program countermeasures. These include the V^2 Matrixes, the Surveillance Matrix, the Vulnerability Matrix, the adversary sequence diagrams, and the circulation path/threat nexus and circulation path/weapons nexus. These will be covered in later chapters in more detail.

Additionally, a proper risk analysis report usually also includes security program recommendations (including countermeasure selections) and rough-order magnitude budgeting. These will also be covered in later chapters.

SUMMARY

Introduction

Risk analysis requires seven basic skills. These are:

- Skill #1: How to gather data including
  - Interviews
  - Research
    - Threat actor research
    - Bibliography
      - Unique for each project
      - Master database
  - Surveys
  - Asset classifications
  - Criticalities
  - Consequences
- Skill #2: Research and evidence gathering
  - Internet research
  - Telephone research
  - Bibliography building
  - Countermeasures research

- Skill #3: Critical thinking in the risk analysis process
  - Maintaining focus on purpose: Why examine this, and what is the issue at hand?
  - Identifying key questions to be answered in the analysis
  - Observing and understanding the implications of different points of view
  - Examining evidence and its implications on the analysis
  - Drawing inferences from the evidence
  - Concepts affecting the evidence
    - What theories, definitions, axioms, laws, and principles or models underlie the issue?
    - What is the reliability of the evidence?
    - What are the effects of personal prejudices on the reliability of inferences?
    - What are the assumptions and what is their effect on risk conclusions?
  - Drawing implications about the consequences of the risk: What might happen and what does happen?
- Skill #4: Quantitative analysis
  - Data classifications
  - Data input
  - Data crunching
  - Risk analysis results calculations
- Skill #5: Qualitative analysis
  - Converting quantitative data into qualitative data
  - Inductive reasoning
  - Threat analysis
- Skill #6: Countermeasures selection
  - Countermeasures selection
  - Cost-benefit analysis
- Skill #7: Report writing
  - Report organization
  - Expanding and explaining quantitative data
  - Writing qualitative sections
  - Writing the recommendations
  - Writing the executive summary
  - Addendums

Tools

- Tool set A: Asset identification tools
  - List of interviewees and contacts
  - List of assets (the resource for all that follows)
  - Criticalities and Consequences Matrix
- Tool set B: Probability assessment tools
  - Adversary/Means Matrix (to develop the DBT)
  - Adversary sequence diagrams
  - Crime statistics
  - Asset Target Value Matrixes for:
    - Terrorism
    - Economic crimes
    - Violent crimes

- – Subversives
- – Petty crimes
- Tool set C: Vulnerability assessment tools
  - Surveillance Matrix
  - Adversary sequence diagrams
  - Circulation Path/Threat Nexus Points Matrix
  - Circulation Path/Weapons Nexus Points Matrix
  - Vulnerability Matrix
- Tool set D: Risk analysis tools
  - Unsorted Risk Matrix
  - Sorted Risk Matrix
  - V^2 Matrixes (top level and by areas)

REFERENCES

1. McNamara, C. General guidelines for conducting research interviews. Free Management Library. http://managementhelp.org/businessresearch/interviews.htm.
2. McNamara, C. 2006. *Field Guide to Consulting and Organizational Development*. Authenticity Consulting, Minneapolis.
3. Scott, J. 1998. *A Dictionary of Sociology*. Oxford University Press, New York.
4. Schensul, J. J. and M. D. LeCompte. 1999. *The Ethnographer's Toolkit*, p. 195. AltaMira Press, Walnut Creek.
5. Zahm, D. L. 1997. *Designing Safer Communities: A Crime Prevention Through Environmental Design Handbook*, p. 7. National Crime Prevention Council, Washington, DC.

Q&A

Questions

Q1: Risk assessment phases often include
  A. Phase 1, phase 2, and phase 3.
  B. Phase A, phase B, and phase C.
  C. First phase, second phase, and third phase.
  D. Survey and research phase, analysis phase, countermeasures selection and budgeting phase, and report phase.

Q2: The seven basic risk analysis skills include
  A. How to gather data and research and evidence gathering.
  B. Critical thinking and quantitative and qualitative analysis.
  C. Countermeasures selection and report writing.
  D. All of the above.

Q3: Tools needed for security risk analysis include
  A. Asset identification tools (including consequences analysis).
  B. Probability assessment tools.
  C. Vulnerability and risk analysis tools.
  D. All of the above.

Q4: Data gathering may include
    A. Interviews, surveys, asset classifications, criticalities, and consequences
    B. Surveys and interviews.
    C. Surveys.
    D. Interviews.

Q5: Critical thinking in the risk analysis process includes
    A. Maintaining focus on purpose, identifying key questions, observing and understanding the implications of different points of view, examining evidence and its implications on the analysis, drawing inferences from the evidence and others.
    B. Intellectual honesty.
    C. Being guided by preconceived notions more than data.
    D. Being guided by desired outcomes.

Q6: Analysis may include
    A. Qualitative analysis.
    B. Quantitative analysis.
    C. Both qualitative and quantitative analysis.
    D. None of the above.

Q7: Countermeasure selection is
    A. A normal part of most risk analysis projects.
    B. A part of better risk analysis methodologies.
    C. Usually left to vendors.
    D. None of the above.

Q8: Asset identification tools include
    A. A list of interviewees and contacts.
    B. A list of assets.
    C. The Criticalities and Consequences Matrix.
    D. All of the above.

Q9: Probability assessment tools may include
    A. Adversary/Means Matrix, adversary sequence diagrams, crime statistics, and Asset Target Value Matrixes.
    B. Probability Matrix development analysis tool.
    C. Both of the above.
    D. None of the above.

Q10: Risk analysis tools may include
    A. The Unsorted Risk Matrix.
    B. The Sorted Risk Matrix.
    C. The V2 Matrix.
    D. All of the above.

Answers

Q1 – D, Q2 – D, Q3 – D, Q4 – A, Q5 – A, Q6 – C, Q7 – B, Q8 – D, Q9 – A, Q10 – D

CHAPTER 4

Critical Thinking and the Risk Analysis Process

INTRODUCTION

Critical thinking is, well, critical to risk analysis. On completion of this chapter, you will have a good basic understanding of critical thinking as it applies to risk analysis. This will include why analysis requires critical thinking; the eight elements that make up the thinking process; the goals, principles, and elements of critical thinking; the difference between pseudocritical thinking and actual critical thinking; why critical thinking should become a part of your everyday thinking process; applying critical thinking to risk analysis; and the roots of most problems.

OVERVIEW OF CRITICAL THINKING

Critical thinking is to thinking as economics is to money management. Critical thinking applies a scientific process to the act of thinking that helps result in far superior conclusions and helps the thinker to support his/her conclusions with rational and defendable arguments. Critical thinking concepts and practice apply a structure of control to the thinking process that helps assure that all relevant data, evidence, points of view, assumptions, biases, and prejudices are considered (particularly those that are "outside the box"); and that the conclusions are well considered and thorough. Critical thinking helps assure that those conclusions are not false, based on incomplete or inappropriate data, or based on preexisting biases; and that possible unintended consequences are considered.

Critical thinking is not based on a fixed set of procedures but on concepts and principles.[1] Its flexibility helps assure that it can be adapted to many different types of situations and will always help achieve the best possible outcome.

Critical thinking helps assure that personal weaknesses, prejudices, or personal agendas are not forwarded as part of the conclusions. Critical thinking can be used in any field where the quality of conclusions is important, particularly where the application of those conclusions may affect how organizations and people work, live, and interact. Critical thinking helps to achieve complex objectives and handle problems with multiple dimensions. Critical thinking also helps people achieve intellectual humility and strategically important results.

IMPORTANCE OF CRITICAL THINKING

Critical thinking is important because it enables one to think about a problem more completely and to consider many factors that may not be intuitively apparent. It also helps to assure that the results of thinking about the problem are intellectually honest and objective in nature. Furthermore, the conclusion reaching process is more likely to involve the consideration of factors that would likely be missed otherwise, thus helping to assure that the conclusions reached are thoroughly considered.

Critical thinking

- Assures that conclusions are all relevant to the issue under consideration.
- Helps the thinker reach conclusions that are true to the purpose of consideration of the issue.
- Helps assure that relevant theories, definitions, axioms, laws, principles, or models underlying the issue are considered in their proper context.
- Reduces the likelihood of personal biases, prejudices, self-deception, distortion, misinformation, and so on being injected into the conclusion process.
- Assures that all relevant stakeholders' points of view are considered, including their concerns, goals, objectives, and intended outcomes. This is true not only for positive stake holders but also for stake holders of opposing points of view.
- Considers all relevant evidence and excludes irrelevant evidence, including relevant and irrelevant data and experiences.
- Clarifies for the thinker what assumptions are being taken for granted and considers the relevance of those assumptions to the issue at hand.
- Considers the implications and possible consequences of various possible recommended courses of action.
- Helps the thinker infer conclusions from the evidence in the light of all other considerations listed above.

Normal intuitive human thinking, left to itself, can often lead to self-deception, both for individuals and for societies.[2] Experience shows that many people (including such critical professionals as intelligence analysts) often reach decisions intuitively before thinking about a problem and then look for evidence to support the conclusions, often discarding any contradictory evidence along the way.*

This natural process of intuition-driven conclusions can be disastrous for individuals and organizations and can wreck budgets and careers. Entire programs have been based on faulty thinking that, in retrospect, was obvious to everyone concerned.†

---

* "The claims of Tony Blair, George Bush, and other senior British and American figures, powerfully made in numerous speeches and several dossiers, including the February presentation to the UN Security Council by Colin Powell, the US Secretary of State, were undermined by a stream of contradictory evidence. This included the leak of a classified document in the United States, the public comments of former intelligence officials, endorsed in private by their still-serving colleagues—and the testimony of Hans Blix, outgoing head of the UN weapons inspectors."[3]

† "New Coke. New Coke came out because in blind taste tests, people preferred Pepsi to Coke. The revelation was startling and Coca Cola decided that it was time to change their formula to make it sweeter like Pepsi. After months of tweaking the formula, doing blind taste tests, and changing their packaging, New Coke was launched.

It failed miserably. Why? Mainly because Coca Cola did not understand their customers. In blind taste tests, people usually only take a small sip of cola, whereas in real life, they drink full glasses of cola. People prefer sweetness in moderation, so when it came to drinking a can of cola, Coke drinkers preferred Coke's less sweet formula to Pepsi's sweetness.

But, it wasn't just the new formula that Coke drinkers opposed. The new packaging and marketing alienated them. They didn't want something new. They wanted the same old Coca Cola they knew and loved. New Coke failed because Coca Cola didn't know its customers. When the company returned to its old formula and re-launched Coca Cola Classic, they did much."[4]

Critical thinking is important wherever the quality of thinking and the programs and expenditures for those programs affect the quality of people's lives. This is certainly true in matters of security, where inconveniences and costs can be high, and mitigation values can be debatable.

Unfortunately, everyone has biases. There is no simple way to overcome people's biases, as most people assume incorrectly that they have no biases or else minimize the consequences of those biases they agree that they may have.* Biases have a way of finding themselves injected subtly into our findings and recommendations.†

Critical thinking is also important if

- You want to assure that you are addressing the real issue and are not being misdirected to a red herring
- You want to assure that you are examining the issue for the correct purposes and are not addressing an aspect of the issue that is itself a misdirection‡
- You want to be certain that you are addressing all of the points of view and arguments that will be raised by any opposition
- You want to acquire and address as much evidence as possible and as objectively as possible, regardless of which direction it may point
- You want to eliminate any false assumptions and take into consideration any other presuppositions and assumptions
- You want to deduce correctly what might happen and know what does happen
- You want to draw correct inferences from the evidence

ANALYSIS REQUIRES CRITICAL THINKING

One simply cannot analyze any problem without thinking about it carefully. Yet the so-called analysis of some ill-prepared security industry workers who position themselves as security consultants, often without any qualifications other than a sales training course, is sadly often lacking in evidence of thought. There is sometimes evidence of opinion, of scant observation, of references to past experiences,

---

* Northwestern University Psychologist Professor Galen Bodenhausen tested the responses of 24 white university students who classified themselves sincerely as having no racial prejudice.[5] In the first experiment, students watched a movie of a computer-generated face changing expression from hostility to happiness and back again. Researchers asked the participants to press a button when the facial expression changed. The participants also took tests to determine their explicit and implicit racial attitudes. In the second experiment, 15 computer-generated faces were morphed to contain racially ambiguous facial structures, skin tone, and hairstyles. Each face was then manipulated to show either a happy or a hostile expression. This time, as in the first study, "When faces were seen to display relatively hostile expressions, individuals high in implicit prejudice tended to categorize them as African-American," Bodenhausen said.

† "The examiner's one-sided findings on credibility clearly evidenced bias and vitiated the board's short-form order adopting his report. *Pittsburgh Steamship Co. v. National Labor Relations Board* 167 F.2d 126 (C.C.A. 6th 1948)."[6]

‡ Some Liquefied Natural Gas (LNG) community activists have implied that LNG is dangerously explosive. The website http://timrileylaw.com/LNG.htm cites an erroneous CNN report: "According to the CNN report on Nov. 15, 2002, 'The company said the vessel, which had just unloaded a cargo of explosive natural gas in Barcelona, Spain, struck a submerged object.'"

In truth, LNG is not explosive when released into the atmosphere. "7: LNG vapors in an open environment cannot explode. To create an explosion, LNG vapors would need to be mixed with air and be in a confined space (i.e., inside a room in a building). *[Exactly like normal piped gas; the author's insertion.]* In the remote event of an LNG spill from the facility or a tanker, there would be no explosion. As a liquid, LNG is not explosive. LNG vapor will only explode if in an enclosed space. LNG vapor is only explosive if within the flammable range of 5%–15% when mixed with air (http://www.energy.ca.gov/lng/faq.html#1000)."

and of conclusions reached that often mostly provide evidence of an agenda that is not fully in the best interests of the client but that serves the so-called analyst, who may represent a company that sells the specific products or services that analyst is recommending.

Let me just say up front that any "analyst" who works for a company whose products or services are being recommended is inherently involved in a conflict of interest. I have read countless risk analysis reports that touted the provider's products and/ or services while completely ignoring recommendations that could certainly be less expensive and more effective. Alarmingly, most of these reports missed entire categories of vulnerabilities, leaving the client unprepared to counter known and apparent threats.

Observing, offering opinions, or focusing on only part of the problem; this is not analysis. Yet this is too often what passes for analysis. I am often asked to review the analysis work of other consultants, contractors, and vendors in the context of preparing for a project. I am frequently shocked at what passes for risk analysis. In one analysis that reportedly cost the client over $100,000, there was not one single reference given to support either the data or the conclusions. The report was filled entirely with references to "experience" and "we were told by [anonymous] persons of authority," with no validating reference. On reading the report, I counted only 22 points of analysis, while that particular case called for thousands.

The report, typical of so many, lacked the following elements of critical thinking:

- Threat assessment was apparently "off the shelf" and did not appear to have been refreshed for this project.
- The focus was primarily on basic vulnerabilities, and those were limited to the obvious, without any evidence of a search for environmentally unique vulnerabilities.
- Risk conclusions were drawn directly from the vulnerabilities, without reference to the type of threat actor.
- The report was written entirely from an authoritarian single point of view.
- Little reference was made to research, no reference to interviews, no reference to the source of facts (therefore making "facts" suspect), no reference to concepts, and only one reference to an applicable law.
- No context for interpretations.
- No options offered.
- No mitigation effect offered for countermeasures recommended.
- No budget.
- No evidence of architectural or aesthetic considerations for countermeasures, or their effect on the efficiency of daily operations.
- No consideration of the effect of recommended countermeasures on the quality of life for the customer and employee base.
- The qualifications of the consultant were not identified.

This was a classic risk assessment report, the type of which I have seen many times. It represented a straight line from assumptions to conclusions with no stops in between, supporting a preconceived point of view. Any data cited supported only the point of view offered. There was no evidence of analysis whatsoever, just a statement of "findings" and then straight off to recommendations. This is not analysis. This barely passes for thinking at all. We can do better.

THE EIGHT ELEMENTS THAT MAKE UP THE THINKING PROCESS

There are eight basic elements that make up all thinking processes, whether structured or unstructured, done by anyone, anywhere, at any time (Figure 4.1):

- We think for a purpose (we are thinking about some idea, thing, or person).
- We bring to the thought a point of view.
- We bring certain assumptions to the thought process.
- We use information at hand to think about it.
- The information may include facts, experiences, data, and so on to give our interpretations context.
- We use concepts, ideas, and theories to interpret the information and give it meaning in the context of what we are thinking about.
- We interpret the information and draw inferences, consider implications, and formulate conclusions.
- We extend our conclusions to think about what would happen if we were to act on the basis of our conclusions.

The process becomes iterative, so that we compare our thoughts about our conclusions to the original data and determine if the outcome of our conclusions is beneficial to our point of view and fits our assumptions. This may sound straightforward enough. But much thinking is unstructured and undisciplined, often leading to erroneous conclusions, because we are all innately biased by our experiences, our thinking distorted by our minimal perspective, partial to our own point of view, uninformed about anything other than what we have been exposed to, and sometimes prejudiced, knowingly or unknowingly.

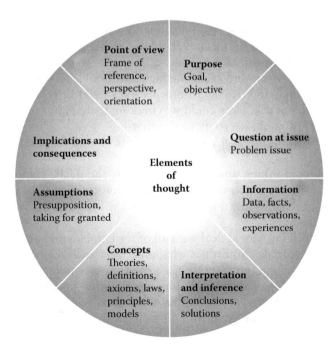

FIGURE 4.1 The elements of thought.

If we want to think better, we must take thinking apart, understand each of its elements, and recognize them as we use them. This is the foundation of insight into our own thinking processes and the seed of better thinking.

THE CONCEPTS, GOALS, PRINCIPLES, AND ELEMENTS OF CRITICAL THINKING

Critical Thinking Concepts and Goals

Critical thinking applies intellectual standards to the elements of reasoning in order to develop intellectual traits. The goals of critical thinking are to

- Overcome biases in thinking
- Be thorough and accurate
- Consider all relevant data
- Apply a methodology to the thinking process to ensure quality results
- Develop results that are true to the purpose of the issue
- Develop conclusions and recommendations that take every relevant issue and point of view into consideration
- Develop conclusions that are optimal outcomes for the participants

Principles*

Critical thinking principles include (Figure 4.2)

- Clarity: Our thinking and our recommendations should be clear and understandable and easily grasped by the stakeholders. Elaborate as required to explain. Give examples and illustrate the ideas.
- Veracity: Our thinking and recommendations should be free from errors and distortions, factual, and true. Our information should be complete enough that stakeholders do not ask: How could we check on that? How could we find out if that is true? How could we verify or test that?
- Precision: Our thinking and recommendations should be precise and provide adequate detail.
- Relevance: Our thinking and recommendations should be completely relevant to the issue. We should encourage stakeholder questions such as: How does that relate to the problem? How does that bear on the question? How does that help us with this issue?
- Depth: Our thinking should deal with all of the complexities and multiple interrelationships involved. This defines what make up the difficulties of the problem.
- Breadth: Our thinking should encompass multiple viewpoints and perspectives.
- Logic: Ultimately, our recommendations should bring together the multiple elements of the problem and solution into a logical network that addresses all of the dimensions of the problem and satisfies or deals with the concerns of

---

* Drawn from www.criticalthinking.org/CTModel/CTModel1.cfm#.

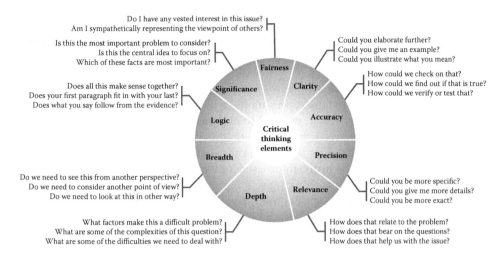

FIGURE 4.2   Critical thinking principles.

stakeholders. Our conclusions and recommendations should follow from the evidence.

- Significance: Our thinking and recommendations should be focused on the important, not on the trivial.
- Fairness: Our thinking and recommendations should be justified by fairness, not self-serving or one sided. There should be no vested interests served over others, and our recommendations should be sympathetic to the viewpoints of others.

Elements of Critical Thinking*

Purpose

We begin with a purpose for thinking. It is our goal, our objective; it may be what we are trying to accomplish. The term also may include functions, motives, and intentions.

One examines purpose by asking, for example,

- What is our purpose for doing…?
- What is the objective of this assignment, task, job, experiment, policy, strategy, and so on?
- What is our central aim in this line of thought?
- What do we hope to achieve by approaching this line of thought?

All thinking has a purpose. We should take time to understand and state our purpose clearly and in a way that anyone can understand, to distinguish our primary purpose from any related purposes, to check periodically to see that we are still on target, and to choose significant and realistic purposes.

---

* Drawn from www.criticalthinking.org/CTModel/CTModel1.cfm#.

The Question at Issue: Most Thinking Is about Problem Solving

All reasoning is an attempt to figure something out, perhaps to settle an argument or question about something, or to solve a problem. We begin by stating the question clearly and precisely.

It is best to express the question in several ways in order to fully understand and clarify its meaning. Ideally, the question should be broken down into its constituent components. By breaking things down, we tend to understand them better. Distinguish questions that have definitive answers from those that are merely opinion or that might have multiple viewpoints. This helps us to focus on the issue more clearly.

The question lays out the problem or issue and guides our thinking. When the question is vague or ambiguous, our thinking will naturally follow with a lack of clarity and distinctness. Questions should be clear and precise enough to guide our thinking.

Questions that can target the issue and help us to focus us on it:

- What are the important questions imbedded in the issue?
- Is there a better way to put the question?
- Is the question clear or complex? And, if complex, how can it be stated more clearly, by breaking it down or rephrasing?
- What do we have to know to settle this question?

Understand Our Own and Others' Points of View

- Surprisingly for many, their own point of view may not be the only one worth considering! In fact, their own point of view may only be worth considering in the context of those of others. That is, if everyone held our point of view, it is likely that everyone's thinking about problems would be quite similar or identical. Thus, there might not even be a problem to consider.

Why look at others' points of view? We do not exist in a vacuum as individuals alone. We exist in an environment in which virtually everything we want to do requires the participation or cooperation of others. Thus, in order to gain the help and support of others, we must present something of value for them to exchange for that help and support. And when we are facing opponents, understanding their point of view is critical to being able to either sway their opinion to our point of view or to overcome their position.

Value those points of view as relevant. Others' points of view *are* relevant to the challenges we face. Our work and personal lives are made up primarily of the interchanges we have with others. Thus, fully understanding and appreciating the value of their points of view is critical to our ability to interact effectively.

In David T. Moore's excellent work on critical thinking for the intelligence community,[7] he illustrates how President John Fitzgerald Kennedy utilized the critical thinking skill of comparing points of view to deal with the Cuban missile crisis of 1962, which brought the world to the brink of nuclear war, and how Kennedy effectively avoided nuclear war by utilizing this important principle. Kennedy compared the points of view of Fidel Castro and Nikita Khrushchev with his own (Kennedy's) on the elements of the conflict. By successfully analyzing the elements of the points of view and knowing what Khrushchev's capabilities and position were, Kennedy was able to skillfully accommodate the critical political needs of the Russian, Cuban, and American leaders to reach a negotiated and face-saving agreement.

It is possible to conclude that problem solving that does not take into consideration the points of view of other stakeholders only delays and often worsens the problem. It is also useful to understand that the failure to understand, appreciate, and take into consideration the points of view of other stakeholders only entrenches the positions of others and makes it increasingly difficult to reach an accommodation later.

Gather Assumptions

Assumptions are beliefs that we take for granted. Usually, assumptions operate at the subconscious or unconscious level of thought.

Every thought and problem-solving effort includes assumptions about the environment in which the problem exists. Assumptions include both our own and the assumptions of others (both shared assumptions and opposing assumptions). Many conflicts have occurred in the absence of understanding of our own or others' assumptions. When the assumption is finally stated, we say "Oh! I didn't know you viewed it this way!" Assumptions are closely related to points of view. In fact, points of view are derived from our assumptions about the facts and our assessment about how things should be. No one ever gets it exactly right. We all color our attitudes about others and our environment by our assumptions about how things should be, rather than simply accepting things for what they are.

The very act of acting out the feeling of anger is an expression of one's discontent over the difference between one's view of things as compared to a realization of how things actually are, and a realization that an idea, thing, or person is not within one's power to control or change. When one realizes that something to which one is attached cannot be had or controlled in the way one would like, anger and conflict can result.

All reasoning is based upon assumptions. Clearly identify and state your assumptions and try to state why they are justifiable. Consider how your assumptions are shaping your point of view. Consider what assumptions other stakeholders could be working from. Consider how their assumptions could be shaping their point of view. Do this by taking two steps:

- What do we think is their point of view and how could these assumptions be shaping that point of view?
- How could these assumptions shape another point of view that we might not know the stakeholder has? Thus, we can perhaps understand more fully a point of view that the stakeholder has not stated or we did not know that they hold.

Gather Information

All reasoning is based on data, information, and evidence. It is important to restrict conclusions to those that are supported by data. One should search for information that opposes one's position as well as information that supports it. Make sure that all information cited is accurate, relevant, and easy to understand. Provide sufficient information to support your findings.

Information may include facts, interview notes, research, evidence, and experiences. Information sources are not necessarily accurate or correct, and it is important to sort out any information that is found to be incorrect or for which there may be questions of accuracy.

The following are questions that can help guide the process of gathering information:

- What information is needed to answer the questions raised by the issue?
- What data are relevant to the issue?
- Is more information needed?

- From what sources can we get the information?
- Is the information relevant to our purpose and goals?
- What experiences are relevant?
- What are the sources of the information, data, and evidence?
- How certain is the accuracy of the various pieces of information?
- Have we left out any information that is needed?

Examine the Implications and Possible Consequences Related to the Issue

All reasoning leads somewhere or has implications and consequences. Implications are claims or truths that logically follow from other claims or truths. Implications follow from thoughts. Consequences follow from actions.

Trace the implications and consequences that follow from your reasoning. Search for negative as well as positive implications. Ask how these consequences affect the environment, relationships, and so on. Ask how those consequences could cause changes between people and their environment and between people and other people (in order to avoid the law of unintended consequences).

Implications are inherent in our thoughts, whether we recognize them or not. The most successful thinkers think through the logical implication in a situation before acting on it.

Implications can often be seen when we compare one possible action against another. By comparing what might happen if we do one thing versus another, we can see possible consequences.

Some consequences are more significant than others. It is important to always compare the consequences to the purpose and points of view of stakeholders in order to help assure the success of the outcome.

Implications can also be drawn from facts, sometimes correctly and sometimes with wrong inferences. ("All cats are mortal. Socrates is mortal. Therefore, Socrates is a cat.") For example, if we ask what it means that prisons are filled more with poor people than the wealthy, we could conclude any of the following:

- Poor people are naturally more inclined to criminal activity than wealthy people.
- Poor people do not have access to excellent lawyers.
- Poor people do not have the financial resources to keep them from the edge of financial hardship, thus creating more emergencies in their lives and thus more possibilities for conflict.
- Poor people do not have the personal relationship resources to fall back on for help in emergencies, thus creating more opportunities for desperate behavior.
- Poor people are poor because of their inability to deal with problems constructively.
- Poor people are uneducated in problem solving.
- It is fruitless to try to help the poor because society cannot overcome such life-long entrenched behaviors.

Thus, it is important to understand that implications are just that, implications, rather than valid facts, and that those inferences are themselves based upon our own biases, prejudices, and points of view. Iteratively, it is thus important to consider others' points of view even when considering implications and consequences.

By reviewing implications and extending the implications to their logical consequences, we can formulate recommendations that can optimize outcomes for the stakeholders. We can validate those recommendations using intellectually honest logic and argumentation processes.

Determine What Concepts, Theories, Definitions, Axioms, Laws, Principles and/or Models Are Applicable to the Issue

All reasoning is expressed through, and shaped by, concepts and ideas. Concepts are ideas, theories, laws, principles, or hypotheses we use in thinking in order to make sense of things. In the absence of concepts, we cannot draw conclusions. This is because these are the benchmark we use to determine if what is happening and what could happen fit our idea of what should happen.

This can be easily illustrated by comparing the thought processes of ordinary citizens of a state with those of terrorist organizations who oppose the leadership of a state. It would be unthinkable for the state to simply destroy the entire country from which terrorists might strike. However, it would not be unthinkable for a terrorist organization to want weapons of mass destruction (nuclear for example) that could wipe a country entirely off the map. The killing of innocent women and children is unthinkable to a state and changes the feelings of citizens toward their leaders when it occurs.* However, the killing of innocent civilians including women, children, and the elderly is considered an effective tool for change by terrorists precisely because of the pressure it puts on governments by their people. As pressure mounts, governments often respond by limiting personal freedoms and conducting investigative and judicial excesses against suspected, though often innocent, civilians, therefore undermining popular support for the government.

Draw Interpretations, Inferences, and Conclusions from the Data; Validate the Data; and Formulate Recommendations Based on the Results

All reasoning contains inferences or interpretations by which we draw conclusions and give meaning to the data. Inferences are interpretations or conclusions we come to. Inferring is what the mind does while trying to figure something out. Inferences should logically flow from the data at hand. We should infer no less or no more than what is implied in the situation. Check inferences for their consistency with each other. Identify any assumptions that are underlying our inferences.

What conclusions are we coming to? Is the inference logical? Are there other conclusions that we could come to that do not fully fit our point of view? What inferences would others come to with another point of view? How did we reach this conclusion? What alternative conclusions could we reach? What are we basing our reasoning on? Does this conclusion make perfect sense, or do elements of the problem remain, and for which stakeholders?

Recommendations should be made after it has become possible to map a successful outcome for ourselves and other stakeholders. Alternatively, we can make recommendations that limit the possibility for opposing people to take action against those whose interest in the issue we serve. Validate the data where possible with a stress test so that an opposing point of view is applied to test the conclusions.

---

* The American psyche was deeply harmed and offended by the discovery of the behavior of two U.S. Army companies during the Vietnam War. On March 16, 1968, the companies massacred 504 innocent civilians, mostly women, children, and the elderly, in the hamlets of My Lai and My Khe of Son My village. This event helped turn Americans against the war.

Pseudocritical Thinking[8]

There is not only good and bad thinking, which are obvious as such, but there is also bad thinking that masquerades as good thinking, causing disastrous results when it is relied on for important decisions. Often, bad thinking is defended and rationalized in highly sophisticated ways.

Pseudocritical thinking is a form of intellectual arrogance, masked in self-delusion or deception, in which thinking that is deeply flawed is not only presented as a model of excellence of thought, but is also, at the same time, sophisticated enough to take many people in. No one mistakes a rock to be a counterfeit diamond. It is obviously not a diamond. But a zircon mimics a diamond and is easily taken for one and hence can be said to be a pseudodiamond. There is much apparently "sophisticated" but deeply flawed thinking that is presented as a model for thought.

Since most people are victims of their own bad thinking, it is very difficult for people to recognize their own thinking as self-serving, incomplete, irrational, or bad. The practice of confusing questions and issues easily diverts people from the relevant to the irrelevant. Many people do virtually no reading. Many cannot speak knowledgeably outside of a narrow field. And many people are not even up to date in their own field.

Much of what passes as critical thinking is merely the use of logic to address a simple question. There is not much coherent understanding of the role of reasoning and intellectual standards in disciplined thought. The practice of confusing recall with knowledge, subjective preference with reasoned judgment, irrational persuasion with a rational discussion of issues, along with the use of vague and ambiguous key terms and arbitrary scoring, results in both invalid and unreliable results.

One of the most common forms of pseudocritical thinking is the use of logic to address problems rather than a comprehensive process of analysis. Logic is part of analysis and critical thinking, but it is not a substitute for critical thinking any more than a wheel is a substitute for a car.

Intellectual Traits[9]

Intellectual traits that allow for successful critical thinking include

- Intellectual humility
- Intellectual courage
- Intellectual empathy
- Intellectual integrity
- Intellectual perseverance
- Faith in reason
- Fair-mindedness

Importance of Integrating Critical Thinking into Everyday Thinking

Critical thinking can be used in virtually every aspect of our lives. While most decisions do not have great consequences, we can often find that what we assumed to be minor decisions can have major consequences (whom we date, what debt we take on, what car we drive [in the case of an accident occurring], etc.).

If critical thinking is left to be used only in the case of major decisions, it will likely not be used at all, or when used, the applicant will be ineffective due to lack of practice. Critical thinking requires practice, like piano playing, math, speaking a foreign language, or any other valuable skill. One cannot learn the principles of critical thinking and be proficient without daily application of the skill, any more than one can only read about the vocabulary and grammar of a foreign language and speak proficiently in the language at a conference.

Integrating critical thinking effectively into one's analysis work requires integrating it into one's daily life. This is a two-step process:

- Step 1: Grasp the concepts of critical thinking, including its basic ideas, principles, and theories. This is a process of internalization.
- Step 2: Begin effectively using the ideas, principles, and theories of critical thinking and make them relevant in the lives of students of critical thinking. This is the process of application. It is at this stage that a person begins to see improvements in reasoning about virtually every subject considered. This is because the person begins to see the world differently, from a standpoint of critical reasoning. The person begins to see fallacies in arguments, weaknesses in the conclusions of colleagues, and so on. The more the person sees, the more he or she begins to understand and appreciate the value of critical thinking in every aspect of his or her life.

So how can one become proficient at critical thinking? I suggest that the person creates a poster of the concepts of critical thinking, places it prominently in the workplace, and contemplates the elements of critical thinking whenever any decision is at hand.

While every decision does not allow time for a fully fledged process of research, evidence gathering, assumption declaration, consequence consideration, and so on, by considering elements of critical thinking in each decision, the person will quickly grasp the principles and also the importance of each of these principles in the process of reaching quality conclusions.

To become truly proficient, each week the person should focus on one element of critical thinking and give it constant attention. To wit: for each decision, however small, asking "What assumptions and presuppositions am I working from?" will make the person more aware of assumptions.

By asking oneself "What are the other views on this issue?" and "Have I performed adequate research from opposing points of view?" one will become aware of the value of opposing ideas to the decision process, be able to deconstruct invalid arguments from different points of view, and assure that the conclusions put forward will stand up to the scrutiny of opposing points of view.

By asking oneself "What could be the consequences of doing nothing or doing A, B, or C?" one will become more aware of the value of considering alternative actions. By asking oneself "What can be inferred from this evidence?" and "Does the evidence point to any other conclusions?" one can become more skilled in developing inferences.

Applying Critical Thinking to Risk Analysis

The risk analysis report is the product of analysis. Analysis is the product of thinking. Thinking that is haphazard, unstructured, biased, and incomplete will always result in a risk analysis report that is haphazard, unstructured, biased, and incomplete. Moreover, it will most often result in incorrect conclusions that do the client more harm than good by giving the client the impression that risk has been fully analyzed, when it has not.

Critical thinking persuades the analyst to maintain focus of purpose, to focus on the issues at hand, and to not be distracted by irrelevant questions having little to do with the issue or purpose; it guides the acquisition of information, data, facts, observations, interview findings, and experiences; it guides the interpretation and inferences of the data; it helps the analyst control the analysis by staying relevant to the concepts, theories, definitions, laws, and principles of the exercise; it helps the analyst to clarify assumptions as such and validate them as true or false and relevant or irrelevant; it helps the analyst draw implications and conclusions; and it helps the analyst to understand, appreciate, and have due consideration for relevant points of view of stakeholders. In short, it helps assure complete and accurate analysis.

By applying critical thinking processes, the analyst can

- Better understand and clarify the purpose of the analysis for a specific project
- Better understand the unique issues of the project
- Define relevant assumptions that could affect the interpretations of data by different stakeholders
- Define a full set of relevant risk related stakeholders, including potential threat actors, and gather their relevant points of view based on interviews or open-source references
- Gather much more complete information of all types and make sure that the information is completely relevant to the project, including information about potential threat actors, vulnerabilities, asset target value, and so on
- Define assumptions and biases that will help to create a more transparent and intellectually honest, unbiased report, complete with interpretations, inferences, implications, and consequences that are unemotional and unbiased by limited points of view
- Make sure that the analysis is based on relevant laws, codes, definitions, and models; and correct concepts, theories, and axioms
- Draw conclusions more accurately, taking into consideration more accurate threat evaluations, budget realities, aesthetic and operational demands, cultural realities, and so on

Following the failures of intelligence analysis on weapons of mass destruction in Iraq by many intelligence communities around the world, there has been a new emphasis on the application of critical thinking skills in the role of intelligence analysis, especially among those Western governments whose decisions to go to war were based on the flawed analysis.

Inductive versus Deductive Reasoning

Analysis can use both inductive and deductive reasoning. Deductive reasoning takes stock of data-driven evidence (quantitative data) such as threat and vulnerability conditions and reaches conclusions from that evidence. Inductive reasoning takes stock of conditions that can affect outcomes (qualitative information) and reaches conclusions from the implications of that evidence. Deductive reasoning can provide useful static risk assessments. Inductive reasoning is the basis for predictive risk assessments.

Most of the information in this book relates to deductive reasoning. The sections on predictive risk analysis rely on inductive reasoning.

The Analysis Process

Information on the risk analysis process is contained in Chapters 5 through 11. Analysis relating to the development of appropriate policies, countermeasures, and budgets is discussed in Chapters 12 through 19.

More about Critical Thinking

I suggest that readers interested in developing critical thinking skills should check out www.criticalthinking.org, which has a wealth of resources.

The Root of Problems*

All problems are the result of an awareness of an impediment to our desired progress toward a goal or are a struggle to avoid suffering. Problems grow from our desire to maintain or grow our position in relation to our environment or to others and the need to overcome obstacles to that growth or maintenance. Conflict evolves out of the ebb and flow of society's natural tendency to move forward from its current position. That move creates change, and change is better for some and worse for others.

This is the single most important element in understanding assumptions and points of view. Where change is better, there is acceptance or even gratitude. Where change results in a lessening of someone's position or their concept of their position, suffering results. Suffering sometimes evolves into conflict as people try to reclaim or improve their position or control what is not easily controllable.

Perception is everything. Where people perceive that their situation is the same or improved, acceptance follows. And where people perceive that their position is harmed or that the effort to effect the change is not worth the resulting benefits, discontent and conflict can emerge.

All emotional suffering comes from only three things:

- Attachment to an idea, a thing, or a person
- Aversion to an idea, a thing, or a person
- Delusion about an idea, a thing, or a person

From emotional suffering comes conflict. Conflict, especially conflict that does not resolve the underlying issue to the general welfare of all stakeholders, assures the continuation of suffering. We can minimize suffering by accepting what is. Where it cannot be accepted, we can optimize the results by applying critical thinking to problem solving.

It is also worth noting that the attempt to solve many problems actually masks an attempt to solve one's feelings about the problem. That is, some problems are only problems because we see them as such. They (the problems we see) are not a problem to others

---

* By this author.

because they do not see them as such.* Additionally, the very existence of a problem in our mind indicates that we are not satisfied about something.

Our overall level of satisfaction can be raised significantly simply by approaching the thing from a standpoint of gratitude rather than from a standpoint of entitlement. The thing that people want to change is fine to those who accept it as it is. For those who are grateful for a thing, its presence brings satisfaction rather than concern.

SUMMARY

1. Critical thinking is to thinking like economics is to money management. Critical thinking applies a scientific process to the act of thinking that helps result in far superior conclusions and helps the thinker to support his or her conclusions with rational and defendable arguments. Critical thinking is not based on a fixed set of procedures but on concepts and principles.[1] Its flexibility helps assure that it can be adapted to many different types of situations and will always help achieve the best possible outcome.

2. Critical thinking helps assure that personal weaknesses, prejudices, or personal agendas are not forwarded as part of the conclusions. Critical thinking can be used in any field where the quality of conclusions is important, particularly where the application of those conclusions may affect how organizations and people work, live, and interact. Critical thinking helps to achieve complex objectives and handle problems with multiple dimensions. Critical thinking also helps people achieve intellectual humility and strategically important results.

3. Critical thinking is important because it enables one to think about a problem more completely and to consider many factors that may not be intuitively apparent.

4. One simply cannot analyze any problem without thinking about it carefully.

5. Eight elements make up the thinking process:
   a. We think for a purpose (we are thinking about some idea, thing, or person).
   b. We bring to the thought a point of view.
   c. We bring certain assumptions to the thought process.
   d. We use information at hand to think about it. The information may include facts, experiences, data, and so on, to give our interpretations context.
   e. We use concepts, ideas, and theories to interpret the information and give it meaning in the context of what we are thinking about.
   f. We interpret the information and draw inferences, implications, and conclusions.
   g. We extend our conclusions to think about what would happen if we were to act on our conclusions.
   h. The process becomes iterative, so that we compare our thoughts about our conclusions to the original data and determine if the outcome of our conclusions is beneficial to our point of view and fits our assumptions.

6. Critical thinking principles include
   a. Clarity
   b. Accuracy or veracity

---

* "For years, I thought that everyone else in the world was an idiot. Then one day it occurred to me that maybe I was the idiot." David Letterman.

    c. Precision
    d. Relevance
    e. Depth
    f. Breadth
    g. Logic
    h. Significance
    i. Fairness

7. Critical thinking applies intellectual standards to the elements of reasoning in order to develop intellectual traits. The goals of critical thinking are to
    a. Overcome biases in thinking
    b. Be thorough and accurate
    c. Consider all relevant data
    d. Apply a methodology to the thinking process to ensure quality results
    e. Develop results that are true to the purpose of the issue
    f. Develop conclusions and recommendations that take every relevant issue and point of view into consideration
    g. Develop conclusions that represent optimal outcomes for the participants

8. The elements of critical thinking
    a. Focus on purpose
    b. Focus on the issue
    c. Gathering information
    d. Interpretation and inference of the data
    e. Focus on concepts, theories, definitions, axioms, laws, principles, and models
    f. Clarifying and validating assumptions
    g. Determining implications and possible consequences
    h. Understanding, appreciating, and taking into consideration the various points of view of relevant stakeholders

9. Pseudocritical thinking: One of the most common forms of pseudocritical thinking is the use of logic to address problems rather than a comprehensive process of analysis. Logic is part of analysis and critical thinking; it is not a substitute for critical thinking any more than a wheel is a substitute for a car.

10. Intellectual traits of critical thinking:
    a. Intellectual humility
    b. Intellectual courage
    c. Intellectual empathy
    d. Intellectual integrity
    e. Intellectual perseverance
    f. Faith in reason
    g. Fair-mindedness

11. The root of problems

All problems are the result of an awareness of an impediment to our desired progress toward a goal or are a struggle to avoid suffering. Problems grow from our desire to maintain or grow our position with our environment or with others and the need to overcome obstacles to that growth or maintenance. Perception is everything. Where people perceive that their situation is the same or improved, acceptance follows. And where people perceive that their position is harmed, discontent and conflict can emerge.

All emotional suffering comes from only three things:
    a. Attachment to an idea, a thing, or a person

b. Aversion to an idea, a thing, or a person
c. Delusion about an idea, a thing, or a person

From emotional suffering comes conflict. Conflict, especially conflict that does not resolve the underlying issue to the general welfare of all stakeholders, assures the continuation of suffering. We can minimize suffering by accepting what is. Where it cannot be accepted, we can optimize the results by applying critical thinking to problem solving.

It is also worth noting that the attempt to solve many problems actually masks an attempt to solve our feelings about the problem. That is, some problems are only problems because we see them as such. They (the problems we see) are not a problem to others because they do not see them as such. Additionally, the very existence of a problem in our mind indicates that we are not satisfied about something. Our overall level of satisfaction can be raised significantly simply by approaching the thing from a standpoint of gratitude rather than from a standpoint of entitlement.

REFERENCES

1. Paul, R. and Elder, L. 2008. *The Miniature Guide to Critical Thinking Concepts and Tools*. Foundation for Critical Thinking Press, Dillon Beach, CA.
2. Hindery, R. 2001. *Indoctrination and Self-Deception of Free and Critical Thought*. Edwin Mellen Press, Lewiston, NY.
3. Whitaker, R., Lashmar, P, and Buncombe, A. Wheels fall off Iraq WMD 'mobile labs' story. *The Independent, UK*. http://www.rense.com/general38/wwmd.htm.
4. Krista. 2006. Why new Coke failed: Knowing your customers is key. LawyerBizCoach. com, June 8.
5. Bodenhausen, G. 2004. Think you're not biased? Prof says you are. FreeRepublic. com, March 17.
6. n.a. 1948. Trial examiner's bias evidenced by findings as ground for reversing administrative order. *Columbia Law Review* 48(6): 970–972.
7. Moore, D. T. 2007. Critical thinking and intelligence analysis (Occasional paper No. 14). National Defense Intelligence College, Washington, DC, p. 20.
8. Foundation for Critical Thinking. n.d. Pseudo critical thinking in the educational establishment. Foundation for Critical Thinking, Tomales, CA. www.criticalthinking. org/articles/pseudo-ct-educ-establishment.cfm.
9. Foundation for Critical Thinking. 1996. Valuable intellectual traits. Foundation for Critical Thinking, Tomales, CA. https://www.criticalthinking.org/pages/ valuable-intellectual-traits/528.

Q&A

Questions

Q1. Critical thinking applies
A. To every instance of thinking, from remembering the smell of flowers to the feelings about one's loved ones.
B. An additional process to thinking after conclusions have been reached.

C. A scientific process to the act of thinking that helps result in far superior conclusions and helps the thinker to support his or her conclusions with rational and defendable arguments.

D. None of the above.

Q2. Critical thinking helps assure

A. That good products are available in the marketplace.

B. That personal weaknesses, prejudices, or personal agendas are not forwarded as part of the conclusions.

C. That you will win every argument regardless of the merit of your argument.

D. None of the above.

Q3. Critical thinking can be used in any field

A. Where the quality of conclusions is important.

B. Where the outcome of the process must meet a predetermined conclusion.

C. Where the needs of the few are more important than the needs of the many.

D. None of the above.

Q4. Normal intuitive human thinking, left to itself,

A. Can help a person reach the best outcome reliably, every time.

B. Can often lead to self-deception, both for individuals and for societies.

C. Will always lead to self-deception.

D. None of the above.

Q5. Which of the below is *not* a goal of critical thinking?

A. Overcome biases in thinking

B. Be thorough and accurate

C. Apply a methodology to the thinking process to ensure quality results

D. Develop conclusions from preexisting opinions

Q6. Which of the below is *not* part of critical thinking principles?

A. Clarity, veracity, and precision

B. Relevance, depth, and breadth

C. Logic, significance, and fairness

D. Assured outcomes, suppression of alternative ideas, and self-congratulation

Q7. Which below are *not* elements of critical thinking?

A. Begin with a purpose for thinking, examine the implications and possible consequences related to the issue

B. Determine the question at issue, determine what concepts, theories, axioms, laws, principles, and/or models are applicable to the issue

C. Gather assumptions and information, draw interpretations and inferences from the data, validate the data, and formulate recommendations based on the results

D. Write the report based on the assumptions and validate the findings using data that support the assumptions

Q8. Validate the data where possible
   A. With a stress test so that an opposing point of view is applied to test the conclusions.
   B. With a supporting point of view so that the assumptions can be shown to be validated.
   C. Neither of the above.
   D. Both of the above.

Q9. Intellectual traits that make up successful critical thinking include which of the below?
   A. Intellectual humility, intellectual courage, intellectual empathy
   B. Intellectual integrity, intellectual perseverance, faith in reason, fair-mindedness
   C. Both of the above
   D. Neither of the above

Q10. Which below is true?
   A. The risk analysis report is the product of analysis.
   B. Analysis is the product of thinking.
   C. Thinking that is haphazard, unstructured, biased, and incomplete will always result in a risk analysis report that is haphazard, unstructured, biased, and incomplete, and most often will result in incorrect conclusions that do the client more harm than good by giving the client the impression that risk has been fully analyzed, when that has not happened.
   D. All of the above.

Answers

Q1 – C, Q2 – B, Q3 – A, Q4 – B, Q5 – D, Q6 – D, Q7 – D, Q8 – A, Q9 – C, Q10 – D

CHAPTER 5

Asset Characterization and Identification

INTRODUCTION

In this chapter, you will learn to identify and characterize the organization's assets in the context of critical thinking, which is the basis for all good analysis. This is the basis for criticality and consequence analysis (Chapter 6) and indeed for much of probability analysis (except for threat analysis), as well as for all vulnerability analysis and finally for risk analysis itself, which comprises the elements of all four analysis steps above (consequence analysis, probability analysis, vulnerability analysis, and risk analysis).

THEORY

The first step of risk assessment is to understand the assets at risk, determine their criticality to the mission of the organization, and determine the possible consequences if those assets are compromised. Simply put, risk can only exist against assets.

PRACTICE

Asset List

The list of assets you develop will be used in all of the following tools:

- Asset/Attack Matrix: Which assets are vulnerable to what types of entry methods, weapons, and attack scenarios
- Criticalities and Consequence Matrix
- Vulnerabilities Matrix: Establishing the vulnerabilities of the assets listed
- Surveillance Matrix: Establishing the surveillance opportunities of the assets listed (one component of vulnerability)
- All of the Asset Target Value Matrixes
  - Terrorism
  - Economic criminals
  - Violent criminals
  - Subversives
  - Petty criminals

- Hazards Matrix
  - Safety hazards
  - Natural disaster hazards
  - Man-made hazards
- Risk Analysis Matrixes (the composite of vulnerabilities and asset target value)

Asset Categorization

The first step in developing all of these matrixes is to develop a comprehensive list of assets and to categorize these into their four classes (Figure 5.1). All organizational assets fall into four main categories:

- People
- Property
- Proprietary information
- Business reputation

Some analysts add to this list the following:

- Business processes
- Dependencies and infrastructure

People

The people category will include management, employees, contractors, vendors, visitors, and customers. Each type of organization may also have other unique categories worth listing. People are the primary target of terrorism and violent crimes.

Property

The property category will include real property, fixtures, furnishings and equipment, supplies, cash vaults, bank accounts, and so on. Property is the primary target of economic crimes.

FIGURE 5.1   Asset classes.

Proprietary Information

Proprietary information includes paper files, computer files, forms, notes, and so on. Proprietary information is also a key target of economic crimes because it provides the intelligence needed to conduct a crime or terrorism event.

Business Reputation

Business reputation is self-evident. An organization begins with little if any business reputation. What reputation it may have will result from general knowledge or impressions about the principals who started the firm, the marketing campaign, location, type of buildings, and so on. That is, people get an impression only about what to expect from the organization. As the organization begins to serve its constituency, that impression solidifies or melts as its constituency develops a new impression by actual interaction with the organization, or from hearing stories or news reports about interactions with the organization. Business reputation is a key asset that, if lost, can destroy an entire organization.* Over time, the organization's brand develops to embrace the organization's business reputation. The two become one. After that, damage to the organization's business reputation is damage to the organization's brand. That kind of damage can be strategic and, when the brand is damaged, it can change the arc of the financial future.

For example, one airline may be a standout as news reports on its number one rating are announced and passengers hear from their colleagues about the pleasant experience of using that airline. This may happen even while the industry as a whole is suffering from negative press and word of mouth. However, one airline crash that is related to poor maintenance or management negligence could wipe out all that good will and destroy the airline's business. An organization's business reputation is essential to its carrying out its mission in that it creates support in the marketplace for its products or services.

Business processes include things like production lines and special processes that are unique to that particular organization. For the purposes of this book, property and proprietary information will include business processes.

The category of dependencies and infrastructure includes all outside resources that the organization is dependent on to maintain its operations. This could include nearby rivers that could flood, rail spurs that come into the property, nearby highways, the water system, and so on. For the purposes of this book, these can be considered under the category of property.

The analyst may wish to break business processes and dependencies and infrastructure out as independent categories for analysis, as some do.

Interviews

I usually begin a risk analysis project with interviews. Interviews are a gold mine of information about the organization's assets; they also help to introduce the stakeholders to the purpose and the process, and to gain their willing participation. A typical opening interview

---

* "Arthur Andersen (1913 to 2002) spent decades as a leading accounting and consulting firm. Founded in 1913, it was once a member of the 'Big 8' accounting firms, which later became the 'Big 5.' Andersen was the accountant for MCI and Worldcom. ... The lesson is to resist the lure of big money to pull you away from your values. Enron's pile of cash was irresistible to Andersen's leaders. And their lack of moral fiber cost a storied and proud firm its existence."[1]

is with a key stakeholder, usually the project manager assigned by the organization to guide the risk analysis project. Subjects include

- The organization's mission statement
- The programs that the organization has developed and how those relate to its mission statement
- The assets the organization has acquired in support of its programs, including
  - Physical assets, including
    - Real property
    - Vehicles
    - Fixtures, furnishings, and equipment
    - Information technology equipment
  - People
    - Senior management
    - Management and staff
    - Contractors and vendors
    - Visitors and customers
  - Proprietary information
    - Unique business processes
    - Customer lists
    - Vital records
    - Strategic plans, and so on
  - The organization's business reputation: Here I ask the interviewee to characterize the organization's business reputation:
- The reason this risk analysis is being undertaken
  - Was there any triggering event that prompted the analysis?
  - Will a security program be developed or modified as a result of the analysis?
  - Is it being carried out at the request of an insurance company?
- What security events have occurred at each property within the last 5 years?
  - Terrorism events or threats
  - Violent crimes
    - Felonies
    - Assaults
    - Muggings
    - Rapes
    - Murders
  - Economic crimes
    - Equipment thefts
    - Burglaries
    - Break-ins
    - Robberies
    - Information thefts
    - Vehicle crimes (thefts of for from vehicles)
  - Subversive acts
    - Activist organization activities
    - Civil disorder
    - Riots
    - Protests
    - Intimidation

- – Drugs in the workplace
- – Sabotage
- – Corporate spying
- Petty crimes
  - – Purse snatching
  - – Desk pilfering
  - – Pickpocketing
  - – Vandalism
  - – Prostitution
  - – Other petty crimes

Much of this information can come from either the risk analysis project manager or the security director/manager. It is valuable to interview the head of any division or department. Interviews can be either cursory or extensive. They should be in proportion to the scope of the project. I have had projects where interviews took only two hours (an office suite in a high-rise building) and others that took two weeks (involving every department of a city government). Keep a list of persons interviewed, including their full name, title, department, and contact information (phone and e-mail). Keep notes. I use either a standard interview form or Microsoft OneNote®, which is an amazing product that I cannot recommend enough as a project organization and note-taking tool.

Facility and Asset List

For all of the matrixes in this book, which will evaluate every aspect of the organization's assets, a full facility and asset list is required. This list should be comprehensive and inclusive. One does not need extreme levels of details, however, due to the excessive number of data analysis points that can drive the analysis into redundancy. Redundant data should be avoided. For example, one would not include both "equipment" and "office equipment." Generally, the list should include something like the following (an example only, indented for clarity):

- People
  - Senior management
  - Management and employees
  - Contractors
  - Vendors
  - Visitors
  - Customers
- Property
  - Site
  - Underground parking levels
    - – Vehicle entrances
    - – Passenger elevator lobbies
  - Tower 1
    - – Basement level
    - – Loading dock
    - – Lobby level

- – Meeting and conference rooms
- – Business center
- – Restaurants level
- – Hotel room levels
- – Premier hotel room levels
- – Passenger elevators
- – Passenger elevator lobbies
- – Freight elevators
- – Freight elevator lobbies
- – Fire stairwells
- – Utility and mechanical areas
- Tower 2
  - – Loading dock
  - – Lobby level
  - – Anchor tenant offices
  - – Free leasehold office levels
  - – Passenger elevators
  - – Passenger elevator lobbies
  - – Freight elevators
  - – Freight elevator lobbies
  - – Fire stairwells
  - – Utility and mechanical areas
- Retail mall
  - – Loading dock
  - – Passenger drop-off area
  - – Main concourse
  - – Events area
  - – Back-of-house areas
- Low-rise building
  - – Lobby area
  - – Loading dock
  - – Office levels
- Proprietary information
  - Information technology system
  - Electronic security system
  - Voice communications systems
  - Paper files
- Business reputation

The example above serves only to give the reader an idea of what type of assets to list. The list should be large enough to be comprehensive but not so large as to duplicate assets of a similar type within a similar area. For organizations with multiple sites, this list can be expanded as required.

Each of the categories of assets above (people, property, information, and reputation) will receive detailed attention as we proceed through the book and into the analysis matrixes. Remember, risk analysis can be performed using any quality program, qualitatively in text from detailed notes, or using a detailed matrix as is described in this book. I have no agenda to drive one type of analysis over another. All can work equally well in the hands of a good analyst.

As we progress through the book, you will learn how to evaluate each of the organization's assets thoroughly, from many points of view, and multidimensionally. The result will be a very thorough analysis. This process can be truncated for very small projects, such as an office suite, but the complete understanding of the analytical process will guide you to a successful conclusion on every project. The use of all of these tools and methods will also assure conformance with any DHS-approved methodology.

If you intend to use the software templates that are presented in this book as an exemplar of how to perform analysis, those templates will be useful in every project of any size. Alternatively, these items fully encompass almost all commercial software products, so the knowledge is fully transferrable.

Research

Research may include Internet, telephone, and records research. Chapter 3 provides a good foundation for the tools of research.

Surveys

Surveys are most illuminating. In surveys, one finds any and all of the following kinds of information:

- Environmental context
  By environment, I mean everything about the organization as it resides at a specific facility. This includes the physical environment, security, political aspects, weather, hours of operation, limitations of operation, and nearby factors.
  - Information about the area where the facility resides: This should include information about the nation, state, city, neighborhood, and street (and water and rail facilities, if applicable.) This provides a context so that the analyst and reader can better understand factors that might not be immediately apparent to unfamiliar readers. For example, if there is only one approach road and the property backs up to a river, this could affect evacuation, should it become necessary. Taken with other information—for example, the fact that an up-street neighbor stores significant amounts of toxic chemicals— this could mean that "shelter in place" rather than evacuation could be the only viable option in the event of a leakage.
  - Political factors: Political factors are often overlooked but can have a profound effect on an organization's security, especially in countries with fragile internal political relationships and countries that have fragile relationships with their neighbors. For example, any organization in a major city in India or Pakistan is at risk of political events there. A friend of mine was the U.S. ambassador to Pakistan when a demonstration erupted into violence. Over a day later, his entire staff emerged from an underground safe room to find that the entire embassy had been burned to the ground.
  - Social factors: Social factors can affect the security of organizations as well. For example, in the wake of the Rodney King verdicts in Los Angeles, California, racial tension erupted into riots that destroyed large parts of the city, including many commercial businesses and government offices.

Regardless of whether or not there has been any violence in the past, any social tension between factions of a city, state, or country should be noted, along with indications for contingency for civil disorder planning.

- Security factors: This may include police response times, past security events, and so on. Any significant past security events should be noted, along with their resolutions. General trends for security in the area, city, and property should be noted.
- Weather and natural environmental conditions (extremes, averages, rainfall, snow days, potential for natural disasters, etc.)
- Hours of operation and occupancy: The hours of operation and occupancy affect the facility's vulnerability to burglary and nighttime employee abuse. If the facility has different hours of occupancy for different departments, list each.
- Limitations of operation: List any development restrictions, hazards, and so on.
- Neighboring factors: Do neighboring business stock toxic chemicals, what is their disaster coordination plan, and so on? Is there an embassy of a country that draws large or potentially violent protesters nearby? List any other neighboring factors that could affect safety or security.
- Property context
  - Information about the property where the facility resides: Use Google Maps® or another service to plot the location of the facility relative to major environmental features such as rivers, streams, major roads, fire department, police department, and so on.
  - Road, air, rail and water ingress/egress: Evaluate the access routes to the property. List the access routes by category (helipad, water taxi, VIP driveway, loading dock entry, etc.) and any unique attributes vis-à-vis possible vulnerabilities. Review any features such as choke-points and sharp turns that could pause VIP arrivals and exits, and list what types of vehicles will access the facility along which routes.
  - Fence line access: Where are the pedestrian and vehicle gates along the fence line?
  - Robustness of natural perimeter defenses (storm walls, water barriers, etc.)
  - Robustness of man-made perimeter: Note the property fence line by path, type, height, quality of maintenance, weaknesses, gate access points, and what lies beyond the gate (road, waterway, pasture, etc.). Also note overhanging access from bridges and other structures, from which a person could jump down into the property.
  - Building types: List the types of uses and types of construction, including numbers of floors, their areas in square feet/meters, and allocation of spaces by departments, functions, and occupancy counts.
  - Access sneak-paths: List any weak gates, manholes, tunnels, concealed access points, and so on.
  - Access control points and equipment/procedures/hours of operation: List which building perimeter locations are normally used for access and which are used exclusively for maintenance. Identify the access control procedures for employees, contractors, vendors, and visitors. Identify the hours of operation for each access point and the type of people who may clear through the access point.

- Organizational context
  - The organizational context includes elements of the operation of the organization that impact on the security environment. These include aspects relating to the daily operation of the facility. This is where normal criminal losses occur, as it is these interactions that create the opportunity for crimes against the organization and its staff.
  - Functional organization chart: Obtain a functional organization chart. This is a document that shows the hierarchy of management and the departments each manager serves. Also it should show or make reference to a document that identifies the charter or mission of each department and departmental unit. Especially important is the location of the security department or unit in the organization.
  - Organizational elements: The organizational elements will detail how each department helps fulfill the overall mission of the organization.
- Functions of elements
  - Customers: Whom does the organization serve? Whom does each department serve? Some departments serve customers outside the organization and others serve customers who are themselves part of the organization, that is, other organization departments.
  - Coordinating entities to deliver the services: On whom do the departments rely to service their own needs? These outside contractors often have access to sensitive information and physical assets including organization planning and projections.
  - Quantity of staff, space allocation: How are staff allocated by space? How many staff are in each department?
  - Access control requirements: What are the access control needs of each department? What screening is necessary for employees, contractors, vendors, and visitors? Is it possible, for example, to restrict all vendor access to a single area to include purchasing and department representatives instead of having vendors visit every department? Is positive access control necessary? That is, does the organization need to control visitors by escort or by issuing them badges that act as access control credentials? Do the visitor access control credentials need to be used to control access both in and out?
  - Proprietary information protection requirements: What kinds of proprietary information are kept and used in each department? Is proprietary information restricted to certain areas or is there wide access to such? What is the department's policy regarding visual access to proprietary information while contractors, vendors, and visitors visit the department? What are the policies regarding
  - Hours of operation: What are the hours of operation for each department? During what hours do cleaning, plant maintenance, and other contractors have routine access?
  - Parking: Is parking space adequate for visitors, staff, management, and contractors and vendors? Is there adequate parking for contractor and delivery trucks? Is there adequate queuing for the loading dock? Do different parking areas operate under different hours of operation?
  - Vehicle access: How is access to parking and the front entry controlled? Is it possible to limit access proximity to vehicles of different sizes? For

example, while much has been made about the need to check the underside of vehicles entering properties, in fact bombs placed under vehicles are generally very small; they have only ever been used to assassinate the vehicle occupants and have not proven to be a significant threat to others, except only for those in the immediate vicinity of the car. Such bombs do not generally pose an overall risk to the facility. It is far more important to limit access by large vehicles, especially trucks, to areas that are structurally robust.

– Shipping/receiving and loading dock: Ideally, all deliveries for high-risk facilities should take place at a dedicated off-site receiving dock, where all deliveries can be properly checked. Then, transit delivery by controlled vehicles bearing seals from the dedicated receiving dock can assure the safety of the facility from unverified vehicles. Failing that, the loading dock should be located well away from the front entrance and away from large expanses of glass façade. Vehicles should be queued, checked, and sealed at some distance from the facility if possible. It is important to note everything about the physical and operating environment of the shipping/receiving and loading dock area including risk/theft mitigation strategies. Try to stay around the area long enough to see if these strategies are actually adhered to.

– Mail/deliveries room: Similar to the shipping/receiving and loading dock, the mail/deliveries room handles packages internal to the organization. This process is also best handled off-site if possible, but that rarely happens. It is important to locate the mail room in a place that can be easily isolated if hazardous chemicals or bio-hazards are found in packages. Also, a negative pressurization environment is ideal, drawing air in from the outside and thus containing any biohazard to the mail room itself. Note the physical and operating environment for the mail room, especially the policies in place for handling hazardous chemicals and suspicious packages.

• Security context
  • Physical security vulnerabilities: After fully understanding the operating environment, note any physical security vulnerabilities that could be exploited by threat actors in this operating environment. These may include unintended access points; abuse of normal access points by stealth, trickery, or intimidation; and the types of assets any threat actor might be interested in.
  • Vetting of contractors, vendors, and visitors: How are these regular visitors granted access? Are contractor or visitor badges used, or are escorts used for either regular or infrequent visitors? What is the policy regarding regular and infrequent visitors to no-escort areas?
  • Lighting levels: What are nighttime lighting levels in parking lots, parking garages, walkways, and so on? During unoccupied hours, are lights left on in any areas to discourage threat actors? Is the landscape near the building lighted sufficiently to display the actions of anyone near the buildings?
  • Security zones: How is the building divided by security zones (public, semi-public, controlled, and restricted zones)? Are these zones formal or informal? Are they controlled by an access control system, by security staff, or by informal means? Do employees, contractors, and visitors wear access credentials

so that their presence by access authorization is clear, or can anyone stray into any area unimpeded?

- Type of security organization:
  - Security management: What is the level of qualifications of the organization's security management? Security management should have the training and experience to conduct its role. This is often not the case, with minimally qualified people placed in this vital role. When I have questioned C-level executives about the qualifications of their vital departments, the executives often talk proudly about the care taken in their selection of the department head and highlight the qualifications of the executive. Then, when they are asked the same question regarding the security chief, the answer is often that the person was promoted to the position from some unrelated function and has received little or no training since, and that neither has the security staff.
  - Staff/dogs/contractors: What is the quantity of security staff including employees, contractors, and dogs? Is staffing sufficient based on the number of posts and patrols and staff positions?
  - Policies and procedures: Review the organization's security policies and procedures. Note the organization, completeness, and relevance of sections and text to the mission and functional organization of the facilities. Note if the policies and procedures appear to be in constant reference and use or if the security chief has to search to find these. Policies and procedures should make reference to relevant laws, codes, and standards and should be based on industry best practices where possible and on accepted industry practice at the minimum.
  - Hours of operation and staffing: What are the hours of operation and staffing of the security department and unit and its constituent components? What are the hours of operation of security management, customer service office, badging, post and patrol shifts, and so on?
  - Training of management and staff:
    - Ask about the training for new security staff and about the continuing training program for security management and staff.
    - Security management training should be across all disciplines of security, and should be especially focused on security operations. The organization should have a budget for continuing training of its management, especially for courses that offer Continuing Education Units (CEUs).
    - All staff training should be based on the policies and procedures. These should be the basis for training, which is not unrelated. All training should derive from laws, codes, policies, and procedures.
  - Programs
    - Posts and patrols: How many security posts are there, and how many patrols? Are patrols by foot, cycle, or vehicle? What are the hours of posts and patrols? Is video utilized to augment patrols? What are guards trained to observe while on patrol? How are notes taken? How do guards communicate urgent or important findings, and what actions are taken when these are communicated? Are there fixed policies to cover such findings?

- Photo ID badging: Most organizations use security badging to augment their access control program and to help identify users and the areas for which they have access.
- Security awareness program: A security awareness program is vital in order to spread the security culture in any organization. A good security awareness program should include written and verbal elements. Written elements may include handouts for visitors and employees and a newsletter or e-mailing program, including security alerts both unique to the organization and of a general nature, such as warnings about new credit-card fraud tactics. These are often highly appreciated by the employees of an organization and help to build both the culture of security and enhance the security organization's esteem in the minds of its constituents. Verbal guidance and handouts for visitors and staff help way finding and help new employees to understand their responsibilities and the security policies of the organization. Review and note the elements and any deficiencies.
- Investigations: Many organizations need an internal investigations program to deter internal crime and to detect and prosecute employee crime, external crime, and crimes of collusion against the organization. Security management should be trained in investigations and interviewing and should know the laws of both as regards their rights and responsibilities, the rights of those being investigated, and the rights of those who are peripheral to the investigation.
- Law enforcement liaison: An important and often overlooked element of a good security program is a law enforcement liaison program.
- Emergency management program: Also called a crisis management program, this should include contingency plans for civil disorder, riot, natural disasters of all types, bomb threats and bomb events, shootings, medical emergencies, and more. Review and note the elements and any deficiencies.
- Disaster recovery program: Part of every organization's critical planning includes both a crisis management program and a disaster recovery program. The security unit is essential to both of these. Review and note the elements and any deficiencies.
- Intelligence program: A good intelligence program is an important if not essential component of the overall security program for any high-risk facility. The program should include commercial intelligence news feeds and public agency liaison, such as the FBI's Infragard or U.S. Secret Service liaison program. The organization's security management should receive basic training in intelligence analysis so that they can put the information into the context of their overall risk in order to advise the organization's management on emerging risks and what steps should be taken to counter them.
- Priority of the security program to upper management
  - Budget: What is the budget of the security organization vis-à-vis the assets they have to protect? Look around the security organization and see how it appears in terms of the condition of equipment and its organization. This often offers clues to the budget itself or the efficiency with which the available budget is applied (a clue to the quality

of management). Look to see if the quality of the security organization's facilities and equipment is consistent with or substantially below that of other departments.

– Position: What is the position given the security chief (director, manager, supervisor, etc.)? Does he or she have a direct line of report to the CEO or president? Is the position commensurate with the importance to the facility? I am not advocating that every organization needs direct access to the president or CEO. But where security is a core part of the organization's mission, such as at a financial institution or NGO,* it is essential that it has a direct line of report in order to succeed at its mission.

– Organization: Security will only receive the emphasis it is granted by the management of its department head. For example, if the security unit is placed under the mantle of the facilities management department, it will likely be treated as a commodity, similar to housekeeping and supplies, with the department head striving to cut costs above all other considerations, as is common to facility departments everywhere.

  The manager of the department should be a trained security professional in order to understand the challenges of security and its role in protecting the mission of the organization. For larger organizations and any organization that is a high security risk, the security function should be a department with a direct line reporting to the president or CEO. If not, any message from security management will be filtered by the department head to which it reports. *This is assured* to dilute, distort, or delete the message that the CEO or president receives and helps assure also that it is not possible for the security chief to counter any thoughtless or uninformed responses by the CEO/president or anyone else in the room at the time the message is rendered. I have seen this happen virtually every time that a department head has presented a message from security to the CEO or president.

– Interface between physical and information security programs: There is often an unfortunate gap between the security program and the information technology security program. This is not helpful to the organization, but as these two functions are often derived from completely different departments, it is natural for such separation to occur. Ideally, both programs should be mutually supporting and should be mutually developed to assure that. Wherever possible, I recommend that the security chief and the information technology security chief have lunch together at least once a week so that they can share concerns and develop a close working relationship.

TOOLS

One of the primary benefits of this book is the teaching of a spreadsheet approach to risk analysis. Either commercial software or custom spreadsheets can perform a quality risk

---

* NGO: nongovernmental organization, such as the United Nations, etc.

analysis. You may either use this approach or use commercial software to document your findings and estimates and to perform calculations. But it is useful for understanding the principles of risk analysis to build the databases at least once. And, once built, they can be easily modified to fit the needs of any project.

Listing assets is straightforward. Make a comprehensive list of four kinds of assets:

- People
- Property
- Proprietary information
- Business reputation

For the first three of these categories, list major assets, for example,

- People
  - Senior executives
  - Management
  - Employees
  - Contractors
  - Vendors
  - Visitors
  - Customers
- Property
  - Perimeter
    - Main campus entry/exit
    - Visitor center
    - Service entry
    - East fence
    - North fence, etc.
  - Parking structure
  - Basement levels
    - Loading dock
    - Chiller plant, etc.
  - Office tower
    - Main lobby
    - Employee entrance
    - Elevator lobbies
    - Executive elevator
    - Building management office
    - Floors 2–6 corporate HQ offices
    - Floor 7 finance and real estate
    - Floor 8 personnel
    - Floor 9 executive offices, etc.
  - Hotel
    - Porte cochere
    - Security checkpoints
    - Main lobby
    - Employee entrance
    - Elevator lobbies
    - Low rise

  - Mid rise
  - High rise
  - Restaurant levels, etc.
- Convention center
  - Main lobby
  - Loading docks
  - Administrative offices
  - Convention floor, etc.
- Proprietary information
  - Vital records
  - Secret formulas and patents
  - Information technology system
  - Security system
  - Telecommunications system
  - Paper records
- Business reputation has no subsets

The information above is an exemplar only. We will fill out information specific to a project beginning from Chapter 6. The information you create in the assets list will be used to populate most of the other matrixes you will develop, so it pays to be sufficiently detailed.

SUMMARY

Theory

The first step of risk assessment is to understand the assets at risk, determine their criticality to the mission of the organization, and determine the consequences that could occur if those assets are compromised.

Practice

The list of assets you develop will be used in all of the following steps:

- Asset/Attack Matrix: Which assets are vulnerable to what types of entry methods, weapons, and attack scenarios
- Criticalities and Consequence Matrix
- Vulnerabilities Matrix: Establishing the vulnerabilities of the assets listed
- Surveillance Matrix: Establishing the surveillance opportunities of the assets listed (one component of vulnerability)
- All of the Asset Target Value Matrixes
  - Terrorism
  - Economic criminals
  - Violent criminals
  - Subversives
  - Petty criminals
- Hazards Matrix
  - Safety hazards

- Natural disaster hazards
- Man-made hazards
- Risk Analysis Matrixes (the composite of vulnerabilities and asset target value)

The first step in developing all of these matrixes is to develop a comprehensive list of assets and to categories those into their four classes. All organizational assets fall into four main categories:

- People
- Property
- Proprietary information
- Business reputation

It is usual to begin a risk analysis project with interviews. Subjects include

- The organization's mission statement
- The programs that the organization has developed and how those relate to its mission statement
- The assets the organization has acquired in support of its programs
- The reason this risk analysis is being undertaken
- The security events that have occurred at each property within the last 5 years

Facility and Asset List

For all of the matrixes in this book, which will evaluate every aspect of the organization's assets, a full facility and asset list is required.

- Research: Research may include Internet, telephone, and records research. Chapter 3 provides a good foundation for the tools of research.
- Surveys: In surveys, one finds any and all of the following kinds of information:
  - Environmental context
  - Property context
  - Organizational context
  - Security context

Tools

One of the primary benefits of this book is the teaching of a spreadsheet approach to risk analysis. You may either use this approach or use commercial software to document your findings and estimates and to perform calculations. But it is useful for understanding the principles of risk analysis to build the databases at least once.

This information will be used as the basis for most of the other matrixes, as we will see in later chapters.

REFERENCE

1. Cohan, P. 2008. Companies that vanished: Arthur Anderson succumbs to the lure of big money. www.bloggingstocks.com. June 8.

Q&A

Questions

Q1: The first step in risk assessment is to
   A. Understand the assets at risk.
   B. Understand the assets at risk, determine their criticality to the mission of the organization, and determine the consequences that could occur if those assets are compromised.
   C. Determine their criticality to the mission.
   D. None of the above.

Q2: Which tools will use the list of assets you develop?
   A. Asset/Attack Matrix, Criticalities and Consequence Matrix, and Vulnerabilities Matrix
   B. Surveillance Matrix, Asset Target Value Matrixes, Hazards Matrix, and Risk Analysis Matrix
   C. Neither of the above
   D. Both of the above

Q3: All organizational assets fall into which four categories?
   A. People, equipment, furnishings, and fittings
   B. People, equipment, proprietary information, and brand loyalty
   C. People, property, proprietary information, and business reputation
   D. None of the above

Q4: The people category will include
   A. Employees, visitors, and vendors.
   B. Employees, contractors, and visitors.
   C. Employees, contractors, visitors, and vendors.
   D. None of the above.

Q5: Over time, the organization's
   A. Brand develops to embrace the organization's business reputation.
   B. Management develops plans for its strategic elements by tactical inclines.
   C. Management develops its brand into a malleable tool for elegance.
   D. None of the above.

Q6: Interviews are a _____ of information about the organization's assets.
   A. Portfolio
   B. Limited amount
   C. Gold mine
   D. None of the above

Q7: Good surveys require what kinds of context?
   A. Environmental context, property context, organizational context, and security context
   B. Security context

    C. Security context and property context
    D. Security context, property context, and environmental context

Q8: Which below is true?
    A. Commercial software is the only reliable way to perform a risk analysis.
    B. Custom spreadsheets are the best way to perform a risk analysis.
    C. Either commercial software or custom spreadsheets can perform a quality risk analysis.
    D. None of the above.

Q9: Make a list of the _____ kinds of assets.
    A. Four
    B. Five
    C. Six
    D. Seven

Q10: Proprietary information includes
    A. Vital records, secret formulas, and information technology system.
    B. Security system, telecommunications system, and paper records.
    C. Both of the above.
    D. Neither of the above.

Answers

Q1 – B, Q2 – D, Q3 – C, Q4 – C, Q5 – A, Q6 – C, Q7 – A, Q8 – B, Q9 – A, Q10 – C

CHAPTER **6**

Criticality and Consequence Analysis

INTRODUCTION

On completion of this chapter, you will understand the difference between criticality and consequences and how to determine both criticality and consequences. You will also understand how consequence analysis is the key to prioritizing security program resources in order to get the best results for the least program expenditure. Risk can be prioritized by consequences so that limited funds can be spent on protecting the most important assets.

Understanding criticality and consequence analysis is the key to applying the limited budget for countermeasures in the most efficient manner. It is imperative that countermeasures be applied to secure the most critical assets first and then others in descending fashion. Usually, this involves a twofold approach, described in the next section.

TWOFOLD APPROACH

While every project should receive a *baseline security program* and *specific countermeasures to address specific vulnerabilities*, the programs that work best are those designed to assure the best protection for the most critical assets within the context of these two approaches. That is, rather than applying a generic baseline security program, a good analyst will recommend a program that biases the countermeasures to assure the best protection for the most critical assets.

CRITICALITY VERSUS CONSEQUENCE

Criticality and Consequence are not interchangeable and they occur at different points in the Risk Analysis process. For this reason, each term has different meanings. Criticality is a qualitative judgment call made as an antecedent to the Risk Analysis process. Consequence can be both a qualitative and/or quantitative term carrying the weight of data and evidence and is made in the latter part of the Risk Analysis process. (Mr. Charles Goslin, CPP, CISSP, personal communication)

There is a distinct difference between the terms criticality and consequence. Many security professionals mistakenly use the terms interchangeably. Criticality has to do

FIGURE 6.1   Consequences graphic.

with the effect that an asset has on the organization's ability to carry out its mission, or the criticality to the sustainability of the organization, while consequence identifies the effect that the loss of an asset would have on the organization.

It is in this latter role that criticality gets confused with consequences. The loss of a critical asset can have a serious consequence for the organization. The consequence is the effect of the loss on the organization. The criticality is the aspect of the asset that causes the consequence.

It is this factor that serious threat actors take into consideration when deciding what attack scenario to use to inflict the greatest damage on an organization with the least effort and to have the greatest probability of success of the attack. In every operational system, there are critical nodes that if damaged or destroyed will cause the entire operational system to collapse. For a bridge, there are generally no more than four points that if damaged with small amounts of tools, weapons, or explosives will cause the total collapse of the entire bridge.

So it is with all operational structures. Simple critical nodes (single points of failure) control everything. Sophisticated threat actors understand this and exploit this principle with dramatic effect. Risk analysts must also. Any risk analyst that cannot identify the critical nodes of an organization's structures, operations, and procedures is useless in his role. The ability to identify critical nodes is the key difference between fair, good, and great risk analysts because critical nodes control consequences.

Criticality in operational systems can be difficult to see. Who would imagine that a few box cutters could be used to effect the worst terrorist attack the world had ever seen? Who would imagine that sloppy tradecraft during an apparently unimportant burglary could bring about the downfall of a president of the United States? Again, critical nodes control consequences.

Criticality and consequence ranking can be used as a component of other calculations including asset target value and risk analysis calculations and also countermeasure cost-effectiveness (Figure 6.1).

CRITICALITY

There are two measures of criticality. The first is the impact that an asset actually has on the carrying out of the mission of the organization. If an asset (person, property, information, or business reputation) is essential to the mission of the organization, it can be said to be critical. The second is the impact the asset has on the sustainability of the organization.

Basic criticality is the measure or estimate of a business unit or asset's importance to the mission of the organization. Certain of the organization's assets are more important than others to the mission of the organization. An asset's sustainability criticality is a measure of how important the asset is to the sustainability of the organization. These can be different. For example, when John D. Rockefeller began Standard Oil Company, he relied on trains to carry his oil east to the large population centers. The railroads became critical to the daily operations of Standard Oil and also critical to the sustainability of the company's business model. As railroads began to see large volumes of oil moving, they began to raise the prices of transporting Mr. Rockefeller's oil, sensing how critical their transportation was to the success of his company. Mr. Rockefeller invested in pipelines as a second mode of transport that eliminated the criticality of the railroad system to his daily operations. The pipelines became critical to the daily operations of Standard Oil instead. But, by doing so, he also eliminated the criticality of both the rails and the pipeline to the sustainability of Standard Oil, as each served as a backup to the other.

Criticality may be intrinsic or derivative. Intrinsic criticality is the extent to which a specific asset is directly important to the mission of the organization, while derivative criticality is estimated by the impact that the loss of the asset would have consequentially. For example, the loss of the accounts receivable database might not immediately cause the collapse of the organization, however the loss of revenues that could occur because the organization cannot prove amounts owed to it could cause its bankruptcy. So while the database is not itself a critical component, the consequences make it so.

It is necessary to place a criticality measure on every major asset so that countermeasures can be appropriately derived. Criticality is best estimated not by a security consultant, but by the organization's own senior management.

At a minimum, each major asset should be estimated for the following:

- Criticality to operations.
  - Absolutely critical to daily operations: loss would cause immediate shutdown of operations.
  - Very critical, but operations could continue for up to several days.
  - Critical, but operations could continue at diminished capacity.
  - Somewhat critical, but operations would be seriously impacted.
  - Not critical, but helpful to operations.
  - Absolutely not critical to the mission.
- Criticality to sustainability.
  - Absolutely critical to Sustainability and no suitable and affordable work-around could be arranged. Loss of asset would cause the loss of the organization.
  - An affordable work-around could be arranged.
  - A work-around could be arranged but would seriously affect operations or profitability.
  - Absolutely not critical to the mission.

VISUALIZATION

Assets that are critical to both operations and sustainability should receive the highest attention. A consultant could prepare a *heat map* (X–Y Matrix) showing escalating operations criticality in the Y scale and escalating sustainability criticality in the X scale, such that the most critical assets land in the upper left corner. This will help the consultant and client to visualize the criticality of all major assets.

Taking the list of assets developed earlier from the interviews and surveys, the consultant, with help from a representative from senior management, should address the criticality of each asset as described above. Often a good place to begin this is with the organization's disaster recovery plan, for which a criticality analysis will already have been conducted.

Develop a criticality/consequences chart with the assets in rows on the left and the first column labeled criticalities. Use the following scale for criticalities:

10. Absolutely critical to daily operations
 7. Very critical, but operations could continue for up to several days
 5. Critical, but operations could continue at diminished capacity
 3. Somewhat critical, but operations would be seriously impacted
 1. Not critical, but helpful to operations
 0. Absolutely not critical to the mission

and place an X next to each asset and under the appropriate criticality ranking.

CONSEQUENCE ANALYSIS

For every unwanted event, a range of consequences are possible, and within most of these, there is a range of severity. Possible consequences include

- Mass casualties
- Loss of property
- Loss of production
- Loss of proprietary information
- Environmental impact
- Loss of business reputation (members of the public's confidence in the organization)

Similar to the measurement for criticality, the measurement of consequence is best conducted in collaboration with a representative from the organization's senior management. It is best to consider not what will happen, but what could happen (Murphy's law).

As for criticality analysis, the analyst should prepare a spreadsheet that illustrates a row for every major asset and columns for the possible consequences. Then, after noting a score between 1 and 10 (10 being the worst) at every appropriate box, the analyst can determine those assets (targets) with the greatest consequences (Figure 6.2).

Another measure of criticality is the cost to the organization to replace the asset if lost:

- Absolutely critical as the cost to replace would be impossible to bear
- Very critical, replaceable at very great cost in dollars or lost production
- Critical, replaceable at significant cost in dollars or lost production
- Somewhat critical, cost would impact other operations or development plans
- Not critical, easily replaceable

FIGURE 6.2   Risks have consequences.

BUILDING YOUR OWN CRITICALITY/CONSEQUENCES MATRIX

For readers who are interested in building their own risk analysis program spreadsheets, read on through the rest of the chapter. Those readers who wish to use a commercially available software product or who are reading only for interest in the subject of risk analysis may skip the rest of this chapter.

This book will explain each element of risk analysis and countermeasure selection in terms of its theory, practice, and tools. The book will explain in adequate detail how to assemble MS Excel® or similar spreadsheets for each element. Those readers who prefer to use a commercial software tool may skip the sections explaining how to build the spreadsheets. For those who are interested in building and using their own world-class risk analysis software tool, the first two Tabs on the Excel Workbooks are explained in cell-by-cell detail and after that in adequate detail to build the remaining sheets. The first of these is the Consequence Matrix. The Consequence Matrix also includes the basic template on which most other matrixes will be built, that is, the list of assets/targets.

CRITICALITY/CONSEQUENCE MATRIX INSTRUCTIONS

These instructions should be combined with a close look at the illustrations in this chapter in order to assemble working spreadsheets. It is most useful to place all of the matrixes described in this book together into a single Excel Workbook. At the bottom of a blank Excel Workbook, you will notice that there are several tabs marked Sheet 1, Sheet 2, Sheet 3, and so on. Right-click on the tabs and rename them to match the matrix you are developing as you go through this book. The tab at the far right (Excel 2007) generates new empty worksheets, while on Excel new worksheets are created by clicking on Insert>Worksheet in the Toolbars at the top of the page.

The instructions that follow will create empty worksheets. You will need to average the values of the columns to form the Score column and rank the rows to fill the Rank column. The row contents given are examples only. You should use the actual assets/ targets that are applicable for your facility.

1. Open an empty Excel or similar spreadsheet.
2. Save as "Consequences".
3. Right-click on a tab on the bottom of the spreadsheet and select Rename.
4. Rename the tab "Consequences".
5. Row 3, Column C. Enter "Project Name". Bold this. Change the font to 14.

6. Row 4, Column C. Enter "Consequences Matrix". Bold this. Change the font to 14.
7. Row 5, Column C. Enter "Note: Criticality is for Reference Only".
8. Select Column C, align the text to the right except for cells C3, C4, and C5. Keep them aligned to the left.
9. Select Column D, right-click>Column Width>Enter "0.2".
10. Row 6, Column C. Enter "Targets". Bold this.
11. Row 6, Column E. Enter "Criticality". Bold this.
12. Go to Cell E6, right-click>FormatCells>Alignment>Orientation>Enter "75 Degrees".
13. Select Column F, right-click>Column Width>Enter "0.2".
14. Copy formatting (use the copy format paintbrush) from E6 through Q6 (this tilts all those cells 75°).
15. Row 6, Column G. Enter "Mass Casualties".
16. Row 6, Column H. Enter "Loss of Property".
17. Row 6, Column I. Enter "Loss of Production".
18. Row 6, Column J. Enter "Loss of Proprietary Information".
19. Row 6, Column K. Enter "Environmental Impact".
20. Row 6, Column L. Enter "Loss of Business Reputation".
21. Select Column M, right-click>Column Width>Enter "0.2".
22. Row 6, Column N. Enter "Score".
23. Select Column O, right-click>Column Width>Enter "0.2".
24. Row 6, Column P. Enter "Rank".
25. Row 7, Column C. Enter "People" (heading for below). Bold this.
26. Row 9, Column C. Enter "VIP Executives & VIP Visitors".
27. Row 10, Column C. Enter "Employees".
28. Row 11, Column C. Enter "Contractors".
29. Row 12, Column C. Enter "Visitors".
30. Row 13, Column C. Enter "Delivery Personnel".
31. Row 14, Column C. Enter "Transportation Personnel".
32. Row 15, Select Cells C15 through Q15, right-click>Format Cells>Patterns>choose Gray Color.
33. Row 16, Column C. Enter "Property" (heading for all property classes below). Bold this.
34. Select Row 17, right-click>Row Width>Enter 2.
35. Row 18, Column C. Enter "Site" (heading for below). Bold and italic this.
36. Select Row 19, right-click>Row Width>Enter 2.
37. Row 20, Column C. Enter "VIP Drop-Off".
38. Row 21, Column C. Enter "Employee Drop-Off".
39. Row 22, Column C. Enter "Visitor Drop-Off—Hotel (South)".
40. Row 23, Column C. Enter "Main South Entry Gate House Area".
41. Row 24, Column C. Enter "North Perimeter Fence".
42. Row 25, Column C. Enter "East Perimeter Fence".
43. Row 26, Column C. Enter "South Perimeter Fence".
44. Row 27, Column C. Enter "West Perimeter Fence".
45. Row 28, Column C. Enter "North Perimeter Freight Gate".
46. Row 29, Column C. Enter "East Perimeter Emergency Gate".
47. Row 30, Column C. Enter "West Perimeter Emergency Gate".
48. Row 31, Column C. Enter "Hotel Loading Dock Area".

49. Row 32, Column C. Enter "Hotel East Entrance".
50. Row 33, Column C. Enter "Hotel West Entrance".
51. Row 34, Column C. Enter "Ramp Down to Underground Parking".
52. Select Row 35, right-click>Row Width>Enter 2.
53. Row 36, Column C. Enter "Underground Structure" (heading for below). Bold and italic this.
54. Select Row 37, right-click>Row Width>Enter 2.
55. Row 38, Column C. Enter "P1 Level Parking".
56. Row 39, Column C. Enter "P1 Level Elevator Lobby".
57. Row 40, Column C. Enter "P2 Level Parking".
58. Row 41, Column C. Enter "P2 Level Elevator Lobby".
59. Row 42, Column C. Enter "P3 Level Parking".
60. Row 43, Column C. Enter "P3 Level Elevator Lobby".
61. Row 44, Column C. Enter "P3 Level Utility Rooms".
62. Select Row 45, right-click>Row Width>Enter 2.
63. Row 46, Column C. Enter "Hotel Tower" (heading for below). Bold and italic this.
64. Select Row 47, right-click>Row Width>Enter 2.
65. Row 48, Column C. Enter "Main Lobby Area".
66. Row 49, Column C. Enter "Lobby Level Reception Desk".
67. Row 50, Column C. Enter "Lobby Level Bell Desk and Storage".
68. Row 51, Column C. Enter "Security Checkpoint Outside".
69. Row 52, Column C. Enter "Lobby Level Concierge Area".
70. Row 53, Column C. Enter "Passenger Elevator Lobby".
71. Row 54, Column C. Enter "Stairwells".
72. Row 55, Column C. Enter "Freight Elevator".
73. Row 56, Column C. Enter "Lobby Level Utility Rooms".
74. Row 57, Column C. Enter "Low-Rise Levels".
75. Row 58, Column C. Enter "Mid-Rise Levels".
76. Row 59, Column C. Enter "High-Rise Levels".
77. Row 60, Column C. Enter "Passenger Elevator Lobbies".
78. Row 61, Column C. Enter "Freight Elevator Lobbies".
79. Row 62, Column C. Enter "Utility Rooms".
80. Row 63, Column C. Enter "Mechanical Floor".
81. Row 64, Column C. Enter "Roof".
82. Row 65, Select Cells C65 through Q65, right-click>Format Cells>Patterns>choose Gray Color.
83. Row 66, Column C. Enter "Proprietary Information". Bold this.
84. Select Row 67, right-click>Row Width>Enter 2.
85. Row 68, Column C. Enter "IT System".
86. Row 69, Column C. Enter "Security System".
87. Row 70, Column C. Enter "RF Communications System".
88. Row 71, Column C. Enter "Paper Files".
89. Row 72, Select Cells C72 through Q72, right-click>Format Cells>Patterns>choose Gray Color.
90. Row 73, Column C. Enter "Business Reputation".
91. Row 77, Column C, Enter "Legend". Bold this.
92. Row 78, Column C, Enter "Major Effect".
93. Row 79, Column C, Enter "Medium Effect".

94. Row 80, Column C, Enter "Minimal Effect".
95. Row 78, Column E, Enter "10". Go to Formats>Conditional Formatting.
96. Under Condition 1, choose Cell Value Is between 0 and 3.25.
97. Under Condition 1, click on Format Tab then on the Patterns Tab and Choose the Color to be Green.
98. Still in the Conditional Formatting Window, click on the Add>> Tab.
99. Under Condition 2, choose Cell Value Is between 3.25001 and 6.55.
100. Under Condition 2, click on the Format Tab then on the Patterns Tab and choose the Color to be Yellow.
101. Still in the Conditional Formatting Window, click on the Add>> Tab.
102. Under Condition 3, choose Cell Value Is between 6.55001 and 10.
103. Under Condition 3, click on the Format Tab then on the Patterns Tab and choose the Color to be Red. Click on "OK".
104. Row 78 Column E, should turn to red filled instantaneously.
105. Copy formatting (use the copy format paintbrush) from E78 through E80 (this copies the conditional formatting to the cells).
106. Row 79, Column E, Enter "5". The cell should turn to yellow filled instantaneously.
107. Row 80, Column E, Enter "1". The cell should turn to green filled instantaneously.
108. Copy formatting (use the copy format paintbrush) from E78 to Cell E7 through Cell N7 (this fills the cells with the green color).
109. Repeat Step 108 above for Cells E9 down to Cell N14.
110. Repeat Step 108 above for Cells E16 through N16.
111. Repeat Step 108 above for Cells E18 through N18.
112. Repeat Step 108 above for Cells E20 down to Cell N34.
113. Repeat Step 108 above for Cells E36 down to Cell N36.
114. Repeat Step 108 above for Cells E38 down to Cell N44.
115. Repeat Step 108 above for Cells E46 through N46.
116. Repeat Step 108 above for Cells E48 down to Cell N64.
117. Repeat Step 108 above for Cells E66 through N66.
118. Repeat Step 108 above for Cells E68 down to Cell N71.
119. Repeat Step 108 above for Cells E73 through Cell N73.
120. Row 7, Column E, Enter "= AVERAGE(E9:E14)" (this is the formula to calculate the average of the cells E9 through E14).
121. Copy Cell E7, select Cells G7 through L7 and paste the formula. (This will copy the formula to the selected cells.) Do not panic if you get "#DIV/0!". This is because your matrix is still not filled.
122. Repeat Step 121 above for Cell N7. (This will calculate the average of Cells N9 through N14.).
123. Row 9, Column N, Enter "= AVERAGE(G9:L9)" (this will calculate the average of Cells G9 through L9).
124. Copy Cell N9, Select Cells N10 through N14 and paste the formula.
125. Row 16, Column E, Enter "=AVERAGE(E18,E36,E46)" (this will give the average of the three selected Headings).
126. Copy Cell E16, Select Cells G16 through L16, and paste the formula.
127. Repeat Step 126 above for Cell N16.
128. Row 18, Column E, Enter "=AVERAGE(E20:E34)".
129. Copy E18, Select Cells G18 through L18, and paste the formula
130. Repeat Step 129 above for Cell N18.

131. Row 20, Column N, Enter "=AVERAGE(G20:L20)" (this will calculate the average of Cells G20 through L20).
132. Copy Cell N20, Select Cells N21 through N34, and paste the formula.
133. Row 36, Column E, Enter "=AVERAGE(E38:E44)".
134. Copy E36, Select Cells G36 through L36, and paste the formula.
135. Repeat Step 134 above for Cell N36.
136. Row 38, Column N, Enter "=AVERAGE(G38:L38)" (this will calculate the average of Cells G38 through L38).
137. Copy Cell N38, Select Cells N39 through N44, and paste the formula.
138. Row 46, Column E, Enter "=AVERAGE(E48:E64)".
139. Copy E46, Select Cells G46 through L46, and paste the formula.
140. Repeat Step 139 above for Cell N46.
141. Row 48, Column N, Enter "=AVERAGE(G48:L48)" (this will calculate the average of Cells G48 through L48).
142. Copy Cell N48, Select Cells N49 through N64, and paste the formula.
143. Row 66, Column E, Enter "=AVERAGE(E68:E71)".
144. Copy E66, Select Cells G66 through L66, and paste the formula.
145. Repeat Step 144 above for Cell N66.
146. Row 68, Column N, Enter "=AVERAGE(G68:L68)" (this will calculate the average of Cells G68 through L68).
147. Copy Cell N68, Select Cells N69 through N68, and paste the formula.
148. Row 73, Column N, Enter "=AVERAGE(G73:L73)".

Following this, populate the cells with appropriate estimates on a scale of 1 to 10. Then, average the Score Column and rank the results in the Ranking Column. I suggest using averaging of rows to create the score, because it provides a relative view of the issues at hand for each row of each spreadsheet. As you build your own spreadsheets and begin to work with them, you may find that you prefer another formula for determining the score, but I have found that averaging is simple and results in a consistently meaningful display of the relationships of the various rows. The spreadsheet can also be made much more useful if you apply conditional formatting to the Data and Score cells so that high scores color red, low scores color green, and medium cells color yellow. Conditional formatting is applied differently in various versions of Excel, so it is best to use the Help file or look up "Conditional Formatting Excel" in Google. (Substitute your version of Excel if different.)

Refer back to these instructions as you prepare the data for other spreadsheets, as these instructions apply to all matrixes throughout the book.

SUMMARY

Criticality and consequence analysis is key to applying the limited budget for countermeasures in the most efficient manner. While every project should receive a baseline security program and specific countermeasures to address specific vulnerabilities, the programs that work best are those designed to assure the best protection for the most critical assets within the context of these two approaches.

Criticality has to do with the impact that an individual asset has on carrying out the mission of the organization, while consequence identifies the effect that the loss of an asset would have on the organization. Criticality and consequence ranking can be used as a component of other calculations including asset target value and risk analysis calculations and also countermeasure cost-effectiveness.

Criticality

There are two measures of criticality. The first is the impact that an asset actually has on the carrying out of the mission of the organization, and the second is the impact that cost or time to replace the asset would have on the organization.

Basic criticality is the measure or estimate of a business unit or asset's importance to the mission of the organization. Certain of the organization's assets are more important than others to its mission. Criticality may be intrinsic or derivative. Intrinsic criticality is the extent to which a specific asset is directly important to the mission of the organization, while derivative criticality is estimated by the impact that the loss of the asset would have consequentially.

Consequence Analysis

For every unwanted event, a range of consequences are possible, and within most of these, there is a range of severity. Possible consequences include

- Death
- Injury
- Economic loss to the organization
- Economic loss to the organization's constituents
- Environmental impact
- Loss of production or operations
- Loss of business reputation (members of the public's confidence in the organization)
- Loss of assets

Q&A

Questions

Q1: Criticality is
   A. The same as consequences.
   B. Different from consequences.
   C. The same as vulnerability.
   D. None of the above.

Q2: Risk can be prioritized by _____ so that limited funds can go to protect the most important assets.
   A. Criticality
   B. Asset target value
   C. Vulnerabilities
   D. Consequences

Q3: Criticality has to do with
  A. The effect that the loss of an asset would have on the organization.
  B. The impact that an individual asset has on carrying out the mission of the organization.
  C. The degree of vulnerability of an asset.
  D. None of the above.

Q4: Criticality and consequence ranking can be used as a component of other calculations including
  A. Asset target value.
  B. Risk analysis calculations.
  C. Countermeasure cost-effectiveness.
  D. All of the above.

Q5: It is necessary to place a criticality measure on every major asset so that countermeasures can be appropriately derived. Criticality is best estimated not by a security consultant, but by
  A. The level of vulnerability of the asset.
  B. Both A and C.
  C. The level of risk.
  D. The organization's own senior management.

Q6: A good place to begin with criticality is with
  A. The organization's disaster recovery plan.
  B. The vulnerability assessment.
  C. The risk assessment.
  D. None of the above.

Q7: For every unwanted event, a range of consequences are possible, with a range of severity. Possible consequences include
  A. Mass casualties, loss of property.
  B. Loss of production, loss of proprietary information.
  C. Environmental impact, loss of business reputation.
  D. All of the above.

Q8: Another measure of criticality is the cost to the organization to replace the asset if lost. Which of the following is considered?
  A. Absolutely critical, as the cost to replace would be impossible to bear
  B. Very critical, replaceable at very great cost in dollars or lost production
  C. Not critical, easily replaceable
  D. All of the above

Q9: The criticality of major assets should be estimated for which of the following:
  A. Absolutely critical to daily operations
  B. Very critical, but operations could continue for up to several days
  C. Very vulnerable to attack
  D. A and B, but not C

Q10: The analysis matrixes may be built and filled out either from a commercially available software tool or by using a spreadsheet program. This statement is
  A. True.
  B. False.
  C. Mostly true.
  D. Mostly false.

Answers

Q1 – B, Q2 – D, Q3 – B, Q4 – D, Q5 – D, Q6 – A, Q7 – D, Q8 – D, Q9 – D, Q10 – A

CHAPTER 7

Threat Analysis

INTRODUCTION

Threats are at the core of probability, so threat analysis is at the core of probability analysis. Probability is the composite of a threat actor with intent and capabilities acting on a vulnerable asset. The process of probability analysis, then, is the process of first defining capable threat actors and then estimating their possible intent to harm or attack the assets of the organization we are analyzing. Probability analysis itself is discussed in Chapter 9, Estimating Probability.

This chapter contains a section on predictive threat analysis. In my humble opinion, any threat analysis that is not predictive in nature is virtually useless. The entire point of risk analysis is to develop strategies that can counter threats. Being able to predict potential threats is central to that effort. This chapter also contains a section on deductive versus inductive reasoning, which is a necessary skill for predictive threat analysis.

On completion of this chapter, you will have a good working understanding of threat analysis, including the difference between threats and hazards, sources for information about hazards, types of threat actors, sources for threat analysis information, and tools to use in threat analysis.

THEORY

Threats versus Hazards

Many security professionals and their clients confuse threats and hazards. Hazards can be either natural or man-made and are generally unintentional or without malice, while threats are always man-made and are intentional and with malice. This chapter begins with a discussion on hazards, which is followed by a comprehensive presentation on threats (Figure 7.1).

A *hazard* is a precondition for an accident or a natural event having negative consequences. Hazards may include

- Safety hazards
- Security hazards
- Natural disaster hazards
- Local or regional political or military hazards

Hazards may be environmental or behavioral. Either type can establish the preconditions for an unwanted consequence.

FIGURE 7.1   Threats vs. hazards.

Examples of *safety hazards* range from an unexpected road obstruction or a candle placed near flammable draperies to the fact that your neighbor never looks before backing his car into the street. Safety hazards may include

- Fires due to safety hazards
- Fires due to negligence
- Human error
- Poor design
- Safety violations (blocked exits, etc.)
- Faulty or poorly maintained buildings, vehicles, and technology
- Institutional failure
- High societal tolerance to safety hazards

Examples of *security hazards* include

- Persistent rule violators (e.g., employees who routinely leave perimeter doors open for their convenience for smoking breaks or leave important documents left lying on desks for any unauthorized person to see)
- Environmental factors
  - For example, if the organization's facilities are located in an area with a high incidence of crime, this is a security hazard.
  - High business culture tolerance for security hazards.

Natural hazards may include acts of God, such as tornados and floods, and other incidents quantifiable in terms of statistical probability, such as mean time between failure (MTBF) of equipment. Natural hazards may include

- Earthquakes
- Hurricanes and tropical storms
- Tornados
- Hailstorms
- Thunderstorms and lightning
- Snow and ice

- Floods including tsunamis
- Landslides and mudslides
- Fires from natural causes
- Fog
- Hail
- Heat
- Wind
- Safety hazards

An *accident* is an incident or event, frequently involving humans, with negative consequences, which is caused by the presence of a hazard and a triggering event. Accidents can be prevented in one of two ways:

- Eliminate or mitigate the hazard so that the accident cannot occur
- Modify the behavior of the person, machine, or thing initiating the triggering event so that the accident will not occur

Either can prevent accidents, but risk professionals should try to do both. In order to modify the preconditions so that the accident cannot occur, one must appreciate that there could be preconditions and identify what they are. Critical thinking in security and safety matters can greatly improve the chances of spotting accident preconditions.

For example, where I do much of my work in the Middle East and in a certain Arabian Gulf state, traffic safety is virtually nonexistent. Despite the fact that people understand that in a collision any unattached objects within the car could be propelled through the windshield or out an open window, in several countries I see almost all small children riding without seat belts, often bouncing and playing in the back seat and sometimes hanging well out of the window. (I have even seen small children reaching out to touch other cars as they go by.) This sets up the preconditions for the loss of the life of the child. All it takes then is a triggering event of someone's bad driving (of which there is plenty).

Political and economic risks: In certain areas, political and economic instability can also affect security conditions. This should also be considered.

Descriptive statistics can provide historical data for the frequency of past occurrences of accidents and suggest expected levels of future occurrence, but specific accidents cannot be predicted using inferential statistical techniques. Examples include traffic accidents on a bridge and falls down stairs at facilities. Accidents, by definition, are not malicious acts.

Security analysts should cite data for their findings and conclusions. Likelihood and consequence information can be obtained from any of the following sources:

- U.S. Coast Guard
  - National Response Center
  - Marine accident database
- Federal Railroad Administration
- Railroad accident database
- Pipeline and Hazardous Materials Safety Administration
  - Pipeline accident database
  - Hazardous materials incident database
- Federal Motor Carrier Safety Administration
- Truck accident data
- U.S. Bureau of the Census

- Demographic data
- Environmental Protection Agency
  - Hazardous waste facility database
  - National Emissions Inventory
  - Toxic Release Inventory
  - Safe Drinking Water Information System
  - Superfund information system
  - Enforcement and compliance database
- National Oceanic & Atmospheric Administration (NOAA)
  - Storm Events Database
  - Drought information center
  - Tsunami database
- U.S. Bureau of Transportation Statistics
  - Political boundaries
  - Urban areas
  - Transportation networks
- U.S. Geological Survey
  - Spatial Hazard Events and Losses Database
  - National Hydrography Dataset
  - Landslide incidence and susceptibility data
  - Earthquake hazard and incident data
  - Volcano incident data
  - Tornado data
- U.S. Fire Administration, fire incident data
- Federal Emergency Management Agency, flood data
- Federal Bureau of Investigation, crime database
- Local law enforcement data and statistics
- Cap index, including local and regional security historical data
- A list of current active terrorism threat actors for any region can be obtained from
  - U.S. State Department: threats to the United States
  - British Foreign & Commonwealth Office (FCO) home
  - Stratfor: strategic forecasts
  - South Asia Terrorism Portal
  - The Nine Eleven Finding Answers (NEFA) Foundation
- Economic risks
  - *The Economist* research database www.economist.com≥ResearchTools ≥CountryBriefings
  - U.S. Department of State www.state.gov/misc/list/index.htm
- Political risk
  - *The Economist* research database www.economist.com≥ResearchTools≥ CountryBriefings
  - U.S. Department of State www.state.gov/misc/list/index.htm

All-Hazards Risk Analysis

I recommend an all-hazards risk analysis approach for major projects that takes all of these factors into consideration.

Since September 11, 2001, there has been a hard shift in risk analysis to a focus on threats of terrorism, and this book deals with terroristic threats more completely than most risk analysis books. However, much of this shift to focus on terrorism has come at the expense of the historical focus on security and hazards. This is most unfortunate, because security and hazard risks far outweigh terrorism risks for most facilities.

Although my primary field of focus is projects that have very significant risks of terrorism (some of my projects have active threats against specific individuals or facilities), I believe that a risk analyst does his or her client a terrible disservice by focusing primarily (and in some cases I have seen, only) on terrorism. The client has not been serviced if they are spending large amounts of money to deter or mitigate possible terrorist attacks while more likely risks are ignored.

Additionally, at the time of writing this book, it is in vogue with many risk analysts to emphasize terrorism risks for virtually every type of facility. While terrorism is certainly a valid risk, it is not a valid risk for a nontoxic landfill (for which I have seen a risk assessment that dealt only with the threats of terrorism). Not every facility is at risk of terrorism. The risk analyst should focus on appropriate risks and not emphasize terrorism on every project.

A good risk analysis report should present all potential threats and hazards and rank and prioritize them, then focus on those that are most relevant. This should typically include natural hazards, man-made security hazards, and intentional acts related to "ordinary decent crime" (ODC).*

All security risk management has a common objective: to reduce the possibility or likelihood of undesirable events and their consequences, to protect human life and health, and to improve the quality of life in the environment. I believe that for major projects, a comprehensive listing of hazards and threats is useful and helps the client to not only focus on the most relevant risks, but also to understand the other risks and appreciate the priority placed on the most relevant risks.

Now, on to threats. Threats are all man-made. A threat is a group or individual that has both the capability of and the intent to cause harm. A threat actor is an individual or group that intends to harm people or to conduct an attack against a facility or organization or against exemplars of an opposing point of view.

Without a threat actor, there is no risk. Analysts must identify potential threat actors and then decide (with ownership) which level of threat actor the security program should attempt to deter and which it should attempt to protect against. The first step is to understand who could be potential threat actors.

There are five kinds of potential threat actors. These include

- Terrorists
  - Class I terrorist: the government-trained professional (including foreign intelligence threats)
  - Class II terrorist: the religious extremist professional
  - Class III terrorist: the radical revolutionary or quasi-religious extremist
  - Class IV terrorist: guerrilla/mercenary soldiers
  - Class V terrorist: amateur (civilian, untrained criminal, or militia vigilante)
- Economic criminals
  - Transnational criminal organizations
  - Organized crime

---

* "What the British Police used to call O.D.C. (Ordinary Decent Crime) has suffered a sad decline in this era of predominantly indecent and extraordinary offenses."[1]

- Sophisticated economic criminals
- Unsophisticated economic criminals
- Street criminals
- Nonterrorist violent criminals
  - Workplace violence threat actors
  - Angry visitors
  - Sexual criminals
  - Mugging and parking lot violence
  - Civil disorder event violence
  - Deranged persons
- Subversives
  - Cause-oriented subversives
  - Political and industrial spies
  - Saboteurs
  - Cults and dedicated activist groups
  - Hackers
  - Invasion of privacy threat actors
  - Persistent rule violators
- Petty criminals
  - Vandals
  - Pickpockets
  - Prostitutes, pimps, and panderers
  - Disturbance causers

A detailed description of all the types of threat actors follows.

Terrorists

The five classes of terrorists are described here.[2]

Class I Terrorist The government-trained professional (including foreign intelligence threats): Government-trained professionals are generally very well trained and equipped and often have substantial support systems that are well integrated into the country where they are working due to support from the intelligence community of the government that supports them. These terrorists are trained to carry out missions with great secrecy, and the high level of training and careful selection of candidates help assure that few mistakes are made.

Class I terrorists are normally recruited from key party personnel, loyal military members, secret police, and intelligence communities. Such terrorists may be working with official (consular, etc.) or nonofficial cover, including posing as businessmen, students, merchants, immigrants, or opposition group volunteers.

A good example of the work of government-trained professional terrorists was the targeted assassinations of Palestinian Black September terrorists by Israeli Mossad agents following the killings of 11 Israeli athletes at the 1972 Munich Olympic Games.

In September 1972, terrorists from the Palestinian Liberation Organization Black September movement, which was a cover for the Palestinian Al-Fatah organization, carried out an attack on the Israeli athletes' compound, killing eleven Israeli athletes. Following that massacre, Israel carried out a methodical campaign to assassinate leaders of the Black September guerrilla group. Israeli Prime Minister Golda Meir authorized the effort and approved each assassination.[3]

Attacks by class I terrorists are typically targeted against the leadership or policies of another country and are sometimes designed to be spectacular, as was the Munich athlete compound attack.

Class II Terrorist The religious extremist professional: Class II terrorists are religious extremists who swear allegiance to an extremist religious cause. These are civilians who live as terrorists with no other duty or career but terrorism. Operatives train and receive advanced combat skills and training, more pay, benefits for their families, and advanced ideological training.

The special characteristics of class II terrorists are that they are professionally trained and experienced, they may be candidates for martyrdom or suicide, they are secretive, and they learn from their mistakes and from the successes of their opposition.

The best known class II terrorism group is Al-Qaeda. Such groups stage both small and spectacular attacks, the most spectacular being the attacks of September 11, 2001.

Class III Terrorist The radical revolutionary or quasi-religious extremist: Radical revolutionary terrorists fit the traditional model of the European and Latin radical revolutionary terrorist of the 1960s and 1970s. In America, the Symbionese Liberation Army (SLA), which kidnapped newspaper heiress Patricia Hearst in 1974, is characteristic of a small class III terrorist organization.[4]

Other examples of class III radical revolutionary terrorist organizations include the Spanish Basque separatist group ETA,[5] the former Irish Republican Army (IRA),[6] and the Tamil Tigers of Sri Lanka.[7]

Class III terrorists are generally small to medium-sized groups, though some, such as ETA, can be extensive and well organized. Operatives are usually trained inside the group. Many active groups are radical nationalists. Attacks are usually small, low-intensity attacks typically injuring and killing only a few civilians, though some attacks have been spectacular, such as the IRA attack on July 21, 1972, "Bloody Friday," when 20 bombs detonated in Belfast within an hour, killing nine people and wounding 30.[8]

Class IV Terrorist Guerrilla/mercenary soldiers: Class IV terrorists are generally the most predictable of terrorists because they fall back on basic military training and equipment used in military or paramilitary experience.

Class IV terrorists are generally ex-military men who have little education and have been recruited by a military or militia to help carry out their operations.

Class V Terrorist Amateur (civilian, untrained criminal, or militia-vigilante groups): These groups have large numbers of people but they have rudimentary terrorist experience. Some form or join militia groups and can become quite organized.

The Ku Klux Klan in the United States is an example of a class V terrorist organization,[9] while individuals such as Timothy McVeigh, Theodore ("Ted") Kaczynski, and Eric Robert Rudolph[10] are examples of individual ("lone wolf") class V terrorists. McVeigh carried out the bombing against the Federal Building in Oklahoma City,[11] Kaczynski was known as the "Unabomber,"[12] and Rudolph was known as the "Olympic Park Bomber." Rudolph killed two people and injured 111 in a series of anti-abortion and anti-gay motivated bombings between 1996 and 1998.[13]

Although class V terrorists are the least organized and typically least educated and least well-equipped, they are nonetheless a threat that can cause major problems to their targets.

- Malcolm W. Nance's foundational book *Terrorist Recognition Handbook*[1] is the single most important book for security consultants if they want to understand terrorism threats. It is essential for the library of all analysts who may write any risk analysis involving terrorism threat actors.
- The International Association for Counterterrorism and Security Professionals (www.antiterrorism.org).
- Force Protection Exhibition and Demonstration (FPED).

Economic Criminals

Transnational Criminal Organizations[14]   Transnational criminal organizations are organized crime syndicates that operate across state and national boundaries. The best examples of these include computer crime, the Mafia, and drug and weapons cartels.

Transnational criminal organizations are noted for their organization, their reach, and their breadth and depth, as well as their focus on their core business. Transnational criminal enterprises are sometimes violent, as in the case of drug cartels, but usually prefer to maintain a low profile so as not to draw too much attention from law enforcement.

Transnational criminal organizations can threaten an organization or subvert its purpose, and they may extort or intimidate an organization into serving the purposes of the criminal enterprise.

Organized Crime[15]   Organized criminal enterprises are modest versions of transnational criminal organizations and have many of the same attributes, skills, methods, and tactics. Like transnational criminal enterprises, their goal is that of using career criminals to conduct lifelong business in crime.

Classic organized crime is local to regional and sometimes national. Many Mafia organizations are considered organized crime versus transnational organized crime due to their limited reach.

Organized crime has focused on drug trafficking, prostitution, loan sharking, and racketeering and has compromised private and public organizations as well as government figures.

> Organized criminal groups are highly sophisticated, are able to draw on specialists, and are able to obtain the equipment needed to achieve their goals efficiently. These groups form efficient, hierarchical organizations that can employ highly paid insiders. Targets of organized criminal groups may involve a high degree of risk in handling and disposal such as large quantities of money, equipment, and other goods.[16]

Sophisticated Economic Criminals   Sophisticated economic criminals include those individuals, gangs, and organizations that apply critical thinking techniques to their criminal planning and operations.

Sophisticated economic criminals include career criminals who specialize in jewels, certain types of retail stores, safe cracking, banks, movie theaters, and so on. Many of these criminals are individuals who work alone or in very small gangs. Sophisticated criminals take time to conduct an operation, sometimes conducting research about and surveilling a potential target for many months. Sophisticated criminals think through many aspects of the crime and carefully calculate the risk to minimize the possibility of being caught.

The goal of sophisticated criminals is usually to steal assets, though some may specialize in assassinations or other contract work for an organized crime group. Most sophisticated criminals are either part of an organized crime group or else work alone in order to avoid discovery and capture.

> Sophisticated criminals are skilled in the use of certain weapons and tools and are efficient and organized. They plan their attacks and have sophisticated equipment and the technical ability to employ it. Sophisticated criminals are often assisted by insiders. They target high-value assets, frequently steal in large quantities and target assets with relatively low risk in handling and disposal.[16]

Unsophisticated Economic Criminals   Unsophisticated Economic Criminals are unskilled in the use of weapons and tools and have no formal organization. Their targets are those items that meet their immediate needs, such as drugs, money, and pilferable items. Unsophisticated criminals are interested in opportune targets that present little or no risk. Breaking and entering or smash-and-grab techniques are common. Theft by insiders is also included in this category.[16]

Street Gangs[17] and Street Criminals   Street criminals or street gangs focus primarily on the drug and sex trades and have a history of sometimes extreme violence.

Gangs may include Hispanic gangs; the Crips and the Bloods; the People Nation and the Folks Nation; Jamaican posses; Asian/South Sea Islander gangs; Colombian gangs; Cuban Marielito gangs; motorcycle gangs; racially, ethnically, or religiously oriented gangs; and prison gangs.

Gangs compel discipline and obedience from their members and often recruit the very young and most impressionable. Gangs may destroy neighborhoods and commercial districts with graffiti; belligerent behavior toward civilians; shake-downs of civilians and businesses; pimping, pandering, and prostitution; and the drug culture.

Special Notes on Lone Criminals   Lone criminals are individuals who commit crimes without the knowledgeable aid or assistance of others. Lone criminals include computer criminals, sophisticated criminals, and unsophisticated criminals. Lone criminals may be very successful or chronic petty criminals who seem to always get caught.

Lone criminals have included the Unabomber (Theodore Kaczynski), Eric Rudolph, and the alleged 2001 Anthrax attacker, Bruce Ivins.* Other lone criminals include individual insiders who target proprietary information and company assets.

Nonterrorist Violent Workplace Criminals[19]

- Workplace violence threat actors. These include two main classes:
  - Domestic violent criminals
        Domestic violence workplace crimes account for a large number of violent crimes in the United States and around the world. Domestic violent criminals are individuals who are involved in unstable personal relationships with employees of an organization and who attack the domestic partner in

---

* "An unsatisfying end to the Anthrax Attacks Mystery: The FBI reportedly was ready to charge an Army scientist, but he apparently committed suicide this week."[18]

the workplace. Increasingly, this kind of workplace violence is receiving the attention of the human resources industry in order to identify possible victims of such violent crimes and provide early intervention. This is not only to protect the intended victim but also innocent bystanders in the workplace who are sometimes targeted either intentionally or randomly.

Violence by such attackers is often sudden and very violent, often involving firearms.

- Disgruntled employee or ex-employee

    Violence inflicted by coworkers and former workers of an organization may include fighting, threatening behavior, assault, harassment, stalking, and the like.

    This type of violent attacker is known to target specific individuals, which may include his current or former manager(s) and specific coworkers whom the individual feels may have either wronged him or gossiped about him. Disgruntled violent employees are almost entirely male and most often use knives or guns to attack their intended victims, though acid and flammable chemicals have also been used.*

- Angry visitors: Angry visitors can sometimes cause violence when their unreasonable (and sometimes reasonable) demands are not met. Frustration mounts as they are unable to achieve their desired results, and after escalating their interaction, they may eventually resort to violence.

- Sexual criminals: Sexual criminals usually prey on women and children who are in vulnerable circumstances. Sexual criminals may act alone or in a group. Some criminals may be playing out a fantasy in their mind and research indicates that they are likely to experience violent sexual fantasies well before they begin to act them out.[21] According to the American Medical Association (AMA), sexual assault is the most rapidly growing crime in the United States.[22] The National Victim Center reports that more 700,000 women are raped or sexually assaulted annually.[25]

- Muggings/parking lot violence/robberies gone wrong

    - Muggings/parking lot violence:

        Muggings and parking lot violence can be a problem at any organization where street crime can spill onto the organization's property.

    - Robberies gone wrong

        Some workplace violence events are related to robberies. This is particularly true of taxis, convenience stores, filling stations, and other stop-and-shop facilities.

        In one famous event, gunmen seized 30 hostages at a large electronics store in Sacramento, California. The incident ended after 8 hours when police stormed the store after gunmen "walked systematically down the line shooting hostages."[23]

        In another, two heavily armed and body-armored gunmen robbed a North Hollywood bank and, when confronted by police outside, they touched off a gunfight with the police that redefined the use of high-powered weapons in policing situations; this incident remains one of the bloodiest days in U.S. law enforcement history.[24]

---

* "Janitor Jonathan D'Arcy, enraged when his February paycheck was late, poured gasoline on the company's bookkeeper and set her on fire."[20]

- Deranged persons and stalkers:

  Deranged or mentally ill people can strike out with violence without any notice. Their violent behavior can accompany alcoholism, drug abuse, and certain types of mental illness, particularly paranoid schizophrenia.[25]

  - Stalkers: Celebrities such as John Lennon, Jill Dando, and Rebecca Schaeffer[26-28] were killed by stalkers. Businesses that cater to celebrities and the wealthy must be constantly aware of the risks their clientele faces from celebrity stalkers. Many more ordinary citizens have been attacked, mutilated, and killed by stalkers. In the book *Blind-Sided* by Gregory K. Moffatt, the author states that

    > Research has repeatedly shown that stalkers usually know their victims before the stalking begins. One study on stalking demonstrated that nearly all stalkers knew their victims: 57% of the victims had prior relationships with their stalkers and another 34% of the victims were at least acquaintances before the stalking began. Only 6% did not know their stalkers.[29]

Subversives

Subversives and saboteurs include

- Cause-oriented subversives: Cause-oriented subversives may include activist groups with an agenda opposed to a government, religion, cause, or industry. These can include such groups as the Animal Liberation Front (ALF), the Environmental Liberation Front (ELF), and others.
- Nonaligned subversives: Other subversive acts can include civil disorder events that are related to protests or civil riots. For example, the city of Los Angeles, California, was gripped by civil disorder and riots in 1992 following the trial of Rodney King, a black motorist who was beaten by LAPD officers; the beating was caught on camera and played on local television news stations.[30] Many businesses were damaged in the riots that followed.
- Political and industrial spies: Increasingly, organizations are being targeted by political and industrial spies. One article noted that industrial spies play a very big role behind the scenes at World Trade Organization talks.[31] There have been many cases of industrial and political spies prying into the secrets of large and small organizations alike.
- Hackers: Hackers may deface websites, damage networks, or act as spies to extract important information. In one recent case, hackers stole highly sensitive data concerning the U.S. Pentagon's newest fighter jet, the Joint Strike Fighter, from a military contractor's computers, which were connected to the Internet.
- Invasion of privacy threat actors: Paparazzi and celebrity stalkers are the bane of celebrities due to their invasion of privacy. Businesses that cater to the wealthy and celebrities are often confronted with aggressive celebrity seekers, photographers, and autograph seekers who interrupt the private moments of their clientele and subvert the purpose of a commercial enterprise for their own purposes.
- Persistent rule violators: These are individuals who frequent the organization's facilities either as employees or as visitors and who act as though the organization's assets are their own to use or abuse as they wish. Though warned of rules of conduct, they persist in violating the rules. Such individuals create problems for the organization in several ways.

- They set a bad example for behavior for others.
- They often require special attention to accommodate their demands or actions.
- They often create safety or code of conduct preconditions that could lead to either injuries or to conduct problems on a larger scale (when one person acts out, it is common to see others follow their example).
- They disrupt a normally orderly environment.
- Their behavior may be illegal or affect the good business reputation of the organization, in some cases putting the organization itself at risk of prosecution for not abating the behavior, such as in racial or sexual misconduct cases; for example, where a manager is abusing his or her power over an employee.
- Persons who abuse parking privileges, cut in line, demand special treatment, act abusively toward employees—all these are subversive influences.

While organizations do not like to have to deal with such individuals, they are a special class. These are individuals who, through their own narcissism and belligerence, become a law unto themselves and demand that the world accommodate their perspective. Such people are threat actors.

Petty Criminals

Petty crimes are offenses that are less than felonies and are usually punishable by a fine, a penalty, forfeiture of property, or imprisonment in a jail facility rather than in a penitentiary (misdemeanors).

- Vandals: Vandals destroy property's value by defacing it. Vandals have caused millions of dollars in damage to property and have damaged the business opportunities of entire communities.[32]
- Pickpockets: Pickpockets ply their trade in many public places including in hotels, restaurants, retail malls, parking lots and parking structures, elevator lobbies, and literally anywhere two or more people come into contact and especially where one of those people may be distracted. Businesses that provide such environments can be harmed by the damage to their reputation as a safe environment to frequent.
- Prostitutes, pimps, and panderers: Prostitution can affect hotels, retail malls, and other public spaces and can damage the reputation of the business.
- Other petty crimes include disturbing the peace, public nuisance, and drunkenness in public.

Design Basis Threat

Risk analysts must determine a design basis threat (DBT), which will be used as a baseline for the countermeasures. A DBT is the level of threat actor that the countermeasures should be able to address with reasonable effectiveness.

There are actually two DBTs. The first is the DBT that the security program will be designed to protect against, and the second is the DBT that the security program will be designed to deter and mitigate. One can deter a terrorist attack in a commercial environment, but it would be prohibitively costly to protect against one. However, an organization can mitigate some of the potential for the damages of a terrorist attack.

For example, during Al-Qaeda's attack on the Marriott Hotel in Islamabad on September 20, 2008, a truck carrying one ton of explosives detonated 20 meters away from the building due to its having been stopped at that distance by a hydraulic barrier; 53 people were killed in the attack. The truck's explosive charge, which was also surrounded with aluminum powder (accelerating the resulting fire) and artillery shells (increasing the resulting shrapnel), would certainly have killed many more if it had been able to get close to the hotel's main entry.*

However, an organization can do much to prevent "ordinary decent crime" (ODC).† ODC includes economic crimes, nonterrorist violent crimes, subversive criminal acts, and petty crimes. These can all be addressed in a baseline security program.

Table 7.1 illustrates the characteristics of terrorist and various types of criminal threat actors. This table shows that each type has very different characteristics.

PRACTICE

One can effectively assess threats in four steps:

1. Identify potential threat actors: An analyst can identify potential threat actors in two steps. List the five types of threat actors, as listed above. Then identify potential individual organizations and classes of individuals that most fit the descriptions of the five types of threat actors.

   For example, as regards potential terrorism threat actors, again there are five types as listed above. Local law enforcement will have a list of each of the potential threat actors who fit the descriptions of the five classes that are active in the area of operations of the law enforcement agency. For projects within the United States, a good source of this information is the FBI's local terrorism task force. For other countries, similar sources exist within their local law enforcement agencies.

   Other sources are also valuable including internet research. This is covered in detail in Chapter 3: Risk Assessment Skills and Tools. Numerous reputable organizations have excellent reference material on both terrorism and ODC criminal activity and groups.

2. Identify their motivation, capabilities, and history (and thus their level of intent, skills, weapons, and tactics, and what types of targets they have chosen in the past): Although this changes constantly, an analyst can follow the news and create a bibliography. Better consultants do this in an ongoing fashion. This is also discussed in detail in Chapter 3: Risk Assessment Skills and Tools. Other good sources also exist‡: see Refs. [2, 31, 34–43]. These books and articles comprise a wealth of resources on the methods and tactics used by terrorists and criminals of all types and the implications of those methods and tactics for the organizations they attack.

---

* "As sniffer dogs start barking around the truck, the vehicle starts ramming the hotel's hydraulic barrier and guards shout at people to run as a fire breaks out in the cab. Seconds later the screens flash blue as the huge bomb obliterates the area."[33]

† "The IRA has never been a stranger to what people in Northern Ireland used to refer to as 'ordinary decent crime'."[34]

‡ *Protection of Assets (POA) Manual*, by Timothy J. Walsh[45] is available through the ASIS International Bookstore (+1-412-741-1495). This four-volume set of books is absolutely recommended.

TABLE 7.1   Offender Characteristics

Characteristics	Terrorists	Economic Criminals	Violent Criminals	Subversives	Petty Criminals
Depth of Violence					
Mass casualties	X				
Few casualties	X		X		
Single casualties	X	X	X	X	
Injuries	X	X	X	X	X
Property Crimes					
Destruction of property	X	X	X	X	
Theft of property		X	X	X	X
Damage of property	X	X	X	X	X
Information Crimes					
Destruction of information	X	X		X	X
Theft of information	X	X		X	X
Damage to information	X	X		X	X
Crimes against Reputation					
Damage to business reputation	X	X	X	X	X
Attack Methods					
May attack in plain view	X	X	X		
Usually attack in stealth		X		X	X
On Interruption of Attack					
Will likely give up on interruption	X	X	X	X	X
Will likely give up on forcible response					
Will repel forcible response	X				
May repel forcible response	X	X	X	X	

A terrorist targeteering screen involves the development of a targeteering list for each of the classes of potential threat actors. Defense departments of various countries have made this into a fine art. Good sources of targeteering information include Malcolm Nance's book *Terrorist Recognition Handbook*. Nance is one of the world's leading experts on terrorist targeteering and is referenced by many articles and thesis papers both within and outside the military (Figure 7.2).

In Alicia L. Welch's 2007 naval postgraduate school thesis titled *Terrorism Awareness and Education as a Prevention Strategy for First Responders*,[46] she quotes Nance:

FIGURE 7.2   Terrorist targeteering.

The targeteer uses three basic tactical actions in deciding on a specific target, all of which are designed to achieve maximum dramatic impact:

- Speed: the target must be struck quickly to enhance the effect of fear
- Surprise: the victims must be taken completely unaware; nothing should transmit the impending operation except only the vaguest of threats.
- Violence of Action: the incident should strike terror and fear into the hearts of its victims through the absolute, horrific violence.[2]

In her thesis, Welch expands on Nance's work and states

The three elements of targeteering include Motive, Opportunity and Means (MOM). Motive: Does the terrorist group have a reason for selecting the target? Does the group have the opportunity to affect a strike against its enemies that is both meaningful and effective? The targeteer will make it a priority to create or wait for the appropriate time, circumstances, and environment to strike. Means: Does the group have the materials, manpower, secrecy, and support to carry out the mission?

As described in this book, the Khalid Sheikh Mohammed (KSM)-Asset Target Value for Terrorism Matrix is a very good surrogate for determining terrorist targeteering in the absence of more specific data. The KSM-Asset Target Value for Terrorism Matrix was developed by the author as a screen for targeteering for organizations allied with Al-Qaeda (many of which were targeted by Khalid Sheikh Mohammed). It is derived from evaluation of numerous Al-Qaeda attacks and the elements that each have in common.

Similarly, the Asset Target Value Matrixes for economic and violent crimes presented herein are useful for establishing targeteering information for those types of crimes.

3. Asset/Attack Matrix: Develop a list of the organization's assets and determine which of the weapons and tactics are most likely to be of use in attacking the organization.

Chapter 5 explained how to develop a list of the organization's key assets. By using the Asset/Attack Matrix (described in Chapter 8: Vulnerability), you will be able to determine which weapons and tactics are the most likely to be of use in attacking the organization.

Although the Asset/Attack Matrix is in fact a vulnerability tool, its use is also essential in helping to define the DBT. This is because the Asset/Attack Matrix defines which types of weapons and attack scenarios are most likely to succeed against the organization's facilities. By matching this information to the targeteering information about the threat actors, you can more easily identify which threat actors are most likely to be interested in this organization's facilities.

A complete listing of terrorist attack tactics and appropriate tactical countermeasures can be found in Nance's aforementioned book *Terrorist Recognition Handbook* (pp. 363–385). Some of those countermeasures mentioned are appropriate for counterinsurgency environments. See Chapter 16 of this book for appropriate antiterrorism countermeasures that are suitable for governments, nongovernmental organizations (NGOs), and commercial environments.

A comprehensive listing of baseline security program countermeasures to address economic crimes, nonterrorist violent crimes, subversives, and petty criminals can also be found in Chapter 16 of this book.

4. Compare that data to information about the organization's assets to be protected and determine which potential threat actors are likely to be most effective against the organization.

By matching up the methods and tactics used against the vulnerabilities of the organization, an analyst can identify those potential threat actors who are most likely to take action against the organization. The DBT worksheet discussed in this chapter accomplishes this task.

TOOLS

This book presents two software tools to assist in threat analysis:

- The Adversary/Means Matrix helps the analyst identify the types of weapons, entry methods, and attack scenarios that are used by various types of threat actors.
- The Asset/Attack Matrix helps the analyst identify what types of weapons, entry methods, and attack scenarios would be most effective against the organization's various assets.

The objectives of these tools are as follows.

- Adversary/Means Matrix: As the analyst moves to establish the organization's vulnerabilities, the analyst will need to understand the characteristics, entry methods, and attack scenarios used by various potential threat actors and keep these capabilities in mind as the analyst is identifying exploits for vulnerabilities. For example, a prison is inherently less vulnerable to intrusion than a warehouse because in a prison, most of the classic entry methods are of no use.
- Asset/Attack Matrix: The Asset/Attack Matrix assists the analyst in identifying the DBT by identifying which types of entry methods and attack scenarios could be eliminated due to the unique attributes of the organization's facilities and assets. Also, by helping to identify those assets that are most vulnerable and to which types of weapons and attack scenarios, it assists the analyst in focusing risk mitigation recommendations on countermeasures that can mitigate those vulnerabilities.

Adversary/Means Matrix

Purpose

The Adversary/Means Matrix helps the analyst define various potential threat actors and their potential for creating problems for the organization.

Functions

The Adversary/Means Matrix should accommodate all of the following:

- List and categorize potential threat actors by types and, where possible, by the name of the group. Some can only be identified by type (e.g., sophisticated criminals).
- Identify their level of professionalism, including their motivation, capabilities, and history; training level including operations* and tradecraft† knowledge; surveillance capabilities; planning skills; and organization and support.
- List the types of weapons the potential threat actor may have access to.
- List if possible the types of entry methods this type of threat actor may use.
- List what types of weapons the threat actor may be known or suspected to use.
- List typical anticipated attack scenarios.

Attributes

The Adversary/Means Matrix can be created using an off-the-shelf software tool such as SVA-Pro® or a build-it-yourself software template, such as Microsoft Excel®, Access®, or MS Word®. In each case, the information listed above should be included. Some analysts prefer a more text oriented approach, while others prefer a numeric rating. The text based approach offers more information, but is also more difficult and time consuming to read and assess overall data from. Certain tools, such as SVA-Pro, combine both text and numeric ratings and so offer both overview (numeric) and deeper reference when

---

* *Operations knowledge* refers to their ability to carry out a criminal or terrorism operation, including use of weapons, suppression and control of subjects, ability to move against the objective, and so on.

† *Tradecraft knowledge* refers to their training in covert operations including surveillance, communications, maintenance of cover or pretense, and so on.

questioning the analysis. A self-developed database approach such as Microsoft Access can also do this.

Example

This section is for those readers who wish to use the Excel risk analysis templates, which can assist in performing the analysis for any size of project from small to global and also can be used as report inserts to illustrate the discussion points of the risk analysis report. Although other tools exist as mentioned above, this approach is very low cost (not counting your time) and provides results that equal or exceed the most expensive software tools available.

In the first two examples in the book, we will be setting up the master templates for all other templates throughout the rest of the book; these will take a little longer to assemble than all the others in the book, as these will be used as the basis for all others that follow. Once these two are formatted and programmed, all the others can be assembled in very short order.

The first tool is called an Adversary/Means Matrix, and the second tool is called an Asset/Attack Matrix. These are both used to develop the threat analysis and the DBT. The Adversary/Means Matrix helps the analyst identify the DBT by identifying the type of threat actors that could carry out operations against the organization (terrorism and ODC). The Asset/Attack Matrix helps the analyst identify the DBT by identifying the types of weapons and attack scenarios that are of most concern to the organization.

By combining the results of both, it becomes clear first what types of weapons and attack scenarios are of the greatest concern and then which types of attackers utilize those attack scenarios and weapons.

Coupled up with the later findings of asset target value (which types of facilities are of most interest to which types of attackers), it can become clear whether to establish the DBT as terrorism (and what type) or as ODC.

In any event, every organization needs what I call a *baseline security program*. Every facility also exhibits certain unique vulnerabilities that should be addressed in addition to the baseline security program, and some (not all) facilities exhibit the historic characteristic of targets of terrorism. For those facilities, terrorism should be the DBT. The DBT then dictates the types of countermeasures that must be used to effectively deter or counter the DBT.

The Excel templates perform quantitative analysis. Any of the tools mentioned in the previous section can work just as practically. The example in Figure 7.3 (Overall Adversary/Means Matrix sheet view) shows a typical Adversary/Means Matrix for a large project with potential terrorist and criminal threat actors.

It should be noted that the approach of entering both text (qualitative) and numeric (quantitative) data is superior to using either text or numeric data alone. The author converts quantitative analysis results into qualitative in the report phase of the work. Software tools such as SVA-Pro accommodate both qualitative and quantitative in the data entry process; arguably, however, its data are much more difficult to digest and process. An analyst can also accomplish simultaneous qualitative/quantitative entry either with a database application or by parallel document entries (text in one document and data in another), thus building the report at the same time as entering the resource data. I do it in sequence (just my personal preference) though you could make the argument that simultaneous data entry is superior, if nonetheless mind-bogglingly tedious. In my mind, the sheer number of data points considered in this approach more than makes up for any other shortcomings.

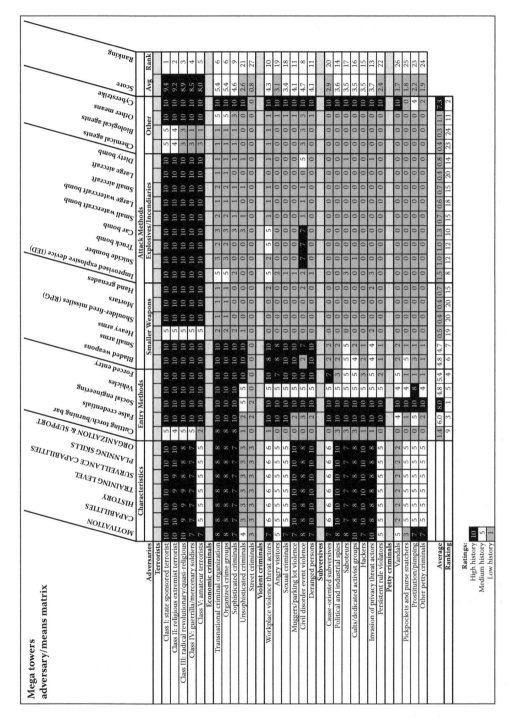

FIGURE 7.3 Adversary/Means Matrix.

In any event, critical thinking principles should be applied to the analysis portion prior to report writing in order to help determine what the risk level is and what types of countermeasures are appropriate. Although the worksheets described herein provide the grinded data for the analysis, they do not perform the actual analysis. That is for the analyst to do.

Professionalism   Professionalism is to threat actors as it is to anything else. The more professional the threat actor, the more dangerous he is. More sophisticated countermeasures must be developed to address the threat actor. For example, Al-Qaeda has used tandem heavy trucks to breach hardened perimeters, where the lead truck was equipped with a ramming device and the second truck followed closely behind. Protecting against this type of entry requires more robust barriers. Factors to consider in professionalism include

- Motivation
- Capabilities
- History
- Training level
- Surveillance capabilities
- Planning skills
- Organization and support

Access to Types of Weapons   The extent of access to weapons is also a factor in establishing the DBT. The more weapons the threat actor has access to and training to use, the more dangerous he is. As with other sections herein, the following are only examples and these should be modified depending on the environment, type of facilities, and so on. Weapons categories include

- Bladed weapons
- Small arms
- Heavy arms
- Shoulder-fired missiles (rocket-propelled grenades [RPGs], etc.)
- Mortars
- Hand grenades
- Explosives
- Chemicals
- Vehicles
- Watercraft
- Aircraft
- Suicide volunteers
- Computers and hacking skills

Entry Methods   Without access by a threat actor, there is no risk, so access control is a key concept in security. Entry methods may vary depending on the type of facility. The following list is an example only. Typical entry methods used by threat actors include

- False credentials
- Social engineering
- Entry by threat

- Forced entry
- Breaking and entering
- Insider
- Hacking

Threat Scenarios Used   Each type of threat actor uses different attack scenarios, and each has different consequences, thus the categories. Threat scenarios may vary depending on the type of assets and the types of facilities under consideration. The following are examples only. Typical threat scenarios include

- Terrorism attack scenarios
  - Improvised explosive devices (IED)
  - Suicide bomber
  - Vehicle-borne IED (VBIED)
  - Airborne IED
  - Waterborne IED
  - Dirty bomb
  - Nuclear weapon
  - Chemical, biological, radiological, and nuclear weapons
  - Cyberterrorism
- Economic crimes
  - Robbery
  - Burglary
  - Insider theft
  - Proprietary information theft
  - Crimes against the organization's business reputation
  - Computer crimes
- Violent crime attack scenarios
  - Violence against employees
  - Violence against the public on the organization's property
  - Bladed weapons
  - Handguns
  - Available weapons
- Subversive acts
  - Civil disorder
  - Riots
  - Protests
  - Intimidation
  - Drugs in the workplace
  - Sabotage
  - Corporate spying
- Petty crimes
  - Purse snatching and pickpocketing
  - Vandalism
  - Prostitution, pimping, and pandering
  - Other petty crimes

How to Set Up the Matrix   This book will explain each element of risk analysis and countermeasure selection in terms of its theory, practice, and tools. The book will explain in adequate detail how to assemble Excel spreadsheets for each element. Those readers who prefer to use a commercial software tool may skip the sections explaining how to build the Excel spreadsheets.

For those who are interested in building and using their own world-class risk analysis software tool, the first two tabs on the Excel workbooks are explained in cell-by-cell detail and after that in adequate detail to build the remaining sheets. The first of these was the Consequence Matrix and the second is this, the Adversary/Means Matrix. The Consequence Matrix builds the basic matrix on which most other matrixes are formed (the list of assets). The Adversary/Means Matrix is built on the list of threat actors.

Following are instructions on how to set up the matrix in Excel. These are basic instructions and will result in a workable matrix that calculates and ranks results. Instructions for setting up the first of these matrixes are described in very great detail. The instructions for others will be simplified, as after the first matrix the reader will have an understanding of how to set these up and how they work. Accordingly, bear with the instructions for the first matrix, the Adversary/Means Matrix, as the detail helps assure that all the matrixes are set up correctly.

Open Excel to a new worksheet: enter the data as shown on the figures and as noted below:

1. Go to Cell 2B, enter the project name. Bold this. Select the font to be 14.
2. Cell 3B, enter "Adversary/Means Matrix". Bold this. Select the font to be 14.
3. Cell 7B, enter "ADVERSARIES". Bold this.
4. Cell 8B, enter "Terrorists". Bold this.
5. Cell 9B, enter "Class I—State Sponsored Terrorist".
6. Cell 10B, enter "Class II—Religious Extremist Terrorist".
7. Cell 11B, enter "Class III—Radical Revolutionary/Quasi-Religious".
8. Cell 12B, enter "Class IV—Guerrilla/Mercenary Soldiers".
9. Cell 13B, enter "Class V—Amateur Terrorists".
10. Cell 14B, enter "Economic Criminals" Bold this.
11. Cell 15B, enter "Transnational Criminal Organization".
12. Cell 16B, enter "Organized Crime Groups".
13. Cell 17B, enter "Sophisticated Criminals".
14. Cell 18B, enter "Unsophisticated Criminals".
15. Cell 19B, enter "Shrinkage/Pilfering".
16. Cell 20B, enter "Violent Criminals" Bold this.
17. Cell 21B, enter "Workplace Violence Threat Actors".
18. Cell 22B, enter "Angry Visitors".
19. Cell 23B, enter "Parking Area Violence".
20. Cell 24B, enter "Rapists/Muggers".
21. Cell 25B, Enter "Civil Disorder Event Violence".
22. Cell 26B, enter "Subversives" Bold this.
23. Cell 27B, enter "Protesters/Non-Violent Civil Disorder".
24. Cell 28B, enter "Political and Industrial Spies".
25. Cell 29B, enter "Saboteurs".
26. Cell 30B, enter "Cults".
27. Cell 31B, enter "Hackers".
28. Cell 32B, enter "Lone Wolfs".
29. Cell 33B, enter "Paramilitary Group".
30. Cell 34B, enter "Persistent Rule Violators".

31. Cell 35B, enter "Petty Criminals" Bold this.
32. Cell 36B, enter "Vandals".
33. Cell 37B, enter "Pickpockets and Purse Snatchers".
34. Cell 38B, enter "Prostitution".
35. Cell 39B, enter "Other Petty Criminals".
36. Cell 40B, enter "Average" Bold this.
37. Cell 41B, enter "Ranking" Bold this.
38. Cell 42B, enter nothing (blank cell).
39. Cell 43B, enter "Ratings:" Bold this.
40. Cell 44B, enter "High Indicator".
41. Cell 45B, enter "Medium Indicator".
42. Cell 46B, enter "Low Indicator".
43. Select column B, align the text to the right except for the two cells B2 & B3, keep them aligned to the left.
44. Cell 44C, enter "10". Go to Formats>Conditional Formatting.
45. Under Condition 1, choose Cell Value Is between 0 and 3.25.
46. Under Condition 1, click on Format Tab then on the Patterns Tab and choose the color to be green.
47. Still in the Conditional Formatting Window, click on the Add>> Tab.
48. Under Condition 2, choose Cell Value Is between 3.25001 and 6.55.
49. Under Condition 2, click on the Format Tab then on the Patterns Tab and choose the color to be yellow.
50. Still in the Conditional Formatting Window, click on the Add>> Tab.
51. Under Condition 3, choose Cell Value Is between 6.55001 and 10.
52. Under Condition 3, click on the Format Tab then on the Patterns Tab and choose the color to be red. Click on "OK".
53. Cell 44C should turn to red filled instantaneously.
54. Copy formatting (use the copy format paintbrush) from C44 through C47 (this copies the conditional formatting to the cells).
55. Cell 45C, enter "5". The cell should turn to yellow filled instantaneously.
56. Cell 46C, enter "1". The cell should turn to green filled instantaneously.
57. Go to Cell C5, Right Click>FormatCells>Alignment>Orientation>Enter 75 Degrees.
58. Cell C5, enter "Motivation".
59. Copy formatting (use the copy format paintbrush) from C5 through BR5 (this tilts all those cells 75 degrees).
60. Cell D5, enter "Capabilities".
61. Cell E5, enter "History".
62. Cell F5, enter "Training Level".
63. Cell G5, enter "Surveillance Capabilities".
64. Cell H5, enter "Planning Skills".
65. Cell I5, enter "Organization & Support".
66. Select columns C through I, right click and change the column width to be 3.
67. Cell J5, enter nothing (blank): This is the beginning of the "Entry Methods".
68. Select column J, right click and change the column width to be 0.2.
69. Cell K5, enter "Cutting Torch/Burning Bar".
70. Cell L5, enter "False Credentials".
71. Cell M5, enter "Social Engineering".
72. Cell N5, enter "Vehicles".

73. Cell O5, enter "Forced Entry".
74. Select columns K through O, right click and change the column width to be 3.
75. Cell P5, enter nothing (blank): This is the beginning of the "Attack Methods".
76. Select column P, right click and change the column width to be 0.2.
77. Cell Q5, enter "Bladed Weapons".
78. Cell R5, enter "Small Arms".
79. Cell S5, enter "Heavy Arms".
80. Cell T5, enter "Shoulder-Fired Missiles (RPG)".
81. Cell U5, enter "Mortars".
82. Cell V5, enter "Hand Grenades".
83. Select columns Q through V, right click and change the column width to be 3.
84. Cell W5, enter nothing (blank): This is the beginning of the "Explosives/Incendiaries".
85. Select column W, right click and change the column width to be 0.2.
86. Cell X5, enter "Improvised Explosive Device (IED)".
87. Cell Y5, enter "Suicide Bomber".
88. Cell Z5, enter "Truck Bomb".
89. Cell AA5, enter "Car Bomb".
90. Cell AB5, enter "Small Watercraft Bomb".
91. Cell AC5, enter "Large Watercraft Bomb".
92. Cell AD5, enter "Small Aircraft".
93. Cell AE5, enter "Large Aircraft".
94. Cell AF5, enter "Dirty Bomb".
95. Select columns X through AF, right click and change the column width to be 3.
96. Cell AG5, enter nothing (blank): This is the beginning of the "Other".
97. Select column AG, right click and change the column width to be 0.2.
98. Cell AH5, enter "Chemical Agents".
99. Cell AI5, enter "Biological Agents".
100. Cell AJ5, enter "Other Means".
101. Cell AK5, enter "Cyberstrike".
102. Select columns AH through AK, right click and change the column width to be 3.
103. Cell AL5, enter nothing (blank).
104. Select column AL, right click and change the column width to be 0.2.
105. Cell AM5, enter score.
106. Cell AN5, enter "Ranking".
107. Select columns AM through AO, right click and change the column width to be 6.
108. Cell C6, enter "Professionalism". Bold this.
109. Group cells C6 through I6 and click on merge cells. This centers the word across the section.
110. Cell K6, enter "Entry Methods". Bold this.
111. Group cells K6 through O6 and click on merge cells.
112. Cell Q6, enter "Attack Methods". Bold this.
113. Group cells Q6 through AK6 and click on merge cells.
114. Cell Q7, enter "Smaller Weapons". Bold this.
115. Group cells Q7 through V7 and click on merge cells.
116. Cell X7, enter "Explosives/Incendiaries". Bold this.
117. Group cells X7 through AF7 and click on merge cells.
118. Cell AH7, enter "Other". Bold this.
119. Group cells AH7 through AK7 and click on merge cells.
120. Cell AM7, enter "Avg". Bold this.

121. Cell AN7, enter "Rank". Bold this.
122. Copy formatting (use the copy format paintbrush) from C44 to cells C9 down to cell AM13 (this fills the cells with the green color).
123. Repeat step 122 above for cells C15 down to cell AM19.
124. Repeat step 122 above for cells C21 down to cell AM25.
125. Repeat step 122 above for cells C27 down to cell AM34.
126. Repeat step 122 above for cells C36 down to cell AM39.
127. Repeat step 122 above for cells K40 through AK40.
128. Select the cells from C8 through AN8, right-click>Format Cells>Patterns>Choose light gray color.
129. Repeat step 127 above for cells C14 through AN14.
130. Repeat step 127 above for cells C20 through AN20.
131. Repeat step 127 above for cells C26 through AN26.
132. Repeat step 127 above for cells C35 through AN35.
133. Step Unused.
134. Cell AM9, enter "=AVERAGE(C9:AK9)" (this will calculate the average of the subject cells). Do not panic if you got " #DIV/0"! This is because your matrix is still not filled.
135. Copy cell AM9, select cells AM10 through AM13 and paste the formula.
136. Repeat step 134 above for cells AM15 through AM19.
137. Repeat step 134 above for cells AM21 through AM25.
138. Repeat step 134 above for cells AM27 through AM34.
139. Repeat step 134 above for cells AM36 through AM39.
140. Cell K40, enter "=AVERAGE(K9:K39)".
141. Copy cell K40, select cells L40 through O40 and paste the formula.
142. Repeat step 140 above for cells Q40 through V40.
143. Repeat step 140 above for cells X40 through AF40.
144. Repeat step 140 above for cells AH40 through AK40.

Following this, populate the cells with appropriate estimates on a scale of 1 to 10. Then average the Score column and rank the results in the Ranking column. I suggest using averaging of rows to create the score because it provides a relative view of the issues at hand for each row of each spreadsheet. As you build your own spreadsheets and begin to work with them, you may find that you prefer another formula for determining the score, but I have found that averaging is simple and results in a consistently meaningful display of the relationships of the various rows. The spreadsheet can also be made much more useful if you apply conditional formatting to the Data and Score cells so that high scores color red, low scores color green, and medium cells color yellow. Conditional formatting is applied differently between various versions of Excel, so it is best to use the Help file or look up "conditional formatting Excel" in Google. (Substitute your version of spreadsheet if different.)

PREDICTIVE THREAT ASSESSMENT

In addition to the quantitative approach above, which utilized deductive reasoning, I recommend that all risk analysts should become conversant with predictive threat assessment, which utilizes inductive reasoning. Inductive reasoning is the entry door to predictive threat assessment, which allows for much more specific and useful threat assessments.

Following is a quote from a blog by Mr. Charles Goslin, CPP, CISSP (http://www. butchkoinc.com/blog/threat-led-risk).*

Threat is the "fissile material" needed to activate the individual components of asset, vulnerability, impact, consequence, and likelihood in the calculation of risk. It is threat that initiates the sequence of relationships and events that together, combine to elevate or lower risk. It is important to understand threat in this context because all too often the element of threat is minimized or abstracted when security assessments are done. Why?

Unlike the examination and assessment of asset value or weaknesses in the facility or organization's security defenses, a "threat" can be deceptively hard to define. Reliable intelligence about the intent, timing, nature, size, and capability of the threat actor's goals are difficult and costly to obtain. Threats, at least in terms of an actor/actors who are actively planning and have the intent and capability to execute an act that could cause harm or destruction to your facility or organization, exist outside of the organization's control. This is true whether it is a trusted "insider" intent on facilitating access to sensitive material for an adversary, or an outside criminal group plotting to kidnap a corporate executive. The contours of threat events take form in plots and planning well outside of the knowledge of the targeted organization, or individual.

Since threat is hard to assess or control, organizations often "abstract" threats via a generic design basis threat (DBT) matrix (a DBT is a useful and necessary tool, but should never be the sole substitute for a thorough threat assessment)—applying levels of severity and impact to various threat actors, rather than more detailed descriptors such as intent, capability, presence, or timing. Alternatively, organizations will outsource threat assessment to firms that deliver anodyne products that lack the granularity and specificity that comes from solid, on the ground, up-to-date data. Assessments such as these are rife with conditional terminology—could, should, may, might—because they do not have solid intelligence and thus lack confidence in their analysis and predictions. A threat analysis that is either not predictive, or vaguely predictive, is useless.

In either case, organizations that give short shrift to threat analysis end up overly focused on the internal picture. They identify, and seek to resolve vulnerabilities. The premise is that the vulnerability "could" be exploited by "a threat." With this conditional premise in mind, the vulnerability is closed—and the threat mitigated. Problem solved. The problem with this approach is that it fosters a risk avoidance mentality. Threats that are ill-defined or abstract do one of two things: they are minimized because they lack substance, or they are magnified because they are not understood properly. In either case, minimizing threat analysis skews the risk assessment.

It is true, that risk can certainly be partially defined by looking almost exclusively at vulnerability and potential impact. The outcome will be murky at best. This can lead to mediocre outcomes, particularly if the risk assessment is the foundation of security program and system design. A well-defined threat analysis makes a real difference, because it provides much greater clarity on the critical component of *likelihood*. This in turn, sheds more light on the potential impact of a threat event or actor's manifestation against an asset. Risk cannot truly be quantified in specific, measurable terms without solid threat analysis.

As a general rule, threat assessment should begin with an examination of trends and indicators surrounding a specific threat actor—it is a reading of the tea leaves. Inexact, yes, but a starting point. The assumption that a threat cannot be clearly defined because it exists outside of the control of the organization, is false. It just requires a different

---

* Mr. Goslin is an analyst for Butchko, Inc. He has spent approximately 35 years in security for high-security U.S. government and corporate facilities, and for over 25 of those years, he conducted intelligence operations for the CIA around the world in India, Africa, Central South America, Europe, and the Middle East. Mr. Goslin also worked previously as a journalist, and his work often appeared in the publications of major media organizations. Mr. Goslin also has exceptional insight into the risk and vulnerability process from an adversarial perspective, and he is a specialist in predictive risk analysis.

set of skills. For example, a terrorist attack does not take place in a vacuum. It requires planning—they all do. While terrorists have free reign with regard to target sets, they are—as are security forces—constrained by operational considerations such as money, manpower, weapons, and intelligence. They need to resolve each of these issues, to successfully accomplish their mission. Targets must be reconnoitered, security forces must be probed for weaknesses, weaponry and explosives must be obtained and stockpiled, personnel recruited, trained and tested. Quite often, smaller operations in similar environments are used as test beds to "blood" terrorist attackers. All of these tasks are indicators, and leave traces in the execution of each.

This constitutes a pattern that taken together give substance and definition to the likelihood of an event. The more refined the assessment of likelihood that a threat actor is planning or will attack, the more refined the risk equation becomes and the subsequent security planning to mitigate the risk.

As noted before, obtaining information about threat is not easy. The analysis of incomplete information is likewise difficult; it requires a trained analyst to deduce from incomplete evidence the bigger picture that comprises an active and gathering threat. Organizations today, to keep information current and relevant for their operations require the development of an effective intelligence capability within their own security ranks. Intelligence-driven security programs ultimately provide the best value for the organization, because security systems and design are refined to address threat and risk with much more specificity than the old "gates, guards and guns" approach to securing a facility or operation.

Threat-led risk analysis refines an assessment so that capital cost expenditures on security countermeasures needed to protect a client's assets are sharply focused, effective and necessarily efficient.

INDUCTIVE VERSUS DEDUCTIVE REASONING

Deductive Reasoning

Deductive reasoning uses patterns and indicators (seeing the pieces and putting them together). Deductive reasoning can be used to assemble a static picture from readily available and quantifiable data, such as what types of weapons a particular threat actor may use, what their logistical capabilities are, what their history of attacks is, and what goals the threat actor has stated, if available.

- Deductive reasoning takes the big picture and reduces it down to causes.

Inductive Reasoning

Inductive reasoning involves the understanding of precursors, understanding red flags, relevant and irrelevant aspects and putting it into the context of what is normal for the environment (what should be there), and the presence or absence of what is normal for the environment.

- Inductive reasoning requires having a good sense of what is normal for the environment.
- Inductive reasoning takes the small things and works out the big issues that could result from them.
- Inductive reasoning allows the reader to build their own conclusions.

- Inductive reasoning can be used to either build a case for or against.
- Inductive reasoning requires access to an analyst with great knowledge of the environment in which the specific threat actor works, and of the specific threat actor.

Inductive Context

- A good inductive threat assessment cannot be developed on a spreadsheet.
- The context includes the environment, history, politics, agendas, over time, development of capacity, potential for acquisition of weapons and logistics, and so on.
- The arc and intensity and motivators of a threat actor all offer context for analysis.
- Inductive threat assessment also looks at weapons, tactics, and statements of objectives.

Predictive Threat Analysis

- Threat analysis has got to be predictive.
- Threat analysis operates within the context of logistical capabilities and proximity to available targets that meet the goals and stated objectives of the threat actor.
- Predictive threat analysis either gives you a sense of urgency or complacency.

PREDICTIVE RISK EXAMPLE

On September 21, 2012, the Somali terrorist group Al-Shabaab conducted an attack on the Westgate Shopping Mall in Nairobi, Kenya, in which 67 people died and over 175 people were wounded in a mass shooting attack by multiple Al-Shabaab gunmen. The attack raged for over 48 hours. Previously, Al-Shabaab had stated their objections to the Kenyan military's participation in the counterterrorism efforts by the African Union in Somalia.

On October 24, 2011, the U.S. Embassy in Kenya had received "credible information of an imminent threat of terrorist attacks directed at prominent Kenyan facilities and areas where foreigners are known to congregate such as malls and night clubs." This warning indicated an intelligence leak somewhere in Al-Shabaab. Following the leak, Al-Shabaab conducted attacks against several soft targets (bus stops and a low-profile gathering spot).

Taking into consideration that large quantities of explosives were difficult to obtain in Kenya and that Al-Shabaab had significant training and expertise in small arms conflict, it seemed to us that a small arms attack against a public place was the most likely.

Venues where this type of attack could be most effective against foreigners included hotels and shopping malls. The greatest casualty count would be against shopping malls. The most high-profile shopping mall that attracted foreigners in Nairobi was the Westgate Shopping Mall. Westgate Shopping Mall was the most likely target for Al-Shabaab, using an assemblage of small arms in a swarm attack. This proved to be true.

SUMMARY

Threats are at the core of probability. So threat analysis is at the core of probability analysis.

Threats versus Hazards

Many security professionals and their clients confuse threats and hazards. Hazards can be either natural or man-made and are generally unintentional or without malice, while threats are always man-made and intentional and with malice.

A hazard is a precondition for an accident or a natural event having negative consequences.

Hazards may include

- Safety hazards
- Security hazards
- Natural disaster hazards
- Local or regional political or military hazards

Hazards may be environmental or behavioral. Both can establish the preconditions for an unwanted consequence. Hazards may include safety hazards, security hazards, natural hazards, and accidents.

Threats are all man-made. A threat is a group or individual that has both the capability of and the intent to cause harm. A threat actor is an individual or group that intends to harm people or to conduct an attack against a facility or organization or against exemplars of an opposing point of view.

Without a threat actor, there is no risk. Analysts must identify potential threat actors and then decide (with ownership) which level of threat actor the security program should attempt to deter and which it should attempt to protect against. The first step is to understand who could be potential threat actors.

There are five kinds of potential threat actors:

- Terrorists
  - Class I terrorist: the government-trained professional (including foreign intelligence threats).
  - Class II terrorist: the religious extremist professional
  - Class III terrorist: the radical revolutionary or quasi-religious extremist
  - Class IV terrorist: the guerrilla/mercenary soldier
  - Class V terrorist: the amateur (civilian, untrained criminal, or militia vigilante)
- Economic criminals
  - Transnational criminal organizations
  - Organized criminals
  - Sophisticated economic criminals
  - Unsophisticated economic criminals
  - Street criminals
- Nonterrorist violent criminals
  - Workplace violence threat actors

- Angry visitors
- Sexual criminals
- Mugging and parking lot violence
- Civil disorder event violence
- Deranged persons
- Subversives
  - Cause-oriented subversives
  - Political and industrial spies
  - Saboteurs
  - Cults and dedicated activist groups
  - Hackers
  - Invasion of privacy threat actors
  - Persistent rule violators
- Petty criminals
  - Vandals
  - Pickpockets
  - Prostitutes, pimps, and panderers
  - Disturbance causers

Another aspect of threat actors is how they may behave when their attack is interrupted or when met by a response force. Table 7.1 (page 134) outlines the generally held experiences of each type of offender.

Design Basis Threat

Risk analysts must determine a DBT that will be used as a baseline for the countermeasures. A DBT is the level of threat actor that the countermeasures should be able to address with reasonable effectiveness.

There are actually two DBTs. The first is the DBT that the security program will be designed to protect against, and the second is the DBT that the security program will be designed to deter and mitigate. This threat is known as "ordinary decent crime" (ODC). One can deter against terrorist attack in a commercial environment, but it would be prohibitively costly to protect against one. However, an organization can mitigate some of the potential for damages of a terrorist attack.

However, an organization can do much to prevent ODC. ODC includes economic crimes, nonterrorist violent crimes, subversive criminal acts, and petty crimes. These can all be addressed in a BSP.

Practice

One can effectively assess threats in four steps.

- Identify potential threat actors
- Identify their motivation, capabilities, and history (and thus their level of intent, skills, weapons, and tactics; and what types of targets they have chosen in the past)
- Develop a list of the organization's assets and determine which of the weapons and tactics are most likely to be of use in attacking the organization

- Compare that data to information about the organization's assets to be protected and determine which potential threat actors are likely to be most effective against the organization

Tools

This book presents two software tools to assist in threat analysis:

- Adversary/Means Matrix: The Adversary/Means Matrix helps the analyst identify the types of weapons, entry methods, and attack scenarios that are used by various types of threat actors.
- Asset/Attack Matrix: The Asset/Attack Matrix helps the analyst identify what types of weapons, entry methods and attack scenarios would be most effective against the organization's various assets.

Predictive Threat Assessment

Predictive Threat Assessment utilizes a combination of quantitative and qualitative analysis in order to offer predictions of what type of attack may occur, where, and by which threat actor.

REFERENCES

1. Mortimer, J. 1997. To catch a thief. *The New York Times* (online), August 24.
2. Nance, M. 2008. *Terrorist Recognition Handbook*, 2nd edn. CRC Press, Boca Raton.
3. Hoffman, D. 1993. Israeli confirms assassinations of Munich Massacre Plotters; Meir Aide's comments in TV interview were censored for a year. *The Washington Post*, November 24.
4. Jenkins, B. M. 1974. Terrorism and kidnapping. Rand Corporation, paper P-5255, p. 1.
5. *The Economist*. 2006. Talking peace; Spain and ETA, July 8.
6. *Christian Science Monitor*. 2005. Calls grow to disband the Irish Republican Army, March 17.
7. *The Economist*. 2002. The Tiger comes out of his lair; Sri Lanka (The Tamil Tigers are talking about peace), April 13.
8. *Associated Press*. 2005. Death toll, targets, worst attacks from 35-year campaign of Provisional IRA, July 28.
9. *The Pantagraph Newspaper*. 2006. History of KKK gives warning for today, Bloomington, IL, April 23.
10. *Telegraph-Herald*. 2003. Worries linger about homegrown "lone wolves"; The arrest of Eric Rudolph rekindles some concerns, Dubuque, June 4.
11. *The Independent*. 2001. US executes its public enemy no. 1: The Oklahoma Bomber Timothy McVeigh goes to his death in silence, London, June 12.
12. Chase, A. 2003. *Harvard and the Unabomber: The Education of an American Terrorist*. W.W. Norton, New York.

13. Pederson, D. 1998. A mountain manhunt (hunt for suspected bomber Eric Rudolph). *Newsweek*, July 27.
14. Freeh, L. J. 1997. Federal Bureau of Investigation before the House Committee on International Relations. Congressional Testimony. Federal Document Clearing House, October 1.
15. Abadinsky, H. 2003. *Organized Crime*. Wadsworth Publishing, Belmont, CA.
16. Krauthammer, T. and E. J. Conrath. 1999. *Structural Design for Physical Security*, p. A-3. American Society of Civil Engineers, Reston, VA.
17. Valentine, B. 1995. *Gang Intelligence Manual: Identifying and Understanding Modern-Day Violent Gangs in the United States*. Paladin Press, Boulder, CO.
18. Whitelaw, K. 2008. An unsatisfying end to the anthrax attacks mystery: The FBI reportedly was ready to charge an army scientist, but he apparently committed suicide this week. *U.S. News & World Report*, August 1.
19. Douglas, J and M. Olshaker. 1999. *The Anatomy of Motive: The FBI's Legendary Mindhunter Explores the Key to Understanding and Catching Violent Criminals.* Simon and Schuster, New York.
20. DiLorenzo, L. P. and D. J. Carroll. 1995. Screening applicants for a safer workplace (part 2). *HRMagazine*, March 1.
21. Gale, T. 2005. Sexual predation characteristics. *World of Forensic Science*. Highbeam Research, April 23. http://www.highbeam.com.
22. *Jet Magazine*. 1995. Why sexual assault is the most rapidly growing crime in the nation. Highbeam Research, Johnson Publishing Co., April 23. http://www.highbeam.com.
23. Paddock R. C. and C. Ingram. 1991. Five killed in Calif. Hostage rescue; Police storm store where gunmen seized 30 people in foiled robbery. *The Washington Post*, April 5.
24. Coffin, B. 2007. War zone: The north Hollywood shootout 10 years later:.... *Risk Management Magazine*, March 1.
25. Friedman, R. A. 2006. Violence and mental illness: How strong is the link? *The New England Journal of Medicine* 355: 2064–2066.
26. Barrett, T. 2004. Why I shot Lennon; I was tired of being a nobody says Mark Chapman. *Liverpool Echo* (Liverpool, England), October 15.
27. *Evening Standard*. 2001. Guilty: Jill Dando's killer gets life, London, July 2.
28. *The New York Times*. 1989. "Man is being held in Actress's Death" regarding the death of Rebecca Schaeffer, July 20.
29. Moffatt, G. K. 2000. *Blind-Sided: Homicide Where It Is Least Expected,* p. 82. Greenwood, Westport, CT.
30. Cannon, L. *Official Negligence: How Rodney King and the Riots Changed Los Angeles and the LAPD.* Basic Books, New York.
31. Blumenthal, L. and M. Doyle. 1999. Spies bring trade secrets to the table at WTO talks. *Star Tribune* (Minneapolis, MN), November 27.
32. Rivera, J. 2008. *Vandal Squad: Inside the New York City Transit Police Dept.* Miss Rosen Editions, Brooklyn.
33. *The Mirror*. 2008. It's our 9/11; 53 killed in Pakistan hotel bomb attack, London, England, September 22.
34. O'Neill, B. S. and D. Lister. 2005. MI5 given task of boosting intelligence on money-making. *TimesOnline*, London, England, February 25.
35. Garland, N. M. and G. B. Stuckey. 1999. *Criminal Evidence for the Law Enforcement Officer*, 4th edn. McGraw-Hill, Glencoe.

36. Douglas, J. and M. Olshaker. 2000. *The Anatomy of Motive: The FBI's Legendary Mindhunter Explores the Key to Understanding and Catching Violent Criminals.* Pocket Books, New York.

37. Cromwell, P. F. and Olson, J. N. 2004. *Breaking and Entering: Burglars on Burglary.* Wadsworth, Belmont, CA.

38. Helfgott, J. B. 2008. *Criminal Behavior: Theories, Typologies and Criminal Justice.* Sage, Los Angeles.

39. Demey, D. L., J. R. Flowers, and M. L. Sankey. 1999. *Don't Hire a Crook! How to Avoid Common Hiring (and Firing) Mistakes.* Facts on Demand, Tempe.

40. Wiener, I. A. 1990. *Economic Criminal Offenses: A Theory of Economic Criminal Law.* Akademiai Kiado, Budapest.

41. Hellman, D. A. 2006. *Economics of Crime: Theory and Practice*, 6th edn. Pearson Custom Publishing, New York.

42. Farrington, D. P., L. Sherman, and B. C. Welsh. 2001. *Costs and Benefits of Preventing Crime: Economic Costs and Benefits.* Westview Press, Boulder, CO.

43. De Jong, D. 1994. Civil disorder: Preparing for the worst. *The FBI Law Enforcement Bulletin*, March 1.

44. Ortmeier, P. J. 2005. *Security Management: An Introduction*, 2nd edn. Prentice Hall/ Criminal Justice, Upper Saddle River, NJ.

45. Walsh, T. J. 2009. *Protection of Assets (POA) Manual.* Merrit Company, ASIS International, Alexandria, VA.

46. Welch, A. L. 2006. *Terrorism Awareness and Education as a Prevention Strategy for First Responders.* Naval Postgraduate School, Monterey, CA.

Q&A

Questions

Q1: Threats are at the core of probability, so threat analysis is at the core of
  A. Threat analysis.
  B. Vulnerability analysis.
  C. Probability analysis.
  D. All of the above.

Q2: Hazards can be either natural or man-made and are generally unintentional or without malice, while threats are
  A. Always without malice.
  B. Always man-made.
  C. Always intentional.
  D. Always man-made and intentional and with malice.

Q3: A Hazard is a _____ for an accident or a natural event having negative consequences.
  A. Probability
  B. Condition
  C. Precondition
  D. None of the above

Q4: Predictive threat assessment utilizes
  A. A combination of quantitative and qualitative analysis in order to offer predictions of what type of attack may occur, where, and by which threat actor.
  B. Predictions from psychics.
  C. Predictions from the government.
  D. Predictions from the military.

Q5: Much of the shift to focus on terrorism has come at the expense of the historical focus on security and hazards. This is most unfortunate because security and hazard risks
  A. Are more consequential than terrorism attacks.
  B. Far outweigh terrorism risks for most facilities.
  C. Both of the above.
  D. Neither of the above.

Q6: Threats
  A. Are all man-made.
  B. Are all natural occurrences.
  C. Can be either man-made or natural occurrences.
  D. None of the above.

Q7: Without a threat actor,
  A. There is no vulnerability.
  B. There is no criticality.
  C. There is no hazard.
  D. There is no risk.

Q8: Threat actors may include
  A. Terrorists.
  B. Economic criminals.
  C. Petty criminals.
  D. All of the above.

Q9: Threat actors may include
  A. Nonterrorist violent criminals.
  B. Subversives.
  C. Both of the above.
  D. Neither of the above.

Q10: A design basis threat is
  A. The level of threat actor that will design the security systems.
  B. The level of threat actor that will attack the facility.
  C. The level of threat actor that the countermeasures should be able to address with reasonable effectiveness.
  D. None of the above.

Answers

Q1 – C, Q2 – D, Q3 – C, Q4 – A, Q5 – B, Q6 – A, Q7 – D, Q8 – D, Q9 – C, Q10 – C

CHAPTER **8**

Assessing Vulnerability

INTRODUCTION

On completion of this chapter, you will be familiar with the vulnerability assessment model; be able to define scenarios and evaluate specific consequences; have learned how to use the Asset/Attack Matrix to determine which facility assets are subject to what kinds of attack scenarios; understand the Threat/Target Nexus Matrix, which identifies where high-value individuals may encounter potential threat actors within the facility; understand the Threat/Weapons Nexus Matrix, which identifies what types of weapons can be used at the nexus points identified by the Threat/Target Nexus Matrix; understand the adversary sequence diagrams, which evaluate how threat actors move in a facility; review how that affects the vulnerability assessment; and have learned how surveillance affects vulnerability and how to assess surveillance opportunities. Finally, the chapter teaches how to develop matrixes that help you assess all these factors, which together comprise vulnerability.

A vulnerability is any condition that could be exploited by a threat actor to carry out an intrusion or escape or to easily destroy property or processes. Different threat actors have different goals and thus look for different kinds of vulnerabilities. An economic criminal is looking for different types of vulnerabilities than a violent criminal. A terrorist is looking for different kinds of vulnerabilities than a subversive.

For a violent criminal robber, a vulnerability could be the age and fragile manner of walking of an elderly couple across a large parking lot. For a hotel prostitute, a vulnerability could be a flirtatious bartender who will accept a cut of her business. For a corrupt warehouse manager, a vulnerability could be poor warehouse accounting processes. For a kidnapper, a vulnerability could be the regular departure and arrival of a CEO from his easily accessible home. For a terrorist with plans to blow up a Western target, a vulnerability could be an easily approachable porte cochere at a Western hotel in a foreign city that can be seen from a great distance across a large plaza.

Some threat actors want to "shave" a little off the top of a business process for their own use, leaving the process intact for a future exploit. Other threat actors have little concern for the organization's long-term survival. For this reason, a risk analyst must look at vulnerabilities differently for each type of potential threat actor. One must look at vulnerabilities differently for each class of threat actor. This chapter provides vulnerability assessment information that is useful for all types of threat actors.

Some aspects of vulnerability apply equally to all types of threat actors. For example, surveillance opportunities work to the advantage of all types (Figure 8.1).

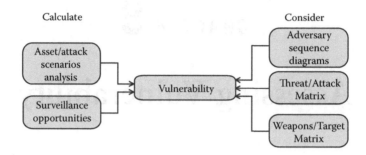

FIGURE 8.1   Vulnerability.

REVIEW OF VULNERABILITY ASSESSMENT MODEL

Assessing vulnerability used to be easy when the threats were limited to "ordinary decent criminals." The use of criminal vulnerability assessment in an environment of possible terrorism, however, is woefully inadequate. The method described in this chapter works equally well for both criminals and terrorists and is far more likely to uncover vulnerabilities that terrorists could easily exploit, which would be completely unnoticed using criminal assessment methods alone.

- Define scenarios and evaluate specific consequences
- Identify which scenarios could be used against the organization's critical nodes most effectively
- Evaluate the effectiveness of existing security measures
- Identify vulnerabilities and estimate the degree of vulnerability

Let me pause here to remind the reader that this is just one chapter dedicated to vulnerability within an entire book. The topic deserves its own book, and in my opinion the ultimate book on vulnerability assessment is by Mary Lynn Garcia (Sandia National Laboratories). I recommend that every reader of this book own a copy of her book.[1]

DEFINE SCENARIOS AND EVALUATE SPECIFIC CONSEQUENCES

It is necessary to understand that to carry out an attack, whether criminal or terrorist, two things must happen in favor of the attacker. First, the attacker must be able to infiltrate the facility; and second, the attacker must be able to carry out a successful attack. For common criminals, a third factor is present, and that is the ability to leave the facility (undetected if possible). All countermeasures for criminal and terrorism protection should be focused on reducing the probability of the success of all of these objectives.

Assessing vulnerabilities for terrorism is more of a challenge than for common criminals. Because terrorist targeteers use simple methods and tactics (scenarios) in unique ways that ordinary people would not easily imagine, it is easy to overlook vulnerabilities in protection systems that a terrorist will easily see and exploit. The challenge, then, is not only to review vulnerabilities to criminal attacks but also to existing and possible terrorist attacks. This takes imagination and a process that helps assure that all possible terrorist methodologies are considered.

The key to being successful in this analysis is the proper identification of the organization's operational critical nodes. Each critical node is susceptible to certain kinds of attacks and certain kinds of weapons. By identifying the critical nodes, one can then identify what types of weapons and attack scenarios could be used against them.

Easy to say, but how does one do that? The answer is to evaluate vulnerabilities the same way terrorists do. In evaluating the characteristics of targets of Al-Qaeda, Salafist, Lashkar-e-Taiba (LeT), and other militant operatives and managers, including Khalid Sheikh Mohammed (KSM), it becomes clear how terrorist organizations conduct target selection, attack planning, scenario testing, and attack operations. Additional insight can be gained from the captured Al-Qaeda 180-page manual titled *Military Studies in the Jihad against the Tyrants*, which was found by authorities in the home of an Al-Qaeda supporter in Manchester, England, in 2000. It also confirms the KSM-asset target value for terrorism model, identified by this author and described in detail in this book.

Terrorism methods and tactics represent a constantly evolving process, but one with a relatively stable agenda. As the first edition of this book was being written, the attacks in Mumbai against the Taj Mahal Palace Hotel, the Oberoi Hotel, rail stations, and other locations went underway.

This attack is a lesson for all risk analysts everywhere who plan defenses for terrorist attacks. In an article in *The Times of India* (December 28, 2008), Rohan Gunaratna makes an excellent point:

> Were the masterminds and perpetrators of the Mumbai carnage influenced by al-Qaida, the chief proponent of global jihad? In future, will sub-continental terrorists prefer to attack the "crusader and Jewish" target set identified by the global jihadists as opposed to 'Indian government and Hindu' targets? The Mumbai attack was unprecedented in target selection; of the five pre-designated targets. Was the target selection influenced by India's alliance with the US and Israel? The method of operation was classic al-Qaida style—a coordinated, near simultaneous attack against high profile and symbolic targets aimed at inflicting mass casualties. The only difference was that it was a fidayeen* attack, a classic LeT modus operandi. ... groups ... that began with local agendas transformed into groups with regional and international agendas. ... Mumbai has demonstrated that the pre-eminent national security challenge facing both India and Pakistan is terrorism and not each other.[2]

The lesson is clear: terrorism is becoming a franchise in which the best organized and trained organizations are becoming available to collaborate with less well trained and imaginative organizations in order to enhance the overall capabilities of all terrorists everywhere.

The key elements in regional and international terrorism strategies include the following (author's analysis). These elements have been used as a common strategic thread in many regions and countries, including Afghanistan, India, Pakistan, Lebanon, Syria, Palestinian Territories, Israel, Indonesia, Thailand, Chechnya, Columbia, Guatemala, Egypt, Jordan, Saudi Arabia, Northern Ireland, and Great Britain. Expect to see them used in Mexico, the United States, and China as time goes on.[†]

---

* Fidayeen: A suicide tactic used by terrorists.
† At the time of the second edition of this book, both China and Mexico have seen this realized on their soil: in China the Uyghur ethnic terrorism attacks and in Mexico various drug cartels attacked targets using the Al-Qaeda handbook. In the United States, "workplace violence" incidents by radicalized Islamists include Maj. Nidal Hassan's Ft. Hood attack and the beheading of an innocent woman at an Oklahoma food processing plant allegedly by radicalized Islamist Alton Nolan, immediately following a call for beheadings in the United States by the "Islamic State" ISIS.

- Create incidents that exploit common vulnerabilities, especially in civilian targets
- Use the media to help the attackers during and after the attacks and prolong media coverage of the attacks as long as possible
- Utilize synchronized attacks to amplify fear and emphasize the organization and skills of the terrorists
- Highlight the ineptitude of local police and counterterrorism forces in protecting the populace
- Terrorize the police by attacking them
- Terrorize the population by individual and mass attacks on innocent civilians
- Encourage governments to take repressive measures, which will inevitably include innocent members of the public, in their efforts to find and suppress terrorism
- Incite the populace to retaliation, especially during election cycles
- Destabilize the government
- Encourage the ascent of militant political parties to power
- Involve elements of neighboring countries where possible
- Create conditions for international armed conflict between countries
- Destabilize any weak regime whose country could be used as a platform for terrorism training and operations
- Overthrow governments that are friendly to Western governments
- Keep up the pressure until the above results are achieved
- Use a strategy of attack, retreat, regroup, attack, retreat, and regroup, never faltering from the long-term goals of overthrowing governments friendly to the West
- Finally, establish Sharia law caliphates in place of existing governments in all Muslim countries and in as many other countries as possible without regard to any existing national borders

This strategy has been identified by the terrorists themselves, and many or all of these footprints can be seen in all the countries identified above.

So we get back to the core of antiterrorism vulnerability assessment, which is to identify possible threat scenarios and identify consequences. One of the major weaknesses of most security vulnerability books is that they do not address this important issue. I have, over the course of my career, read numerous books that talk about facility penetration; rings of protection; checking windows, shrubs, fences; and so on, but do not focus on what kinds of attacks can actually occur. This has resulted in a phenomenon that is almost unique to the United States; that is, facilities that are robustly protected at their points of entrance but are highly vulnerable almost everywhere else. For example, it is common in the United States to see high-risk facilities that have a single chain-link fence around the facility. In other countries, one would see a double fence with detection equipment in between. Many Western risk analysts perceive a psychological barrier as a real barrier; that is, that a chain-link fence, window, or gypsum wall is a barrier. These are not barriers, but in fact only create momentary inconveniences in the progress of an attacker.

So an effective process of vulnerability assessment must include the following steps:

- Identify the organization's most valuable and most critical assets
- Identify the organization's operational critical nodes
- Utilize an Asset/Attack Matrix, which identifies which attack scenarios are most likely to be used by what class of threat actors

- Utilize a Threat/Target Nexus Matrix, which identifies what areas are most likely to be used by threat actors to carry out their action
- Utilize a Weapons/Target Nexus Matrix, which identifies what types of weapons are most likely to be used at each threat/target location
- Review surveillance opportunities for each major asset under consideration
- Assemble vulnerabilities in the light of all the information above

Asset/Attack Matrix

An Asset/Attack Matrix identifies which attack scenarios are most likely to be used by what class of threat actors. This matrix has two dimensions: assets and threat scenarios. Like every other matrix discussed in this book, this matrix can be developed in a professional program such as SVA-Pro® or by using a spreadsheet program like Microsoft Excel®. There are two steps to developing the Asset/Attack Matrix (Figure 8.2). The first is the list of major assets that was developed in Chapter 5: Asset Characterization and Identification. The second is the list of possible threat scenarios that was developed in Chapter 7: Threat Analysis (the Adversary/Means Matrix).

This is a good time to review the threat scenarios listed in the threat analysis section in order to be sure that they are inclusive of every type of attack. For example, many threat scenario lists did not include moving shooter attacks before the Mumbai attacks on the Taj Mahal Palace and Oberoi hotels in 2008. This type of attack is different from other types of ballistic attacks in that the shooter is not stationary but moves throughout the facility, attacking victims as he moves and taking up sniping positions to attack forces assembling outside, and then moving on to a new location in the building. In the Mumbai attacks, the shooters moved in a zigzag pattern up through the building to the top floors, causing casualties as they went. There are effective countermeasures for this attack scenario, but they are different from those for other types of scenario and involve deploying barriers within the building that limit the movement of the shooter and containing him to an area where he can be easily taken out by the special forces team. This countermeasure also limits casualties to the area of containment. Threat scenarios must be constantly updated in order to keep up with current attack models.

With assets in rows from the left and threat scenarios in columns to the right, the analyst can estimate the severity of a given attack scenario on the organization's key assets. For example, attacks on people have less effect on the organization's information technology system but can have a dramatic effect on its business reputation.

Threat/Target Nexus Matrix

A Threat/Target Nexus Matrix (Circulation Path/Threat Nexus Matrix) identifies what areas are most likely to be used by threat actors to carry out their action.

The Threat/Target Nexus Matrix can be developed either in a professional program such as SVA-Pro or by using a spreadsheet program such as Microsoft Excel. The example herein uses Microsoft Excel, which anyone can use to develop a suitable matrix.

The Threat/Target Nexus Matrix creates a link between areas and possible targets (people who might be targets for a terrorist attack). This uses a different list from asset-driven matrixes such as the Asset/Attack Matrix. In the case of the Threat/Target Nexus Matrix, we want to examine vehicle and pedestrian circulation paths in the context of possible victims (Figure 8.3).

Mega towers

Asset/attack matrix

Targets		Entry Methods					Weapons					Incendiaries and Explosives												Other				
	Tools	Cutting torch/burning bar	False credentials	Social engineering	Vehicles	Forced entry	Bladed weapons	Small arms	Heavy arms	Shoulder-fired missiles (RPG)	Mortars	Hand grenades	Incendiary device	Improvised explosive device (IED)	Suicide bomber	Truck bomb	Bus bomb	Car bomb	Small watercraft bomb	Large watercraft bomb	Small aircraft	Large aircraft	Dirty bomb	Chemical agents	Biological agents	Cyberstrike	Score	Rank
People																												
VIP executives and VIP visitors	6	6	3	3	4	3	7	8	8	8	8	8	8	8	8	8	8	8	7	7	7	7	7	7	7	6	7	2
Employees	8	8	6	5	7	6	6	10	10	10	8	8	7	10	10	10	10	10	10	10	10	10	10	8	8	8	8	4
Contractors	8	8	6	6	8	5	8	10	10	10	8	8	7	10	10	10	10	10	10	10	10	10	10	8	8	8	9	1
Visitors	6	6	2	2	5	5	5	7	7	7	7	7	7	7	7	7	7	7	7	7	7	7	7	7	7	6	6	39
Delivery personnel	8	8	1	1	2	1	7	7	6	6	8	7	8	8	6	6	6	4	4	4	3	3	4	4	4	2	5	51
Transportation personnel	8	8	1	1	1	1	7	7	6	6	8	7	8	8	6	6	8	4	4	4	3	3	7	7	7	2	6	50
Property																												
Site	6	6	5	6	6	8	5	9	9	10	9	10	8	8	8	8	8	8	4	7	8	8	7	6	6	1	7	1
VIP drop-off	5	5	4	6	6	7	4	8	8	8	10	7	10	10	10	10	10	10	4	9	9	9	8	3	3	2	8	31
Employee drop-off	3	3	6	8	8	8	8	8	8	10	8	10	10	10	10	10	10	10	8	8	8	7	7	7	5	5	8	10
Visitor drop-off: hotel (south)	3	3	2	6	6	8	8	8	8	7	10	10	10	10	10	10	10	10	8	8	8	8	10	10	7	1	8	5
Main south sntry gatehouse area	2	2	8	8	6	6	8	8	8	7	8	10	10	10	10	10	10	8	8	8	8	8	7	7	5	5	8	12
North perimeter fence	8	8	1	1	6	6	2	8	8	8	8	5	10	10	10	10	10	10	1	10	10	8	8	1	1	1	6	42
East perimeter fence	8	8	1	1	6	7	2	8	8	8	8	5	10	10	10	10	10	10	1	7	10	8	8	1	1	1	6	42
South perimeter fence	8	8	1	1	6	7	2	8	8	8	8	5	10	10	10	10	10	10	1	10	10	8	8	1	1	1	6	42

FIGURE 8.2   Asset/Attack Matrix.

Hotel and convention center
circulation paths and threat nexus points

PATHS/ACTORS	On-property actors								Adjacencies	
	VIPs	Employees	Public	Contractors	Food service	Vendors	Delivery vans	Exhibition workers	Public transporation	Adjacent rooftops
Site										
VIP entry areas	X								X	X
Employee entry areas		X						X	X	X
Public			X	*		X			X	X
Transportation	*	X	X	X		X	X	*	X	X
Basements										
VIP parking	X									
Public parking			X	X		X				
Loading docks		X		X	X	X	X	X		
Convention center										
Retail circulation		X	X	X		X				
Exhibition/convention circulation	*	X	X	X	X	X		X		
Employee circulation		X		X		X				
Service areas		X		X	X	X				
Food service circulation		X		X	X	X				
Roof deck										
Roof deck	X	*	X		X					

Legend	
X	**Likely intersection**
*	**Possible intersection**
	Intersection with high risk
	Intersection with medium risk
	Lower risk

FIGURE 8.3 Threat/Target Nexus Matrix.

Different targets (possible victims) and different types of attackers will use different areas, and it is where these areas cross paths that attacks may occur. For example, VIPs will almost always enter through a VIP entry, if one is provided. So the approach by vehicle and pedestrians to the VIP entry area is a critical nexus point for attacks on VIPs. Infiltration and attack vulnerabilities:

- Blends aspects of threat and vulnerability assessment.
- Is an important part of vulnerability analysis.
- Almost like method acting.
- If you purposely adopt a position that allows you to look at vulnerabilities in the same way an adversary looks at them, it gives you insight into how adversaries will attack.

VIPs circulate through a building in different ways from normal visitors. The attack by Sirhan Sirhan on Robert Kennedy in the kitchen area of the Los Angeles Ambassador Hotel demonstrates how Sirhan understood VIP circulation paths and took advantage of this to isolate his target from the mass of public admirers and corner him into a more vulnerable space. Similarly, in his attack on Lee Harvey Oswald, Jack Ruby used circulation-path knowledge to create an opportunity to get close to his target. Other examples abound. The attack on Rafic Al Hariri in February 2005 in Beirut, Lebanon, illustrated the attackers' foreknowledge of the victim's transportation habits. Most kidnappings happen at locations selected for the purpose of isolating the victim from movement options. The better the risk analyst understands how circulation paths play an important role in target acquisition, the better they can identify and assess circulation paths for determining where attacks might take place.

One project I worked on involved a red-carpet area for a major media awards ceremony. This is an obvious nexus point for terrorists wishing to cause large numbers of public casualties in the full glare of the media.

The main lobby of buildings, the employee entrance, food circulation paths, housekeeping paths, delivery paths—all these create opportunities for threat actors to exploit crossing paths with potential victims. So once a victimology profile is understood (what types of victims designated threat actors prefer), a risk analyst can easily understand the areas of a facility that present targets to potential attackers.

Weapons/Target Nexus Matrix

A Weapons/Target Nexus Matrix (Circulation Path/Weapons Nexus Matrix) identifies types of weapons that are most likely to be used at each threat/target location. The Weapons/Target Nexus Matrix can be developed either in a professional program such as SVA-Pro or by using a spreadsheet program such as Microsoft Excel. The example herein uses Microsoft Excel, which anyone can use to develop a suitable matrix.

Similar to the Threat/Target Nexus Matrix, the Weapons/Target Nexus Matrix helps the risk analyst understand what types of weapons can be useful to potential threat actors at each of the circulation path nexus points that were identified using the Threat/Target Nexus Matrix (Figure 8.4).

Not all weapons can be used in all locations. For example, rocket-powered grenades (RPGs) would have been less useful to the Mumbai moving shooter threat actors than the small arms they carried because RPGs need distance to work. However, hand grenades

Hotel and convention center
circulation paths and weapons nexus points

PATHS/WEAPONS	Entry methods					Smaller weapons					Explosives						Other			
	Tools	False credentials	Social engineering	Vehicles	Forced entry	Small arms	Heavy arms	Shoulder-fired weapons	Mortars	Hand grenades	Improvised incendiary devices	Improvised explosive device	Conventional bomb	Vehicle bombs	Dirty bomb	Suicide bomber	Chemical agents	Biological agents	Other means	Cyberstrike
Site																				
VIP entry areas		X	X	X	X	X	X	X	X	X	X	X	X	X	X	X	X	X	X	
Employee entry areas	X	X	X	X	X	X	X	X	X	X	X	X	X	X	X	X	X	X	X	
Public				X	X	X	X	X	X	X	X	X	X	X	X	X	X	X	X	
Transportation		X	X	X	X	X	X	X	X	X	X	X	X	X	X	X	X	X	X	
Basements																				
VIP parking		X	X	X	X	X	X			X	X	X	X	X	X	X	X	X	X	
Public parking				X	X	X	X			X	X	X	X	X	X	X	X	X	X	
Loading docks		X	X	X	X	X	X			X	X	X	X	X	X	X	X	X	X	
Convention center																				
Retail circulation				X	X	X	X	X	X	X	X	X	X	X	X	X	X	X	X	
Exhibition/convention circulation		X	X	X	X	X	X	X	X	X	X	X	X	X	X	X	X	X	X	
Employee circulation		X	X	X	X	X	X	X	X	X	X	X	X	X	X	X	X	X	X	
Service areas		X	X	X	X	X	X	X	X	X	X	X	X	X	X	X	X	X	X	
Food service circulation		X	X	X	X	X	X	X	X	X	X	X	X	X	X	X	X	X	X	
Roof deck																				
Roof deck		X	X		X	X				X	X	X	X	X		X	X	X	X	

Legend

X	**Likely intersection**
*	**Possible intersection**
■	Intersection with high risk
□	Intersection with medium risk
▨	Lower risk

FIGURE 8.4   Weapons/Target Nexus Matrix.

are highly useful within a building to clear a room from defenses or to kill victims in a single stroke, especially if they might be armed.

The closer the threat actor to the potential victim, the smaller the preferred weapon will be. An AK-47 would have been useless in the Robert Kennedy assassination because it would have identified the attacker as such before he could use the weapon. He chose instead a handgun, which was easy to conceal until needed.

In the Columbine High School attack, the threat actors chose propane bombs, which, had they detonated properly, would have caused casualties in the hundreds. Such bombs, though ideal for creating casualties, also created problems in transportation to the attack site, slowing down the attackers and giving some warning to their potential victims. Similarly, the Columbine attacker, Eric David Harris, kept a journal that identified "good hiding places" and areas with poor lighting that could be utilized. The attack was to start at exactly 11.17 a.m., when Harris had calculated that the largest possible number of students would be located in the cafeteria.* So the lesson here is that it is not only where, but also when opportunities for contact between threat actors and victims arise.

The Weapons/Target Nexus Matrix should illustrate what types of weapons the risk analyst should be concerned about in each of the areas considered. This will also limit the number of probable threat scenarios for these areas.

Adversary Sequence Diagrams (ASD) and Path Analysis

Adversary sequence diagrams (ASD) and path analysis† (described in detail in Chapter 7: Threats) identifies the pathways from perimeter to target that potential attackers might follow on their way to the target(s).

The ASD path analysis can be conducted in either of two ways:

- Flowchart
- Graphically

To prepare an adversary sequence diagram path analysis, one must first identify the locations of all high-value assets within the buildings. Then one should examine all of the entries to the facility, including frontal, side, and rear perimeter entries; underground (utility) entries and overhead entries from adjacent buildings; helicopter fast rope entries; and so on. Once inside the perimeter, the analyst should evaluate all pathways into the buildings where high-value assets are located. The diagrams should illustrate progressively the nexus between the locations of high-value assets and the building perimeter entries until all logical pathways are resolved. Finally, the analyst should identify the locations along those pathways where detection, assessment, and delays can be placed (Figure 8.5).

Surveillance Opportunities Matrix

The Surveillance Opportunities Matrix identifies surveillance opportunities. It can be developed either in a professional program such as SVA-Pro or by using a spreadsheet

---

* http://en.wikipedia.org/wiki/Eric_Harris_and_Dylan_Klebold.
† This is explored in detail in Mary Lynn Garcia's book.[1]

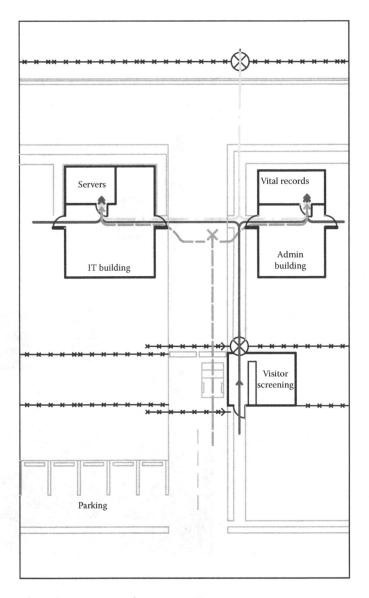

FIGURE 8.5   Adversary sequence diagram (ASD).

program such as Microsoft Excel. The example herein uses Microsoft Excel, which any-one can use to develop a suitable matrix (Figure 8.6).

Before any terrorist attack or criminal attack is carried out, it is necessary for the attacker to perform some kind of surveillance. This is necessary so that the threat actor can understand what assets there may be to attack, understand what the vulnerabilities are that can be exploited, gain advantage to control the area, obtain cover and conceal-ment while approaching and withdrawing, and all the other elements necessary to suc-ceed in the attack.

Whether the intended act is criminal or terrorist, surveillance is required. The more important success is to the mission and the more complicated the attack location, the more important surveillance is to the operation.

Mega towers

Surveillance nexus matrix

Targets	Fixed visual surveillance	Off-site mobile visual Surveillance	Acoustic eavesdropping	Electronic surveillance	IT system surveillance	Interception of info/docs	Score	Rank
People	8	8	4	3	4	6	6	1
VIP executives and VIP visitors	7	6	2	2	4	6	5	39
Employees	10	7	7	5	7	7	7	6
Contractors	8	7	3	5	5	5	6	23
Visitors	8	7	7	4	3	5	6	20
Delivery personnel	8	10	2	2	2	7	5	33
Transportation personnel	8	10	2	2	2	7	5	33
Property	8	7	5	7	2	2	5	3
Site	9	8	6	6	3	3	6	*16*
VIP drop-off	10	10	2	6	5	6	7	8
Employee drop-off	10	8	8	6	6	6	7	3
Visitor drop-off: hotel (south)	10	8	8	6	3	1	6	14
Main south entry gatehouse area	10	8	2	7	1	5	6	23
North perimeter fence	8	8	6	7	1	2	5	27
East perimeter fence	8	8	6	7	1	2	5	27
South perimeter fence	8	8	6	7	1	2	5	27

FIGURE 8.6 Surveillance Opportunities Matrix.

The task of surveillance is also the best opportunity any organization has to prevent an attack that is in the planning stage. Surveillance is a task like any other task. As such, there are certain steps that must be carried out that can identify the act of surveillance.

A threat actor surveilling a potential target is looking for different things than anyone else would be, except possibly for a risk analyst. Both the surveillant and the risk analyst are looking for vulnerabilities that can be exploited. I have actually been stopped by an astute security manager in an airport because my actions fit the description of surveillance. After I showed the security manager my credentials, he understood that my tendency to notice security provisions was industry based and not out of interest in surveillance for planning an attack.

Surveillance has many possible components, only some of which may be used in support of planning an attack. These may include

- Fixed visual surveillance
- Mobile vehicular surveillance
- Mobile pedestrian surveillance
- Acoustic eavesdropping
- Electronic surveillance
- Information technology surveillance (multiple modes)
- Interception of information or documents

Using the asset list developed in Chapter 5: Asset Characterization and Identification, the risk analyst will develop a spreadsheet identifying the list of assets by rows on the left (broken down by asset class: people, property, proprietary information, and business reputation), and surveillance types by columns, including those identified above, as appropriate.

This matrix will allow the risk analyst to determine what assets are prone to what types of surveillance, and can help the analyst rank those assets most vulnerable to surveillance. The results of this matrix are components for asset target values and risk calculations.

EVALUATE VULNERABILITY

Determining the effectiveness of existing security measures is done differently for existing and new facilities. For existing facilities, a security survey is required. As this is not possible for new facilities, a vulnerability estimate can be made from architectural drawings and renderings.

For new facilities, the process includes the following steps, described in detail below.

- Determine surveillance opportunities
- Determine accessibility
- Identify intrinsic vulnerabilities
- Natural countermeasures
- Physical countermeasures
- Electronic countermeasures
- Operational countermeasures

For existing facilities, a full vulnerability survey is recommended. A vulnerability survey should include the following elements:

- Determine the physical nature of the facility (campus, building, perimeter, etc.).
- Determine the operational nature of the facility (hospital, factory, office building, military base, etc.).
- Determine the functional operating elements of the facility (administration, human resources, marketing, research and development, etc.; list all).
- Determine the distribution of the functional operating elements throughout the facility (e.g., marketing, fourth floor; human resources, fifth floor; executive offices, sixth floor; etc.).
- Determine the number and type of people who are distributed through the functional operating elements (employees, all floors; managers, all floors; executives, sixth floor and executive lift; delivery personnel, loading dock and mail room; visitors, lobby, ground floor conference rooms, and executive floor; etc.).
- Then review the facility as described above for new facilities. For existing facilities, this can best be done by a comprehensive walkabout with knowledgeable security representatives. A combination of a security manager and a security supervisor is recommended. The security manager will help to maintain a strategic focus, while the supervisor is more likely to be familiar with the intimate details of the facility.

Survey Points

The commitment of management to the mission of the security organization should be noted. From there, the survey involves observing, questioning, verifying, investigating, and evaluating. Every survey should begin with field interviews of key management, including security management. The history of security events should be available and will be used in the identification of and estimates of significance of various threat scenarios. Obtain organization charts; a functional description of each business unit, along with its location in the facility; any satellite activities of the organization; and any outside services that are critical to the organization.

Obtain access to information about the flow of information in the organization: information on paper, financial information, and through the information technology system. Maintain focus on the problems outlined by management in the opening interviews, as these will be front and center in their minds for the report. Ask about and focus on procedures that have been put in place to deal with problems. Ask if these procedures have largely resolved the problems, and what concerns still exist.

Make a flowchart of the business operations in terms of flow of products, information, money, financial records, and services. The resulting information can be entered into the vulnerability matrix as described below for quantitative analysis. From there, the analysis process is the same for existing and new facilities, as described below.

Quantitative Analysis Matrixes

Consider surveillance opportunities as described above.

Determine Accessibility

Accessibility is the key to any threat action. Inaccessible assets are safe from attackers. So the degree of accessibility is a direct and most important factor in vulnerability. No access equals no attack. More access equals a higher opportunity for an attack.

For some types of attacks, any access will do. The assassination of former Pakistani prime minister Benazir Bhutto is an example of this. All the attacker needed was 10-meter proximity to Madam Bhutto in the midst of a large crowd. Suicide bombers need only approximate access. Leave-behind backpack bombs need only access to a crowd. A road-side bomber will place the bomb and then wait for an appropriate target to pass by before triggering his attack.

For most targeting, a direct line of sight is required for ballistic attacks, RPG attacks, and the like. The more accessible a potential target is, the more easily an attack can be carried out. Access equals possibility. More access equals more probability.

For ordinary decent crime, reducing access can be easily accomplished with physical, technical, or procedural means. As you survey an area, think how each type of threat actor would approach access to the area. Would they confront directly? Would they try to fit in? Would they wait for a quiet period, or for those who might notice them to be distracted? Would they look for a weak point and punch through?

Identify Intrinsic Vulnerabilities

Intrinsic vulnerabilities are important to understand and are often overlooked. They are so intuitive that they are most often not considered as a component factor but only as part of an aggregate of intrinsic vulnerability and other countermeasures. This is important to understand, because the environment can change, and when it does, so does the vulnerability equation.

Intrinsic vulnerabilities are those vulnerabilities that an asset has in the absence of any other countermeasures. That is, if the asset is sitting in an open field with no building or other protection, what kinds of attacks can be carried out against it? Different assets have different intrinsic vulnerabilities.

For example, people are subject to ballistic attacks, bombs, fire, and armed robberies. While paper files are less vulnerable to ballistic attacks, they are still vulnerable to bombs, fires, and burglaries (it is very rare for an armed robbery to occur for which the target is a file). Cyber attacks do not directly attack people or property but are targeted against the information technology system. Each asset should be scored for its intrinsic vulnerability on a scale of 1 to 5 or 1 to 10.

Surprisingly, intrinsic vulnerabilities are often overlooked by many surveyors in favor of technical or physical vulnerabilities. Intrinsic vulnerabilities can often include the polite helpfulness of staff or victims and other similar factors that are important to threat actors but are just considered part of the normal landscape by the organization.

Natural Countermeasures

After the consideration of intrinsic vulnerabilities, we begin to consider the effect that natural countermeasures have on the vulnerability. Examples of natural countermeasures include

- A liquefied natural gas (LNG) terminal that is surrounded on the land side by a storm berm (a 21 ft [7 m] high raised levy) to keep hurricane storm surges out; this also serves as a natural countermeasure against the entry of conventional vehicles.
- A facility on a small island with only ferry access makes access and getaway more difficult as it creates a "choke point" through which all threat actors must come and go.
- Any facility located on a waterway is only accessible by watercraft on that side.
- A facility located on a hillside cliff has very limited access from that side.
- A facility that is located up a dead-end road offers little chance for escape if the threat actor is discovered.

Most often, natural countermeasures affect access to assets. The deterrent or access attributes of natural countermeasures should be subtracted from the asset's intrinsic vulnerability.

Evaluate Effectiveness of Existing Security Measures

Existing man-made security countermeasures also limit vulnerably. Man-made countermeasures should also be subtracted from the intrinsic vulnerabilities. Man-made countermeasures may include

- Physical countermeasures
- Electronic countermeasures
- Operational countermeasures

Sometimes man-made countermeasures overlap natural countermeasures and sometimes they complement each other. For example, a fence on top of the LNG terminal storm berm will not serve to keep out any vehicles that cannot themselves climb the storm berm. So the mitigating effect of the fence on vehicle access is negligible. However, the limiting effect on pedestrians may be significant because they can climb the storm berm more easily than a vehicle.

Man-made countermeasures are of three types: physical, electronic, and operational.

Physical Countermeasures

Physical countermeasures include locks, doors, gates, lighting, signage, fences, walls, and fixed and deployable barriers. Physical countermeasures that are missing or are poorly maintained can add vulnerability. High-quality locks that have keys that cannot be copied reduce vulnerability. A 6 ft. high poorly maintained fence might add vulnerability, while an 8 ft. high well-maintained fence would reduce vulnerability.

Electronic Countermeasures

Electronic countermeasures include alarm systems; access control systems; video systems; communications systems, including electronic signage; telephones; public address systems; and two-way radios. Electronic countermeasures can also include long-range acoustic weaponry, visible light weaponry, electronic jamming equipment, and information technology threat countermeasures. Electronic systems that offer protection in depth reduce vulnerability, while poorly maintained single-point electronic systems do little to reduce vulnerability.

Operational Countermeasures

Operational countermeasures include all uses of security staffing (posts, patrols, reserve staff), security dogs, security policies and procedures, countersurveillance program, investigations, and security intelligence program. Poorly implemented guard solutions can actually add vulnerability, because they can give a feeling of security without real security. Any organization without a security plan that is based on a proper risk analysis is operationally vulnerable regardless of what they think because they have unknown threats and unknown vulnerabilities.

All these should be subtracted from intrinsic vulnerabilities, paying attention to the overlapping and complementary effects of countermeasures on the same asset.

Vulnerability Calculation Spreadsheet

The vulnerability calculation is based on the threat scenarios and identifies the most likely locations for attacks by reviewing both the threat/target nexus locations and the weapons/target nexus locations. Once we know what types of threat actions can occur and the most likely locations for each of these, we can focus on the vulnerabilities of not only the entire facility, but especially the most likely locations for attacks of each type by each type of threat actor. This level of granularity and accuracy is considered unobtainable by many security analysts, but we will review exactly how to achieve it.

The vulnerability calculation spreadsheet adds surveillance and intrinsic vulnerability and subtracts the mitigating effects of natural and man-made countermeasures, including physical, electronic, and operational countermeasures.

Create a new spreadsheet using the asset/consequences spreadsheet as a basis. Name the spreadsheet tab vulnerability calculations. Include the following columns:

- List of targets (assets)
- Access opportunities
- Surveillance opportunities (referenced from the Surveillance Opportunities Matrix)
- Intrinsic vulnerability
- Existing natural countermeasures
- Existing man-made countermeasures
  - High-tech
  - Low-tech
  - No-tech

Add surveillance, access, and intrinsic vulnerability (each from 1 to 10). Subtract existing, high-tech, low-tech, and no-tech countermeasures (each from 1 to 10). The result is the vulnerability of each asset from 1 to 10 (Figure 8.7).

Qualitative Analysis Section

Following the interviews, records gathering, survey, and quantitative analysis, it is important to condense the information into a qualitative analysis. Quantitative analysis information is easily reduced by stepping through the process and noting significant elements of each step, including significant information from the interview, records, survey, and

Mega towers Vulnerability Matrix

Targets	Accessibility	Surveillance	Intrinsic vulnerability	Natural countermeasures	Physical measures	Electronic measures	Operational measures	Score	Rank
People	8	7	3	8	3	1	6	5	3
VIP executives and VIP visitors	5	2	1	7	6	1	8	4	44
Employees	8	10	4	10	5	1	8	7	18
Contractors	8	3	4	5	5	1	3	4	51
Visitors	8	10	4	10	1	1	8	6	22
Delivery personnel	8	7	2	8	1	1	3	4	44
Transportation personnel	8	7	2	8	1	1	3	4	44
Property	8	7	5	7	6	5	4	6	1
Site	8	8	6	6	5	5	4	6	24
VIP drop-off	7	6	6	8	5	5	5	6	22
Employee drop-off	10	0	7	10	7	8	7	8	2
Visitor drop-off: hotel (south)	10	10	7	10	8	8	7	9	1
Main south entry gatehouse area	8	8	7	10	8	8	7	8	4
North perimeter fence	8	8	4	2	3	3	2	4	44
East perimeter fence	8	8	4	2	3	3	2	4	44
South perimeter fence	8	8	4	2	3	3	2	4	44
West perimeter fence	8	8	4	2	3	3	2	4	44
North perimeter freight gate	8	8	4	6	5	3	2	5	35
East perimeter emergency gate	8	6	6	6	5	3	2	5	35
West perimeter emergency gate	8	6	6	6	5	3	2	5	35
Hotel loading dock area	7	8	6	6	4	3	2	5	35
Hotel east entrance	7	8	7	10	8	8	7	8	5
Hotel west entrance	7	8	7	10	8	8	7	8	5
Ramp down to underground parking	7	3	4	6	4	3	6	5	41
Underground structure	7	7	5	8	4	3	3	5	34
P1 level parking	7	7	6	8	4	3	3	5	27
P1 level elevator lobby	7	7	5	8	4	3	3	5	30
P2 level parking	7	7	6	8	4	3	3	5	27
P2 level elevator lobby	7	7	5	8	4	3	3	5	30
P3 level parking	7	7	6	8	4	3	3	5	27
P3 level elevator lobby	7	7	5	8	4	3	3	5	30
P3 level utility rooms	6	6	3	8	4	3	3	5	41
Hotel tower	9	6	5	8	8	6	5	7	17
Main lobby area	10	10	6	8	8	6	6	8	7
Lobby level reception desk	10	7	6	10	10	10	6	8	2
Lobby level bell desk and storage	8	6	6	8	8	6	6	7	14
Security checkpoint outside	10	7	3	4	3	3	3	5	41
Lobby level concierge area	10	6	3	8	8	8	8	7	13
Passenger elevator lobby	10	6	6	8	8	8	6	7	9
Stairwells	10	5	3	8	8	8	6	7	14
Freight elevator	7	3	3	8	8	6	4	6	25
Lobby level utility rooms	7	2	3	8	8	3	3	5	40
Low-rise levels	10	7	7	8	8	6	6	7	9
Mid-rise levels	10	7	7	8	8	6	6	7	9
Hi-rise levels	10	7	7	8	8	6	6	7	9
Passenger elevator lobbies	10	7	4	8	8	8	8	8	8
Freight elevator lobbies	7	5	4	8	8	3	4	6	25
Utility rooms	8	4	3	8	8	3	3	5	30
Mechanical floor	7	4	3	8	8	3	3	5	35
Roof	6	6	7	8	7	6	6	7	18
Proprietary information	6	6	5	6	7	3	7	5	2
IT system	8	8	3	10	10	1	6	7	18
Security system	8	8	7	6	10	1	8	7	14
RF communications system	7	7	7	5	5	6	7	6	21
Paper files	1	1	1	1	1	4	5	2	52
Business reputation	2	6	2	2	2	6	5	4	4

Legend

Major effect	10
Medium effect	5
Minimal effect	1

FIGURE 8.7   Vulnerability Matrix.

quantitative analysis. This is just a process of putting raw data into words, formatted in a fashion that flows logically.

Vulnerability Detail Spreadsheet

Finally, the risk analyst should create a comprehensive list from the vulnerability calculations for every vulnerability to be addressed. This is quite straightforward and its value will become apparent when we proceed to Chapter 18: Security Effectiveness Metrics. Begin with the list of assets, which have been broken down into asset categories (people, property, proprietary information, and business reputation); of course those have been broken down into subcategories (property > sub perimeter > sub north perimeter, east perimeter, south perimeter, west perimeter; perimeter entries > sub main public entry, service entry, employee entry, VIP entry, etc.; main building > sub ground floor > sub main entry, lobby, elevator lobby, etc.). Now, in a spreadsheet as described above, with assets listed in rows to the left, list the vulnerabilities found for each asset row in a new column next to the asset.

Vulnerability Detail Matrix

The Vulnerability Detail Matrix identifies possible vulnerabilities. It can be developed either in a professional program such as SVA-Pro or by using a spreadsheet program such as Microsoft Excel. The example herein uses Microsoft Excel, which anyone can use to develop a suitable matrix (Figure 8.8).

Additionally, between the asset listing and the vulnerability listing, create two new columns labeled infiltration vulnerability or attack vulnerability. Classify the vulnerability appropriately in one or the other, or both, with an X.

Finally, be sure to include columns for criticality and consequence ranking.

Now, you should have a spreadsheet that lists by columns:

- Assets by general classes
- Subclasses of assets under each general class
- Criticality ranking for each asset (from the Consequences Matrix)
- Consequence ranking for each asset (from the Consequences Matrix)
- Infiltration/attack vulnerability columns
- The vulnerability ranking from the Vulnerability Matrix
- A written description of the vulnerability

This matrix will be used as the basis for the Countermeasures Effectiveness Matrix in Chapter 18 and for the Cost-Effectiveness Matrix in Chapter 19.

SUMMARY

Introduction: Review of Vulnerability Assessment Model

Assessing vulnerability used to be easy when the threats were limited to "ordinary decent criminals." The use of criminal vulnerability assessment in an environment of possible

Targets	Accessibility	Surveillance	Intrinsic vulnerability	Natural countermeasures	Physical measures	Electronic measures	Operational measures	Score	Rank
People									
VIP executives and VIP visitors	8	7	3	8	3	1	6	5	3
Employees	5	2	1	7	6	1	8	4	44
Contractors	8	10	4	10	5	1	8	7	18
Visitors	8	3	4	5	5	1	3	4	51
Delivery personnel	8	10	4	10	1	1	8	6	22
Transportation personnel	8	7	2	8	1	1	3	4	44
Transportation personnel	8	7	2	8	1	1	3	4	44
Property									
	8	7	5	7	6	5	4	6	1
Site	8	8	6	6	5	5	4	6	24
VIP drop-off	7	6	6	8	5		5	6	22
Employee drop-off	10	10	7	10	7	8	7	8	2
Visitor drop-off: hotel (south)	10	10	7	10	8	8	7	9	1
Main south entry gatehouse area	8	8	7	10	8	8	7	8	4
North perimeter fence	8	8	4	2	3	3	2	4	44
East perimeter fence	8	8	4	2	3	3	2	4	44
South perimeter fence	8	8	4	2	3	3	2	4	44

FIGURE 8.8   Megatowers Vulnerability Detail Matrix.

terrorism, however, is woefully inadequate. The short version of a quality vulnerability assessment model includes

- Define scenarios and evaluate specific consequences
- Evaluate effectiveness of existing security measures
- Identify vulnerabilities and estimate degree of vulnerability

Define Scenarios and Evaluate Specific Consequences

In interviews and interrogations with Al-Qaeda, Salafist, Lashkar-e-Taiba (LeT), and other militant operatives and managers, including Khalid Sheikh Mohammed (KSM), it becomes clear how terrorist organizations conduct target selection, attack planning, scenario testing, and finally attack operations.

An effective process of vulnerability assessment must include the following steps:

- Utilize an Asset/Attack Matrix, which identifies which attack scenarios are most likely to be used by what class of threat actors
- Utilize a Threat/Target Nexus Matrix, which identifies what areas are most likely to be used by threat actors to carry out their action
- Utilize a Weapons/Target Nexus Matrix, which identifies what types of weapons are most likely to be used at each threat/target location
- Review surveillance opportunities for each major asset under consideration
- Review vulnerabilities in the light of all the information above

Surveillance has many possible components, only some of which may be used in support of planning an attack. These may include

- Fixed visual surveillance
- Mobile vehicular surveillance
- Mobile pedestrian surveillance
- Acoustic eavesdropping
- Electronic surveillance
- Information technology surveillance (multiple modes)
- Interception of information or documents

Evaluate Vulnerability

Determining the effectiveness of existing security measures is done differently for existing and new facilities. For existing facilities, a security survey is required. As this is not possible for new facilities, a vulnerability estimate can be made from architectural drawings and renderings.

For new facilities, the process includes the following steps, listed here:

- Determine accessibility
- Identify intrinsic vulnerabilities
- Natural countermeasures
- Physical countermeasures

- Electronic countermeasures
- Operational countermeasures

For existing facilities, a full vulnerability survey is recommended. A vulnerability survey should include the following elements:

- Determine the physical nature of the facility (campus, building, perimeter, etc.).
- Determine the operational nature of the facility (hospital, factory, office building, military base, etc.).
- Determine the functional operating elements of the facility (administration, human resources, marketing, research and development, etc.; list all).
- Determine the distribution of the functional operating elements throughout the facility (marketing, fourth floor; human resources, 5th floor; executive offices, sixth floor; etc.).
- Determine the number and type of people who are distributed through the functional operating elements (employees, all floors; managers, all floors; executives, sixth floor and executive lift; delivery personnel, loading dock and mail room; visitors, lobby, ground floor conference rooms, and executive floor; etc.).
- Then review the facility as described above for new facilities. For existing facilities, this can best be done by a comprehensive walkabout with knowledgeable security representatives. A combination of a security manager and a security supervisor is recommended. The security manager will help to maintain a strategic focus, while the supervisor is more likely to be familiar with the intimate details of the facility.

Vulnerability Calculation

The vulnerability calculation adds surveillance and intrinsic vulnerability and subtracts the mitigating effects of natural and man-made countermeasures, including physical, electronic, and operational countermeasures.

Qualitative Analysis Section

Following the interviews, records gathering, survey, and quantitative analysis, it is important to condense the information into a qualitative analysis. Quantitative analysis information is easily reduced by stepping through the process and noting significant elements of each step, including significant information from the interview, records, survey, and quantitative analysis. This is just a process of putting raw data into words, formatted in a fashion that flows logically.

Vulnerability Listing

Finally, the risk analyst should create a comprehensive list from the vulnerability calculations of every vulnerability to be addressed. In a spreadsheet, with assets listed in rows to the left, list the vulnerabilities found for each asset row in a new column next to the asset. You can create two columns: infiltration vulnerability and attack vulnerability.

REFERENCES

1. Garcia, M. L. 2006. *Vulnerability Assessment of Physical Protection Systems*. Elsevier Butterworth–Heinemann, Burlington, MA.
2. Gunaratna, G. 2008. LeT is looking at India through the global lens. *The Times of India*, December 28, p. 157.

Q&A

Questions

Q1: In order for an attacker to carry out a successful attack,
  A. The attacker must be able to infiltrate the facility.
  B. The attacker must be able to carry out a successful attack.
  C. For common criminals, the attacker must be able to leave the facility after a successful attack (undetected if possible).
  D. All of the above.

Q2: It is easy
  A. To review vulnerabilities for an enterprise class organization.
  B. To overlook vulnerabilities in protection systems that a terrorist will easily see and exploit.
  C. To overlook vulnerabilities in protection systems at a convenience store.
  D. None of the above.

Q3: In order to consider as many terrorism scenarios as possible, one should
  A. Use a fire evacuation checklist.
  B. Use a natural disasters checklist.
  C. Evaluate vulnerabilities in the same way terrorists do.
  D. Evaluate vulnerabilities in the same way as economic criminals do.

Q4: A useful tool for evaluating terroristic threat vulnerabilities is the
  A. New York terrorism attack model.
  B. Generic terrorism attack model.
  C. Khalid Sheikh Mohammed (KSM) asset target value for terrorism model.
  D. Khalid Sheikh Mohammed (KSM) almanac for terrorism.

Q5: The core of antiterrorism vulnerability assessment
  A. Is to identify possible threat scenarios and identify consequences.
  B. Is to identify threat actors and consequences.
  C. Is to identify workplace violence incidents.
  D. Is to identify all-hazards risks.

Q6: Many Western risk analysts
  A. Perceive a psychological barrier as a real barrier.
  B. Believe it cannot happen here.
  C. Believe that terrorism is a social problem.
  D. Use many fences as perimeter layers in their designs.

Q7: The Asset/Attack Matrix has two dimensions:
  A. Assets and threat actors
  B. Assets and threat scenarios
  C. Attack scenarios and threat actors
  D. None of the above

Q8: The Threat/Target Nexus Matrix (Circulation Path/Threat Nexus Matrix) identifies
  A. What areas are most likely to be used by threat actors to carry out their action.
  B. What areas are most likely to be the best escape routes.
  C. What areas should be reinforced against intrusion.
  D. All of the above.

Q9: The Weapons/Target Nexus Matrix (Circulation Path/Weapons Nexus Matrix) identifies
  A. What types of weapons are most likely to be used in a shopping mall attack.
  B. What types of weapons are most likely to be used during armed conflict between nations.
  C. What types of weapons are most likely to be used at each threat/target location.
  D. None of the above.

Q10: The adversary sequence diagrams (ASD) and path analysis identify
  A. The pathways from perimeter to target that potential attackers might follow on their way to the target(s).
  B. The path best taken by victims to escape attackers.
  C. The path best taken by special operations teams to deal with terrorists.
  D. None of the above.

Answers

Q1 – D, Q2 – B, Q3 – C, Q4 – C, Q5 – A, Q6 – A, Q7 – B, Q8 – A, Q9 – C, Q10 – A

CHAPTER 9

Estimating Probability

INTRODUCTION

At the end of this chapter, you will understand the issue of probability for all types of threat actions, how to obtain statistical data for criminal action probability, and how to estimate probability for terrorism, economic crimes, violent crimes, subversive crimes, and petty crimes (Figure 9.1).

Basic Risk Formula

$$\text{Risk} = \text{Probability} * \text{Vulnerability} * \text{Consequences, or}$$

$$\text{Risk} = (\text{Probability} + \text{Vulnerability} + \text{Consequences}) / 3$$

Classical risk analysis methodologies including all of the Department of Homeland Security (DHS)-approved methodologies assume the existence of a threat actor, times probability, times the vulnerability to be the risk. (This calculation works equally well by summing the three variables and averaging the result.)

ISO 31000 risk formula:

$$\text{Risk} = \text{Likelihood} * \text{Consequences or}$$

$$\text{Risk} = (\text{Likelihood} + \text{Consequences}) / 2$$

Likelihood

Likelihood (probability) is the composite of

- A particular type of threat actor's potential interest in a target
- The vulnerabilities that threat actor could exploit on that target
- The potential for a desired outcome (economic, subversive, or violent criminals) or the potential for achieving the desired consequences (for terrorists)

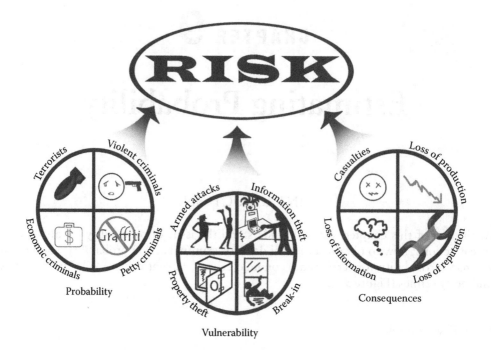

FIGURE 9.1   Risk factors.

Likelihood assumes a threat actor that is both interested and capable and has the logistical resources and adequate proximity to the target, which has exploitable vulnerabilities. The nexus of these two variables results in likelihood.

While the existence of a threat actor is presumed (no threat actor = no threat action), and vulnerability can be estimated from the data at hand, it is probability, or likelihood, that is virtually impossible to calculate for terrorism acts. However, we will discuss methods of estimating likelihood in this chapter.

In most communities, data are available from reliable sources to help the risk analyst estimate violent and nonviolent crimes including felonies and misdemeanors (more about that later in this chapter.) But for terrorism, the picture is different. For terrorism, the challenge is determining the probability or likelihood of an event. This is for all practical purposes impossible, but still it must be done in order to make a legitimate case for antiterrorism expenditures. It is impossible because unlike criminal incidents, where occurrences are common enough to build up a solid database that can be extrapolated to the facility in question with statistical surety, the only sure way to determine that a terrorist attack will occur would be to have clear and present intelligence of an attack being planned against a specific facility. This sort of intelligence almost never occurs, and when it does, it is better to disrupt the attack plan than to begin building defensive countermeasures.

So while we can use statistical data to determine the likelihood of a criminal attack, the same is not possible for terrorist attacks. There are simply an insufficient number of terrorist attacks to build a useful predictive database. But, they do occur, and when they occur, they are catastrophic to an organization. The loss of lives, business continuity, facilities, and business reputation is both tragic and arguably avoidable. The absence of an attack does not mean that there will not be an attack. Nor does it mean that there will be an attack. But the continued existence of terrorist groups with agendas that include organizations that fit the description of yours infers that the organization you are serving could be a target. And that emphasizes the need for preventative risk management planning.

Additionally, terrorism is not monolithic. No two terrorist organizations have exactly the same agenda. No two have the same target preferences. No two use exactly the same mix of methods and tactics. No two will select the same target or attack it in the same way. So it is also necessary to understand which terrorist organization(s) is most likely to be most interested in the specific target.

Terrorism Probability Estimates and Surrogates

So how can a risk analyst estimate probability for terrorism? It is not uncommon for risk analysts to simply state that the probability for a terrorist attack = 1 and simply assume that it will occur. However, this does not answer the question of where the most resources should go. With two-lane K-12 barriers costing well over $100,000 each, blast-resistant glazing costs running into the hundreds of thousands, and fencing costs also running into the hundreds of thousands, should an organization protect everything equally? Or would it be better to understand what assets are most attractive to the most likely terrorist organization(s)? I think the latter. This allows the risk analyst to focus recommendations for countermeasures onto those countermeasures and those attributes of the organization that will do the most to deter an attack from the most likely source of an attack.

RESOURCES FOR LIKELIHOOD

Viewing the Range of Possible Threat Actors

As said above, there are multiple types of threat actors and each is interested in different aspects of the organization. This is important, because what is attractive to a suicide bomber is probably not important for a pickpocket or information technology criminal. What is most interesting for a paramilitary terrorist organization is not likely to be the most interesting for a disgruntled employee. Transnational organized crime groups do not want to disrupt the operations of the organizations they feed on. Prostitutes are more interested in the hotel restaurant/bar than the porte cochere or lobby.

So it is necessary to understand the threat actors and the things that interest them the most in order to understand what should be protected. As a risk analyst, your job is to recommend countermeasures that most of all make the organization an unattractive playing field for both criminals and terrorists. You cannot do that unless you understand what it is about the organization that is attractive to their intentions.

Terrorist Threat Actors

All terrorists are not equal. Terrorists join their causes for different reasons and have different objectives. Those differences determine what type of facility they want to target and in what way they will attack it. Terrorists fall into five classes:[1]

- Class I terrorist: Government-trained professionals (including foreign intelligence threats) are among the most potent threat actors for assassinations, sophisticated bombings, and abductions. Their area of operations is generally international or regional. Their training, equipment, and discipline are all of very high quality, and they have excellent support structures. Planning and execution are highly professional. Intelligence sources to support them are keen. Examples of Class I terrorists include those who carried out the Pan Am Flight 103 bombing over Lockerby, Scotland.

A second subgroup of Class I terrorists is those who are trained by quasi-governmental organizations or under the knowing eye of a legitimate government. These include Black September, who perpetrated the Munich massacre of 1972, trained by Yasser Arafat's Palestine Liberation Organization,[2] and Lashkar-e-Taiba (LeT), trained in Pakistan at one time under the knowing eye of the Pakistani Inter-Services Intelligence Agency (ISI).

- Class II terrorist: Religious extremist professionals are arguably the most dangerous in terms of the number of casualties. Religious extremists swear dedication to an extremist cause in the name of their religion and have sworn allegiance to a group that is dedicated to destroying others who do not share their extremist view of their religion. This may include their own and other governments, those of its own and other religions who do not share their radical interpretation of their religion, and also other ethnic groups who it sees as infidels. Examples of Class II terrorists include the "Islamic State" (IS), Al-Qaeda, Hezbollah, Hamas, and LeT.

- Class III terrorist: The radical revolutionary or quasi-religious extremist. Examples include the Red Army Faction, Basque Homeland and Freedom Movement (ETA), and certain individuals such as "Yigal Amir, a radical right-wing Orthodox Jew who opposed the signing of the Oslo Accords and believed that he was saving his country from a dire fate."* Amir assassinated Israeli Prime Minister Yitzhak Rabin on November 4, 1995.

- Class IV terrorist: Guerrilla/mercenary soldier. Examples include Hutu guerrillas who massacred rival Tutsis and the Janjaweed of Sudan, who were drawn from nomadic Arabic-speaking African tribes. The Janjaweed have massacred, raped, and tortured hundreds of thousands of Darfur's sedentary population and rebel groups reportedly at the behest of the Sudanese government. Other examples include the child soldiers of Ivory Coast, the Revolutionary Armed Forces of Colombia (FARC), and Abu Sayyaf (the Philippines). Other examples include transnational organized criminal groups that conduct "narcoterrorism," such as Pablo Escobar's organization. Such individuals and groups serve political puppeteers and carry out atrocities in furtherance of the cause of their masters. Such groups usually attack in small or large groups and use military weaponry.

- Class V terrorists: Amateur (civilian, untrained criminal, or militia/vigilante) terrorists include Timothy McVeigh and Terry Nichols, who bombed the Alfred P. Murrah Federal Building in Oklahoma City, Oklahoma (radical antigovernment terrorists), and Eric Robert Rudolph, also known as the Olympic Park Bomber (a radical Christian terrorist associated with the white supremacist Christian Identity movement). All over the world, militia organizations and individuals with radical leanings attack symbols of their hatred. Such groups and individuals usually use small explosives and firearms.

- Certain terrorist organizations, such as the "Islamic State," encompass multiples of these groups (guerrilla/mercenary, religious extremist, radical revolutionary).

---

* http://en.wikipedia.org/wiki/Yitzhak_Rabin.

The risk analyst should constantly maintain familiarization with all classes of terrorist threats within his/her area of operation; agendas, size, potency, preferred weaponry, methods, and tactics should all be known to the risk analyst beforehand. It is especially important to understand the agenda and preferred targets of each type of terrorist organization operating in his/her area of consulting operations.

From the list of active terrorist organizations that are operating in the area of the facility, the risk analyst must determine two things:

- Which of these is interested in facilities like the one under consideration?
- What methods and tactics do these groups use to attack their targets?

Those most interested in the facility type in question will become obvious as we begin to delve into the Asset Target Value Matrixes. The second point is important so that the correct attack scenarios are used in the Asset/Attack Matrix.

It should also be noted that terrorist organizations sometimes change target models and methods of attack. An example of this was LeT's Mumbai attacks in 2008. These attacks were a radical departure from previous attacks for LeT in terms of both targets and methods. Having said that, if one ran LeT through the Asset Value on Terrorism (KSM) Model described here, one would find that all of the targets of that attack came up as high probabilities from LeT's terrorist agenda. This shows the model works even when tactics change, because their agenda had not changed, only their tactics.

Criminal Threat Actors

- Economic criminals, like terrorists, come in many types, including
  - Transnational criminal organizations: These organizations are a superset of organized crime that operate across national boundaries. Obvious examples include the Medellín and Cali drug cartels. Transnational criminal enterprises engage in nuclear smuggling, drug trafficking, trafficking in persons, intellectual property (IP) crimes, and money laundering.
  - Organized crime: Organized crime groups operate primarily within a nation's borders and focus on criminal enterprises that are more locally based. Organized crime groups may have ties to transnational crime organizations, but treat them as a service for money laundering or to facilitate the group's operations when traveling outside the country of origin. Examples of organized crime groups include the various groups of the Mafia in the United States and Europe. Typical activities including targeting businesses through the use of extortion, theft, and fraud including hijacking cargo trucks, robbing goods, smuggling, bid rigging, counterfeiting money or products, gambling, prostitution, drugs, gunrunning, murder for hire, and human trafficking.*
  - Sophisticated economic criminals use surveillance and planning to carry out economic crimes as individuals or as small closely knit groups. Examples include the Great Train Robbery of 1963, Internet criminals who collect and sell consumers' identities, real-estate criminals, check fraudsters, Ponzi scheme criminals, and jewel thieves.
  - Unsophisticated economic criminals, also known as opportunistic criminals, use little planning and sophistication in carrying out their crimes. Examples include common burglars, pickpockets, muggers, con men, and the like.

---

* http://en.wikipedia.org/wiki/Organized_crime.

- Information technology (IT) criminals: IT criminals may or may not be economic criminals. IT criminals use computers and the Internet to conduct crimes that may include breaking into other computers, stealing data, interrupting active network communications and placing themselves between the users, fake websites designed to garner personal information, destruction of data, and the like.
- Nonterrorist violent criminals: While all terrorists use violence, not all violence is terrorism. Almost anyone can be prompted to violent action, but for those with less impulse control, this may happen more often. Violent criminals may act out of planning or spontaneously. Violence may be used as a means to control the victims while carrying out the crime or as an end in itself.
- Subversives: Subversives are individuals who are working against the interests of the organization. These may include political or industrial spies, disturbance causers (including civil disorder), and persistent rule breakers.
- Petty criminals: Petty criminals are a class of unsophisticated criminals who may or may not be economic criminals. These often include vandals, pickpockets, prostitutes, and pimps.

Each class of criminals use targeteering that is relatively consistent for the class. Thus, a potential target can be estimated for its asset target value by using those attributes as an estimating rule.

CRIMINAL VERSUS TERRORISM LIKELIHOOD RESOURCES

General Comparison for Resources

As said above, there are no useful databases for terrorism to estimate the likelihood of the facility in question being of interest to a potential terrorist. Note that wording. This is the central question for terrorism risk analysis. Is a specific facility likely to be of interest to a given terrorist organization?

Terrorism Asset Target Value Estimates

In the early days after September 11, 2001, government risk analysts searched for a formula that could help them determine whether or not a terrorist organization might be interested in targeting specific classes of facilities:

CARVER+Shock

As governments often do, they turned to the military to learn about targeting. As militaries often do, they relied on their own tried and true method of targeteering as a rule. For many years, U.S. Special Forces used the CARVER method of target selection. CARVER stands for Criticality, Accessibility, Recuperability, Vulnerability, Effect on Population, and Recognizability. "CARVER is a target selection methodology originally designed by U.S. Special Operations Forces to determine the value of a target to military attackers. The CARVER target selection factors assist planners and operators in identifying choke points and critical damage points." After 9/11, the military added a seventh tool, which helps evaluate "the combined health, economic, and psychological impacts of an attack, or the SHOCK attributes of a target."

To use CARVER or CARVER+Shock, one evaluates the components of a facility using the seven attributes, ranked on a scale of 1 to 10 for each and then adds the sum of the estimates for each component. This shows the analyst what component of a facility would be best to target for military purposes.

Both CARVER and CARVER+Shock are made by and for military special forces and do a very good job of determining what targets would be good for military operations (i.e., to take a facility out of operations for as long as possible). However, CARVER and CARVER+Shock do nothing to help the analyst understand if a target would be interesting to a particular terrorist organization due to the fact that terrorists are not necessarily interested in taking out a facility but are very interested in communicating through the use of violence.

Terrorists use violence as language. The language of violence causes a public debate, not only about the terrorist act, but also about the causes of it and what can be done about it. Terrorists speak through violence to the public directly, past the national leadership. The language of violence can affect elections, such as in Spain in 2004 after the Madrid train bombings.* Terrorism can affect the stability of governments, as evidenced by Pakistani President Asif Ali Zardari's statement "Terrorists wanted to destabilize Pakistan."† Terrorists may want to drive out foreign nationals and foreign workers from their own lands.‡

So if a risk analyst wants to know what component of a facility to strike in order to take out the facility for a long time, CARVER and CARVER+Shock are good tools. But if a risk analyst wants to know *if* a terrorist organization would be interested in this facility, CARVER and CARVER+Shock are woefully inadequate.

KSM Asset Target Value Model

Responding to this, I developed the KSM Asset Target Value Model, named after Khalid Sheikh Mohammed, who was the principal architect of the 9/11 attacks. KSM selected the targets for the September 11, 2001, attacks and also had a principal or influencing role in the 1993 World Trade Center attack, Operation Bojinka, an aborted 2002 attack on Los Angeles's U.S. Bank Tower, the Bali bombings, the failed bombing of American Airlines Flight 63, the Millennium Plot, and the murder of Daniel Pearl. KSM knows Al-Qaeda's model for targeting well and reports of his interrogations have him saying that during his first meeting, bin Laden discussed targeting. Discussions included economic, political, and military targets. Interrogations of KSM have become a wealth of information about how Al-Qaeda operates and selects its targets. The specifics of Al-Qaeda targeting include

- Does the target fit the strategic objectives of Al-Qaeda?
- Are mass casualties possible?
- Can the attack generate prolonged media coverage, especially of the attack itself?
- Is the target of economic importance?
- Is the target of cultural importance, to the constituent community of the victim, the constituent community of Al-Qaeda, or both?
- Is the target highly vulnerable to attack?

---

* http://www.pbs.org/newshour/updates/europe/jan-june08/spain_03-07.html.

† http://www.geo.tv/10-21-2008/27336.htm.

‡ "The killing of two French sightseers in Peru's Andean highlands on Friday highlights how terrorist attacks are forcing a wide withdrawal of foreign aid workers, archaeologists and tourists from remote areas of this country's mountainous interior."[3]

- What is the probability of success of the attack?
- Does this attack benefit recruiting and fund-raising for Al-Qaeda?

Using this model, one can easily see how past attacks by Al-Qaeda and attacks in which Al-Qaeda have contributed planning and organization have all fit the KSM Targeting Model. For example, the Mumbai attack of 2008 on a railway station, a cinema, hotels, a hospital, and a Jewish center fits all these criteria. The 2001 World Trade Center attack was planned in such a fashion that the television cameras of the world would be focused on live coverage of the towers when the second plane struck, causing shock and impact far beyond a postevent account of the attack by the media.

Al-Qaeda are experts at exploiting obvious vulnerabilities. Few risk analysts before September 11, 2001, seriously considered attacks by airplanes on high-rise buildings. But in hindsight, the attack mode was obvious to all who had previously rejected it.

To use the KSM Targeting Model, create a spreadsheet with rows on the left identifying the facility and its key assets. Then create columns above for each of the targeting criteria. Score each cell from 1 to 10, sum the columns for each asset, and average the sum. Then rank the results by individual asset and by asset class (people, property, information, and business reputation).

The proof of the KSM Targeting Model is in evaluating it against targets that have been struck by Al-Qaeda and Al-Qaeda-related groups. Without exception, all of their targets fit the model. The "Islamic State" uses a similar model, although their objectives are strategically focused on utilizing terrorism in pursuit of the destruction of existing nations for the long-term purposes of building an Islamic caliphate.

Similar models can be built for each terrorist group by analyzing their public statements and interrogation reports of senior leaders for the organization's agenda and targeting preferences, thus creating a model for each organization that is accurate for use. Terrorist organizations are surprisingly open about their targeting preferences, but a risk analyst must interpret these public statements into strategic criteria.

CRIMINAL INCIDENT LIKELIHOOD ESTIMATES

There are two main sources for criminal criteria estimates: criminal statistics and asset target value estimates.

Criminal Statistics

The best source is actual criminal statistics, which should be used whenever available. Criminal statistics should include records that go back at least 5 years and should cover the following types of crimes:

- Major crimes
  - Murders
  - Rapes
  - Assaults
  - Major economic crimes
- Minor offenses

- Vehicle crimes
- Misdemeanor crimes

Some local authorities maintain records in a fashion that makes them easily usable by risk analysts, but some question the validity of police records, which might have been falsified in order to qualify for higher federal funding. Failing availability of crime statistics from local authorities that are complete, organized, and reliable, in many areas analysts can turn to private sources such as CAP Index, Inc.® Such sources offer highly organized and graphically presented data that are useful for risk analysis.

Alternatively, in the absence of usable data, an analyst can use an asset target value estimate, similar to that used for terrorism.

Economic Crime Asset Target Value Estimate

The elements for economic crime asset target value estimates include the following:

- Is there an opportunity for economic gain?
- What is the probability of success?
- What is the probability of escape?
- What is the probability of escape without subsequent capture?

Remember, this is not a vulnerability analysis but rather an estimate of how attractive key assets are to economic criminals. Vulnerability may be a factor in the probability of success, along with other factors including hours of operation, accessibility, and vigilance. Depending on the type of economic crime, the size of the organization planning the crime, the sophistication of the criminal, and the assets in question, what may be a low probability of success for one type of economic criminal may be a high probability of success for another offender.

The analyst should consider the type of economic crime that would be most concerning to the organization and use that as a baseline for estimation.

To use the Economic Crime Asset Target Value Model, create a spreadsheet with rows on the left identifying the facility and its key assets. Then create columns above for each of the targeting criteria. Score each cell from 1 to 10, sum the columns for each asset, and average the sum. Then rank the results by individual asset and by asset class (people, property, information, and business reputation).

Nonterrorism Violent Crime Asset Target Value Estimate

As stated above, terrorists use violence, but not all violent crimes involve terrorism. Violent crimes include planned and spontaneous murders, rapes, aircraft hijacking, child abuse, elder abuse, kidnapping, happy slapping, and police brutality.

Violent crimes are often committed by people with poor impulse control. Often these are people who have difficulty controlling their own lives and so attempt to control those around them. Often when such a person fails to maintain control, they resort to violence instead of just "moving on."

One example of such is David Pardo, who arrived at the front door of his former in-laws' home on Christmas Eve wearing a Santa suit. The door was opened by an 8-year-old girl whom he shot in the face. He then proceeded through the home, which was filled with about 25 holiday visitors and killed a total of 9 in the extended family including his former wife, both her parents, and others. He then used a custom-made incendiary device to set the home on fire, which burned to the ground. While the extent of Pardo's obsession is not common, it is not uncommon for many domestic partners to resort to violence when their lives go wrong.

Other queues to violent behavior include drunkenness, acute depression, schizophrenia, psychopathic personality, brain damage, flawed brain chemistry, genetic defects,[4] and criminals who use violence to control their victims during the execution of a crime, such as in the case of home-invasion robberies.*

Whatever the cause, almost all violent criminals use some judgment in committing their crimes. The lone exception is the rage-aholic, who may attack anyone nearby without concern for the consequences. Rage-aholics are typically highly mentally disturbed individuals, often paranoid schizophrenics who are very out of touch with reality at the time.[†]

But most violent criminals who are aware of their actions use certain criteria to determine if and when to conduct a violent attack. These include the following:

- Is there an available surveillance position to reconnoiter the target before finally selecting it?
- Is access identification required before entry? (No violent criminal wants to be identified, so any form of identification including cameras and ID checks are a strong deterrent to violent crimes.)
- Is forcible entry possible?
- Is there any sneak-path for entry and/or exit?
- Is the asset or subject vulnerable to direct physical attack or intimidation through the use of force?
- Can entry be made through social engineering? ("Hello, I accidentally damaged your car with mine. Could you open the door so that I can give you my insurance information?")
- What is the probability of success of the physical attack? (Is the victim likely to be overwhelmed by force, or am I about to attack Chuck Norris?)
- What is the probability of escape? (Yes, I may be able to strike down the elderly woman to get her purse, but what about the 50 people at the festival who would see me do that?)

To use the Violent Crime Asset Target Value Model, create a spreadsheet with rows on the left identifying the facility and its key assets. Then create columns above for each of the targeting criteria. Score each cell from 1 to 10, sum the columns for each asset, and average the sum. Then rank the results by individual asset and by asset class (people, property, information, and business reputation).

Petty Crimes Asset Target Value Estimate

For some facilities, particularly those hosting masses of the public such as hotels, convention centers, retail malls, and the like, petty crimes are a constant concern. Even for

---

* http://www.popcenter.org/problems/pdfs/home_invasion_robbery.pdf.
† http://www.schizophrenia.com/New/Dec2002/violenceDec02.htm.

facilities such as factories and distribution centers, a constant stream of vandalism and graffiti can be a deterrent to good business.

For such facilities, it is useful to consider Petty Crimes Asset Target Value. Criteria may change from one type of facility to another, so the Asset Target Value Matrix will not be constant. For example, hotels tend to attract prostitution and pimps, while retail malls may have a problem with pickpockets and purse snatchers.

The risk analyst should develop an Asset Target Value Matrix that focuses on the type of petty criminal the facility will confront.

SUMMARY

$$Risk = Probability * Vulnerability * Consequence), \ or$$

$$Risk = (Probability + Vulnerability + Consequence) / 3$$

(This calculation works equally well by summing the three variables and averaging the result.)

Likelihood

While the existence of a threat actor is presumed (no threat actor = no threat action), and vulnerability can be estimated from data at hand, it is probability, or likelihood, that is virtually impossible to estimate for terrorism acts.

However, for criminal acts, the picture is different. In most communities, data are available from reliable sources to help the risk analyst estimate violent and nonviolent crimes including felonies and misdemeanors.

- Terrorist threat actors
  - Terrorists fall into five classes:
    - Class I terrorist: the government-trained professional (including foreign intelligence threats)
    - Class II terrorist: the religious extremist professional
    - Class III terrorist: the radical revolutionary or quasi-religious extremist
    - Class IV terrorist: guerrilla/mercenary soldier
    - Class V terrorist: amateur (civilian, untrained criminal, or militia/vigilante)
  - The risk analyst should constantly maintain familiarization with all classes of terrorist threats within his/her area of operation. The risk analyst should have knowledge of agendas, size, potency, preferred weaponry, methods, and tactics beforehand. It is especially important to understand the agenda and preferred targets of each type of terrorist organization operating in his/her area of consulting operations.
- Criminal threat actors
  - Economic criminals: Like terrorists, There are many types of economic criminal, including

- Transnational criminal organizations
- Organized crime
- Sophisticated economic criminals
- Unsophisticated economic criminals, also known as opportunistic criminals: use little planning
- Information technology (IT) criminals
- Nonterrorist violent criminals
- Petty criminals

Terrorism Asset Target Value Estimates

Two usable asset target value estimating tools for terrorism are CARVER+Shock and the KSM Asset Target Value Model. The latter asks the following:

- Does the target fit the strategic objectives of Al-Qaeda?
- Are mass casualties possible?
- Can the attack generate prolonged media coverage, especially of the attack itself?
- Is the target of economic importance?
- Is the target of cultural importance to the constituent community of the victim or the constituent community of Al-Qaeda or both?
- Is the target highly vulnerable to attack?
- What is the probability of success of the attack?
- Does this attack benefit recruiting and fund-raising for Al-Qaeda?

Criminal Incident Likelihood Estimates

There are two main sources for criminal criteria estimates: criminal statistics and asset target value estimates.

Criminal Statistics

The best source is actual criminal statistics, which should be used whenever available. Criminal statistics should include records that go back at least 5 years and should cover the following types of crimes:

- Major crimes
  - Murders
  - Rapes
  - Assaults
  - Major economic crimes
- Minor offenses
  - Vehicle crimes
  - Misdemeanor crimes

Failing availability of crime statistics from local authorities that are complete, organized, and reliable, in many areas analysts can turn to private sources such as CAP Index, Inc.

Alternatively, in the absence of usable data, an analyst can use an asset target value estimate, similar to that used for terrorism.

Economic Crime Asset Target Value Estimate

The elements for economic crime asset target value estimates include the following:

- Is there an opportunity for economic gain?
- What is the probability of success?
- What is the probability of escape?
- What is the probability of escape without subsequent capture?

Nonterrorism Violent Crime Asset Target Value Estimate

Violent criminals who are aware of their actions use certain criteria to determine if and when to conduct a violent attack. These include:

- Is there an available surveillance position to reconnoiter the target before finally selecting it?
- Is access identification required before entry? (No violent criminal wants to be identified so any form of identification including cameras and ID checks are a strong deterrent to violent crimes.)
- Is forcible entry possible?
- Is there any sneak-path for entry and/or exit?
- Is the asset or subject vulnerable to direct physical attack or intimidation through the use of force?
- Can entry be made through social engineering? ("Hello, I accidentally damaged your car with mine. Could you open the door so that I can give you my insurance information?")
- What is the probability of success of the physical attack? (Is the victim likely to be overwhelmed by force, or am I about to attack Chuck Norris?)
- What is the probability of escape? (Yes, I may be able to strike down the elderly woman to get her purse, but what about the 50 people at the festival who would see me do that?)

Petty Crimes Asset Target Value Estimate

For some facilities, particularly those hosting masses of the public such as hotels, convention centers, retail malls, and the like, petty crimes are a constant concern. Even for facilities such as factories and distribution centers, a constant stream of vandalism and graffiti can be a deterrent to good business.

For such facilities, it is useful to consider petty crimes asset target value. Criteria may change from one type of facility to another, so the Asset Target Value Matrix will not be constant. For example, hotels tend to attract prostitution and pimps, while retail malls may have a problem with pickpockets and purse snatchers.

The risk analyst should develop an Asset Target Value Matrix that focuses on the type of petty criminal the facility will confront.

REFERENCES

1. Nance, M. W. 2008. Who they are: Identifying terrorist operatives. In *Terrorist Recognition Handbook*, 2nd edn. CRC Press, Boca Raton.
2. Mannes, A. 2006. Black September: How terrorism got its start. *National Review Online*, September 11.

3. Brooke, J. 1990. Attacks in Peru drive out foreigners. *The New York Times*, January 15.
4. Bernstein, M.; American Chemical Society. 2003. Possible causes of violent behavior explored in C&EN article. *Research News: Medical News*, June 3.

Q&A

Questions

Q1: The basic risk formula is
  A. Risk = Probability * Vulnerability * Consequences.
  B. (Risk = Probability + Vulnerability + Consequences)/3.
  C. Both of the above are correct.
  D. None of the above are correct.

Q2: In most communities, data are available from reliable sources to help the risk analyst estimate
  A. Violent crimes.
  B. Violent and nonviolent crimes including felonies and misdemeanors.
  C. Nonviolent crimes.
  D. Felonies and misdemeanors.

Q3: We can use _____ to determine the likelihood of a criminal attack:
  A. Statistical evaluations of orders of magnitudes
  B. Statistical data
  C. Statistical empericalism
  D. None of the above

Q4: The continued existence of terrorist groups with targeting agendas that include
  A. Organizations that fit the description of yours infers that the organization you are serving could be a target.
  B. Child care centers.
  C. Restaurants.
  D. None of the above.

Q5: The risk analyst should constantly maintain familiarization with all classes of terrorist threats
  A. In Detroit.
  B. Everywhere in the world.
  C. Within his/her area of operation.
  D. None of the above.

Q6: The KSM Asset Target Value Model includes:
  A. Does the target fit the strategic objectives?
  B. Are mass casualties possible?
  C. Can the attack generate prolonged media coverage?
  D. All of the above.

Q7: The best source for estimating the probability of criminal acts is
   A. Actual police records for the area in question.
   B. CAP Index.
   C. Both A and B.
   D. None of the above.

Q8: Asset target value charts can be prepared for
   A. Potential acts of terrorism.
   B. Economic criminals.
   C. Violent and petty criminals.
   D. All of the above.

Q9: Violent crimes are often committed by people
   A. Just like you and me.
   B. With poor impulse control.
   C. Who feel bad.
   D. None of the above.

Q10: Terrorist organizations are surprisingly open about their targeting preferences,
   A. But a risk analyst must interpret these public statements into strategic criteria.
   B. But this is generally useless for predicting attacks.
   C. Both of the above.
   D. Neither of the above.

Answers

Q1 – C, Q2 – B, Q3 – B, Q4 – A, Q5 – C, Q6 – D, Q7 – C, Q8 – D, Q9 – B, Q10 – A

CHAPTER 10

Risk Analysis Process

INTRODUCTION

As we have seen in Chapter 2, the US Department of Homeland Security (DHS)-approved risk assessment methodologies vary substantially in the formulas used. The two most complete methodologies are the NIST 780 methodology and the Sandia methodologies.

However, all of the better DHS-approved methodologies have two things in common:

- They all use the elements of probability, vulnerability, and consequence.
- They all result in comparatively similar findings, even considering the differences in the formulas and approaches.

The key to approval by the DHS appears to be that the ranking of risks should be similar, not that the formulas result in exactly the same numbers. *It seems to be that it is the mathematical relationship, not the mathematical result, that is important.*

This is also illustrated by the fact that the NIST 780 methodology can be interpreted in a table, rather than in a formula, where the table ranks its findings by position in the table (no actual mathematical result at all). And in the end, the objective is all about providing the evidence for countermeasure selection decisions. Thus, it is the ranking rather than the formula that matters.

Don't get me wrong. In a perfect world, I would rather have a team of Sandia engineers performing every risk analysis. I have enormous respect for the model and the approach. But for most commercial, governmental, industrial, and critical infrastructure projects, the cost of the Sandia-style analysis with its abundant team of subject matter experts is not bearable for the project. For most organizations, a competent risk analyst or small team of experts can achieve the same general results at completely affordable costs using either the Sandia formula or the NIST 780 model.

So let us begin to look at how to achieve those results using a simple spreadsheet program. Remember, these results can also be achieved using a commercial program such as SVA-Pro.

OBJECTIVE

Remember, the actual formulas used do not matter as long as the relationships of the variables remain the same. We can substitute the Sandia formula and the various versions of NIST 780 formulas for the same risk values and the risk relationship always remains the same (Table 10.1).

TABLE 10.1   Comparison of Sandia and American Petroleum
Institute/National Petrochemical and Refiners Association
(API/NPRA) Formulas (0 to 1)

Risk	Probability	Vulnerability	Consequence
Sandia $R = P * (1-V) * C$		$(1-V)$	
0.42	1	0.6	0.7
0.25	0.7	0.6	0.6
0.08	0.5	0.4	0.4
0.04	0.4	0.3	0.3
API/NPRA			
Using $R = P*V*C$			
0.49	1	0.7	0.7
0.25	0.7	0.6	0.6
0.08	0.5	0.4	0.4
0.04	0.4	0.3	0.3
Using $R = (P+V+C)/3$			
0.80	1	0.7	0.7
0.63	0.7	0.6	0.6
0.43	0.5	0.4	0.4
0.33	0.4	0.3	0.3

Examples

Further, except for the Sandia model, which must use component numbers between 0 and 1, with NIST 780 and other similar models, we can use any component numbers such as 0–1, 0–10, 0–100, or 0–1,000,000, and the risk relationship will always remain the same. Also, note that the Sandia model uses $(1-V)$ instead of V because the component numbers are fractions of 1 and using three variables with fractions of 1 will result in inverse relationships. (Risk would appear to reduce as vulnerability goes up.) For NIST 780, all assumed formulas use 1–5, 1–10, and so on. If one were to use 0–1 for NIST 780, then one would also have to use $(1-V)$ instead of V in the formula (Tables 10.2 through 10.4).

All of the examples above result in relatively similar risk rankings. Though the actual risk results may vary slightly, the relationships always remain the same.

The balance of this book will use the NIST 780 methodology formulas for simplicity. It could be confusing to compare Sandia and NIST 780 throughout the rest of the book. However, rest assured, the principles taught herein work equally well using both formulas and in fact, work equally well using any methodology that combines probability, vulnerability, and consequence to comprise risk, as do all of the DHS-approved methodologies. Any approach that does not use probability, vulnerability, and consequence does not result in a valid risk result.

Displaying Risk Formula Results

In the NIST 780 methodology, the formula is expressed as a matrix of Probability and Vulnerability (two dimensions), then ranked later by Consequences. I always thought that

TABLE 10.2   Comparison of Sandia and NIST-780
Formulas Using 0 to 10 Component Numbers

Risk	Probability	Vulnerability	Consequence
Sandia R = P * (1 − V) * C		(1 − V)	
0.42	1	0.6	0.7
0.25	0.7	0.6	0.6
0.08	0.5	0.4	0.4
0.04	0.4	0.3	0.3
API/NPRA			
*Using R = P * V * C*			
490	10	7	7
252	7	6	6
80	5	4	4
36	4	3	3
Using R = (P + V + C)/3			
8.00	10	7	7
6.33	7	6	6
4.33	5	4	4
3.33	4	3	3

TABLE 10.3   Comparison of Sandia and NIST-780
Formulas Using 0 to 100 Component Numbers

Risk	Probability	Vulnerability	Consequence
Sandia R = P * (1 − V) * C		(1 − V)	
0.42	1	0.6	0.7
0.25	0.7	0.6	0.6
0.08	0.5	0.4	0.4
0.04	0.4	0.3	0.3
API/NPRA			
*Using R = P * V * C*			
490000	100	70	70
252000	70	60	60
80000	50	40	40
36000	40	30	30
Using R = (P + V + C)/3			
80.00	100	70	70
63.33	70	60	60
43.33	50	40	40
33.33	40	30	30

TABLE 10.4   Comparison of Sandia and NIST-780 Formulas
Using Different Component Numbers (0 to 1)

Risk	Probability	Vulnerability	Consequence
Sandia R = P * (1 − V) * C		(1 − V)	
0.30	1	0.6	0.5
0.35	1	0.7	0.5
0.40	1	0.8	0.5
0.45	1	0.9	0.5
API/NPRA			
*Using R = P * V * C*			
0.30	1	0.6	0.5
0.35	1	0.7	0.5
0.40	1	0.8	0.5
0.45	1	0.9	0.5
Using R = (P + V + C)/3			
0.70	1	0.6	0.5
0.73	1	0.7	0.5
0.77	1	0.8	0.5
0.80	1	0.9	0.5

Facility Name			
	Asset target value (probability)		
Vulnerability	**High**	**Medium**	**Low**
High	***Most consequence assets are shown in bold/italics*** *Medium consequence assets shown in italics* Least consequence assets are shown normally	Medium ATV and high vulnerability	Low ATV and high vulnerability
Medium	High ATV and medium vulnerability	Medium ATV and medium vulnerability	Low ATV and medium vulnerability
Low	High ATV and low vulnerability	Medium ATV and low vulnerability	Low ATV and low vulnerability

FIGURE 10.1   V² Summary Matrix.

was a bit abstract, so I developed a method to express all three dimensions in one spreadsheet. I do this by showing consequence in three levels with different text: **Bold** = High, *Italics* = Medium, and Standard Text = Low (Figure 10.1).

The spreadsheets taught in this book are capable of illustrating all three dimensions. Alternatively, these can be reduced using any of the formulas above and illustrated as a list or as an array.

COMPLETE RISK ANALYSIS PROCESS

So far, we have compared the best risk analysis methodologies and found that their results are comparable. NIST 780 provides wide latitude in how risk is calculated and always results in comparable results. As such, I typically utilize the NIST 780 methodology for most risk analysis projects and it fits the needs of most DHS-sponsored projects (except for those few where a specific approach is dictated by DHS, such as Chemical Facility Anti-Terrorism Standards [CFATS], for chemical industry sites). The steps shown herein meet or exceed all risk analysis methodologies except for the full Sandia subject matter expert team approach, which is too excessive in its depth for most commercial applications.

The results that we will achieve include

- Step-by-step spreadsheet process to risk results.
- The results can be expressed either in numbers or graphically.
- Prioritization of risk results will be illustrated in Chapter 11.

Let us now review the resources we have assembled and how they contribute to the risk analysis calculation. Each of these has an important role in the overall risk calculation.

We begin by evaluating the complete list of major assets, their criticalities to the operation of the organization, and the consequences of the loss of those assets for the sustainability of the organization. We then determine what type of threat actors constitute a threat to the facility in question. Then we review probability (the aspects of the facility that make it a likely target for the different threat actors). Then we review the facility's vulnerability (the aspects of the facility that could be exploited by a threat actor). Next, we review risk, using a formula that includes probability, vulnerability, and consequences, keeping in mind that although certain threat scenarios may have a high probability but low consequence, and thus represent a low risk to the organization, other threat scenarios may present a low probability but a very high consequence, and thus a higher risk. Finally, we prioritize, or rank, risk by consequences. Risk only occurs if an action has consequences; the more significant the consequences, the greater the risk.

Probability (Likelihood) Factors

- Threat considerations
  - Terrorist organization targeteering[*]
  - Adversary/Means Matrix[†]
- Asset target value considerations
  - Crime statistics[‡]
  - CAP Index report[§]

---

[*] Identifies which terrorist organizations are operating in the region of the facility and whether or not they have shown any interest in this type of facility.

[†] Illustrates potential threat actors (for terrorism) and their relative capabilities.

[‡] Crime statistics and CAP Index reports provide ratings for the address only, not for individual assets at the address.

[§] See footnote ‡.

- • CARVER+Shock Matrix*
- • Khalid Sheikh Mohammed (KSM) Asset Target Value for Terrorism Matrix†
- • Circulation Path/Threat Nexus Matrix‡
- • Circulation Path/Weapons Nexus Matrix§
- • Economic Crimes Matrix¶
- • Violent Crimes Matrix**
- • Petty Crimes Matrix††
- • Exploitable vulnerabilities at the target

Vulnerability Factors

- • Asset/Attack Matrix‡‡
- • Circulation Path/Threat Nexus Matrix§§
- • Circulation Path/Weapons Nexus Matrix¶¶
- • Attack path analysis***
- • Surveillance Matrix†††
- • Vulnerability Matrix‡‡‡

Consequence Factors

- • Criticality and Consequence Matrix§§§

RISK ANALYSIS PROCESS

Let us go back to the basic risk formula. Remember that of the various forms of valid risk formulas, the simplest form of the formula is

$$R = (P + V + C) / 3, \text{ or}$$

$$\text{Risk} = (\text{Probability} + \text{Vulnerability} + \text{Consequences}) / 3$$

---

* Basic terrorism calculation.
† Advanced terrorism calculation.
‡ Determines where threat actors and high-value individuals may encounter each other.
§ Determines what types of weapons can be used at the locations where threat actors and high-value individuals could encounter each other.
¶ Determines the attractiveness of various assets/locations for different types of economic crime threat actors.
** Determines the attractiveness of various assets/locations for different types of violent criminals.
†† Determines the attractiveness of various assets/locations for different types of petty criminals.
‡‡ Determines which assets are most susceptible to various attack scenarios.
§§ Determines where threat actors and high-value individuals may encounter each other.
¶¶ Determines what types of weapons can be used at the locations where threat actors and high-value individuals could encounter each other.
*** Determines the path(s) that potential attackers might take and analyzes the protective system's ability to deal with the attack. Also guides the analyst to what types of countermeasures might be required to cope with an attack along the path.
††† Determines which assets are most susceptible to various surveillance methods.
‡‡‡ Determines overall vulnerability (including existing countermeasures).
§§§ Illustrates criticality and consequences for ranking.

In ISO 31000, it is

$$R = (L * C) \text{ or } R = (L + C) / 2$$

Let us see how we can build up the components to obtain the result.

Probability Factors

Probability comprises a capable threat actor combined with the intent to attack a facility under question. So the first element of risk is threat identification. As there are multiple types of threat actors, the first step is to consider the design basis threat (that threat against which the security program is designed to defend).

The most serious threat actors are terrorists. Of the five kinds of terrorists, not all are likely to be interested in the facility in question. So the first question is what group of terrorists might be interested in targeting the facility in question? This information can be derived from terrorist organization targeteering histories. Targeteering involves two main factors:

- The area of operations (AO) of the terrorist organization
- The characteristics of the facility vis-à-vis the agenda of the terrorist organization

AO Information

Few terrorist organizations operate worldwide. Most have a primary or active AO. For each region of the planet, the AO will be different. This may change from time to time. The best organizations for information as to which terrorist organizations are operating in the region of the facility in question include

- Jane's World Insurgency and Terrorism Service
- The Nine Eleven Finding Answers (NEFA) Foundation
- Terrorism Center for Defense Information
- Raman's Terrorism Analysis
- The U.S. Diplomatic Security Service of the Department of State (US-DOS-DSS)
- British Foreign and Commonwealth Office (FCO)

Targeteering Information

Targeteering is the preference of a type of target and attack scenario by a terrorist organization or threat actor. This information is more complex and may be somewhat difficult to discern compared to simple AO information. In general, though, for larger and more active terrorist organizations where there is a history of strikes against targets, much may be written on the types of facilities struck by the organization. For less active and newer terrorist groups, little may be available. One should also be concerned about emerging terrorist threat actors who have not acted yet. These are the most difficult to get information on due to their lack of action. Targeteering information is rarely discussed in news articles and official reports. One may not be able to find precise targeteering information (as such) about a specific terrorist organization in any public report. However, targeteering information on existing active terrorist organizations can be derived from past attacks.

Terrorist Group Attack Scenarios

Each terrorist organization has its own preferred attack scenarios. While some such as Abu Sayaf (Philippines) may prefer kidnappings, others such as Islamic Jihad (Gaza) may prefer suicide bombings. It is important to note that while a specific type of attack scenario may not ever have been used in a specific geographic region, that attack scenario may have been used by that organization in other regions. In such cases, the risk analyst would be well advised to include the attack scenario in the list of possible attack scenarios for the region where it has not ever been used. Additionally, terrorist organizations often work together to develop skills and resources. For example, Al-Qaeda have worked with both the Taliban and Lashkar-e-Taiba (LeT) in Pakistan to develop and enhance the sophistication of their attack scenarios. So while neither of these organizations had used coordinated attacks and suicide bombers previously, the use of these tactics could be predicted as news reports of the alliance of these groups spread in advance of the use of these tactics. Finally, it is also useful to scan terrorism news blogs such as NEFA and the Investigative Project on Terrorism daily to note the emergence of new terrorist groups and their agendas, which can imply targeteering information.

The other types of threat actors include

- Economic criminals
- Violent criminals
- Subversives
- Petty criminals

For each of these threat actors, probability can be determined either from historical data (crime statistics, etc.) or from asset target value. Asset target value is the estimation of the degree of compliance with the factors that make an asset interesting to a particular type of threat actor.

For all classes of criminal threat actors, an Asset Target Value Matrix has been developed and is discussed in this chapter. Asset target value can also be applied to terrorists using the KSM Asset Target Value Model and, to a lesser extent, the CARVER+Shock Asset Target Value Model.

The point of crime statistics is crime forecasting. We study the undesirable results of history in order to avoid them in the future. We avoid them by moving "off the railroad tracks" of the freight train that will come again on the same track. By studying how the train has come in the past, we can hear its sound, feel the vibration of the tracks, and move away from its path. When it comes to crime, history does repeat itself. Criminals of a type target again and again in certain predictable ways.

Historical data can be assembled using either crime statistics or CAP Index reports. Crime statistics can be obtained from local law enforcement with varying results. Some jurisdictions keep very meticulous records and segment that information into data that can allow for highly refined searches. Other jurisdictions provide data that some would say is designed to confound any analyst. If the data cannot be combined into searches such as facility types, locations, and types of crimes, then it is of little practical use.

CAP Index Inc.® is a crime statistic product available on the Internet that offers graphically oriented data in a uniform fashion. This is a very useful product, especially when available local law enforcement data is not so useful. CAP Index is available at www.CAPIndex.com.

DIAGRAM ANALYSIS

- Adversary sequence diagrams (ASD) and path analysis identify the pathways from perimeter to target that potential attackers must follow on their way to the target asset. These help to identify the locations within the facility that should be studied for vulnerabilities and where aggressors can be detected, assessed, and delayed.
- The Circulation Path/Threat Nexus Matrix identifies the locations within a facility where high-value individuals might encounter potential threat actors.
- The Circulation Path/Weapons Nexus Matrix identifies the types of weapons that could be used in the locations where threat actors might encounter high-value individuals.
- Circulation path/threat nexus and circulation path/weapons nexus analysis can be performed either graphically using diagrams or as a matrix. To perform these graphically, one will evaluate drawings and diagram the pathways taken by both high-value individuals and potential threat actors. To define these in a matrix, one must create a matrix that shows nexus points as rows and both high-value individuals and other classes of individuals (for the Threat Nexus Matrix) or one that shows nexus points as rows and types of weapons as columns (for the Weapons Nexus Matrix). Then one places an X at each cross point where high-value individuals might be found and where other types of individuals might cross the path of the high-value individuals (for the Threat Nexus Matrix). For the Weapons Matrix, one would place an X at each nexus point for the type of weapon that could be used at that location. This identifies not only where VIPs might encounter potential threat actors, but also what type of weapon might be used at that location.

ASSET TARGET VALUE MATRIXES

When historical data useful for statistics are not available, probability can be estimated from Asset Target Value Matrixes. Asset target value analysis lends itself well to quantitative analysis.

Additionally, and perhaps more importantly, Asset Target Value Analysis lends itself extremely well to quantitative analysis, while diagrammatic processes and targeteering do not. Accordingly, I use diagrammatic processes, crime statistics, CAP Index and targeteering information as precursor studies preliminary to performing asset target value studies. Together, these methods comprise a much more thorough approach to estimating probability.

One should use a separate Asset Target Value Matrix for each type of threat actor within the design basis threat. I know analysts who only analyze for terrorist threats or only for terrorism and a few economic threats. However, no security program can be successful that only deals with terrorism or major economic crime. The security program director will have to cope with a wide range of criminal and subversive activity on the facility and so the risk analyst should help the program director by preparing a risk profile for all types of threat actors including all types of anticipated criminal activity. Many people misperceive the design basis threat as only the *worst* threat that the security program must counter, but no security program can be effective if it is not prepared to

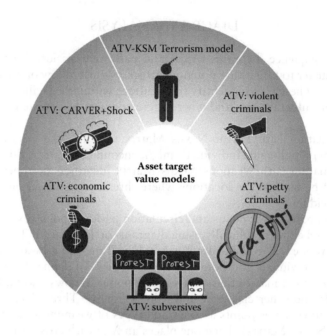

FIGURE 10.2 Typical asset target value categories.

counter every type of threat actor it will face. In fact the design basis threat is a range of threats up to and including the *worst* threat that the security program must counter and not only that threat, as some ill-informed risk analysts seem to believe.

For each Asset Target Value Matrix, the analyst should prepare a spreadsheet matrix that includes all of the assets and security nexus points categorized by logical groupings as rows and the asset target value characteristics as columns. The rightmost two columns should be a score and ranking, as shown in Figure 10.2. The asset target value categories for each of the various types of matrixes are as follows:

- CARVER+Shock Matrix
  - Criticality
  - Accessibility
  - Recuperability
  - Vulnerability
  - Effect
  - Recognizability
  - Shock
- KSM Asset Target Value for Terrorism Matrix
  - Fits the strategic objective of the terrorist organization
  - Mass casualties possible
  - Media event possible
  - Target is of economic importance
  - Target is culturally important
  - Vulnerability
  - Probability of success
  - Success on target has recruiting and fund-raising value

- Economic crimes matrix
  - Economic gain possible
  - Probability of success
  - Probability of escape
  - Escape without subsequent discovery
- Violent Crimes Matrix
  - Surveillance possible
  - Access identification required
  - Forcible access is possible
  - Sneak-path access is possible
  - Target is vulnerable to physical attack
  - Vulnerable to social engineering
  - Probability of success
  - Probability of escape
- Subversives and Petty Crimes Matrix
  - Useful environment for exploitation
  - Can establish temporary domain over environment
  - Can go largely unnoticed
  - Minimum resources applied to resolving my crimes
  - Acceptable penalties for discovery

PROBABILITY SUMMARY MATRIX

The results of all of the individual Asset Target Value Matrixes should be summarized together in a *Probability Summary Matrix*. This matrix, like most others, should list all assets (targets and public and VIP/threat actor nexus points) as rows and the scores of all the asset target value matrixes as columns. The Probability Summary Matrix will include columns for the final scores from the following Probability Matrixes, including

- CARVER+Shock Matrix
- KSM Asset Target Value for Terrorism Matrix
- Economic Crimes Asset Target Value Matrix
- Violent Crimes Asset Target Value Matrix
- Subversives and Petty Crimes Asset Target Value Matrix

For example, the result cells (Scores) of the CARVER+Shock Matrix should reference the Probability Summary Matrix CARVER+Shock column. The result cells (scores) of the KSM Asset Target Value for Terrorism Matrix should reference the Probability Summary Matrix, and so on, until the results of all of the constituent probability matrixes are represented into the Probability Summary Matrix. A sample of a Probability Summary Matrix is shown in Figure 10.3.

VULNERABILITY COMPONENTS

It saddens me to see risk analysts pull a vulnerability rating out of the air. This is done so often that most people in the industry think that is how it should be done. The truth is quite the opposite. Like everything else about risk, vulnerability is a

Mega towers					
Probability worksheet					
Targets	Criminal threats	Terrorism threats	Score	Rank	
People	7	6	7	1	
VIP executives and VIP visitors	6	7	6	10	
Employees	8	9	8	1	
Contractors	8	5	6	9	
Visitors	8	6	7	6	
Delivery personnel	7	5	6	19	
Transportation personnel	7	5	6	19	
Property	5	5	5	4	
Site	5	5	5	28	
VIP drop-off	6	7	7	7	
Employee drop-off	7	8	8	2	
Visitor drop-off: hotel (south)	7	7	7	5	
Main south entry gatehouse area	7	6	6	14	
North perimeter fence	4	5	4	45	

FIGURE 10.3   Probability Summary Matrix.

composite of many elements. Unless one considers all those elements, one cannot estimate vulnerability.

Some of the elements for probability are also useful for considering vulnerability. This is not extraordinary, as this only presents a different point of view on the same subject. So even though these have been considered before under probability, they are worth considering again from a vulnerability standpoint. The core elements include

- Aspects to consider while reviewing vulnerability
  - What kinds of attacks are the assets vulnerable to?
  - Where on the facility could high-value individuals come into contact with potential threat actors?
  - What kinds of weapons could be used in areas where high-value individuals might interact with potential threat actors?
  - What paths would adversaries have to take to reach the assets of the facility from outside its perimeter?
- Vulnerability components
  - What surveillance opportunities exist for each asset?
  - Finally, we roll up all these and other factors when considering all of the constituent elements of vulnerability including
    - Accessibility
    - Surveillance (from above)
    - Intrinsic vulnerability
    - Natural countermeasures

    – Physical countermeasures
    – Electronic countermeasures
    – Operational countermeasures

Vulnerability Tools

- The Asset/Attack Matrix lists all of the facility assets and the same threat scenarios that were considered under the Adversary/Means Matrix. While the Adversary/Means Matrix provides insight into what types of threat scenarios various threat actors may use, the Asset/Attack Matrix provides similar insight into what types of threat scenarios each asset is vulnerable to.
- The Circulation Path/Threat Nexus Matrix was used for probability considerations in order to determine the possibility of attacks against high-value individuals (VIPs) within a facility. Similarly, the same matrix gives insight into areas of vulnerability in the facility that would otherwise go unnoticed.
- The Circulation Path/Weapons Nexus Matrix was used for probability considerations in order to understand the types of weapons that might be used in areas where high-value individuals might encounter potential threat actors. The other side of that coin is the vulnerability that such an encounter would present. It is important to consider not only what assets are at risk in a facility, but where and to what threat scenarios.
- ASD analysis illustrates the pathways that threat actors must take from the property perimeter to reach an asset. This gives insight not only into probability, but also into vulnerabilities that must be addressed along those pathways. The ASD is also useful when considering potential countermeasures that can be used to detect, assess, and delay threat actors.

    Not all of the above elements are direct contributors to the vulnerability calculation, but are preparatory to the quantitative calculations. The next two elements are used to perform quantitative analysis.
- Surveillance is a basic element of vulnerability. Surveillance is a prerequisite of all threat actions by all threat actors. No security program can be effective that does not fully consider surveillance in its risk and countermeasure elements. Yet, I rarely find surveillance being given serious consideration. I have reviewed countless countermeasure programs that never mention surveillance at all. An understanding of surveillance is especially important for terrorist act prevention. The Surveillance Matrix lists the assets by category from previous matrixes and the various elements of surveillance in columns, including

    - Fixed visual surveillance opportunities
    - Off-site mobile visual surveillance opportunities
    - Acoustic eavesdropping opportunities
    - Electronic surveillance opportunities
    - IT system surveillance opportunities
    - Opportunities for interception of documents and information

- The Vulnerability Matrix combines the results of the Surveillance Matrix with the other factors listed above to create a composite picture of overall target (asset) vulnerability. The results of this matrix are also used in the

CARVER+Shock Matrix, the KSM Asset Target Value for Terrorism Events Matrix, and the Risk Summary Matrix. This is done by referencing the Vulnerability cells of those matrixes to the comparable Score cell of the Vulnerability Matrix. In this fashion, the vulnerability data is computed automatically into the other matrixes.

Consequence Components

The three legs of risk are probability, vulnerability, and consequences; but often consequences are not fully studied. There are several dimensions to consequences, as there are to other factors we have studied. The consequence factors are estimated using the Criticality and Consequence Matrix, the factors of which are as follows:

- Criticality to business operations: How critical is the asset in question to the mission of the organization? Is the asset truly critical, or does it serve a supporting role that could be replaced in part or in whole by other resources? Score 1–10, 10 being absolutely critical such that the mission could not be carried out without the presence of this asset.
- Casualties: Could an attack result in casualties? If so, how severe could casualties be? Would it result in mass casualties or perhaps just a single injury? Score for severity 1–10, 10 being large numbers of mass casualties, and 1 being a single injury.
- Loss of property: Could property be lost in an attack on this asset? If so, how severe could that be? Would the severity be as much as the loss of an entire campus (such as the attack on the World Trade Center in 2001) or just on a single asset such as a computer workstation? Score for severity 1–10, 10 being the loss of many buildings or much property of very high value.
- Loss of production: Could an attack result in loss of production or loss of support operations to the mission of the organization? If so, how severe could that loss be? Score 1–10, 10 being worst such as total unrecoverable loss of operations resulting in the permanent collapse of the organization, and 1 being very minor disruption for a short period of time such as a few days.
- Loss of proprietary information: Could an attack result in the loss of proprietary information? If so, how severe could that loss be? Score 1–10, 10 being worst such as total exposure of mission critical information such as strategic product development that would permit competitors to gain a significant advantage.
- Loss of business reputation: Could an attack result in loss or exposure of highly sensitive information, which if released out of context could result in unrecoverable loss of business reputation (such as the complete private financial data of all customers of a financial institution), or in other ways damage the good business reputation of an organization? Score 1–10, 10 being worst.

Risk Formulas

Risk calculation is a two-step process. The basic formula combines probability, vulnerability, and consequences to determine unranked risk. That is, it is possible to have an asset for which probable events are highly likely and which is relatively highly vulnerable, but for which the consequences are quite low. This could score highly on risk and yield a possible misrepresentation of overall risk.

To mitigate this result, use a second step, which ranks the final risk results by order of consequences. This assures that the final risk rankings are relevant to the consequences so that budgets for countermeasures are allocated by consequences rather than by probability or vulnerability. There are other methods that may be appropriate for certain projects, discussed in Chapter 11.

Risk Results (Unranked)

Finally, we are at the risk calculation stage! The Risk Calculation Matrix follows the form of most previous matrixes. That is, all relevant assets (targets and VIP-public/threat actor nexus locations) are listed as rows and the columns will include the scores of three other matrixes:

- Vulnerability Matrix
- Probability Summary Matrix
- Consequences Matrix

To score the Unranked Risk Matrix, one can multiply probability by vulnerability by consequences to achieve a score, or one can use (Probability + Vulnerability + Consequences)/3 as a score. Both will yield roughly similar results. Regardless of which is used, the final ranking by consequences will generally ensure that they are all sorted correctly for countermeasure budget allocation.

It is often useful to create two unranked risk results models (one for terrorism and a separate one for criminal risks). These are combined for simplification of the illustrations in this book (Figure 10.4).

In the next chapter, we will look at how to rank the risk results for more meaningful evaluation and especially how to create the V^2 Matrixes, which will help illustrate risk to decision makers. The V^2 Matrixes are one of the most valuable tools in helping decision makers reach consensus on how to best budget to protect the organization.

SUMMARY

Introduction

The DHS-approved risk assessment methodologies vary substantially in the formulas used. The two most complete methodologies are the NIST 780 methodology and the Sandia methodologies (all of which use variations of the same formula).

The better DHS-approved methodologies have two things in common:

- They all use the elements of probability, vulnerability, and consequence.
- They all result in comparatively similar findings, even considering the differences in the formulas and approaches.

The key to DHS approval appears to be that the ranking of risks should be similar, not that the formulas result in exactly the same numbers. *It is the mathematical relationship, not the mathematical result, that is important.*

Mega towers					
Risk calculation worksheet (unsorted)					
Targets	*Probability*	*Vulnerability*	*Consequences*	*Score*	*Rank*
People	**7**	5	4	5	3
VIP executives and VIP visitors	6	4	4	5	24
Employees	8	7	6	7	2
Contractors	6	4	4	5	29
Visitors	7	6	5	6	12
Delivery personnel	6	4	2	4	39
Transportation personnel	6	4	2	4	39
Property	**5**	**6**	**3**	**5**	**4**
Site	*5*	*6*	*4*	*5*	*21*
Employee drop-off	8	8	7	8	1
VIP drop-off	7	6	5	6	10
Visitor drop-off: hotel (south)	7	9	5	7	4
Main south entry gatehouse area	6	8	3	6	9
North perimeter fence	4	4	3	4	46
East perimeter fence	4	4	3	4	43
South perimeter fence	4	4	3	4	43

FIGURE 10.4   Unranked risk results.

Displaying Risk Formula Results

In the NIST 780 methodology, the formula is expressed as a matrix of Probability and Vulnerability (two dimensions), then ranked later by Consequences. I always thought that was a bit abstract, so I developed a method to express all three dimensions in one spreadsheet. I do that by showing consequence in three levels with different text: **Bold = High**, *Italics = Medium*, and Standard Text = Low.

Complete Risk Analysis Process

The steps shown herein meet or exceed all risk analysis methodologies except for the deep Sandia model, which is too excessive in its depth for most commercial applications.
   The results that we will achieve include

- Step-by-step spreadsheet process to risk results.
- The results can be expressed either in numbers or graphically.
- Prioritization of risk results will be illustrated in Chapter 11.

   The steps are as follows:

- Review the resources we have assembled and how they contribute to the risk analysis calculation. Each of these has an important role in the overall risk calculation.

- Step through the calculation by first determining what type of threat actors constitute a threat to the facility in question.
- Review probability (the aspects of the facility that make it a likely target for the different threat actors).
- Review the facility's vulnerability (the aspects of the facility that could be exploited by a threat actor).
- Finally, review consequences. Risk only exists if there are consequences to the action and the more significant the consequences, the greater the risk. Risk should also be prioritized by consequences.

Probability Factors

- Threat considerations
  - Terrorist organization targeteering
  - Adversary/Means Matrix
- Asset target value considerations
  - Crime statistics
  - CAP Index report
  - CARVER+Shock Matrix
  - KSM Asset Target Value for Terrorism Matrix
  - Circulation Path/Threat Nexus Matrix
  - Circulation Path/Weapons Nexus Matrix
  - Economic Crimes Matrix
  - Violent Crimes Matrix
  - Petty Crimes Matrix

Vulnerability Factors

- Asset/Attack Matrix
- Circulation Path/Threat Nexus Matrix
- Circulation Path/Weapons Nexus Matrix
- Attack Path Analysis
- Surveillance Matrix
- Vulnerability Matrix

Consequence Factors

- Criticality and Consequence Matrix

Risk Formulas

Risk calculation is a two-step process. The basic formula combines probability, vulnerability, and consequences to determine unranked risk. That is, it is possible to have an asset for which probable events are highly likely and that is relatively highly vulnerable, but for which the consequences are quite low. This could score highly on risk and yield a possible misrepresentation of overall risk.

To mitigate this result, use a second step that ranks the final risk results by order of consequences. This assures that the final risk rankings are relevant to the consequences so that budgets for countermeasures are allocated by consequences rather than by probability or vulnerability.

Risk Results (Unranked)

Finally, we are at the risk calculation stage! The Risk Calculation Matrix follows the form of most previous matrixes. That is, all relevant assets (targets and VIP-public/threat actor nexus locations) are listed as rows and the columns will include the scores of three other matrixes:

- Vulnerability Matrix
- Probability Summary Matrix
- Consequences Matrix

To score the Unranked Risk Matrix, one can multiply probability by vulnerability by consequences to achieve a score, or one can use (Probability + Vulnerability + Consequences)/3 as a score. Both will yield roughly similar results. Regardless of which is used, the final ranking by consequences will generally assure that they are all sorted correctly for countermeasure budget allocation.

Q&A

Questions

Q1: All of the better DHS-approved methodologies have two things in common:
   A. They all use the elements of probability, vulnerability, and consequence and they all result in vastly different findings.
   B. They all use the elements of probability, vulnerability, and consequence and they all result in comparatively similar different findings.
   C. They all use the elements of surveillance, vulnerability, and consequence and they all result in comparatively similar different findings.
   D. None of the above.

Q2: The objective of the risk analysis process:
   A. In the end, the objective is all about providing a perfectly accurate risk assessment. Thus, it is the formula that matters.
   B. In the end, the objective is all about providing the evidence for countermeasure selection decisions. Thus, it is the ranking rather than the formula that matters.
   C. In the end, the objective is all about providing a perfectly accurate vulnerability assessment. Thus, it is the formula that matters.
   D. None of the above.

Q3: When comparing the Sandia risk analysis model with the NIST-780 model using a variety of different examples,
    A. One gets quite different results, which must be justified in the report.
    B. One gets exactly the same results.
    C. All of the examples above result in relatively similar risk rankings.
    D. None of the above.

Q4: Any risk analysis approach that does not use probability, vulnerability, and consequence
    A. Does not result in a valid risk result.
    B. Results in a valid risk result.
    C. May result in a valid risk result.
    D. None of the above.

Q5: To get a risk analysis project started,
    A. We begin by evaluating probability.
    B. We begin by evaluating the complete list of major assets, their criticalities to the operation of the organization, and the consequences of the loss of those assets for the sustainability of the organization.
    C. We begin by evaluating the likelihood of a terrorist attack on the facility.
    D. None of the above.

Q6: After that we should
    A. Determine what type of threat actors constitute a threat to the facility in question.
    B. Determine which type of threat actors are most likely to strike the facility.
    C. Determine if petty criminals will be a major problem to the facility.
    D. None of the above.

Q7: Then we should
    A. Review response capabilities.
    B. Review the level of force necessary to repel threat actors.
    C. Review probability (the aspects of the facility that make it a likely target for the different threat actors).
    D. All of the above.

Q8: Then we review
    A. Risk and consequences.
    B. Consequences.
    C. Risk.
    D. The facility's vulnerability (the aspects of the facility that could be exploited by a threat actor).

Q9: Then we review
    A. Risk using a formula that includes probability and vulnerability.
    B. Risk using a formula that includes vulnerability and threat.
    C. Risk using a formula that includes threat and probability.
    D. None of the above.

Q10: Finally, we prioritize or rank
   A. Risk by consequences.
   B. Risk by vulnerabilities.
   C. Risk by probability.
   D. All of the above.

Answers

Q1 – B, Q2 – B, Q3 – C, Q4 – A, Q5 – B, Q6 – A, Q7 –C, Q8 – D, Q9 – A, Q10 – A

CHAPTER 11

Prioritizing Risk

INTRODUCTION

Every organization must prioritize their security budgets. Determining exactly how to do this has caused security directors and managers and C-level executives more grief than almost anything else about security. Arguments ensue as different stakeholders jockey to forward their agendas. And agendas abound. Various departments have their own interests, and they often compete with security for the same budget.

First, let us understand that prioritization is all about developing a budget and determining the schedule for implementation. As we discuss this subject, let us remember our purpose; that is, that prioritization is the first step. The second step is getting budget commitment and scheduling the implementations. The first is a requirement for the second, and the second will not be successful without the first.

So two skills become paramount:

- Prioritizing risk
- Communicating priorities effectively to management to gain their support

In this chapter you will

- Learn five common ways to prioritize risk, including the best practices method, which is prioritization by consequences
- Learn how to formulate arguments to gain consensus on budget priorities

PRIORITIZATION CRITERIA

There are five potential ways of prioritizing risk. By request of colleagues, I am discussing all of these, but it is my opinion that the only correct way to prioritize risk is by sorting the fundamental risk analysis on consequences. The complete list of approaches includes

- Natural prioritization (prioritizing by formula)
- By probability
- By consequences
- By criticality
- By cost (not recommended)

NATURAL PRIORITIZATION (PRIORITIZING BY FORMULA)

Both the Sandia formula and the NIST 780 formula facilitate intrinsic prioritization. For Sandia, the formula is $Risk = Probability * (1 - Vulnerability) * Consequence$. For NIST 780, the formula is $Risk = Probability * Vulnerability * Consequence$, or $(Probability + Vul\text{-}nerability + Consequence)/3$.

All three of these formulas will result in perfectly actionable results all by themselves. However, this can sometimes result in items of very high vulnerability and very high probability but very low consequence rising to the top of the risk chart. The analyst can further prioritize the results in order to focus and guide the implementation process. And I have found that different organizations place a different emphasis on each element.

For example, a good security program is comprised of two main elements:

- A baseline security program (focused on day-to-day risks and reinforcing good behavior)
- Special countermeasures to address unique vulnerabilities (usually focused on terrorism or a criminal problem that may be unique to the area, industry, or facility)

The baseline security program is a comprehensive program of elements that deter, detect, delay, respond, and collect evidence, intended primarily to reduce the overall probability of occurrence. Such programs include a full complement of countermeasures, including hi-tech, low-tech, and no-tech countermeasures. These are woven into a comprehensive security program that addresses all of the day-to-day risks and known criminal risks (economic crime, violent crime, and petty crime). Similar to an organization's accounting effort, marketing program, or research and development program, the baseline security program should be developed to support the mission of the organization.

Special countermeasures are either focused on dealing with threats of terrorism or with criminal activity that is unique to the area, property, or industry. Certain industries, such as transport or depot firms, have known risks that are unique to their industry (transport: hijackings; depots: smuggling). And some areas or properties may have regional problems that are unique (vandalism, gang activity, remote dark parking lots, etc.). (Refer to the example of special countermeasures in Chapter 13.)

The extent of the baseline security program and of special countermeasures to address unique vulnerabilities may be driven by probability, consequences, criticalities, or cost.

PRIORITIZATION OF RISK

Often organizations place a different emphasis on prioritization, depending on their circumstances. For example, organizations that face little risk of terrorism but are located in a high-crime area often want their risk prioritized by probability, while critical infrastructure facilities should address risks by consequences.

The other two ways of prioritizing risk are by criticality and cost. These are not recommended because criticality is an incomplete and arguably poor surrogate for consequences, and cost should be examined after either probability or consequences prioritization has been addressed. Those organizations that address cost as a primary priority completely miss the point of the exercise. While a security program may be "boxed" into a budget, threat actors will not be. Therefore, the security program that is built to a budget as a first priority is doomed to fail at its inception.

Security programs that are prioritized by criticalities also miss the point. Criticalities and consequences do not necessarily go hand in hand. A program may be critical to the operation of the organization but may pose a small risk of consequences. For example, the accounting program (a very critical asset) is so easily backed up that although it is very high on the criticality list, its loss is almost certain not to occur. Thus, prioritizing countermeasures to further protect the information is a waste of money. However, a red-carpet area at an entertainment complex may be low in criticality, but the consequences of a suicide bomber making a political statement at a red-carpet event could have drastic consequences for the organization's business reputation.

Prioritizing by Probability

To prioritize risk by probability, one would first organize risk by formula and then sort the risks by probability. Using the spreadsheet model discussed herein, one would simply use the Probability column of the Risk Analysis Matrix to sort the entire array. This will result in a comprehensive listing of risk to targets, sorted by probability.

Prioritizing by Consequences

To prioritize risk by consequences, one would first organize risk by formula and then sort the risks by the ranking of consequences. Using the spreadsheet model discussed herein, one would simply use the consequences column of the Risk Analysis Matrix to sort the entire array. This will result in a comprehensive listing of risk to targets, sorted by consequences.

Prioritizing by Criticality

To prioritize risk by criticality, one would first organize risk by formula and then sort the risks by criticality. You can do this by creating a new spreadsheet using the raw risk analysis spreadsheet as a template and then adding a column for Criticality from the Criticality and Consequences Matrix. Then sort the whole array by criticality.

Prioritizing by Cost

There are two ways to prioritize by cost. One is simple and direct and the other is more scientific.

Simple Cost Prioritization

To prioritize by cost in a simple manner, one would develop risk by formula and then develop a list of security countermeasures. After budgeting the total list of countermeasures, one would consider cost reductions to a target number based on how those countermeasures relate to the highest risks. That is, for example, one might consider allocating an access control reader to an entire department rather than to individual doors in the department. Both approaches address the risk of unwanted visitors, but one does so at much lower cost.

Process-Driven Cost Prioritization

In the more process-driven approach to prioritizing the risk by cost, one would first organize the risk by formula and then add a column for vulnerabilities with a row under each risk for each threat scenario relating to each risk. For each vulnerability, develop a list of countermeasures that address the vulnerability. Countermeasures may include those that control access, detect, assess, delay, assist in response, or collect evidence. Each of these will have a cost associated with it and a rating for effectiveness. Chapters 18 and 19 explain the process of security effectiveness metrics and cost-effectiveness metrics usage.

COMMUNICATING PRIORITIES EFFECTIVELY

Making the Case

Virtually every organization faces financial challenges. Understanding that many program directors are vying for the same budget dollars, it is necessary for the security program manager to make a clear case for security program budget dollars.

I often say that accounting and security programs have much in common. They both are required to comply with codes and regulations and to limit the organization's exposure to risks (in one case financial risk and in the other, security risks).

But accounting organizations make a far better case for their needs and successes than do most security organizations. We can change that. The very process of developing a comprehensive risk analysis will go a long way toward making the case. Though many may read no more than the executive summary, it should include a summary paragraph of each section and graphics illustrating the risk summary. The proposed countermeasure budget should be based on a comprehensive solution with a caveat that it can be adjusted to accommodate implementation phasing.

Developing the Arguments

- Determine the priorities of management: This simple but often overlooked item is essential to targeting management's interests in budgeting arguments. Priorities can be determined from annual statements and memos issued by management to employees, and by directly asking executive management to outline their priorities for the next fiscal year in an e-mail. They will appreciate your interest.
- Identify the points of view of stakeholders and acknowledge them. In order for the security program to get its own share of the overall budget, you will have to contend with other organization stakeholders who have their own priorities and agendas. By understanding these, you can make the case for security program countermeasures in the context of all these other competing agendas. By preparing the argument in this context and acknowledging the points of view, all of which need executive management's attention, you are more likely to succeed than if the argument is made in the absence of this information. This helps executive management to place the security program in the context of the overall organization's needs. This is one of the most important elements of a successful presentation.

- Provide a list of consequences: The only reason to have a security program at all is to prevent the undesired consequences of not having a security program. This is what risk analysis is all about. By identifying all risks and consequences, executive management can develop the priorities of its budget. It is useful to create a comprehensive list of consequences and to ask executive management which of the consequences would be acceptable losses. This is not a rhetorical question, and it is not intended to provoke management. It is a logical question directly related to prioritizing budgets. Remember, all risks can be dealt with in one of several ways:
  - You can accept the loss.
  - You can duplicate the asset.
  - You can insure the asset.
  - You can protect the asset.

    Executive management needs to make these decisions about all assets, and this list gives them the tools to do so.
- Provide tiered countermeasure budgets versus solutions. Chapters 17, 18, and 19 (Chapter 17: Countermeasures Selection; Chapter 18: Budgeting Tools, Security Effectiveness Metrics; and Chapter 19: Cost-Effectiveness Metrics) will assist in preparing a workable tiered plan. The tiered plan should present achievable goals versus budgets and explain clearly what cannot be achieved (what risks will be accepted) for deferred budgets. Chapter 18: Security Effectiveness Metrics includes a spreadsheet tool (the Decision Matrix) that helps present what can and cannot be achieved with various budget options. Management needs to understand what risks they are accepting for budgets that they defer or program elements they decide not to budget.
- Let management draw their own conclusions.
- Use a Decision Matrix to help committees reach a consensus when there is no agreement on the choice of a particular approach. Chapter 17 explains and illustrates the use of the Decision Matrix.

BEST PRACTICES: RANKING RISK RESULTS

To achieve the final risk rankings, we simply copy the Unsorted Risk Summary Matrix and perform a sort on the Consequences column so that the results descend from the highest consequence targets to the lowest.

Now, finally we have truly meaningful results on which the allocation of countermeasures can be based. However, there is one more final step to complete the analysis. Let us make it ready for presentation to decision makers. Most decision makers have a basic understanding of risk. However, for a large facility, particularly a campus of buildings, a proper risk analysis can easily generate over 10,000 individual points of analysis (each cell on each matrix). This can be a mind-numbing amount of data to consider. Even the Ranked Risk Analysis Matrix for some projects I have completed has contained an astonishing 1,200+ points of analysis, and even a modest project can result in a Ranked Risk Analysis Matrix of over 300 points of analysis. This is just too much data for decision makers to process quickly. The result is all too often that poor decisions can result by decision makers deferring decisions until can fully consider the information or simply asking for a more readily digestible form of the data. That is what the V^2 Matrixes were designed to accomplish (Figure 11.1).

Mega towers						
Risk sorted worksheet						
Targets	*Probability*	*Vulnerability*	*Consequences*	*Score*	*Rank*	
People	7	5	4	5	3	
Employees	8	7	6	7	2	
Visitors	7	6	5	6	12	
VIP executives and VIP visitors	6	4	4	5	24	
Contractors	6	4	4	5	29	
Delivery personnel	6	4	2	4	39	
Transportation personnel	6	4	2	4	39	
Property	5	6	3	5	4	
Site	5	6	4	5	21	
Employee drop-off	8	8	7	8	1	
VIP drop-off	7	6	5	6	10	
Visitor drop-off: hotel (South)	7	9	5	7	4	
Hotel east entrance	6	8	5	6	6	
Hotel west entrance	6	8	5	6	6	
North perimeter freight fence	6	5	5	5	20	

FIGURE 11.1   Sorted risk results.

Displaying the Ranked Results as a Visual Graphic

The V² Matrix in its simplest form assembles the data from the ranked risk results into a color-coded graphic form that is easily digestible by nontechnical decision makers. In its most complex form, it creates the ability for decision makers to "drill down" into the data to see detail behind the recommendations.

The V² Matrixes typically include a Summary Matrix (a matrix of risk rankings by building) and Detail Matrixes (matrixes for each individual building or area).

To create the Summary Matrix, go back to the Unsorted Risk Matrix and select the major headers from that matrix. These will include people, property, proprietary information, and business reputation. Also include minor headers for each area of the property within the facility, such as tower 1, tower 2, hotel, parking, site, and so on.

From that information, looking at the Unsorted Risk Matrix and at an empty V² Matrix, place the first header (People) into the cell related to its score for vulnerability and probability, based on the colors of the cell. If probability is medium and vulnerability is high, place People into the Medium Probability/High Vulnerability cell. Then code the font for the word *people* as normal, italics, or bold text, depending on whether its consequence rating is low, medium, or high. Do this for each major heading and you will have a graphical array that lists the information in three dimensions: X for probability, Y for vulnerability, and consequence shown as different text types. This provides a very easily digestible summary of the overall risk rankings (Figure 11.2).

Now, while the V² Summary Matrix is good at providing an overall picture of risk for the entire project, it is not granular enough to base budgeting decisions on. For that, we need to create a separate V² matrix for each subarea, including

Facility name			
	Asset target value (probability)		
Vulnerability	High	Medium	Low
High	*Most consequence assets are bold/italics* *Medium consequences assets shown in italics* Last consequences assets are shown normally	Medium ATV and high vulnerability	Low ATV and high vulnerability
Medium	High ATV and medium vulnerability	Medium ATV and medium vulnerability	Low ATV and medium vulnerability
Low	High ATV and low vulnerability	Medium ATV and Low vulnerability	Low ATV and low vulnerability

FIGURE 11.2   V² Summary Matrix.

- People
- Each individual property area (building, remote site, etc.)
- Proprietary information
- Business reputation

Together, these provide the reviewer with a drill-down look at risk rankings. So, Tower 1 may be listed on the V² Summary Matrix, and there will also be an individual V² Matrix labeled Tower 1 (with its areas also arrayed), and so on for all of the assets of the facility (Figure 11.3).

This approach provides a comprehensive analysis and results in exceptionally understandable summaries.

Regardless of what method is used, best practices involve displaying the prioritized risk results in an easily understandable graphic form.

Hotel tower			
	Asset target value (probability)		
Vulnerability	High	Medium	Low
High	***Lobby level bell desk and storage*** *Lobby level reception desk* *Passenger elevator lobbies*	*Main lobby area* Low-rise levels *Mid-rise levels* High-rise levels *Roof* Lobby level concierge area Stairwells	
Medium		*Utility rooms* *Mechanical floor* *Security checkpoint outside* *Freight elevator* *Lobby level utility room*	
Low			

FIGURE 11.3   V² Tower 1 Matrix.

SUMMARY

Every organization must prioritize their security budgets. Determining exactly how to do this has caused security directors and managers and C-level executives more grief than almost anything else about security. Arguments ensue as different stakeholders jockey to forward their agendas. And agendas abound. Various departments have their own interests, and they often compete with security for the same budget.

Two skills are paramount:

- Prioritizing risk
- Communicating priorities effectively to management to gain their support

Prioritization Criteria

There are five potential ways of prioritizing risk:

- Natural prioritization (prioritizing by formula)
- By probability
- By consequences
- By criticality
- By cost (not recommended but often a reality)

Natural Prioritization (Prioritizing by Formula)

Both the Sandia formula and the NIST 780 formula facilitate intrinsic prioritization. For Sandia, the formula is Risk = Probability * (1 − Vulnerability) * Consequence. For NIST 780, the formula is Risk = Probability * Vulnerability * Consequence, or (Probability + Vulnerability + Consequence)/3.

All three of these formulas will result in perfectly actionable results all by themselves. However, this can sometimes result in items of very high vulnerability and very high probability but very low consequence rising to the top of the risk chart. The analyst can further prioritize the results in order to focus and guide the implementation process. And I have found that different organizations place a different emphasis on each element.

For example, a good security program is comprised of two main elements:

- A baseline security program (focused on day-to-day risks and reinforcing good behavior)
- Special countermeasures to address unique vulnerabilities (usually focused on terrorism or a criminal problem that may be unique to the area, industry, or facility)

The extent of the baseline security program and of special countermeasures to address unique vulnerabilities may be driven by probability, consequences, criticalities, or cost.

Prioritization of Risk

Often organizations place a different emphasis on prioritization, depending on their circumstances. For example, organizations that face little risk of terrorism but are located in a high-crime area often want their risk prioritized by probability, while all critical infrastructure facilities should address prioritization of risks only by consequences.

The other two ways of prioritizing risk are by criticality and cost. These are not recommended because criticality is an incomplete and arguably poor surrogate for consequences, while cost should be examined after either probability or consequences prioritization has been addressed.

Communicating Priorities Effectively

Making the Case

Virtually every organization faces financial challenges. Understanding that many program directors are vying for the same budget dollars, it is necessary for the security program manager to make a clear case for security program budget dollars.

- Developing the arguments
  - Determine the priorities of management.
  - Identify the points of view of stakeholders and acknowledge them.
  - Provide a list of consequences: The only reason to have a security program at all is to prevent the unwanted consequences of not having a security program.
    - You can accept the loss.
    - You can duplicate the asset.
    - You can insure the asset.
    - You can protect the asset.
    Executive management needs to make these decisions about all assets and this list gives them to tools to do so.
  - Provide tiered countermeasure budgets versus solutions.
  - Let management draw their own conclusions.
  - Use a Decision Matrix to help committees reach a consensus when there is no agreement on the choice of a particular approach. Chapter 17 explains and illustrates the use of the Decision Matrix.

Best Practices: Ranking Risk Results

To achieve the final risk rankings, we simply copy the Unsorted Risk Summary Matrix and perform a sort on the Consequences column so that the results descend from the highest consequence assets to the lowest.

Now, finally, we have truly meaningful results on which the allocation of countermeasures can be based.

Displaying the Ranked Results as a Visual Graphic

The V^2 Matrix in its simplest form assembles the data from the ranked risk results into a color-coded graphic form that is easily digestible by nontechnical decision makers. In its most complex form, it creates the ability for decision makers to "drill down" into the data to see detail behind the recommendations.

The V^2 Matrixes typically include a Summary Matrix (a matrix of risk rankings by building) and Detail Matrixes (matrixes for each individual building or area).

Q&A

Questions

Q1: Every organization must prioritize
   A. Their security budgets.
   B. Their guard schedules.
   C. Their management conflicts.
   D. None of the above.

Q2: Understand that prioritization is all about
   A. Developing budgets and determining the schedule for implementation.
   B. Developing budgets that reflect the issues of the most forceful managers.
   C. Developing budgets that reflect the best public relations issues.
   D. None of the above.

Q3: Two skills that are paramount are
   A. Prioritizing risk and communicating priorities effectively to management to gain their support.
   B. Prioritizing risk and emphasizing that you will quit if you do not get your way.
   C. Prioritizing risk and then accepting that more powerful managers may always get their way, but at least you can blame bad outcomes on them when they happen.
   D. None of the above.

Q4: A good security program is comprised of which elements?
   A. A baseline security program (focused on day-to-day risks and reinforcing good behavior)
   B. Special countermeasures to address unique vulnerabilities (usually focused on terrorism or a criminal problem that may be unique to the area, industry, or facility)
   C. Neither of the above
   D. Both of the above

Q5: Which is the best factor to use to prioritize risk?
   A. Probability
   B. Criticality
   C. Consequences
   D. Cost

Q6: To prioritize risk by consequences, one would
   A. First organize risk by formula and then sort the risks by the ranking of consequences.
   B. First organize the risk by vulnerabilities and then sort the risks by the ranking of consequences.
   C. First organize the risk by consequences and then sort the risks by the ranking of vulnerabilities.
   D. None of the above.

Q7: Accounting and security programs have much in common.
   A. They both deal with money.
   B. They both require close management.
   C. They both can be a big problem for management.
   D. They both are required to comply with codes and regulations and to limit the organization's exposure to risks (in one case financial risk and in the other, security risks).

Q8: To develop the arguments, the security manager or director should
   A. Determine the priorities of management and identify the points of view of stakeholders and acknowledge them.
   B. Prove a list of consequences and provide tiered countermeasure budgets versus solutions.
   C. Let management draw their own conclusions, using a Decision Matrix to help committees reach a consensus when there is no agreement on the choice of a particular approach.
   D. All of the above.

Q9: One way of displaying the ranked risk results as a visual graphic is
   A. The P_2 Matrix
   B. The R^2 Matrix
   C. The V^2 Matrix
   D. None of the above.

Q10: Best practices involve
   A. Displaying risk numerically.
   B. Displaying the prioritized risk results in an easily understandable graphic form.
   C. Displaying the prioritized risk in clear text.
   D. None of the above.

Answers

Q1 – A, Q2 – A, Q3 – A, Q4 – D, Q5 – C, Q6 – A, Q7 – D, Q8 – C, Q9 – C, Q10 – B

Policy Development before Countermeasures

CHAPTER **12**

Security Policy Introduction

INTRODUCTION

On completion of this chapter, you will understand the role that security policies have in the development of all aspects of the security program; what the differences are between policies, standards, guidelines, and procedures; and why security policies should be developed before decisions on other countermeasures are finalized. This is the first of three chapters dealing exclusively with security policies, emphasizing the importance of the role of security policies in the overall security program.

HIERARCHY OF SECURITY PROGRAM DEVELOPMENT

Many years ago, I wrote an article for a security technology magazine titled "How to Plan, Design and Implement a Bad Security System." The focus of the article was that most security systems have no design at all but are in fact a scattering of cameras, card readers, and alarms with no coherent purpose, serving no set of security policies.

It is easy to create a bad security program. It takes no planning at all. In fact, the lack of planning virtually guarantees a bad security program. There are several steps, which, if taken, can also virtually guarantee a good security program. These steps are as follows:

- Perform a competent risk assessment
  - Identify threats.
  - Identify vulnerabilities.
  - Identify consequences.
  - Calculate and prioritize risks.
- Identify appropriate countermeasures
  - Outline security policies (goals and objectives).
  - Develop a security plan, which should include
    - A baseline security program.
      - Detailed security policies and procedures.
      - All other countermeasures derive from policies and procedures.
    - Develop special countermeasures to address unique vulnerabilities.
- Apply the countermeasures in conformance with the security policies.
- Measure the security program performance against the security policies (security metrics).

WHAT ARE POLICIES, STANDARDS, GUIDELINES, AND PROCEDURES?*

A policy is a very brief high-level statement that states the organization's general beliefs, goals, objectives, and acceptable procedures for a specified subject area. A policy should state a problem or objective and outline a plan of action to mitigate the problem.

Policy attributes include the following:

- Require compliance (mandatory).
- Failure to comply results in disciplinary action.
- Focus on desired results, not on means of implementation.
- Further defined by standards and guidelines.

Policies always state required actions and may include pointers to standards and guidelines.

- Policies require compliance (mandatory): This is the most basic fact differentiating policies and guidelines. Guidelines are general in nature and allow for exceptions to be determined by the person interpreting the guideline. That is, a person can judge for themselves whether or not conditions are right for following a guideline, while no such judgment can be made regarding policies. Policies do not allow for exceptions based on personal judgment.
- Failure to comply with a policy results in disciplinary action: Policies are not only mandatory, but have provisions for disciplinary action if the policy is not followed. Each policy should state the disciplinary action (loss of job, loss of position, financial penalty, loss of parking privilege, negative comment in personal file affecting raise evaluation, etc.) One of the easiest ways to determine if a statement is in fact a policy is to ask what the disciplinary action is corresponding to the policy.
- Policies should focus on desired results, not on means of implementation: Each security policy should state a problem and the desired result. Means of implementation should be left to countermeasures, which may include technological solutions, signage, and architectural or landscaping solutions and/or procedures.
- Policies may be further defined by standards and guidelines: Standards and guidelines expand on policies to make them more clear and understandable. For example, a standard may expand on an aspect of a policy to explain it further and break it down into its component parts. Guidelines may give a framework for implementation and should guide the user to better understand how to conform to the policy.
- Most policies are supported by procedures: Procedures define how to implement a policy. Procedures may be rules for action directed either to the security unit or the organization's users. Procedures are more specific than guidelines, which allow for the user's interpretation. Procedures define what a person must do to comply with a policy. Procedures may also be implemented as guidelines (Figure 12.1).

---

* The Introduction section and some other portions are resourced from Sans Institute and Cisco: www.sans. org/resources/policies/policy_primer.pdf.

FIGURE 12.1 Policies form the basis for problem solving.

Other Key Documents

Standards, guidelines, procedures, position papers, and guiding principles all play a role in defining the overall security program. A brief explanation of each follows:

Standards

- Standards are a mandatory action or rule, designed to support and conform to a specific policy.
- A standard should make a policy more meaningful and effective.
- A standard must include one or more accepted specifications for hardware, software, or behavior.

Guidelines

- Guidelines are general statements, recommendations, or administrative instructions designed to achieve the policy's objectives by providing a framework within which to implement procedures.
- A guideline can change as needed based on the environment and should be reviewed more frequently than standards and policies.
- A guideline is not mandatory, but rather a suggestion of a best practice. Hence "guidelines" and "best practice" are in some ways interchangeable.
- Guidelines help convey best practice to users.
- Guidelines are meant to guide users to adopt behaviors that increase the security posture of the organization, but that are not as yet required.
- Guidelines may be used as a "trial balloon" before instituting the guideline as a policy.

Procedures

- Procedures are statements of actions required by users in order to assure conformance to policy.
- Procedures define how to carry out policies or function as the mechanisms to enforce policy.
- Procedures help eliminate the problem of a single point of failure (e.g., an employee suddenly leaves or is unavailable when most needed).

- Procedures, unlike guidelines, are mandatory.
- Procedures are equally important to policies. For example, a badging policy would require the use of photo ID badges at a facility. The badging procedure would describe the process for creating new photo ID badges, distributing them, maintaining them, and collecting them when an employee or contractor leaves.
- There is not always a one-to-one relationship between policies and procedures.

Position Paper

- A position paper describes the security unit management's position on emerging issues and technologies.
- Position papers often act as a precursor to policy.
- Alternatively, position papers may be used where a policy may never be developed.
- Position papers can also fill the gap between policies and guidelines.

Guiding Principles

- These are statements of the philosophy, direction, or beliefs of the organization.
- Guiding principles serve to guide people in making the right decisions in the organization's interests, including
  - What policies and standards are needed.
  - What technologies are appropriate.
  - How goals should be accomplished.
- Guiding principles are not policies, but serve to help management form thoughtful and comprehensive security policies and procedures.
- Highest-level guiding principles:
  - The security unit shall embody integrity.
  - The security unit shall be available when needed.
  - Everyone is responsible for security, especially department managers.
  - Access to the facilities should be limited only to those persons who are authorized.
  - Risk to the organization should be limited through cost-effective risk mitigation.
  - Security measures should be proactively implemented.
  - Security should be propelled through security awareness.
  - Information technology security and physical security should work together to create a more secure environment for people, property, proprietary information, and the organization's business reputation.
  - Wherever possible, the security unit should use technology rather than personnel to grant access, except where direct interaction with the user is compelled by access control requirements (vehicles, weapons and explosives screening, visitor and employee badging, etc.).

The Key Role of Policies in the Overall Security Program

Policies Define All Other Countermeasures

A good set of policies will define all security program countermeasures. Any countermeasure that is not supported by a security policy is an indication of either

- A poorly conceived countermeasure
- A missing policy

In the first case, there is no need for the countermeasure, and its presence may actually be detrimental to the goal of good security. Some countermeasures are put in place to address temporary problems and then become accidentally permanent.

In the second case, where the case for the countermeasure is obvious and there is no supporting policy, it indicates that policies have not been fully considered and should be revised to include the case for this countermeasure.

Under every circumstance, every single countermeasure should be supported by an underlying security policy. This is important for the following reasons:

- Defending against legal challenges
- Defending against challenges by users

Legal Challenges

In the case of a lawsuit, it is common for the plaintiff's attorneys to examine the security countermeasures and their basis in law or security policies, or both. Where countermeasures exist in one part of a facility that might have mitigated a security event in another part of the organization's facilities, a skillful attorney can make a compelling case that the use of the countermeasure could have mitigated the plaintiff's injuries and that the application of a countermeasure in one part of a facility indicated the organization's awareness of the need for the countermeasure. And the fact that the countermeasure was not uniformly applied indicates negligence on the part of the organization's management. Thus, the absence of a security policy for a countermeasure can create the conditions under which an organization can be successfully sued in the event of a security incident occurring elsewhere within its facility, which might have been mitigated by the presence of a countermeasure that was not applied because there was a missing policy (Figure 12.2).

Challenges by Users

It is common for users to challenge applications of security procedures and technical countermeasures, such as cameras. The ability to cite an underlying security policy obviates any complaint about a security procedure or countermeasure. For the persistent complainer, a security officer can not only cite the policy but also the disciplinary action that will result in noncompliance with the policy. This is an effective means of achieving

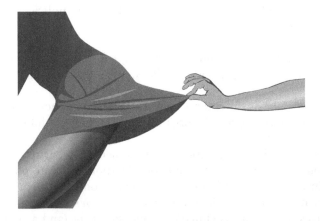

FIGURE 12.2   Policies help prevent offensive and illegal behavior.

compliance. Thus the occasional complainer can actually serve to underscore compliance for any bystanders who hear the exchange between the complainer and the security officer.

There is another category of complainer that this approach is especially effective in dealing with, one that is particularly difficult to address: the organization manager who complains loudly and publicly about a security procedure in the presence of other users. This complainer can be intimidating to security officers, and that is his intent. He is intending to create a special exception to policy for him alone, whether it be permission to park in an area where there is a concern about vehicle-borne improvised explosive devices (VBIEDs) or avoiding having his bags checked at a screening point. The loud manager is a direct challenge not only to the security officer but to security management, and moreover to the security mission of the organization itself. Such challenges must be dealt with effectively. The ability of the security officer to quote security policy by policy number and text can effectively put down such challenges. Every officer should be drilled in policy until he or she knows each without reference to paper. This is part of basic training. In the few cases where a manager continues to challenge the security officer after policy is quoted, it should be referred to the security unit chief.

It is not uncommon for such managers to fabricate claims of misbehavior by the security officer during his or her interaction with the manager at the checkpoint. I recommend that all security checkpoints are observed and recorded for both video and audio in order to provide supporting evidence of the security officer's appropriate behavior. When the manager's superiors are presented with the audio or video evidence of a manager's misbehavior after his claim of a security officer's misbehavior, the manager's claim not only dissolves into vapor, but any future claims are also rendered suspicious. The manager moves suddenly from a position of assumed correctness to a position of having to defend his own inexcusable actions. Such video is best presented to his superiors in the presence of the manager himself, as the effect of his retreat when faced by evidence of his own behavior is that much more pronounced. After one such occurrence, the word gets out to other managers that such behavior at a security checkpoint can be counterproductive to their careers.

Benefits of Having Proper Policies

There are numerous benefits to having well-defined security policies. The list below is a summary of the key reasons:

- Policies dictate a uniform standard of behavior for all including users and security staff. No one is exempt, neither visitors, managers, ordinary users, nor security staff.
- Policies provide a basis for enforcement. If there is no policy against a behavior, then there is no misbehavior. An organization can only prohibit behavior that is proscribed by a policy.
- Policies exemplify the organization's commitment to security. The fact that an organization has taken the time and consideration to create policies regarding security illustrates the position of that organization's management on security. The organization that has well-considered policies on security takes security seriously. Policies provide a benchmark for measurement (and a basis for security management metrics). Policies are the basis against which all behaviors having to

do with security are compared. Additionally, security policies provide the basis for judging the effectiveness of the security organization itself and of its management. The security organization that does not achieve policy compliance is not by any measure effective.

- Policies help provide consistency across business units and facilities and eliminate variances of interpretation by security staff. One of the most important aspects of any security program is its ability to uniformly apply security policy across all business units and facilities and equally for management, employees, contractors, vendors, and visitors. The existence of uniform security policies helps assure uniform compliance. This improves security and business productivity and, very importantly, reduces the chance for litigation due to nonuniform application of security principles between facilities or business units.
- Policies give the security staff the backing of management. Since policies derive from a process that finalizes with senior management authorization, each policy has the backing of the organization's senior management.
- Policies provide a basis for training. Security management, supervisors, and officers all need basic and continuous training in order to define and constantly improve their skills. Security policies provide the basis for all training.
- Policies provide a basis for counseling security officers on their performance. A security officer's performance can be judged against the policies regarding their training; their moral, ethical, and professional behavior; and their enforcement of the security policies.

Control Factors

- Business culture must play a major role in the development of security policies. Any security program that does not take an organization's business culture into account is doomed to fail. Users will complain and revolt and find ways around security policies that do not fit their understanding of the organization's business culture.
- Security policies must balance security control with business productivity. One major cause of the failure of some security policies is that they are conceived in the absence of consideration for business productivity. Users will always find ways to circumvent policies that impede on their ability to do their job or that come and go in the performance of their job. All policies should take the possible effects on business operations effectiveness as one of their first considerations.
- Policies that are too restrictive will be circumvented, thus obviating the intent and effect of the policy. As noted above, policies that are too restrictive will also undermine the entire security program. When users succeed in circumventing one policy, all other policies suffer. When the security organization fails to enforce one policy, it is easy for users to cite that example as a reason why they should not be compelled to obey other policies. For this reason, it is important to review security policy compliance continuously and make changes to any policies that are so restrictive that they are unenforceable, impede normal business conduct, or defy the organization's business culture. Often, well-intentioned policies turn out to be white elephants that must be modified or discarded due to unenforceability.
- Technical controls are not always possible, and personal intervention must be planned and implemented with effective training. Generally, technical controls are better than controls that rely on security staff for the following reasons:

- Technical controls cost less to operate, especially when many control points are needed.
- Technical controls cannot be accused of bias or the preference of one user over another.
- Technical controls are generally well accepted, as users understand that arguing with a card reader, barrier gate, electronic turnstile, or revolving door is fruitless.

    Where it is necessary to use security staffing due to the need for directions, a decision process, personal verification, to enroll visitors, or to present a "face" to visitors, it is important to plan and implement the control point and train the security staff in their duties well enough to assure the success of the control point.

SUMMARY

Hierarchy of Security Program Development

These steps virtually guarantee a good security program:

- Perform a competent risk assessment
  - Identify threats
  - Identify vulnerabilities
  - Identify and prioritize risks
- Identify appropriate countermeasures
  - Outline security policies
  - Baseline security program
    - Detailed security policies and procedures
    - All other countermeasures derive from policies and procedures
  - Develop special countermeasures to address unique vulnerabilities
- Apply the countermeasures in conformance with the security policies
- Measure the security program performance against the security policies

Policies, Standards, Guidelines, and Procedures*

A policy is a very brief high-level statement that states the organization's general beliefs, goals, objectives, and acceptable procedures for a specified subject area. A policy should state a problem or objective and outline a plan of action to mitigate the problem.

Policy attributes include the following:

- Require compliance (mandatory).
- Failure to comply results in disciplinary action.
- Focus on desired results, not on means of implementation.
- Further defined by standards and guidelines.

---

* The Introduction section and some other portions are resourced from Sans Institute and Cisco: www.sans. org/resources/policies/policy_primer.pdf.

Policies always state required actions and may include pointers to standards and guidelines.

Other Key Documents

Policies aside, standards, guidelines, procedures, position papers, and guiding principles all play a role in defining the overall security program.

The Key Role of Policies in the Overall Security Program

Policies define all other countermeasures: A good set of policies will define all security program countermeasures. Any countermeasure that is not supported by a security policy is an indication of either

- A poorly conceived countermeasure
- A missing policy

Under every circumstance, every single countermeasure should be supported by an underlying security policy. This is important for the following reasons:

- Defending against legal challenges
- Defending against challenges by users

Benefits of Having Proper Policies

There are numerous benefits to having well-defined security policies.

- Policies dictate a uniform standard of behavior for all, including both users and security staff.
- Policies provide a basis for enforcement.
- Policies exemplify the organization's commitment to security.
- Policies provide a benchmark for measurement (and a basis for security management metrics).
- Policies help provide consistency across business units and facilities and eliminate variances of interpretation by security staff.
- Policies give the security staff the backing of management.
- Policies provide a basis for training.
- Policies provide a basis for counseling security officers on their performance.

Control Factors

- Business culture must play a major role in the development of security policies.
- Security policies must balance security control with business productivity.
- Policies that are too restrictive will be circumvented, thus obviating the intent and effect of the policy.
- Technical controls are not always possible, and personal intervention must be planned and implemented with effective training.

Q&A

Questions

Q1: It is easy to create a bad security program. Which of the approaches below can achieve that?
  A. One must only use too many cameras.
  B. One must only use too many card readers.
  C. It takes no planning at all. In fact, the lack of planning virtually guarantees a bad security program.
  D. One must only use too few cameras and card readers.

Q2: There are several steps, which, if taken, can also virtually guarantee a good security program. Which of the approaches below are included?
  A. Perform a competent risk assessment
  B. Identify appropriate countermeasures
  C. Apply the countermeasures in conformance with security policies and measure the security program performance against the security policies (security metrics)
  D. All of the above

Q3: A policy is
  A. A very brief high-level statement that states the organization's general beliefs, goals, objectives, and acceptable procedures for a specified subject area.
  B. A very brief high-level statement that states the organization's wishes and hopes for a safe employment environment.
  C. Both of the above.
  D. Neither of the above.

Q4: A policy should
  A. State a problem.
  B. State an objective.
  C. Outline a plan of action.
  D. State a problem or objective and outline a plan of action to mitigate the problem.

Q5: Policy attributes include the following:
  A. They require compliance (mandatory), with failure to comply resulting in disciplinary action.
  B. They focus on desired results, further defined by standards and guidelines.
  C. Both of the above.
  D. Neither of the above.

Q6: Any countermeasure that is not supported by a security policy is an indication of either
  A. A poorly conceived countermeasure.
  B. A missing policy.

C. Both of the above.
D. Neither of the above.

Q7: Every single countermeasure should be supported by an underlying security pol-
    icy. This is important for the following reasons:
    A. Defending against legal challenges
    B. Defending against challenges by users
    C. Both of the above
    D. Neither of the above

Q8: Other key documents for a successful security program include
    A. Standards and guidelines.
    B. Standards, guidelines, and procedures.
    C. Standards, guidelines, procedures, and position papers.
    D. Standards, guidelines, procedures, position papers, and guiding principles.

Q9: A standard must include
    A. One or more accepted specifications for hardware, software, or behavior.
    B. A policy.
    C. A position paper.
    D. A guiding principle.

Q10: Procedures define
    A. How to carry out policies or be the mechanisms to enforce policy.
    B. A policy.
    C. A position paper.
    D. A guiding principle.

Answers

Q1 – C, Q2 – D, Q3 – C, Q4 – D, Q5 – C, Q6 – C, Q7 – C, Q8 – D, Q9 – A, Q10 – A

CHAPTER **13**

Security Policy and Countermeasure Goals

INTRODUCTION

On completion of this chapter, you will understand why security programs that are not based on security policies are so likely to fail, the role of policies in the security program, the role of countermeasures in the security program, the types of security countermeasures, why policies should be developed before countermeasures, security policy goals, security countermeasure goals, and a list of key policies that most facilities should include in their security plan.

THEORY

I have seen countless requests for proposals for security systems consulting tasks, for which no risk assessment has been performed, nor was one wanted; and for which no security policies had been developed by the organization for the facility in question.

I usually turn down such work.

It is not that I do not like the business or enjoy the work; it is for the reason that such projects are almost always doomed to fail, and I do not want my name associated with the failure. Also, I do not want to participate in any potential lawsuit resulting from its failure.

There are many security consultants and contractors who will design card readers and cameras into an architectural space without any risk analysis or security policies, based solely on their experience of what previous clients for similar companies have wanted.

This is like asking your neighbor to go to a car dealer and buy a car for your cousin. He might return with a sub-compact, or a luxury car, or a SUV. It might be red or blue or silver. It may have an automatic transmission or manual. All of these might be good choices for your neighbor, but may not be what your cousin would like to have. Your cousin, who is an executive and who entertains clients, needs a full-sized luxury four-door car with adequate leg room in the rear seat and good shoulder and head room. The car must be black or dark blue, have an automatic transmission, and provide a comfortable ride. Your neighbor does not know this. Your cousin is not likely to get the car he needs in the absence of these specifications being known to the buyer (Figure 13.1).

FIGURE 13.1   Buying a car.

So it is with security systems designed in the absence of a risk analysis or security policies. The client will not get the system he needs in the absence of the designer knowing the assets, threats, vulnerabilities, and risks. The access cards may be incompatible with other facilities if the designer does not know that this is a criteria. Elevators may not have floor-by-floor control if the client needs this feature but does not have a policy for it. There may be no card readers on elevator lobby doors if that requirement is not known. There may be no duress alarms at reception desks if that need is not understood.

So the request to "Design us a security system" truly is equivalent to "Buy my cousin a car."

Accordingly, the security analyst should address the need for security policy goals before recommending any other countermeasures. All countermeasures should derive entirely from the organization's security policies. If a countermeasure is implemented in the absence of a security policy, it is a waste of money. It is not needed. And it may be counterproductive or even expose the organization to unwanted liability. For example, the use of video within a parking structure can actually raise the organization's liability unless it is properly implemented.

Questions that policies answer (just a few out of many):

- Where should access control technology go and where should guards be placed in lieu of card readers?
- When are guards better than card readers?
- Where should cameras be used and what should they view and not be allowed to see?
- Where are alarms needed and where are they likely to be a problem?
- How could crime prevention through environmental design (CPTED) be used to reduce the need for both security manpower and technology?
- In which situations is security technology not helpful but actually detrimental?
- What type of security credential is necessary?
- How should high-tech, low-tech, and no-tech security solutions be mixed to achieve an appropriate balance between best results and best economy?
- How much attention should be paid to perimeter detection?

- Should cameras be used in interior spaces and where?
- How can we achieve effectiveness and still control costs?
- And the list goes on and on and on...

Policies answer all these questions. Without a risk analysis, security policies are not likely to be effective, and without security policies, security countermeasures will almost certainly not be effective.

ROLE OF POLICIES IN THE SECURITY PROGRAM

If a risk analysis is the foundation of a good security program, then policies are the structural columns and beams. Everything hangs on policies and will fall if not supported by policies. Policies are the supporting structure that assures that countermeasures will succeed.

Let us look at the nature of security policies. Policies are mandatory and must be followed. There are penalties for not following policies. These penalties apply equally to the lowest office boy and the highest executive. Policies are universal unless exceptions are expressed in the policy and their application is also universal.

Security policies give strength to enforcement. It is common for employees and visitors alike to complain about security procedures: "Hey, I am not a threat! You should not be asking to check my computer bag!"

Security policies also set goals to achieve and are a metric against which the security program can be measured. The terrorists who struck hotels in Mumbai, India, in November 2008 avoided hotel security by entering through the kitchen, where there was no useful security presence. A security policy of securing all entrances would have been a metric against which this inadequacy would have been apparent.

Policies act as a *roadmap* to success. Security programs that begin without policies develop in a haphazard fashion that often results in a schizophrenic application of disorganized responses. It is common for security programs that are run without policies to be so scattered that a common complaint is that different guards have different interpretations of what their job is. This results in inconsistent applications of what each guard thinks their role is and is assured to generate complaints from employees and guests. It will also result in an ineffective security program.

Security policies are the plan for the security program. If you fail to plan, you are planning to fail. If you have a security program without policies, you are planning to fail. Security policies determine *what* to do.

Security policies create a roadmap for everything else in the security program. Any good security program should include security policies for

- Crime and terrorism prevention elements
- Access control to the campus, buildings, and parking
- Asset protection of equipment and documentation
- Individual responsibilities for security
- Use of security technology
- Emergency planning
- Recurring risk analysis

ROLE OF COUNTERMEASURES IN THE SECURITY PROGRAM

There are three main goals for all security countermeasures:

- Where possible, to identify and deny access to potential threat actors
- To deny access to the facility of weapons, explosives, and dangerous chemicals (except for legitimate exceptions, which should be well controlled and monitored)
- To make the environment suitable for appropriate behavior and unsuitable for inappropriate for criminal or terroristic behavior (CPTED program) and to mitigate the actions of both hazards and threats

If security policies determine *what* to do, then countermeasures get it done. There are three broad types of countermeasures in any good security program:

- High-tech
- Low-tech
- No-tech

High-tech countermeasures are the electronic portions of the security program, commonly including

- Access control system
- Digital video system
- Security alarm system
- Two-way voice communications system
- Information technology security (always a subset of the information technology department) (Figure 13.2)

Except for guards, high-tech elements are the most visible components of the security program. High-tech portions of the system can also be a force multiplier when correctly designed. That is, a well-designed security video system can support video surveillance, video guard tours (many more tours of the facility each hour than a walking guard can

FIGURE 13.2   High-tech element.

perform), and video pursuit (following a subject through the building). Access control systems save many tens of thousands of dollars annually in guard costs. And alarm systems provide alerts in many more places than an organization could afford to have eyes.

Low-tech countermeasures include the physical portions of the security program, commonly including

- Locks
- Barriers
- Lighting
- Signage
- CPTED elements

Low-tech elements can be designed to provide an environment that reduces the possibility of criminal behavior and encourages appropriate behavior. Fencing defines boundaries and indicates intent when an intruder breaches a fence. Signage elements help guide visitors to their destination and inform them of the organization's expectations for appropriate behavior. Locks and barriers maintain control over secure spaces and lighting helps create a safer, more secure environment (Figure 13.3).

No-tech countermeasures include the operational elements of the security program, commonly including (Figure 13.4)

- Authorities and responsibilities
- Reference to charter for security unit
- Statement from the CEO/chairman/president
  - Responsibilities
    - Security unit chief
    - Security supervisors
    - Security officers
    - Security administrative staff
    - Department managers
    - Employees
    - Visitors

FIGURE 13.3 Low-tech element.

FIGURE 13.4   No-tech element.

- • Maintenance of security policies and procedures
- • Protection of life
  - • Weapons and explosives screening program
  - • Chemical weapons defense and mitigation measures
  - • Special countermeasures for unique vulnerabilities
  - • Countersurveillance program
  - • All other aspects of baseline security program
- • Crime prevention
  - • Security awareness program
  - • Post and patrol reports
  - • Incident reporting
  - • Crime investigations program
  - • Law enforcement liaison program
  - • Security intelligence program
  - • Countersurveillance program
- • Access control program
  - • Identify public, semipublic, controlled, and restricted access spaces
  - • Access cards and photo ID badging program
  - • Functions, meetings, and events
  - • Hours of operations and after-hours access
  - • Parking controls for vehicles, cycles, and trucks
  - • Loading dock and mail room access
  - • Control of locks, keys, and access control credentials

- Asset and property protection
  - Security of equipment
  - Security hardware
  - Insurance cover
  - Mail recipients and deliveries
  - Headed paper
- Individual responsibilities for security
  - In the office
  - Drugs and illegal substances in the workplace
  - Weapons in the workplace
  - Property, lost and found
- Guards
  - Posts
  - Patrols
  - Response
  - Administrative duties
  - Training and career development
  - Random countermeasures
- VIP protection program
  - VIP preassessment
  - VIP security team liaison
  - Guard duties
- Emergency security plans
  - Weather emergencies
  - Medical emergencies
  - Civil disorder response
  - Disaster recovery plan
- Recurring risk analysis

WHY SHOULD POLICIES PRECEDE COUNTERMEASURES?

Countermeasures that are applied without supporting policies will be necessarily lacking in completeness, organization, and coordination, resulting in a haphazard and poorly performing security program.

Security programs deployed without appropriate supporting policies often have very bad results. For example, in one institution a touchy senior manager was asked to clear through the security checkpoint on a day when he did not wish to do so. An argument ensued that resulted in the security officer being accused of inappropriate behavior and the manager demanding disciplinary action (remember, he was the one not following security policy here). In a case of his word versus hers, the manager prevailed and the banishment of the security officer stuck. This occurred for the following reasons:

- There was no policy in place requiring *all* employees to follow security policy, and the manager claimed that he was exempt because he was management, not an employee.
- There was no policy or training for officers on how to handle belligerent people, so she was on her own in determining how best to respond (witnesses claimed she was always polite and the video showed this).

- There was no policy in place regarding the treatment of security officers by management, employees, or others (thus no penalty for belligerence).
- There was no audio recording at the security checkpoint, so the manager's claims as to what was said and by who went unchallenged, despite the video evidence.
- The security officer suffered because of a lack of policies.

Without appropriate policies, security programs fail.

SECURITY POLICY GOALS

- Protection of people is the key goal: Security and protection of employees, contractors, vendors, and visitors is the key goal of the security program, as well as having respect for their human rights and dignity.
- Security is an all-management responsibility: Corporate and line management throughout every department must be continually be aware of and take responsibility for the security aspects of its business activities. The security unit must reflect this commitment in its organization and resource allocations.
- Priorities
  - Focus on prevention: Prevention of security events and emergencies is the first priority.
  - Threat and vulnerability assessment and risk analysis must be carried out on a regular basis, at least annually.
  - Routine facility users should be informed of security policy in a professional manner and be made to understand that they are responsible for adhering to corporate security policy while on the premises.
  - Minimize the impact of security on daily operations: All security procedures should be introduced in such a way as to minimize their impact on the normal operations of the organization.
- Security countermeasure hierarchy: All security policies should be focused on using a combination of high-tech, low-tech, and no-tech countermeasures in order to deter, detect, assess, respond, and gather evidence for prosecution.
- Routine events preparedness: The organization and its security unit must be prepared to handle security events as they emerge daily. The security unit shall develop policies and procedures to handle all routine kinds of security events.
- Emergency events preparedness: The security unit shall develop policies and procedures to handle all kinds of predictable emergencies.
- Security program auditing: Security measures and procedures should be inspected regularly and verified and validated by independent security specialists.
- Security unit professionalism: The security unit staff must be held to a high standard of professionalism, knowledge, and integrity and must be exemplary. To that end, the security unit should only hire or contract qualified staff, and appropriate training of security unit management and staff should be continuous, with pay raises and bonuses based on continuous training and on-the-job performance.
- Reporting and follow-up of security events: All incidents, including security breaches and irregularities, should be reported to the security unit manager and logged into a record of security events. Corrective action should be taken as follow-up to

- Determine if the event is routine and requires a routine countermeasure, such as signage to inform users.
- Determine if the event illuminates a vulnerability that could be exploited by potential threat actors and should be remedied by architectural, technical, or procedural countermeasures.
- Determine if the event is minor and infrequent in nature and does not represent a significant vulnerability and so requires no mitigating action.
- Determine if the event requires follow-up, investigation, or prosecution.

- Security unit counseling role: The security unit shall act as a counselor to each department and shall provide periodic security audits of departments to assist management in understanding and improving security within each business unit.
- Weapons in the workplace including arming of guards: Security policy should determine if weapons should be allowed in the workplace and by whom they can be carried. Policy should also determine if guards should be armed or unarmed, based on the type of assets protected and the threats faced (including who else is permitted weapons in the workplace). If armed, the policy should assure qualifications, training, and practice for armed guards and should lay out clear rules of engagement.

SECURITY COUNTERMEASURE GOALS

The primary goal of every countermeasure is to support one or more specific security policies. The primary goals of all countermeasures are prevention, control, and recovery. These can be broken down into the following functions. All countermeasures are capable of only one or more of the following six functions:

- To help control access
- To deter a security event
- To detect a security event underway
- To help a security officer assess a security event
- To help a response to a security event
- To produce evidence of the security event

- Control access: Security is much easier if only you can keep the criminal threat actors and inappropriate users away from your organization's assets. Access control helps assure that only authorized people may access the organization's assets.
- Deter a security event: Deterrence is the best result of any security program. All countermeasures should be undertaken with the goal of deterring inappropriate, criminal, or terrorist acts.
- Detect a security event underway: When a security incident occurs, it is important wherever possible to detect it as it is underway. Security events that are detected after the fact provide no opportunity for control and often only minimal chances for recovery. Detection may be by alarms, cameras, security staff, or employees.
- Help a security officer assess a security event: Once detected, the severity of the incident must be determined in order to mount an effective and appropriate response. The number of threat actors, their dress, weapons, equipment, movements, and aggressiveness, movement toward a goal, entry point and method of entry, preparations for surveillance and detection, and preparations for exit all indicate the measures necessary to counter the threat actors.

- Respond to a security event: Depending on the conditions above, a response can be formulated and dispatched. The response should be observed and managed by the console officer and console supervisor via the console and two-way radios.
- Produce evidence of the security event: Throughout the security incident, special attention should be taken to record and preserve evidence for investigation and prosecution.

POLICY SUPPORT FOR COUNTERMEASURES

- No countermeasure should exist without a corresponding policy to support it.
- Policies should be written in a manner that defines supporting countermeasures.
- Each security policy should state what countermeasures are needed to support it.

KEY POLICIES

The following is a list of key security policies that any good security program should include. These should be augmented by policies that apply uniquely to the organization's industry, facility type (office, warehouse, factory, marine terminal, etc.), and geographic area.

Authorities and Responsibilities

- Reference to charter for security unit: The charter for the security unit is the foundational document on which the entire security program is grounded. This document lays out the need for security for the organization and lays the groundwork for the formation of a unit to specifically address that issue alone. This document underscores the importance that the organization's management places on security.
- Statement from the CEO/chairman/president: This document, from a recognized voice of authority, declares the organization's emphasis on security and directs all users to observe security policies.
- Responsibilities: The responsibilities of each of the organization's personnel responsible for security will be outlined, including
  - Security unit chief: Vision, strategy, countermeasure and policy development, unit metric analysis and high-level investigations, training program development, law enforcement liaison, security intelligence program
  - Security managers: Management of supervisors and staff, training, compilation of logs and reports
  - Security supervisors: Supervision of officers, logs, and reports
  - Security officers: Interfacing with the public, posts and patrols, logs, and reports
  - Security administrative staff: Assistance with record keeping and liaising between security management and its customers
  - Department managers: Responsible for security for their own business unit with the guidance and review of the security unit chief

- Employees: Responsible for preserving company property and a safe workplace, also responsible for their own personal security for themselves and their property
  - Visitors: Responsible for their own personal security for themselves and their property
- Maintenance of security policies and procedures: A specific policy will address the maintenance of security policies and procedures, including the process for the review of policies, the introduction process for new policies, the process for to changing a policy, and the process for submitting the change through management channels for approval.

Protection of Life

Protection of life is the key goal of any security program.

- Weapons and explosives screening program: The greatest threat to life in any workplace is the presence of weapons and explosives in the workplace. A good weapons screening program will include magnetic weapons detectors, x-ray screening, and explosives chemical signature detectors.
- Chemical weapons defense and mitigation measures: Chemical weapons defenses include protecting air intakes and sensing chemicals at air intakes, with automatic shutdown of heating, ventilation, and air-conditioning (HVAC) fans.
- Special countermeasures for unique vulnerabilities: Depending on the vulnerability findings, the risk analyst will recommend special countermeasures to address the unique vulnerabilities found in the analysis.
- Countersurveillance program: The best way to prevent a terrorist attack is to identify the surveillance attempts that precede any attack.
- All other aspects of baseline security program: Taken together, the entire baseline security program forms a deterrent to attacks of all types.

Special Countermeasures Example

Early in my design career, I was confronted with a need for special countermeasures to deal with potential criminal activity. I was designing an extension building next to a banking institution's data center. The property was surrounded by a tall estate fence, but due to zoning restrictions, it was not possible to queue vehicles on the street to enter the property and the zoning officials had ruled that the fence could not be extended across the driveway, so it remained open, thus allowing pedestrians to enter the property. They had many female employees who worked until late hours and who had to walk some distance across the parking area to their cars. Gangs were known to run in the area and violent crimes had occurred nearby. Management was concerned that some employees might be threatened by intruders through the fence opening.

I developed the following special countermeasures for the organization:

- A system to detect pedestrians entering through the vehicle entrance. The pedestrian detector comprised a pair of photo beams placed across the vehicle entry exactly at the fence line, coupled with a vehicle detection loop buried in the pavement exactly below the photo beams. When a vehicle passes through the beams, it is detected by the photo beams and also the vehicle loop detector. Although the photo beams detect the vehicle, the loop also detects it. The loop is programmed to shunt the photo beams so no alarm occurs when a vehicle passes. However, when a pedestrian crosses the photo beams, the vehicle loop does not detect it, so an alarm occurs, thus detecting the pedestrian.

- This was coupled with a video/audio system to "escort" late-leaving employees to their cars and to intervene if they encounter any threatening stranger in the parking lot. This system included these elements:
  - A special dedicated card reader at the main lobby for employees to notify security that an escort is needed
  - A light next to the card reader to notify the person making the request for escort that the request is acknowledged so they can proceed to the parking lot knowing that they are under watch
  - A low-light pan/tilt/zoom video camera mounted on the corner of the building and equipped with a long-range infrared illuminator and a high-power bullhorn mounted on the pan/tilt mechanism
- The escort system worked as follows:
  - When an employee is ready to enter the parking lot late at night, she presents her card to the card reader at the reception counter. This causes an alarm at the security console, notifying the guard that an escort is requested. The guard presses a button causing the light next to the card reader to notify the requestor that the request is acknowledged and an escort is available. The requestor can then leave the building.
  - As the requestor leaves the building, their image is displayed on the pan/tilt/zoom camera, which has moved to view the front door of the building. The guard then manipulates the pan/tilt/zoom camera to follow the requestor to her car.
  - If a suspicious individual appears, the guard presses the intercom talk button, which is already queued to the intercom bullhorn.
  - The guard warns away the offender and dispatches a guard to intervene, assure the protection of the requestor, and direct the offender away from the parking lot.

This example illustrates the typical nature of special countermeasures. That is, they typically employ multiple system elements and procedures to accomplish a task of deterrence, detection, and response. Special countermeasures often comprise elements that form unique responses to unique problems, using combinations of system elements and procedures that you would expect to see in a conventional security program, but which are used in unique ways to address special vulnerabilities.

Crime Prevention

Crime prevention is one of the key goals of any organization's security program. A typical crime prevention strategy includes the following policies:

- Security awareness program: A security awareness program helps users to understand their responsibilities and their role in crime prevention.
- Post and patrol reports: Each post and patrol should note any anomalies found during their shift or patrol. These should be assembled and recorded into the following categories:

- Note of a policy violation
- Note of a safety concern
- Note of a condition not covered by policy but suspicious or of concern
- Note of an unaddressed vulnerability
- Incident reporting
  - Incidents are any behavioral security policy violation by any user. Incidents can involve employees, managers, visitors, contractors, vendors, or offenders who are otherwise unrelated to the facility.
  - Incidents may be either criminal or policy violations.
  - All incidents should be handled in accordance with security policy and recorded by all security officers involved.
  - Management should review all incidents and categorize them by:
    - Life/safety violations
    - Security policy violations
    - Property violations
    - Proprietary information violations
    - Business reputation violations
  - Any trend in incidents should be analyzed monthly over the previous 6 months–2 years so that additional policy or countermeasures can be developed to prevent such and mitigate any actions related to trending incidents.
- Crime investigations program: For criminal violation incidents, either an internal or professional law enforcement investigation is appropriate in the event that the incident is unresolved.
- Law enforcement liaison program: The security unit chief should formalize a relationship with local law enforcement in order to
  - Develop, maintain, and test emergency response procedures
  - Keep law enforcement appraised of security concerns related to their purview (the need for police patrols, etc.)
  - Maintain familiarity and good relations with local law enforcement
  - Obtain up-to-date information on crime trends, strategies, methods, and tactics
  - Assist in maintaining the organization's security intelligence program
- Security intelligence program: Every organization should maintain a security intelligence program to
  - Be aware of crime trends including strategies, methods, and tactics
  - Be aware of terrorism or regional security activities that could be related to the welfare of the organization (potential for demonstrations, etc.)
- Countersurveillance program: Every organization for which terrorism is a legitimate threat should have a countersurveillance program in order to identify surveillance as an possible precursor to an attack and thus to reduce the probability of a terrorist attack by interrupting the surveillance or providing information to law enforcement for follow-up by their counterterrorism task force.

Access Control Program

The key to crime and terrorism prevention is simple: Keep threat actors out of the facility. Every organization should vet all employees and contractors for criminal background and affiliations with known terrorist organizations. Those persons who fail the vetting process should not be hired. All visitors should be allowed access on a "need to access" basis.

- Identify policy for public, semipublic, controlled, and restricted access spaces.
  - Public spaces: Anyone can be allowed access, such as to the main public lobby of a building.
  - Semipublic spaces: Areas available to the public without escort after receiving authorization by the organization's security unit.
  - Controlled spaces: General "back-of-house" employee spaces, only available to vetted employees and contractors and to vendors and visitors by escort.
  - Restricted spaces: Those spaces that require fully vetted access, only for vetted employees and not accessible to visitors or contractors who are not under escort or fully vetted.
- Access cards and photo ID badging program: Policy for development, use, and control of identification and access control credentials, used by an access control system and using a photo ID credential to make obvious that a person is authorized for an area.
- Policy for functions, meetings, and events: Access for functions, meetings, and events should be clearly laid out so that the presence of visitors, especially during other than normal business hours, can be controlled.
- Hours of operations and after-hours access: Normal hours of operation should be identified and after-hours access provisions for employees, contractors, and vendors should be established and maintained.
- Parking controls for vehicles, cycles, and trucks: Parking is a continuous problem at most facilities. Parking for executives, employees, visitors, and others should be identified by signage and access control measures.
- Loading dock and mail-room access: Access to the loading dock should be controlled for antiterrorism and crime prevention reasons. Policy regarding vehicle and driver vetting and access to facilities for drivers should be closely controlled.
- Control of locks, keys, and access control credentials: Lock and key control is essential to maintaining control over spaces not secured by the access control system. A master-keying system and computerized lock and key control are very helpful. Many organizations maintain their own locksmith facilities. If so, these must also be very closely controlled to assure that unauthorized keys are not made.

Asset and Property Protection

Property control is essential to protecting the organization's property, including fixtures, furnishings, equipment, and proprietary information.

- Security of equipment: Develop policy regarding equipment marking and bar coding with a property control system. (This function may be under the facilities department.)
- Security hardware: Security hardware should be inventoried and audited regularly for functionality.
- Insurance cover: Any and all property, fixtures, furnishings, and equipment that is under cover of insurance should be valued and inventoried (This function may be under the facilities department).

- Mail recipients and deliveries: Develop policy to assure that all mail and deliveries are actually delivered to their intended recipients.
- Out-shipments and shipping dock control: Policy should be coordinated with shipping/receiving to assure that out-shipments are all authorized and that company property not intended for export is not exiting through the shipping department.
- Headed paper, checks, and purchase orders: Policy should be developed to protect all letterheads, headed envelopes, checks, and purchase orders; and any other financial instruments or forms indicating that the document carries the authorization of the company should be controlled.

Individual Responsibilities for Security

Personal security resides with the occupants, not with the security unit. However, policy should be developed to help assure a safe and crime-free workplace, including

- In the office: Develop policy such that all employees, contractors, vendors, and visitors shall understand their responsibilities for personal security, the security of their own property, and the security of others and the property of the company.
- Drugs and illegal substances in the workplace: Policy regarding drugs and contraband in the workplace must be clear, unambiguous, and well enforced. Policy may include prohibitions, penalties, and provisions for counseling or rehabilitation.
- Weapons in the workplace: Management must determine their policy regarding weapons in the workplace, not only for visitors and employees but also for the security force. This is a matter for individual organization decision in many districts. But increasingly, laws are being put into place to determine who may and may not carry weapons on private property.
- Property, lost and found: Policy regarding lost and found property and its storage, identification, and return or disposition must be put into place.

Guards

Guards are the "face" of the security unit and present the culture of the organization as it regards its security commitment.

- Posts: Dedicated posts, usually for granting of access control, must be established. Security policy will dictate under which conditions a post should be established and when it should be staffed.
- Patrols: Security patrols present an indication of a constant security presence and the commitment to watching out for criminal activity and to underscoring the watch for security violations. Policy identifying the purpose and scope of patrols and their frequency should be established.
- Response: Policy regarding the nature and methods of response and coordination with emergency responders should be established, along with initial training and scenario testing/continuing training.
- Administrative duties: Policy concerning the administrative duties of the security unit should be established, including telephone answering, log keeping, record keeping, and so on.

- Training and career development: Policy regarding basic and continuing training should be developed for guards. Guards are responsible for their own career training. Those who underperform should have their employment terminated.
- Random countermeasures: All security programs should include provisions for the random application of procedural countermeasures so that observers planning an attack will never know when a patrol or use of a particular vetting method may occur.

VIP Protection Program

Most organizations have some VIPs, either as their own management or as visitors. Policies should be developed to graciously accommodate the special security needs of these special people.

- VIP definition: Policy should determine who is a VIP. An astonishing number of managers, employees, and visitors presume to be treated as such or pressure security to have their visitors treated as such. This can overwhelm a security force with frivolous demands.
- VIP preassessment: A true VIP requires preassessment, and their visit will almost always be preannounced. This is one clear definition of a true VIP: the need for special preparation in advance to accommodate their presence and also the fact that they are accompanied by their own security team. Pretender VIPs will often arrive unannounced and demand special treatment. True VIPs usually require a preassessment by their own security team. The security unit should have accommodation to deal with such.
- VIP security team liaison: Before a VIP arrives and after arrival, the security unit will have to liaise with the VIP's security team. Their team needs to know
  - The layout of the facility, the access and egress path of the VIP, and the security provisions to be made during transit into and out of the facility and meeting space.
  - With whom the VIP will meet and where, and the security provisions for that space and the greeting party.
  - The provisions for the VIP's own security escort team (adjacent anteroom, refreshments, etc.).
  - Policy for minimizing the presence of those who do not need access to the VIP while they are on the premises. Verify that the policy is being observed.
  - Policy regarding access for VIPs and weapons for their security units while on the facility.
- Guard Duties: Make VIPs' security liaisons familiar with the organization's posts and patrols and any special guards who will be assigned to help protect VIPs while visiting.

Emergency Security Plans

Emergencies will occur. The security unit must have policies in place to accommodate them or they will bring chaos with them. Policies should be established to deal with the following types of emergencies:

- Weather emergencies
- Medical emergencies
- Power or communications outages
- Civil disorder/riot response
- Disaster recovery plan

Recurring risk analysis: A policy regarding the frequency of risk analyses should be established (annually is suggested). These may be either a self-assessment or by an SME. SME risk analyses are often well received by senior management, so if significant or costly changes to countermeasures are expected or if security conditions or business functions or campus construction have changed, an SME analysis is often the best way to go.

SUMMARY

Introduction

The request to "Design us a security system" truly is equivalent to "Buy my cousin a car."

Accordingly, the security analyst should address the need for security policy goals before recommending any other countermeasures.

Questions That Policies Answer

- Where should access control technology go and where should guards be placed in lieu of card readers?
- Where should cameras be used and what should they view and not be allowed to see?
- Where are alarms needed and where are they likely to be a problem?
- How could CPTED be used to reduce the need for both security manpower and technology?
- In which situations is security technology not helpful but actually detrimental?
- What type of security credential is necessary?
- How should high-tech, low-tech, and no-tech security solutions be mixed to achieve an appropriate balance between best results and best economy?
- When are guards better than card readers?
- How much attention should be paid in the design to perimeter detection?
- Should cameras be used in interior spaces and where?
- And the list goes on and on and on...

Role of Policies in the Security Program

Policies are the supporting structure that assures that countermeasures will succeed.

Policies are mandatory and must be followed. There are penalties for not following policies. Policies are universal unless exceptions are expressed in the policy and their application is also universal. Policies give strength to enforcement. Policies also set goals to achieve and are a metric against which the security program can be measured. Security policies are the plan for the security program.

Security policies create a roadmap for everything else in the program. Any good security program should include security policies for

- Crime and terrorism prevention element
- Access control to the campus, buildings, and parking
- Asset protection of equipment and documentation
- Individual responsibilities for security
- Use of security technology
- Emergency planning
- Recurring risk analysis

Role of Countermeasures in the Security Program

If security policies determine *what* to do, then countermeasures get it done. There are three broad types of countermeasures in any good security program:

- High-tech
- Low-tech
- No-tech

High-tech countermeasures are the electronic portions of the security program, commonly including

- Access control system
- Digital video system
- Security alarm system
- Two-way voice communications system
- Information technology security (always a subset of the information technology department)

A routine security program should include policies for

- Authorities and responsibilities
- Reference to charter for security unit
- Statement from the CEO/chairman/president
  - Responsibilities
    - Security unit chief
    - Security supervisors
    - Security officers
    - Security administrative staff
    - Department managers
    - Employees
    - Visitors
  - Maintenance of security policies and procedures
- Protection of life
  - Weapons and explosives screening program

- Chemical weapons defense and mitigation measures
- Special countermeasures for unique vulnerabilities
- Countersurveillance program
- All other aspects of baseline security program
- Crime prevention
  - Security awareness program
  - Post and patrol reports
  - Incident reporting
  - Crime investigations program
  - Law enforcement liaison program
  - Security intelligence program
  - Countersurveillance program
- Access control program
  - Identify public, semipublic, controlled, and restricted access spaces
  - Access cards and photo ID badging program
  - Functions, meetings, and events
  - Hours of operations and after-hours access
  - Parking controls for vehicles, cycles, and trucks
  - Loading dock and mail room access
  - Control of locks, keys, and access control credentials
- Asset and property protection
  - Security of equipment
  - Security hardware
  - Insurance cover
  - Mail recipients and deliveries
  - Headed paper
- Individual responsibilities for security
  - In the office
  - Drugs and illegal substances in the workplace
  - Weapons in the workplace
  - Property, lost and found
- Guards
  - Posts
  - Patrols
  - Response
  - Administrative duties
  - Training and career development
  - Random countermeasures
- VIP protection program
  - VIP preassessment
  - VIP security team liaison
  - Guard duties
- Emergency security plans
  - Weather emergencies
  - Medical emergencies
  - Civil disorder response
  - Disaster recovery plan
- Recurring risk analysis

Q&A

Questions

Q1: In the absence of a risk analysis or security policies,
  A. The organization will get the security system it needs.
  B. The organization will get the security system but not the guard force that it needs.
  C. The organization will not get the security system it needs in the absence of the designer knowing the assets, threats, vulnerabilities, and risks.
  D. None of the above.

Q2: The security analyst should
  A. Design the security system as soon as possible after the risk analysis report so that situations do not change too much.
  B. Address the need for security policy goals before recommending any other countermeasures.
  C. Recommend all countermeasures and then set about to recommend security policies.
  D. None of the above.

Q3: Without a risk analysis,
  A. Security policies can be developed from experience.
  B. Security policies can be developed based on interviews.
  C. Security policies are not likely to be effective.
  D. None of the above.

Q4: Without security policies,
  A. Security countermeasures can be developed from experience.
  B. Security countermeasures will almost certainly not be effective.
  C. Security countermeasures can be developed on the basis of interviews.
  D. None of the above.

Q5: Security policies create
  A. A roadmap for the facility.
  B. A roadmap for everything else in the security program.
  C. A roadmap for the risk analysis effort.
  D. None of the above.

Q6: Security policies also
  A. Set goals to achieve.
  B. Are a metric against which the security program can be measured.
  C. Both the above.
  D. Neither of the above.

Q7: Without appropriate policies,
  A. Security programs can succeed if there are good countermeasures.
  B. Security programs fail.
  C. Security programs can be developed that look very good to auditors.
  D. None of the above.

Q8: The key goal of security policies is
A. The protection of people.
B. The protection of property.
C. The protection of people and respect for their human rights and dignity.
D. The protection of the organization's business reputation.

Q9: The primary goals of all countermeasures are
A. Prevention.
B. Control and recovery.
C. Prevention, control, and recovery.
D. Recovery.

Q10: Each security policy should state
A. That everyone should be well behaved.
B. What countermeasures are needed to support it.
C. That executives may be allowed to break security policies.
D. That executive security guards are allowed to break security policies.

Answers

Q1 – C, Q2 – B, Q3 – C, Q4 – B, Q5 – B, Q6 – C, Q7 – B, Q8 – C, Q9 – C, Q10 – B

Developing Effective Security Policies

INTRODUCTION

On completion of this chapter, you will understand the process for developing and introducing security policies, triggers for policy changes, the need for expertise in periodic policy review, policy requirements, basic security policies, and regulation- and non-regulation-driven policies.

PROCESS FOR DEVELOPING AND INTRODUCING SECURITY POLICIES

The process for developing and introducing security policies has five distinct steps. These steps are

- Elements that trigger policy changes
- A policy request review
- A policy impact statement
- Subject matter expert (SME) review
- Senior management review and approval

Triggers for Policy Changes

Aside from the original development of security policies, there are many reasons for an organization to add or change one or more security policies.

- Annual review of security policies vis-à-vis the changing security landscape and revised risk analysis: All security policies should be reviewed annually. Considerations should include
  - Does this policy serve an important purpose (prevention, control, or recovery)?
  - Is the goal of the policy still valid?
  - Is the policy being observed or are there active efforts to get around the policy?
  - Is this the most effective way to achieve the goal of the policy?
- Changes in technology that make a policy obsolete or alter its need:

- Sometimes changes in technology obviate the need for a policy and some-times these changes simply change the nature of how a policy might be imple-mented. For example, as information technology emerged, all policies relating to proprietary information had to be changed as they had previously dealt with paper files. Also, as security technology evolves into a more information technology–based infrastructure, technical standards also need to change.
  - In either case, change in the language of a policy might be needed.
- Evidence of a vulnerability that could be exploited that no policy addresses: Sometimes new tactics of criminals and terrorists cause new vulnerabilities to emerge, which were not previously exploited. In these cases, policy should change to accommodate emerging threats.
- Regulatory compliance requirement: As security programs become more regula-tion-driven, new policies must emerge to address the regulations.
- Client request: Sometimes changes in the organization itself or in the functions of its business units dictate new needs for policies.
- Policy expiration: Some policies are built with expiration dates. For example, some policies are annual and expire automatically unless renewed. These cases beg for revision or renewal.
- Position paper compels need for new policy: The security unit chief will issue an annual position paper on emerging issues relating to security. Sometimes these spark discussion regarding a policy to address the issues discussed.
- It is recommended that the security unit should track all client interactions regarding discussions about the need for or insufficiency or inadvisability of any security policy.

Policy Request Review

- Any need for a security policy should be submitted by the security unit chief to his management, along with a policy impact statement.

Policy Impact Statement

- The policy impact statement should accompany the request for policy or stan-dards changes.
- The policy impact statement should highlight changes and include
  - Description of the new or changed policy.
  - Justification or reason for new or updated policy.
  - Identification of the risks of not changing the policy.
  - Identification of impacted stakeholders.
    - Who will be affected if the policy is not implemented?
    - Who will be affected if the policy is implemented?
  - Identification of the dependencies for implementation of policy changes (i.e., regulatory, technology, organization, etc.).
- Procedure changes do not require policy impact statements but may be changed as needed by the security unit chief to accommodate or improve on implementing security policies.
- Policy changes may be submitted in either of two ways:

FIGURE 14.1   Policy impact: limiting vulnerability.

- Scheduled review once annually.
- Review to address an emerging or recently identified vulnerability for which no policy is effective to mitigate (Figure 14.1).

Subject Matter Expert and Management Review Process

- A security SME should review policy impact statements and the associated proposed policies and either validate the documents or make recommendations for changes in a collaborative way with the security unit chief.
- The SME will return a review report identifying any comments for changes and emphasizing the need for the change or lack of it.
- The security unit chief can either make collaborative changes or make independent changes and submit it to the SME for review and comment. Collaborative changes are best so that it is the most thoughtful process. The SME should send his comments through the security unit chief to help assure full coordination.
- Following the SME review, and any resulting collaborative changes, the security unit chief can submit the changed policy along with the SME report, or may disagree with the SME and submit the policy impact Statement and proposed policy

without the recommended changes along with the SME's report and the security
unit chief's statement supporting the policy in its initial form.

- Security management will then review the policy impact statement and the proposed policies and submit them to senior management for approval or recommend revisions to the security unit chief. If the recommendations do not comply
with the SME's recommendations, those will be resubmitted to the SME for
further review and comment, and the process will re-cycle.
- The proposed policy should also be reviewed by human resources (HR) (if it
affects business operations) and the legal department prior to being reviewed by
senior management. Each of these will add comments, and the comments will
be relayed back to the SME and security unit chief for further comment, if recommendation is not forthcoming. Let me emphasize that it is not wise to "send
the recommendations down the chain" without the security unit chief and SME
being allowed to review the HR and legal department's comments. Very often,
those departments make a comment without fully understanding the document
they are commenting on. This can torpedo a perfectly good document. Most
HR and legal comments can be easily resolved in collaboration and no HR/legal
comment should ever shoot down a recommendation on which the security unit
chief and SME have not been permitted a reply comment or collaboration.
- Finally, senior management will review and approve or deny the change to policy
and will provide a comment. If denied, the policy may be resubmitted either
annually or as vulnerability needs emerge.

POLICY REQUIREMENTS

Policies must

- Be implementable and enforceable
- Be concise and easy to understand
- Balance protection with productivity

Policies should

- State reasons why the policy is needed
- Describe what is covered by the policies
- Define contacts with responsibilities
- Discuss how violations will be handled
- Be reviewed annually and updated if needed

BASIC SECURITY POLICIES

In the process of setting up a new security program, the security unit chief must determine what basic policies are needed. These may include

- Establish management support for security policies
- Establish security policy development and implementation guidelines, including
a policy revision history

- Access control
  - Establish area access levels
  - Establish access authorizations for various classes of users
  - Establish access vetting and authorization granting for:
    - Hiring and contracting
    - Management
    - Staff
    - Contractors
    - Vendors
    - Visitors
      - VIPs
      - Public
      - Department visitors
    - Tenant departments
    - Vehicle access to the property
    - Parking by classes of users
- Establish standards of behavior for
  - Use of the facility
  - Use of internal roadways and curbs
  - Courtesy of interactions between staff, visitors, and security officers
  - Respect for the directions of security officers
- Establish standards for security posts and patrols
  - What is the purpose of posts?
  - What is the purpose and goals of patrols including routine and investigative?
  - Standards for event responders
- Establish standards for use of security technology including alarms, video, monitoring, radios, and coordination with security management and responders
- Establish a weapons policy for the security unit and employees and visitors
- Establish the criteria for a public agency liaison program
- Establish the criteria for a crisis management program
- Establish an information technology security liaison policy
- Establish a department management security liaison policy
- Establish the criteria for a security investigations program
- Establish the criteria for a security intelligence program
- Establish standards for training of
  - Security management
  - Security staff
  - Security contractors
- Establish security management metrics

SECURITY POLICY IMPLEMENTATION GUIDELINES

Security policies need policy statements, references, and enforcement statements.

- Policy statements
  - Why is a specific policy needed?
  - What behaviors is the policy trying to govern?
  - What conflict or problem does the policy intend to resolve?

- What is the overall benefit of having the policy?
- Who must observe the policy?
- Who must understand the policy in order to perform their job?
- What technologies are used to implement the policy?
- What exceptions are there to the policy?
- References
  - Refer to any government regulations, industry standards, and internal authorities
- Enforcement
  - Define penalties for violating the policy
  - Define who shall enforce the policy

REGULATION-DRIVEN POLICIES

Many security policies are driven by government regulations. Increasingly, regulations are becoming the driving force and requirement behind not only policies, but entire security programs. Especially in critical infrastructure organizations such as transportation, energy, chemical, and healthcare, regulations play a key if not *the* key role in determining the nature and extent of security provisions that the organization carries out.

The U.S. Department of Homeland Security (DHS) is the benchmark agency for security regulations and many nations have copied, adopted, or used these as a model for their own security regulations.

Significant guidance is provided by the department in the form of

- The National Infrastructure Protection Plan (NIPP), which can be downloaded at http://www.dhs.gov/xlibrary/assets/NIPP_Plan.pdf. Components of the NIPP include
  - U.S. Citizenship and Immigration Services (arguably the worst possible model for border protection)
  - U.S. Coast Guard (USCG)
  - U.S. Customs and Border Protection
  - Federal Emergency Management Agency (FEMA)
  - Immigration and Customs Enforcement (ICE)
  - Transportation Security Administration (TSA)

Relevant Laws and Standards include*

- Support Anti-Terrorism by Fostering Effective Technologies Act of 2002 (SAFETY Act).
- National Environmental Policy Act (NEPA) of 1969.
- Procedures for Handling Protected Critical Infrastructure Information Act of 2002.
- The U.S. Department of Health & Human Services enforces Public Law 104-191: Health Insurance Portability and Accountability Act of 1996 (HIPAA), which requires significant security measures to protect healthcare information.

---

* www.dhs.gov/laws-regulations.

- The Sarbanes-Oxley (SOX) Act of 2002 was enacted in response to numerous major corporate and accounting scandals including Enron, Tyco International, Adelphia, Peregrine Systems, and WorldCom. The legislation established standards for all U.S. public company boards, management, and public accounting firms, but does not apply to privately held companies. The act addresses the management of accounting records and has penalties for noncompliance. Regarding security, this could apply to the badge and video databases, and e-mails, among others.
- The Foreign Corrupt Practices Act (FCPA), the American Anti-Corruption Act, and sections of Title 18 of the U.S. Code taken together prohibit corrupt business behavior by both enterprises and individuals within the United States and in business dealings with foreign organizations and with all politicians.

Relevant policies include:

- DHS Policy for Internal Information Exchange and Sharing

Additional laws and regulations from the DHS include:

- Information sharing and analysis*
  - HSPD-3: Homeland Security Advisory System (amended by HSPD-5) establishes a comprehensive and effective means to disseminate information regarding the risk of terrorist acts to federal, state and local authorities and to the American people.
  - HSPD-7: Critical Infrastructure Identification, Prioritization, and Protection: Establishes a national policy for federal departments and agencies to identify and prioritize U.S. critical infrastructure and key resources and to protect them from terrorist attacks.
  - Final Rule: Procedures for Handling Protected Critical Infrastructure Information: These procedures govern the receipt, validation, handling, storage, marking, and use of critical infrastructure information voluntarily submitted to the DHS.
  - The Critical Infrastructure Information Act of 2002 (CII Act): The CII Act seeks to facilitate greater sharing of critical infrastructure information among the owners and operators of the critical infrastructures and government entities with infrastructure protection responsibilities, thereby reducing the nation's vulnerability to terrorism.
- Prevention and protection†
  - Border security
    - Real ID Final Rule
    - US-VISIT Air and Sea Exit, Notice of Proposed Rulemaking
    - US-VISIT Final Rule: Enrolment of Additional Aliens, Additional Biometric Data, and Expansion to More Land Ports
    - Western Hemisphere Travel Initiative (WHTI)
  - Travel security
    - Changes to Visa Waiver Program to Implement the Electronics System for Travel Authorization (ESTA) Program: Interim Final Rule

---

* http://www.dhs.gov/isao.
† http://www.fema.gov/media-library-data/1407348347595-b3ed717d37d1f27b8b348015f34d9e3f/2014%20NPR%20Prevention_ProtectionOverview_508.pdf

- – Advanced Information on Private Aircraft Arriving and Departing the United States: Notice of Proposed Rulemaking
- Travel procedures
  - – Issuance of a Visa and Authorization for Temporary Admission into the United States for Certain Nonimmigrant Aliens Infected with HIV
- Infrastructure protection
  - – Critical Infrastructure Information Act of 2002
  - – Final Rule: Procedures for Handling Protected Critical Infrastructure Information
  - – Chemical Facility Anti-Terrorism Standards (CFATS): Interim Final Rule
- Chemical security
  - – Chemical Security (CFATS)
- Employment issues
  - – E-Verify
  - – Social Security No-Match: Safe-Harbor Procedures for Employers Who Receive a No-Match Letter
  - – Optional Practical Training Interim Final Rule
  - – H-2A Temporary Agricultural Worker Program Proposed Changes
- Preparedness and response*
  - HSPD-5: Management of Domestic Incidents: Enhances the ability of the United States to manage domestic incidents by establishing a single, comprehensive national incident management system.
  - HSPD-8: National Preparedness: Identifies steps for improved coordination in response to incidents. This directive describes the way federal departments and agencies will prepare for such a response, including prevention activities during the early stages of a terrorism incident. This directive is a companion to HSPD-5.
  - HSPD-8 Annex 1: Further enhances the preparedness of the United States by formally establishing a standard and comprehensive approach to national planning.

The U.S. TSA issues and administers Transportation Security Regulations (TSRs), which are codified in Title 49 of the Code of Federal Regulations (CFRs), Chapter XII, parts 1500 through 1699.†

- Security Rules for All Modes of Transportation are contained in Subchapter B, CFR 1520. Civil aviation security is covered under Subchapter C, CFRs 1540, 1542, 1544, 1546, 1548, 1550, 1552, and 1562. CFRs 554 and 1560 are reserved.
- Maritime and Land Transportation Security are covered under Subchapter D, CFRs 1570 and 1572, with 1580 reserved.
- Administrative and Procedural Rules are covered under Subchapter A, CFRs 1500, 1502, 1503, 1507, 1510, 1511, and 1515.

NON-REGULATION-DRIVEN POLICIES

Non-regulation-driven policies include all policies that are not required by law or regulation. However, many non-regulation-driven policies are required by organization charters.

---

* http://www.fema.gov/media-library-data/20130726-1635-20490-2790/hazus_response.pdf.
† http://www.tsa.gov/stakeholders/security-regulations.

The key policy development should include policies to

- Protect people
- Protect business operations
- Protect proprietary information
- Protect the organization's business reputation
- Protect property

The goal of every security policy should be to protect one or more of these vital assets. The types of policies that accomplish these goals include

- Policy basis
  - Establish management support for security policies
  - Establish security policy development and implementation guidelines
  - Establish a facility security plan
  - Establish security management metrics
- Protect people
  - Access control policy
  - Weapons/explosives screening policy
  - Crisis management program policy
  - Security intelligence program policy
  - Standards of behavior policy
  - Security posts and patrol policy
  - Security technology policy
  - Weapons policy
  - Security awareness program policy
  - Security training policy
- Protect business operations
  - Access control policy
  - Weapons/explosives screening policy
  - Crisis management policy
  - Disaster recovery policy
  - Security posts and patrol policy
  - Standards of behavior policy
  - Security technology policy
  - Public agency liaison policy
  - Information technology liaison policy
  - Department management liaison policy
  - Security investigations program policy
  - Security intelligence program policy
  - Security training policy
  - Security management metrics policy
- Protect proprietary information
  - Access control policy
  - Weapons/explosives screening policy
  - Crisis management policy
  - Disaster recovery policy
  - Security posts and patrol policy
  - Standards of behavior policy

- Security technology policy
- Information technology liaison policy
- Department management liaison policy
- Protect the organization's business reputation
  - Access control policy
  - Weapons/explosives screening policy
  - Crisis management policy
  - Disaster recovery policy
  - Security posts and patrol policy
  - Standards of behavior policy
  - Security technology policy
  - Public agency liaison policy
  - Information technology liaison policy
  - Department management liaison policy
  - Security investigations program policy
  - Security intelligence program policy
  - Security training policy
  - Security management metrics policy
- Protect property
  - Access control policy
  - Weapons/explosives screening policy
  - Crisis management policy
  - Disaster recovery policy
  - Security posts and patrol policy
  - Standards of behavior policy
  - Security technology policy
  - Public agency liaison policy
  - Information technology liaison policy
  - Department management liaison policy
  - Security investigations program policy
  - Security intelligence program policy
  - Security training policy
  - Security management metrics policy

SUMMARY

Process for Developing and Introducing Security Policies

The process for developing and introducing security policies has several distinct steps. These steps include

- Elements that trigger policy changes
- A policy request review
- A policy impact statement
- Subject matter expert review
- Senior management review and approval

Policy Requirements

Policies must

- Be implementable and enforceable
- Be concise and easy to understand
- Balance protection with productivity

Policies should

- State reasons why the policy is needed
- Describe what is covered by the policies
- Define contacts with responsibilities
- Discuss how violations will be handled
- Be reviewed annually and updated if needed

Basic Security Policies

- Establish management support for security policies
- Establish security policy development and implementation guidelines including a policy revision history
- Access control
- Establish standards of behavior for security officers
- Establish standards for security posts and patrols
- Establish standards for use of security technology including alarms, video, monitoring, radios, and coordination with security management and responders
- Establish a weapons policy for the security unit and employees and visitors
- Establish the criteria for a public agency liaison program
- Establish the criteria for a crisis management program
- Establish an information technology security liaison policy
- Establish a department management security liaison policy
- Establish the criteria for a security investigations program
- Establish the criteria for a security intelligence program
- Establish standards for training of security patrol and security console officers
- Establish security management metrics

Security Policy Implementation Guidelines

- Policy statements
  - Why is a specific policy needed?
  - What behaviors is the policy trying to govern?
  - What conflict or problem does the policy intend to resolve?
  - What is the overall benefit of having the policy?
  - Who must observe the policy?
  - Who must understand the policy in order to perform their job?
  - What technologies are used to implement the policy?
  - What exceptions are there to the policy?

- References: Refer to any government regulations or industry standards.
- Enforcement: Define penalties for violating the policy.

Policies may be driven by regulations or other needs.

Q&A

Questions

Q1: The process for developing and introducing security policies has
   A. Three distinct steps.
   B. Four distinct steps.
   C. Five distinct steps.
   D. Six distinct steps.

Q2: Which below is a trigger for a security policy?
   A. Annual review of security policies.
   B. Evidence of a vulnerability that could be exploited.
   C. Regulatory compliance requirement.
   D. All of the above.

Q3: Any need for a security policy should be submitted by the security unit chief to his management, along with
   A. A description of why the policy will strengthen the power of the security unit.
   B. A description of why the policy will save the organization money.
   C. A policy impact statement.
   D. All of the above.

Q4: A _____ should review policy impact statements and the associated proposed policies and either validate the documents or make recommendations for changes in a collaborative way with the security unit chief.
   A. Committee of neighborhood businesses
   B. Committee of affected employees
   C. Security subject matter expert (SME)
   D. All of the above

Q5: Policies must
   A. Be implementable and enforceable.
   B. Be concise and easy to understand.
   C. Balance protection with productivity.
   D. All of the above.

Q6: Policies should
   A. State reasons why the policy is needed and describe what is covered by the policies.
   B. Define contacts with responsibilities and discuss how violations will be handled.

C. Be reviewed annually and updated if needed.
D. All above.

Q7: Security policies need
  A. Policy statements.
  B. References.
  C. Enforcement statements.
  D. All of the above.

Q8: Security policies may be
  A. Regulation driven.
  B. Nonregulation driven.
  C. Either regulation or nonregulation driven.
  D. None of the above.

Q9: Non-regulation-driven policies
  A. Include all policies that are required by law or regulation.
  B. Include all policies that are not required by law or regulation.
  C. Include both policies that are and policies that are not required by law or regulation.
  D. None of the above.

Q10: Many non-regulation-driven policies
  A. Are required by organization charters.
  B. Are required by employees.
  C. Are required by the organization's customers.
  D. None of the above.

Answers

Q1 – C, Q2 – D, Q3 – C, Q4 – C, Q5 – D, Q6 – D, Q7 – D, Q8 – C, Q9 – B, Q10 – A

Countermeasure Selection and Budgeting

CHAPTER 15

Countermeasure Goals and Strategies

INTRODUCTION

On completion of this chapter, you will understand why security countermeasures are required and the elements of countermeasure objectives, goals, and strategies. The name security countermeasures implies correctly that these are measures taken to counter a threat action. In an ideal world, security countermeasures would be so effective as to completely eliminate the will of potential threat actors to take action.

While most people believe that this is not possible, in fact it has been done. There are actually numerous examples, but perhaps the best known one is the Fort Knox gold depository. As one can imagine, there have been many potential threat actors who would have been interested in accessing the gold at Fort Knox since it was built. But none have even attempted it. Countermeasures, including a formidable building and complex, heavily armed guards, layered detection systems, and automatic weapons, are so well developed that no one has ever attempted a robbery there. And do not forget it sits next to the largest assembly of U.S. Army tanks and tank crews in the world.

Compare that to the average U.S. convenience store, which as a class have the highest incidence of robberies of any fixed asset, including many fatal violent attacks. It is worthwhile to compare the two in order to develop study models of risk mitigation.

Fort Knox has multiple layers of protection for its assets, including heavy arms and multiple layers of detection systems. Its focus is on access control.

Convenience stores have little if any protection; often the cash register drawer is directly accessible by reaching across the counter from the public side. Access to the store is free to anyone, good or bad. There are often no responsive weapons and no detection until a robbery is announced by the threat actor himself. The greatest protection is usually a video camera system, which records the robbery but cannot intervene. Access control is often limited to a hopeful expectation of politeness and the occasional but undependable entry of a police officer.

In the first of these examples, access control is heavy. In the other, access control is virtually nonexistent. The obvious lesson is that keeping bad people out is good for security.

I am not suggesting that all facilities should be equipped like Fort Knox, because most organizations could not function with this level of access control and the presence of automated 50-caliber weapons and guards on parapets with scoped weapons would be not only a deterrent to crime but a deterrent to normal business.

Thus, countermeasures should be focused not only on security measures but also on being balanced with the needs of the organization's daily business needs. Like all other business programs, compromises are necessary. What, then, are the goals of countermeasures, given that compromises are necessary?

COUNTERMEASURE OBJECTIVES, GOALS, AND STRATEGIES

All security countermeasures have the broad goal of adjusting the behavior of potential threat actors so that they do not pose a threat to the organization.

There are three main goals for all security countermeasures. These are

- Where possible, identify and deny access to potential threat actors
- Deny access to weapons, explosives, and dangerous chemicals (except for legitimate exceptions, which should be well controlled and monitored)
- Make the environment suitable for appropriate behavior and unsuitable for inappropriate, criminal, or terroristic behavior; and mitigate the actions of both hazards and threats

Implementation objectives and strategies include

- Control access to the target, denying access to possible threat actors
- Where possible, deter threat actors from acting
- Detect any threat action
- Assess what has been detected
- Respond to any active threat action
- Gather evidence for prosecution, investigations, and training
- Comply with the business culture of the organization
- Minimize any impediment to normal business operations
- Help to create an environment where people feel safe and secure and can focus on the purpose of the organization
- Design programs to mitigate possible harm from hazards and threat actors

Each aspect of the overall security program has the ability to support one of the three main goals. An incomplete example of how to map these is illustrated in Table 15.1. You can use this as an example to help build your own list of countermeasures.

ACCESS CONTROL

Goals

Access control should be sufficient to facilitate access by authorized users and to deny access to unauthorized persons to all critical areas. Unlike Fort Knox, most organizations rely on access by the public to their facilities. However, access should not be universal. All members of the public and all employees do not require full access to all areas of a facility. In the most humble shop, there is a public area and a storeroom or office. In complex facilities, access may be layered so that one needs progressively higher access authorization as one moves deeper into the facility.

TABLE 15.1 Examples of Countermeasure Goals and Functions

Countermeasure Goals	Countermeasure Functions						
	Access Control	Deterrence	Detection	Assessment	Delay	Response	Evidence
Identify and deny access to potential threat actors	Access control, screening posts, and employee screening	Visible devices, signage, guards, and procedures	Guards, dogs and alarm devices including video motion	Console, guards, and security awareness policy	Operable barriers and guard posts	Console, guards, operable barriers, and intercoms	CCTV, intercoms, and witness reports
Deny access to weapons, explosives, and dangerous chemicals	Screening, guard posts, and procedures	Signage, guards, and procedures	Detectors, dogs, guards, and procedures	Screening posts, detectors, dogs, and patrols	Operable barriers and guard posts	Console, guards, operable barriers and intercoms	CCTV, intercoms, and witness reports
Make the environment suitable for appropriate behavior and unsuitable for inappropriate, criminal, or terroristic behavior; and to mitigate the actions of both hazards and threats	CPTED design, policies and procedures, training programs, and security awareness programs	CPTED design, policies and procedures, training programs, and security awareness programs	Patrols and reports by organization members	Patrols and reports by organization members	See above	See above	CCTV, intercoms, and witness reports

Modes

Access control has two modes:

- Passive strategies: screening of employees, contractors, and vendors
  - Develop screening program for employees, contractors, and vendors
  - Screen for criminal background and drug abuse (and financial responsibility where possible)
  - Enforce the screening program strictly
- Active strategies: screening of entry by employees, contractors, vendors, and visitors. Access control should be arranged in *layers*, typically including
  - Public layers will be nearest the main public door(s), such as a public lobby, customer waiting area, or service desks.
  - Semipublic areas are areas where the general public may not freely go but where they may be escorted, such as to an interview or triage room or the emergency department in a hospital.
  - Controlled areas are for those individuals with authorization, such as non-public office floors, mechanical rooms, auto mechanic work areas, airport tarmacs, and so on.
  - Restricted areas are those that require a high degree of vetting and where access is limited to a relatively small number of persons, such as research and development areas, the boardroom, the main information technology server room, cash vaults, counting rooms, and so on.

Access control can be achieved by technology or personnel means. There are two basic types of access control for both

- General access control
- Positive access control

General access control assumes that if one person in a group has access to a space, anyone they are escorting is also permitted. This approach is commonly used in employee work spaces and the like, where an access card reader on a suite door controls access to the space. General access control should not be used where it is important to assure that each person in a group has access privileges. This is because of the phenomena of an unauthorized person "tailgating" entry behind an authorized person as the door is opened. Although many organizations have tried to encourage employees to vet visitors who try to tailgate, none I know have fully succeeded.

Positive access control uses technology or guards to assure that each person is checked to be sure that they are authorized to enter the space. Examples of positive access control include card reader controlled revolving doors and turnstiles, theater or sports event ticket checkers, and airport boarding screening.

DETERRENCE

Goals

Deterrence is the ultimate goal. Deterrence achieves security without intervention against a threat actor. Deterrence builds its own momentum. The longer attacks are

Remove all metal objects before passing through metal detector

FIGURE 15.1   Security checkpoint.

deterred, the less likely it is that an attack may take place. But do not depend on deterrence.

Deterrence occurs when potential threat actors evaluate the risks and rewards of an attack and determine that the risk is not worth the reward.

- For terrorists, this could mean that an attack is not likely to succeed, that their attack would not capture the media's attention, or that they could be perceived negatively by their own constituency.
- For economic criminals, it could mean that they may not be able to access the desired assets, that they may not be able to leave with them, or that the likelihood of capture after the heist would be high.
- For violent criminals, this could mean that the threat actor could not reach his target, could not succeed in the attack, might not escape, or might be captured later.
- For subversives, this could mean that they might not succeed in subverting the normal operations of the organization.
- For petty criminals, this could mean that they might not be able to carry out their crime or would likely be captured in the act or later.

Strategies

Deterrence is achieved through making countermeasures so visible that possible threat actors think twice about their crime. Deterrence countermeasures can include architectural hardness, access control measures, guards, obvious cameras, witnesses, alarms, alarm signs, and so on. To be effective as a deterrent, countermeasures must be visible and must seem to create too much risk to carry out the attack. Ultimately, the entire baseline security program is about deterrence, and it creates the environment for all the other countermeasure functions (Figure 15.2).

There are no such things as deterrent-specific countermeasures. All visible countermeasures can act as deterrents, but no countermeasures deter alone. Deterrence is a side effect of the countermeasure's other (primary) role. Countermeasures deter because the potential threat actor believes that the countermeasure creates risk to him. That risk is

FIGURE 15.2   Deterrence.

the result of the countermeasure serving its primary role of limiting access and enabling detection, assessment, response, or evidence gathering.

DETECTION

Goals

Although at first the reader may be tempted to think that detection means catching the crook in the act, in fact every threat actor must carry out a plan in order to attack a facility, and detection also means detecting this plan. The basic steps in every threat action, whether it is terrorism or vandalism, include

- Select an appropriate target for an attack
- Surveil the target to determine the target's vulnerabilities
- Determine the best way to carry out the attack
- Plan the attack (the approach, the attack, and the escape)
- Test the target to determine if the vulnerability assessment is correct
- Execute the attack
  - Enter
  - Establish and maintain control
  - Establish and maintain countersurveillance
  - Execute the objective
  - Escape

For petty crimes, all these steps may occur in one linear timeline. However, the more valuable the asset, the more important the attack is to the threat actor's strategic goals, the more robust the countermeasures, and the more time is required to carry out all these steps. Interviews with highly successful criminals indicate that the planning cycle for some crimes can take months or even years. This gives the target many opportunities to detect the plan through surveillance and the interception of planning communications.

Strategies

Strategies include surveillance detection and attack detection.

Surveillance Detection

Most people think of detection as occurring during an attack; however, detection can also occur during surveillance. Surveillance is required for virtually every attack in order to

- Select the target
- Surveil target vulnerabilities
- Determine the best way to carry out the attack
- Test the target to determine if the vulnerability assessment is correct

Additionally, the longer a criminal spends time with his eyes on the target, the more interaction he may have with individuals working in the target space. Each individual interaction gives the target an opportunity to recognize surveillance, attack planning, or testing and to interrupt the attack before it occurs.

A good countersurveillance program is highly useful to all organizations where asset values are high and especially where there is a possibility of violence occurring in the carrying out of a crime. For terrorism, a good countersurveillance program is an absolutely essential component of any workable terrorism countermeasures program.

A good countersurveillance program includes

- Ample use of video surveillance in exterior and public spaces
- Trained and alert security officers
- Trained and alert console officers
- Loitering detection software on the video system

Attack Detection

Once an attack of any kind is underway, whether it is terrorism, economic crime, violent crime, subversive action, or petty crime, it is important, where possible, to be able to detect the crime underway. Detection countermeasures may include

- Intrusion detection system on property and building perimeters
- Intrusion detection system applied to critical passageways and internal spaces
- Duress alarms at critical counters and desks
- Hold-up alarms

Intrusion detection systems on property and building perimeters may include fence detection systems, microwave and infrared beams, seismic detectors, pneumatic line detectors, video fence line detection systems, glass break detectors, and door position switches. Internal space detection systems may include door position switches, area motion detectors, and video motion detectors. Duress alarms may include hidden finger switches, footswitches, and so on. Hold-up alarms may include duress alarms and bill traps (the last bill removed in a cash drawer triggers a silent alarm).

Alarms may be either silent or audible. It is best to use an audible alarm if the property is vacant such as at nighttime, when the audible alarm could itself act as a deterrent, frightening the intruder away. Silent alarms are best where an audible alarm could be false or a nuisance, where on-site security staff can respond quickly, and where such a response would not possibly escalate the crime to the point of violence.

ASSESSMENT

Goals

When an attack is detected, it is then necessary to assess the threat for the following characteristics:

- Is the detection itself real, false, or a nuisance detection?
- If the detection is real, what is the level and nature of the threat actors?
- What is their goal?
- What weapons are they carrying?
- What are their tactics?
- Does this appear to be a unfolding as a property or violent crime or a property crime with potential for violence?
- Are the threat actors employing countersurveillance methods?
- How are they dressed? How can law enforcement distinguish the threat actors from ordinary employees or customers?
- What is their apparent exit strategy?

Is the Detection Itself Real, False, or a Nuisance Detection?

Many alarms are either false or nuisance alarms. Before responding to any alarm, it is useful to investigate and assess to see if the alarm is real. This can often be done by using a second alarm device as a confirmation or by using a second technology to confirm it. For example, on perimeter alarms where nuisance alarms are very common, it is useful to have two types of alarm detection technologies, each having different nuisance modes and both working together. Consider, for example, the use of infrared beams and fence line detection, where infrared is subject to nuisance alarms from blowing newspapers or animals and the fence line detection is subject to nuisance alarms from nearby trains. If only one alerts, it could be a nuisance alarm, but when both do, it is confirmed. Video cameras can also be used to confirm the alarm when the presence of an intruder can be seen on camera.

If the Detection Is Real, What Is the Level and Nature of the Threat Actors?

Once confirmed, it is important to know the nature of the threat actors. How many threat actors are there? Does their intrusion seem organized or chaotic? Is there an obvious leader? Is the group cohesive and professional or are they displaying anxiety and fear?

What Is Their Goal?

Are they carrying a sign protesting the activities of the organization or are they carrying automatic weapons? How many threat actors are there? Can their intentions be determined by their actions?

What Weapons Are They Carrying?

If the threat actors are carrying weapons, what type are they? Are they knives, handguns, automatic weapons, RPGs, or mortars? Does the use of the weapons indicate a high degree of training, or do they seem amateurish?

What Are Their Tactics?

The tactics of an individual or group speak to their capabilities and training and their preparation to use force or to counter a security presence. Tactics may indicate that it is appropriate to confront or to stand off.

Could Their Intentions Include Violence?

Based on observations such as their interactions with employees and customers, it may be possible to determine the threat actors' willingness to use violence as a means to control the crime scene or to gain access to specific assets. The willingness to use violence may be important to help dictate your response.

Are They Employing Countersurveillance Methods?

The presence of obvious countersurveillance, such as a person waiting in a car nearby but not at the door, indicates a high level of preparation and planning. This indicates that contingency planning may also be in place to deal with approaching law enforcement or the arrival of external security team members. The presence of countersurveillance will dictate different response strategies.

*How Are They Dressed? How Can Law Enforcement Distinguish
the Threat Actors from Ordinary Employees or Customers?*

Whether the response will be by law enforcement or by internal security, it is important for them to know who are the threat actors and who are the victims. Otherwise, all persons will be treated as threat actors. This is especially true where the threat actors are using violence to control the crime scene.

What Is Their Apparent Exit Strategy?

Although this factor is often overlooked, it is important to determine the probable exit strategies, where possible. These may include

- A waiting car, perhaps with a getaway driver (look for a getaway car at all exits)
- Waiting motorcycles or bicycles
- The use of weapons to exit the premises
- The taking of hostages
- The staging of stolen goods (such as dumping jewelry into a dumpster for later retrieval)

This knowledge can help to cut off the criminals or allow for the interception of the criminals or their stolen goods.

Strategies

Effective assessment countermeasures include video and voice communications systems. Video cameras should be placed at all facility perimeter areas, facility approaches, and facility entries in order to get a positive identification of any threat actors who enter the facility and to determine what external support they have in terms of lookouts and getaways.

It is very useful to have a video camera viewing every area where a threat action could reasonably occur, including all entry control locations. This allows both the detection and assessment of crimes in progress. It is also very useful to have a two-way voice station (intercom station or station without call button) near the camera wherever a threat action could occur. This allows interruption of the threat action by a remote console operator, and, for many crimes, this is enough to end the crime.

RESPONSE

Goals

Once a threat action is detected, a response is possible. Responses to threat actions could include

- Take no direct action to counter the threat actors, instead try to minimize any potential harm to innocent people
- Gather evidence for an investigation and for a post event analysis, resulting in scenario planning and training later
- Call others (such as the police) for help
- Intervene directly against the attack to stop it and/or capture the threat actors

Before any response is undertaken, it is necessary to formulate an appropriate response. I propose that the best time to do this is before any attack, when heads are clear and planning time is leisurely. It may be necessary to adjust the plan if an actual attack takes place, but at least there will be a response plan in place.

For example, before September 11, 2001, it was the policy of airlines to cooperate with airplane hijackers and let negotiators arrange for freedom of the hostages once back on the ground. This strategy included allowing hijackers access to the cockpit to avoid casualties on the plane. However, when United Flight 93 passengers used their cell phones to call loved ones after the plane was hijacked, the passengers learned that another plane had crashed into the World Trade Center, and the passengers themselves changed the strategy from one of cooperation to one of counterforce. Although this strategy did not save their own lives, it did save many lives in the ultimate target in Washington, and as such, it was certainly an act of heroism.

Strategies

Responses may also include delaying the threat actors, denying them access to the target asset, voice communications for negotiations, and ultimately force-on-force.

As a design consultant, I am a big believer in using technology to counter threat actors instead of placing lives at risk. The use of reactive electronic automated protection systems (REAPS technologies) may include two-way voice communications, delaying technologies, disruptive technologies, and active force technology for direct use against threat actors. See Chapter 16 for more on REAPS technologies.* Also REAPs technologies are covered in great detail in my book *Integrated Security Systems Design*.

Intercoms are the forgotten technology of security. Security intercom systems, along with the ample use of security video systems, allow for immediate assessment of threat actions without dispatching a guard, which could escalate the crime to violence. One of the most effective tools against convenience store crimes has proven to be a two-way voice communication system that allows console officers in a remote security command center to speak directly to store robbers, alerting them that they are not only being recorded by video cameras, but that their identification is solid, that police have been called and are on the way, and that any escalation to violence will result in more severe charges by law enforcement. This has proven to be effective in getting robbers to stop the robbery and leave the premises immediately without further harm to the store employees or customers and in many cases also without completing the robbery.

It is very useful to have a two-way voice station (intercom station or station without call button) near the camera wherever a threat action could occur. This allows interruption of the threat action by a remote console operator, and for many crimes, this is enough to end the crime.

EVIDENCE GATHERING

Goals

The goals of evidence include providing resources for investigations, strategy development, and training (Figure 15.3).

Evidence sources may include

- Video footage
- Audio recordings
- Fingerprints
- Crime scene forensics
- Computer forensics

Strategies

The security program should be designed to gather evidence from its outset and personnel should be trained to protect physical evidence. Camera placements should be useful to identify threat actors as they approach and enter the facility and at the locations where crimes are most likely to occur. During the risk analysis, this requires careful consideration of the types of threat scenarios that are most likely and the locations where such scenarios might occur. All these should be noted in the report. Audio should be recorded on all outgoing calls to emergency responder phone numbers (911 in the United States and 112 in other countries) and on all active security intercom stations.

Security officers should be trained to secure a crime scene immediately after a crime until law enforcement arrives. Security barrier marker tape ("Crime Scene—Do Not

---

* For even more on REAPS technologies, see the author's book *Integrated Security Systems Design: Concepts, Design and Implementation*.[1]

FIGURE 15.3   Evidence gathering.

Cross") should be kept in stock for this use. Any computers that could have been involved in a crime should be unplugged from the network but left powered on, secured, and sealed for the arrival of a law enforcement or internal computer forensics team.

COMPLY WITH THE BUSINESS CULTURE OF THE ORGANIZATION

Goal

Each organization has its own unique business culture. It may be formal or relaxed, top-down or lateral, open for free movement of the public or imposing restricted movements. The security program should be configured to comply with the business culture of the organization. All security measures have some consequences both for normal business operations and for the business culture. Both should be minimized as much as possible.

I have been consulted on many projects to correct failed security programs that, on review, were sound in principle but did not take the organization's business culture into account and thus were not accepted by the users. The users are stakeholders in the system. If their points of view and expectations of convenience and perceived intrusion are not taken into account, the security provisions will not be accepted. This is the most important nontechnical element that addresses directly the success or failure of the system.

People will naturally take the path of least resistance. And, if after many years of moving freely, they are suddenly confronted by a queue or a barrier, they will attempt to circumvent it because they are used to being able to move freely through a portal without impediment. If there is a sneak-path, they will use it. If there is a guard, they will argue with him or her. There will be complaints, and pressure will be applied to the security manager to change the procedures or technology. It is important to take traffic flow, throughput, and people's perceptions of how they are being treated by management into account.

Strategies

In the countermeasure planning phase, it is important to understand the organization's business culture as much as possible. This is perhaps the most difficult task that a security practitioner has to carry out. Business cultures are rarely well documented. Culture by definition is that body of knowledge that is common and allows a common communication based on the shared assumptions of those working together.

For example, in one high-security project, the entire campus could have been easily secured by moving all visitor parking to an adjacent parking lot and having all visitors clear through a single visitor center. However, the business culture of that organization required that all visitors be granted access to parking on the campus itself, thus allowing visitors past the visitor center. Security took second place to business culture. It should be assumed that the security program should impede the movements of people as little as possible and should assure that everyone is treated with consideration, kindness, and respect.

MINIMIZE IMPEDIMENTS TO NORMAL BUSINESS OPERATIONS

Goals

As with business culture, all security measures have some impact on normal business operations. The security program should impede normal business operations as little as possible.

Strategies

The key impediment to business operations is almost always in the area of access control. A key strategy of controlling access without creating the sense of an impediment is to rely more on technology than on people for security access control.

It takes more time to clear a staffed checkpoint than to clear through a card reader. And people tend to see technological delays as part of the environment. However, when the delay is associated with a security guard, they tend to personalize the screening action (people sometimes presuppose a bias against the person by the screener and infer an intent on the part of the security officer to delay the person). No such intent can be imposed on a card reader, as technology has no capacity to develop intent or biases or to distinguish any one person from another.

This strategy has other benefits as well. Because technology does not distinguish between people, it treats everyone fairly and cannot be compromised by threat, intimidation, or enticement.

All security officers dealing with the public should be trained to be gracious under fire and not to personalize any verbal abuse. In areas where people are carrying bags or totes, provisions should be made to use as few hand actions as possible. In such cases, the use of photo IDs as an access vetting measure can help speed people along.

SAFE AND SECURE ENVIRONMENT

Goals

The aim is to help to create an environment where people feel safe and secure and can focus on the purpose of the organization.

Strategies

The use of crime prevention through industrial design (CPTED) principles helps to create a safe and secure environment and conveys a feeling of safety and security to all. Good lighting, gracious guards, well-maintained facilities and security equipment, good way-finding signage, and security awareness inserts in the company newsletter all contribute to a feeling of well-being on the part of users.

DESIGN PROGRAMS TO MITIGATE POSSIBLE HARM FROM HAZARDS AND THREAT ACTORS

The security program should include elements to deal with unwanted exceptions such as

- Intruders and offenders
- Disruptive people
- Medical emergencies
- Natural disasters
- Civil disorder and riot
- Loss of business continuity
- Chemical, biological, radiological emergency
- Challenges to the security program from outside and inside sources (Table 15.1)

SUMMARY

Introduction

The name security countermeasures implies correctly that these are measures taken to counter a threat action. In an ideal world, security countermeasures would be so effective as to completely eliminate the will of potential threat actors to take action. Countermeasures should be focused not only on security measures but also on being balanced with the needs of the organization's daily business needs. Like all other business programs, compromises are necessary.

All security countermeasures have the broad goal of adjusting the behavior of potential threat actors so that they do not pose a threat to the organization. This is done in three ways:

- Design an environment that encourages appropriate behavior and discourages inappropriate, criminal, or terroristic behavior
- Detect, assess, and respond to exceptions
- Design the program to mitigate any potential harm from hazards and threats

Implementation strategies include:

- Control access to the target, denying access to possible threat actors
- Deter any threat action from occurring
- Detect any threat action
- Assess what has been detected
- Respond to any active threat action
- Gather evidence for prosecution, investigations, and training
- Comply with the business culture of the organization
- Minimize any impediment to normal business operations
- Help to create an environment where people feel safe and secure and can focus on the purpose of the organization
- Design programs to mitigate possible harm from hazards and threat actors

Access Control

Goals

Access control should be sufficient to facilitate access by authorized users and to deny access to unauthorized persons to all critical areas.

Strategies

Access control should be arranged in layers, typically including

- Public areas
- Semipublic areas
- Controlled areas
- Restricted areas

Access control can be achieved by technology or personnel means. There are two basic types of access control for either

- General access control: access control on a portal
- Positive access control: access control to the individual

Deterrence

Goals

Deterrence is the ultimate goal. Deterrence achieves security without intervention against a threat actor. Deterrence occurs when potential threat actors evaluate the risks and rewards of an attack and determine that the risk is not worth the reward.

Strategies

Deterrence is achieved through making countermeasures so visible that possible threat actors think twice about their crime. Deterrence countermeasures can include architectural hardness, access control measures, guards, cameras, witnesses, alarms, alarm signs, and so on. To be effective as a deterrent, countermeasures must be visible and must seem to create too much risk to carry out the attack.

Detection

Goals

Detect preattack surveillance, planning, and testing where possible and detect attacks in progress. The basic steps in every threat action, whether it is terrorism or vandalism, include

- Select an appropriate target for an attack
- Surveil the target to determine the target's vulnerabilities
- Determine the best way to carry out the attack
- Plan the attack (the approach, the attack, and the escape)
- Test the target to determine if the vulnerability assessment is correct
- Execute the attack:
  - Enter
  - Establish and maintain control
  - Establish and maintain countersurveillance
  - Execute the objective
  - Escape

Strategies

Strategies include surveillance detection and attack detection.

Surveillance Detection   A good countersurveillance program includes:

- Ample use of video surveillance in exterior and public spaces
- Trained and alert security officers
- Trained and alert console officers
- Loitering detection software on the video system

Attack Detection   Once an attack of any kind is underway, whether it is terrorism, economic crime, violent crime, subversive action, or petty crime, it is important, where possible, to be able to detect the crime underway.

Detection countermeasures may include

- Intrusion detection system on property and building perimeters
- Intrusion detection system applied to critical passageways and internal spaces
- Duress alarms at critical counters and desks
- Hold-up alarms

Assessment

Goals

When an attack is detected, it is then necessary to assess the threat for the following characteristics:

- Is the detection itself real, false, or a nuisance detection?
- If the detection is real, what is the level and nature of the threat actors?
- What is their goal?
- What weapons are they carrying?
- What are their tactics?
- Could their intentions include violence?
- Are they employing countersurveillance methods?
- How are they dressed? How can law enforcement distinguish the threat actors from ordinary employees or customers?
- What is their apparent exit strategy?

Strategies

Effective assessment countermeasures include video and voice communications systems.

Response

Goals

Once a threat action is detected, a response is possible. Responses to threat actions could include

- Take no direct action to counter the threat actors, and instead try to minimize any potential harm to innocent people
- Gather evidence for an investigation and for a postevent analysis, resulting in scenario planning and training later
- Call others (such as the police) for help
- Intervene directly against the attack to stop it and/or capture the threat actors

Strategies

Responses may also include delaying the threat actors, denying them access to the target asset, using voice communications for negotiations, and ultimately using force-on-force.

As a design consultant, I am a big believer in using technology to counter threat actors instead of placing lives at risk. The use of reactive electronic automated protection systems (REAPS technologies) may include two-way voice communications, delaying technologies, disruptive technologies, and active force technology for direct use against threat actors. See Chapter 16 for more on REAPS technologies.*

Evidence Gathering

Goals

The goals of evidence include providing resources for investigations, strategy development, and training. Evidence sources may include

- Video footage
- Audio recordings
- Fingerprints
- Crime scene forensics
- Computer forensics

Strategies

The security program should be designed to gather evidence from its outset, and personnel should be trained to protect physical evidence. Camera placements should be useful to identify threat actors as they approach and enter the facility and at the locations where crimes are most likely to occur. During the risk analysis, this requires careful consideration of the types of threat scenarios that are most likely and the locations where such scenarios might occur. All these should be noted in the report. Audio should be recorded on all outgoing calls to emergency responder phone numbers and on all active security intercom stations.

Security officers should be trained to secure a crime scene immediately after a crime until law enforcement arrives. Any computers that could have been involved in a crime should be unplugged from the network but left powered on, secured, and sealed for the arrival of a law enforcement or internal computer forensics team.

Comply with the Business Culture of the Organization

Goal

Each organization has its own unique business culture. The security program should be configured to comply with the business culture of the organization. All security measures have some consequences both for normal business operations and for the business culture. Both should be minimized as much as possible.

Strategies

In the countermeasure planning phase, it is important to understand the organization's business culture as well as possible. It should be assumed that the security program should impede the movements of people as little as possible and the security program should assure that everyone is treated with consideration, kindness, and respect.

---

* For even more on REAPS technologies, see the author's book *Integrated Security Systems Design – Concepts, Design and Implementation*.[1]

Minimize Impediments to Normal Business Operations

Goals

As with business culture, all security measures have some consequences for normal business operations. The security program should impede normal business operations as little as possible.

Strategies

The key impediment to business operations is almost always in the area of access control. A key strategy of controlling access without creating the sense of an impediment is to rely more on technology than on people for security access control.

All security officers dealing with the public should be trained to be gracious under fire and not to personalize any verbal abuse. In areas where people are carrying bags or totes, provisions should be made to use as few hand actions as possible. In such cases, the use of photo IDs as an access vetting measure can help speed people along.

Safe and Secure Environment

Goals

The aim is to help to create an environment where people feel safe and secure and can focus on the purpose of the organization.

Strategies

The use of CPTED principles helps to create a safe and secure environment and conveys a feeling of safety and security to all. Good lighting, gracious guards, well-maintained facilities and security equipment, good way-finding signage, and security awareness inserts in the company newsletter; all these things contribute to a feeling of well-being on the part of users.

Design Programs to Mitigate Possible Harm from Hazards and Threat Actors

The security program should include elements to deal with unwanted exceptions such as:

- Intruders and offenders
- Disruptive people
- Medical emergencies
- Natural disasters
- Civil disorder and riot
- Loss of business continuity
- Chemical, biological, radiological emergency
- Challenges to the security program from outside and inside sources

REFERENCE

1. Norman, T. L. 2007. *Integrated Security Systems Design: Concepts, Design and Implementation.* Butterworth Heinemann, Oxford.

Q&A

Questions

Q1. Security countermeasures
  A. Are policies that can keep burglars away.
  B. Are measures taken to counter a threat action.
  C. Are policies that keep all employees safe from all threats.
  D. None of the above.

Q2. Security countermeasures should be focused not only on security measures,
  A. But also on being balanced with the organization's daily business needs.
  B. But also on safety measures.
  C. But also on the welfare of the natural environment.
  D. None of the above.

Q3. All security countermeasures
  A. Have the broad goal of adjusting the behavior of employees so that they do not take advantage of management.
  B. Have the broad goal of adjusting the behavior of customers so that they do not steal products and services.
  C. Have the broad goal of adjusting the behavior of security guards so that they do not sleep on the job.
  D. Have the broad goal of adjusting the behavior of potential threat actors so that they do not pose a threat to the organization.

Q4. There are _____ main goals for all security countermeasures.
  A. Two
  B. Three
  C. Four
  D. Five

Q5. Implementation objectives and strategies include (but are not limited to)
  A. Controlling access to the target.
  B. Detecting any threat action.
  C. Responding to any active threat action.
  D. All of the above.

Q6. Access control should be sufficient to
  A. Facilitate access by authorized users.
  B. Deny access to unauthorized persons to all critical areas.
  C. Neither of the above.
  D. Both of the above.

Q7. Do not depend on
  A. Detection.
  B. Access control.
  C. Deterrence.
  D. Response.

Q8. Detection includes
   A. Surveillance detection.
   B. Attack detection.
   C. Surveillance detection and attack detection.
   D. None of the above.

Q9. When an attack is detected, it is then necessary to _____ the threat.
   A. Assess
   B. Deter
   C. Surveil
   D. None of the above

Q10. The goals of evidence include
   A. Providing resources for investigations.
   B. Providing resources for strategy development.
   C. Providing resources for training.
   D. All of the above.

Answers

Q1 – B, Q2 – A, Q3 – D, Q4 – B, Q5 – D, Q6 – D, Q7 – D, Q8 – C, Q9 – A, Q10 – D

CHAPTER 16

Types of Countermeasures

INTRODUCTION

All security countermeasures should have the goals of adjusting the behavior of potential threat actors so that they do not pose a threat to the organization and of adjusting the behavior of the organization to effectively mitigate risks.

This is done in three ways:

- Design an environment that encourages appropriate behavior and discourages inappropriate, criminal, or terroristic behavior
- Detect, assess, and respond to exceptions
- Design the program to mitigate any potential harm from hazards and threats

There are two primary types of countermeasure implementations, each having three elements. These are

- The baseline security program (BSP).
- Special countermeasures to address special threats.
- Each of these has high-tech, low-tech, and no-tech components.

Both the BSP and special countermeasures are necessary to cope with all the conditions that an organization may confront. The exact makeup of those programs is the result of recommendations from the risk analysis.

BASELINE SECURITY PROGRAM

The BSP is the heart of the countermeasures. The BSP is designed to accommodate normal day-to-day operations and to allow for the identification of unwanted exceptions so that they can be handled. The BSP is not designed to cope with highly unusual conditions such as acts of terrorism. The BSP should include all the following four elements:

- Design an environment that encourages appropriate behavior and discourages inappropriate, criminal, or terroristic behavior
- Control access to critical assets
- Detect, assess, and respond to exceptions
- Design the program to mitigate likely potential harm from hazards and threats

Typical Baseline Security Program Elements and Implementation

A. Program elements
  1. High-tech program elements
     a. Alarm/access control system
     b. Parking access control system
     c. Security video system:
        i. Fixed and pan/tilt/zoom (PTZ) exterior cameras
        ii. Fixed and PTZ interior cameras
        iii. Video analytics
     d. Security communications systems
        i. Digital two-way radio system (part of the telecommunications package)
        ii. Security intercom system
     e. Command/control elements
        i. Lobby consoles
        ii. Security management console
        iii. Main and archive servers
        iv. Situation awareness software
  2. Low-tech program elements
     a. Perimeter control elements (fencing, etc.)
     b. Pedestrian and roadway barriers such as
        i. Office lobby turnstiles
        ii. roadway barriers (lift-arm gates)
        iii. Automated road blockers
     c. Lighting (part of the electrical package)
     d. Locks (part of the architectural package)
     e. Signage (part of the architectural package)
     f. Crime prevention through environmental design (CPTED) elements
        i. Security landscaping
        ii. Security architectural elements
  3. No-tech program elements
     a. Management elements
        i. Security program planning
        ii. Security management acquisition
        iii. Security policy development
        iv. Security procedures development
        v. Security program metrics development
     b. Security guard program:
        i. Posts (also called a fixed patrol)
        ii. Patrols
        iii. Security guard training program
     c. VIP handling program
        i. Mobile procedures (drop-off areas)
        ii. Fixed procedures (in-house areas)
        iii. Liaison with VIP security staff
     d. Security awareness program
     e. Security communications program
     f. Security investigations program
     g. Law enforcement liaison program

B. BSP implementation
  1. Planning
  2. Security supervisor hiring
  3. Supervisor training
  4. Security officer hiring
  5. Security officer training
  6. Scenario rehearsals
  7. Daily operations training
  8. Security program documentation
C. BSP phasing
  1. Planning
  2. Training
  3. Review

Designing Baseline Countermeasures (and Qualifications)

Qualifications

Security systems should be designed by qualified security system designers, for example, those having a professional certification such as ASIS Certified Protection Professional (CPP) or Physical Security Professional (PSP), or holding a degree in electrical engineering with an extensive background in both security system design and security risk analysis. Alternatively, a qualified technical designer can work with a qualified risk analyst.

Many security systems today are designed by security technicians. Let me just state here that a security technician is a security system designer in the same way that an automobile mechanic is an automobile designer. The qualifications for designing a system are entirely different from those for installing one. While security technicians may fancy themselves as designers, they are not. There are myriad decisions necessary in every security system that have no basis whatsoever in anything technical. A good set of technical skills still leaves the technician completely devoid of analytical skills, which are the basis on which all countermeasure decisions are made.

Design Process

Follow these steps to design countermeasures for a BSP:

- Access control program
  - Define access zones such as
    - Public zones
    - Semipublic zones
    - Controlled zones
    - Restricted zones
  - Define which assets require what level of zoning, then zone to those requirements.
  - Define control points between zones. These will be the access control locations.
  - Determine what kind of access control is required at each control point (card reader, biometric reader, vehicle lift gate, vehicle sliding gate, etc.).
  - Determine which access control locations need guard assistance (visitor badge issuance, etc.).

- Determine which access control points need intercom assistance (vehicle parking gates, etc.).
- Define the access credential program (photo ID badges, etc.).
- Way-finding signage.
  - Define the detection program
    - Perimeter detection
      - Facility perimeter
      - Building perimeter
    - Interior detection
    - Space detection
    - Duress alarms
  - Define the assessment program
    - Video assessment
    - Audio assessment
    - Two-factor alarm assessment
  - Define the deterrence program
    - Patrols
    - Posts
    - Signage
    - Security awareness program
    - Security investigations program
  - Define the response program
    - Communications
    - Guards
    - Vehicles
    - Armed/unarmed
    - Response training requirements
    - Security related medical emergencies
  - Define the evidence gathering program
    - Video and audio archiving elements
    - Crime scene security principles
    - Evidence preservation
    - Witness statements
    - Follow-up investigations and training

SPECIFIC COUNTERMEASURES

During the course of the risk analysis, you may uncover certain threats that are not day-to-day threats but which the security program must be prepared to handle. These will require specific countermeasures over and above the BSP. Three common elements of specific countermeasures are

- Terrorism and major crimes deterrence program
  - Terrorism countersurveillance program.
  - Security intelligence program.
  - Physical hardening of major entries and perimeter boundaries.
  - Blast protection and blast mitigation measures.
- Emergency preparedness program.

- Medical emergencies.
- States of heightened alert.
- Civil disorder preparedness.
- Fire evacuation and response.
- Earthquake, hurricane, or other natural disaster response.
- Postevent activities.
- Disaster recovery program.
  - Short-term disaster recovery: security unit coordination.
  - Long-term disaster recovery should be part of the risk manager's mandate, and the security unit will play a part but will not lead that effort.

Each of these program elements requires its own unique approach, and each individual subject deserves a book dedicated to it, but this list covers the most used program elements.

COUNTERMEASURE SELECTION BASICS

Following the guide in BSP development above, the analyst, security program manager, and security technology designer should work together to develop a coordinated and effective security program. The basic elements of a well-shaped BSP are outlined below, and an appropriate selection of possible countermeasures is listed in each section.

This section also outlines the advantages and disadvantages of various electronic security countermeasures as well as the exploits for them. This is necessary to know in order to use the devices correctly so that they cannot be easily exploited. Note: Exploits have not all been verified by the author, and most exploits will result in false alarms with possible detection of the person setting the false alarms.

All detection countermeasures should be used in layers or pairs or with audio or video assessment measures for independent verification of any alarm detection. This effectively counters the exploits of most technologies.

High-Tech Elements

Access Control Systems

- Card technologies
  - General: Access cards are digital credentials that allow authorized users access through doors and portals, such as revolving doors and turnstiles, that are equipped with access card readers. This helps assure that only authorized people are permitted into controlled and restricted spaces and achieves this with minimal security force staffing. Access cards may also be configured with the user's photo and other identifying information to identify the user and the areas to which the user has access. The latter is usually shown in card colors, where certain colors designating certain locations identify the areas for which the user has access. Finally, some access credentials also contain other data such as biometric information, health records, financial records, and so on.
  - Magnetic stripe cards
    - Description and application: Magnetic stripe cards are similar to credit cards in form and have a magnetic stripe typically using an American

Bankers Association (ABA) stripe with either two or three active stripes. Each stripe holds different information. Stripes may or may not be encrypted to protect the data.
  - Advantages: Magnetic stripe cards are very inexpensive and can be used with a photo ID system.
  - Disadvantages/exploits: Magnetic stripe cards are easily copied and can be insecure.
- Wiegand wire cards
  - Description and application: Wiegand wire cards are credit-card shaped and the card's number is created by laying a series of magnetically encoded wires (Wiegand wires) in an order that represents a distinct binary code, one unique to that individual card. The cards are read by swiping them through a Wiegand card reader and can be equipped with photo ID imprints.
  - Advantages: Wiegand wire cards are permanently magnetized and cannot be modified like magnetic stripe cards. They are also virtually impossible to copy and are therefore much more secure than magnetic stripe cards.
  - Disadvantages: Wiegand wire cards are more expensive than magnetic stripe cards, and the cards must be swiped through their reader, requiring some precision and contact; therefore these card readers have a limited life, require more maintenance, and entail a longer throughput time than proximity cards.
  - Exploits: Disassemble another card and reconfigure the bitmap to match the card to be copied. This is almost impossible to do correctly as the spacing as well as the bitmap must be copied exactly in order for the copied card to work properly.
- Proximity cards and key fobs
  - Description and application: Proximity cards are credit-card shaped and are equipped with a microchip and two antennas. One antenna receives a query from a nearby proximity card reader and the other transmits the card's unique card number back to the querying reader. Another version of this technology configures the credential as a key fob for convenience.
  - Advantages: Proximity cards are relatively inexpensive and can be equipped with photo ID imprints. Proximity cards do not require contact with the reader and thus have a high throughput through an access control portal.
  - Disadvantages: None in practical use.
  - Exploits: Proximity cards can be copied by sophisticated technology.
- Active cards
  - Description and application: Active cards are typically used where some distance is required, such as for automotive access. The cards are typically equipped with batteries.
  - Advantages: Active cards can be read from long distances of up to 100 ft., allowing for very fast throughput, such as in the case of automobiles transiting at high speed. Encrypted cards and readers are available.
  - Disadvantages: The batteries have a limited life span and the cards are relatively expensive.
  - Exploits: Capture the bitmap with a second reader nearby and create a copy of a valid active card using a sophisticated card programmer. This is virtually impossible for encrypted cards.
- Radio-frequency (RF) access devices

- - Description and application: RF access devices are similar in form to garage door openers. When a button is pressed, the device transmits a radio frequency code to a receiver. Unlike active cards, the receiver is not transmitting a query code.
  - Advantages: These permit long-range use in a convenient and familiar form, such as at the main gate of a housing development, allowing ready access for residents and their vehicles.
  - Disadvantages: The codes can be captured and duplicated unless encrypted.
- Barcode cards
  - Description and application: Cards are typically paper cardstock, and barcodes may be either optically readable or readable by infrared reader.
  - Advantages: Very inexpensive, suitable for use for visitors (one-time use).
  - Disadvantages/exploits: Optical type can be easily copied on a normal copier.
- Contactless smart cards
  - Description and application: Contactless smart cards are access control cards with small integrated circuits embedded.
  - Advantages: All of the advantages of proximity cards.
    - Higher level of security over proximity cards due to encryption of data.
    - Card can carry supplementary data for use as an IT access credential, point of sale, or medical data carrier.
    - Cards can also carry biometric data.
    - Cards can coordinate operation with other systems including digital cash, health records, time and attendance, guard tour information, lighting and heating, ventilation, and air-conditioning (HVAC) control and billing, and so on.
    - RF data transmission between cards and readers is encrypted to prevent card "sniffing."
  - Disadvantages: Slightly higher cost than standard proximity card.
  - Exploits: Virtually none if the system is encrypted and configured correctly.
- Transportation worker identification credential (TWIC) cards
  - Description and application: TWIC cards provide a tamper-resistant biometric credential for maritime workers needing unescorted access to secure areas of port facilities, platforms, and vessels that are under Maritime Transportation Security Act of 2002 (MTSA) regulation. The U.S. Coast Guard administers the program. Persons needing access to the above-mentioned facilities and vessels must submit a photo and biometric sample (such as a fingerprint) and pass a U.S. Coast Guard–administered security check.
  - Advantages: TWIC cards provide a high degree of security due to their multiple confirmations that the carrier is the authorized bearer and the security checks. Some facilities use TWIC credentials exclusively, while other facilities use a combination of TWIC and non-TWIC cards, depending on what part of the facility to which one needs access.
  - Disadvantages: Cost is higher than for other types of access cards.
  - Exploits: Virtually none.
- Access credential reader technologies*
  - The three main types of credential readers are

---

* This section lists only card readers that are in common use. For a full list of card readers, refer to the author's book *Integrated Security Systems Design*.[1]

- Readers that let you credential by what you have (cards, fobs, etc.)
- Readers that let you credential by what you know (keypads)
- Readers that let you credential by who you are (reads a physical attribute: biometric)

- Magnetic stripe card readers
  - Description and application: Magnetic stripe card readers come in two types: insertion type and swipe type. Insertion type readers are very rare and are usually seen in older installations. Swipe readers are still sold. Each reader reads the magnetic stripe of a magnetic stripe access card.
  - Advantages: Very inexpensive.
  - Disadvantages: Card must be swiped. Routine maintenance required on the reader. Readers may fail to read accurately as they wear and may need to be replaced periodically.
  - Exploits: Cards for these readers can be copied easily.
- Wiegand swipe readers
  - Description and application: Wiegand access cards are read by Wiegand swipe readers by being swiped, inserted, or laid against a surface.
  - Advantages: Card readers are very secure and reliable. Card cannot be read from nearby devices, as could a proximity card theoretically. Cards are almost impossible to copy.
  - Disadvantages: Card must have contact with the card reader and reader slots may be subject to vandalism.
  - Exploits: None for the reader. Disassemble another card and reconfigure the bitmap to match the card to be copied. This is almost impossible to do correctly as the spacing as well as the bitmap must be copied exactly in order for the copied card to work properly.
- Standard proximity readers
  - Description and application: Proximity readers read cards in near proximity to the card reader.
  - Advantages: Affordable, no routine maintenance in place.
  - Disadvantages: Card readers must not be mounted on metal surfaces (such as on the outside of a metal building) in order to work well.
  - Exploits: Theoretically, cards could be read from a nearby concealed unauthorized card reader and then cloned, allowing an unauthorized user to pose as an authorized cardholder.
- Contactless smart card readers
  - Description and application: Contactless smart cards are access control cards with small embedded integrated circuits.
  - Advantages:
    - All of the advantages of proximity cards.
    - Higher level of security over proximity cards due to encryption of data.
    - Card can carry supplementary data for use as an IT access credential, point of sale, or medical data carrier.
    - Cards can also carry biometric data.
    - Cards can coordinate operation with other systems including digital cash, health records, time and attendance, guard tour information, lighting and HVAC control and billing, and so on.

- – Disadvantages: Slightly higher cost than standard proximity reader and cards.
  - – Exploits: Virtually none when encrypted.
- Long-range card readers
  - – Description and application: Long-range card readers use RF to query and read cards from a distance. Long-range readers come in two types:
    - – Those that read conventional access cards (read from 3 to 6 ft.).
    - – Those that read special access cards (suitable for use in automobiles).
  - – Advantages:
    - – No need to remove card from wallet or purse.
    - – Conventional type can read conventional cards at vehicle entry points without the need to lower the driver's window.
    - – Suitable for reading cards in automobile windshields.
    - – Disadvantages: More costly than conventional card readers. Those suitable for reading automobiles at a distance are comparatively very expensive.
  - – Exploits: Virtually none.
- Barcode readers
  - – Description and application: Barcode readers are commonly used to read temporary (visitor) cards.
  - – Advantages: Can read temporary cards.
  - – Disadvantages: Most barcode readers have ASCII rather than Wiegand connections, requiring a data protocol converter to be compatible with most access control systems.
  - – Exploits: Optical barcode cards can be easily copied.
- Keypad readers
  - – Description and application: Numeric keypads similar to keypads allow access to doors and portals by reading a code unique to each user, or common to all. These come in two types:
    - – Common code: Dry-contact relay interface to door lock or gate.
    - – Unique user code: Wiegand interface to access control system.
  - – Advantages:
    - – Very inexpensive.
    - – No cards to carry.
  - – Disadvantages: Codes can be easily read by person standing nearby, thus compromising portal security.
  - – Exploits: Persons with visual access can memorize access code and then enter it later. This can be easily facilitated by a cell phone video camera allowing the offender to appear to be making a cell phone call while actually recording the keypad entry code.
- Scramble keypad readers
  - – Description and application: Similar to normal keypad readers, but each number is comprised of a seven-segment LED behind a transparent membrane. User first enters "start" button, which causes numbers to appear in random order, never showing the same pattern twice in a row. A user entering the same code will virtually always press different buttons each time the reader is used.
  - – Advantages: Very secure as no one nearby can read the number or remember the sequence of the buttons.

- Disadvantages: Slightly more costly than proximity card reader, provided by only one vendor and must be used with that manufacturer's access control system, obviating their use on other systems.
- Exploits: Extort the code from a valid user.
- Biometric reader technologies
    - Description and application
        - Biometric readers read a person's physical attributes and validate the person against a card or key code sample or against a database of other biometric samples (Figure 16.1).
        - Biometric readers may read a variety of biometric attributes including
            - Hand geometry
            - Fingerprint
            - Blood vessel patterns in the finger, hand, or eye
            - Iris
            - Retina
            - Voice print
            - Facial characteristics (facial recognition)
            - Handwriting
        - There are two main applications of biometric readers.
            - ID verification: ID validation of the biometric credential is conducted against another credential (card, keypad code, etc.). This application

FIGURE 16.1   Biometrics.

validates one biometric credential against one other form of credential (dual factor).
  - True identification: Identification of the person directly from the biometric sample validated against the entire biometric database of all users in the system (single factor).
- Advantages: Biometric credentials provide a more certain assurance that the individual is who he or she claims to be.
- Disadvantages
  - Biometric readers are more costly than card readers or keypads of all types.
  - Biometric readers are slightly slower to use than card readers or keypads.
  - True identification readers may operate slowly if the biometric sample database is large.
- Exploits:
  - Hand geometry: None.
  - Fingerprints: Fingerprints can be copied using special plasticized coating.
  - Blood vessel patterns: None.
  - Retina: None.
  - Iris: None.
  - Voice print: Virtually none.
  - Facial: None.
  - Handwriting: Virtually none.
- Photo ID systems
  - Description and application: Photo ID systems place a photo of the authorized bearer on the access card. The card may also have other identifying information for the individual, the organization, and the area(s) for which the individual has valid authorization. A photo ID system may comprise
    - Digital camera(s)
    - Photo ID workstation and software (captures the photo, prints the card, and coordinates those attributes with the access control database)
    - Photo ID card printer(s)
    - Interface to the alarm/access control database
  - Advantages:
    - Photo ID systems help assure that the bearer is the authorized cardholder.
    - Photo ID systems help visually identify authorized users from nonauthorized visitors.
    - Photo ID systems simplify enforcement of access card security policy.
  - Disadvantages: None
  - Exploits: Numerous exploits have been devised to circumvent photo ID systems, but these systems remain an effective deterrent against all but the most sophisticated criminals.

Detection Systems

- Property perimeter detection systems
  - Capacitance detection systems
    - Description and application: Capacitance detection systems can be configured underground or on a fence fabric or fence topper. They detect by sensing changes in a tuned circuit resulting from the introduction of

water (in the form of a human) near the antenna of the tuned circuit (the sensing cable). This changes the resonant frequency of the tuned circuit and thus "de-tunes" it. The de-tuning results in a detectable change to the resonance of the tuned circuit, which can be measured in mass and location along the sensing cable. Thus, detection software can annunciate the location of a detection along a long line.

- Advantages: Reliable if used correctly. Very little maintenance if installed correctly.
- Disadvantages: Cannot be used underground near pools of water such as puddles.
- Exploits: There are unverified stories of exploits of capacitance systems during very heavy rains. Cutting the line.

- Fiber-optic detection systems
  - Description and application: Long optical fibers attached to fence fabric detect the vibrations caused by a fence climber or an attempt to cut the fence fabric. Detects the location of the forced entry attempt along the sensor line. Some versions also provide audio.
  - Advantages: Highly reliable when installed correctly. Long lines are possible; one manufacturer makes single zones as long as 100 km (60 miles), with sensing accuracy down to ±1.5 m, thus making these systems suitable for use along a nation's border.
  - Disadvantages: Must be installed completely correctly along the entire line.
  - Exploits: Cutting the line; entry is possible downline until repairs are made.

- Seismic detection systems
  - Description and application: Seismic detection systems are microphones, usually in the form of spikes that are driven into the ground and connected by RF or cable to a detection circuit.
  - Advantages: Detect ground noise for short or long distances, such as footsteps or vehicles nearby.
  - Disadvantages: Must be used in the correct type of soil. Loose soil is less effective. Cannot be used in areas with high vehicle traffic (especially large trucks) as the noise of vehicles will drown out any footsteps.
  - Exploits: Use of a large vehicle to mask the sound of footsteps (in one case a jackhammer was used to mask the entry).

- Monostatic microwave detection systems
  - Description and application: Monostatic microwave detectors (transceivers) fill a space with microwave energy and detect the echo of the microwave energy. When an object such as a person moves within that space, it changes the echo, which is measurable.
  - Advantages: Reliable outdoors for short ranges.
  - Disadvantages: Can sense through walls, causing undesired detections. Cannot be used in close proximity to fluorescent lights, as it will also sense the plasma movement in the lamp.
  - Exploits: Cause numerous false alarms, resulting in the guard force to ignore later (and real) detections.

- Bistatic microwave detection systems

- – Description and application: Bistatic microwave detectors do not work on the echo principle, but rather have two units (transmitter and receiver). Detection occurs for the movement of any object between the units within their field of detection, which is widest at the center point between the detectors.
- – Advantages: Very reliable for detection of any moving object.
- – Disadvantages:
  - – Must be used with another detector outdoors to confirm, as many nuisance detections are possible.
  - – Area of detection must be completely free of standing water and small animals; it is best used inside a confined fence enclosure, such as between two perimeter fences, to reduce nuisance alarms.
  - – Detector will detect any motion, including blowing debris, rain, snow, blowing dust, and so on.
- – Exploits: During rainstorm when there may be many nuisance alarms.
- • Pneumatic underground detection systems
  - – Description and application: Comprising a flexible tube and an atmospheric pressure sensor, these detectors reliably sense pressure on the tube, such as a person stepping on the tube. The tubes are typically buried just beneath the surface of the ground.
  - – Advantages:
    - – Inexpensive compared to some other long line detectors.
    - – Because the tube is buried, its location is difficult for an intruder to detect.
  - – Disadvantages:
    - – Imprecise detection. Only the entire zone is detected, not the location along the zone.
    - – Line must be pressurized and pressure must be maintained precisely.
    - – Burrowing animals (moles) could gnaw through the tube, thus disabling it. When this occurs, the entire line must be inspected to find the leak.
  - – Exploits: If the location of the tube could be found, one could create a hole, disabling the entire sensor zone (unverified).
- • Infrared and laser detection systems
  - – Description and application: Infrared and laser detection systems are line detectors that detect a break in the infrared or laser light beam. Laser detectors cover longer distances than infrared beams. As the names of both types of detectors imply, these are both sensing line-of-sight. Best use is as a set of multiple stacked beams.
  - – Advantages: Very reliable sensing of motion between the beams.
  - – Disadvantages: Senses anything between the beams, including animals, blowing objects, and so on. Sensors must be "stacked" so that the beam cannot be crawled under or stepped over.
  - – Exploits: Cause so many false alarms that the zone is ignored.
- • Building perimeter detection systems
  - • Door position switches
    - – Description and application: Door position switches sense a door or gate being opened as the magnet (which is on the door) leaves its position next to the switch (which is in the door frame). Better switches utilize multiple magnets to "bias" the switch so that simple exploits actually create an alarm instead of defeating it.

- Advantages: Detects doors opening as little as two inches.
- Disadvantages: Switch and magnet should both be concealed in the door top and frame where the door sits, rather than on the outside of the door.
- Exploits: Early exploits called for the placement of a magnet next to the switch, thus causing the switch to fail to sense that the door had been opened. Better "balanced bias" switches use multiple magnets to use this exploit against itself. That is, placing a magnet next to the switch will actually cause an alarm immediately, even with the door closed. Saw through the door, leaving it closed in the frame.

- Glass break detectors
  - Description and application: Acoustic and vibration-based glass break detectors detect the sound of breaking glass.
  - Advantages: Almost certain detection of window breakage.
  - Disadvantages: Early acoustic detectors false alarmed on vacuum cleaners and sometimes on keys jangling.
  - Exploits: Better glass break detectors are nearly invulnerable to outside exploits.
- Photoelectric beam detectors
  - Description and application: Photoelectric beam detectors (usually configured as infrared detectors) sense motion between the detectors.
  - Advantages: Very reliable detection of any object or person crossing the beams. Infrared beams are invisible.
  - Disadvantages: In most installations, the location of the beams is obvious, allowing one to step over the beams unless they are used as a stack, which is rare indoors.
  - Exploits: Leave an object blocking the beams before leaving for the night, thus causing the zone to trip into "trouble" condition.
- Outdoor passive infrared detectors
  - Description and application: A few companies manufacture passive infrared detectors that are designed for use outdoors. These have hardened enclosures and specific circuitry to deal with the unique infrared signatures found only outdoors. These include the ability to filter out most infrared noise such as shadows of leaves, wind driven temperature changes, and so on.
  - Advantages:
    - Low cost relative to many other outdoor detectors.
    - Detector visibility may act as a deterrent (most potential intruders would recognize it as a security device but would not understand its workings and thus be fearful of being caught).
  - Disadvantages:
    - Higher false alarms than some other outdoor systems.
    - Does not work well in high-temperature environments or extremely low temperature environments.
  - Exploits: Very, very slow movement
- Interior space detection systems
  - Microwave detection systems
    - Description and application: Microwave detectors (transceivers) fill a space with microwave energy and detect the echo of the microwave energy. When an object such as a person moves within that space, it changes the

echo, which is measurable. Microwave detectors use the Doppler effect to detect. Accordingly, microwave detectors are most sensitive to objects moving toward and away from the detectors.

- Advantages: Reliable indoors in confined areas as long as the energy does not penetrate an adjacent room, where it could also be measured.
- Disadvantages:
  - Can sense through walls causing undesired detections.
  - Cannot be used in close proximity to fluorescent lights as it will also sense the plasma movement in the lamp.
- Exploits:
  - Very, very slow movement directly across the field of the motion detector.
  - Cause numerous false alarms, resulting in the guard force ignoring later (and real) detections.
- Infrared detection sensors
  - Description and application: Infrared motion detectors are wall-mounted units that are usually mounted near the ceiling and view an entire room or corridor. Some types are configured as a "curtain" sensing motion moving through the curtain. In all types, the sensor is configured to view a number of zones (also called fingers) and the sensor detects differences in heat signature between the fingers. Thus, persons moving across the fingers are most readily detected.
  - Advantages: Reliable detection, within normal temperature zones, of any motion across the fingers.
  - Disadvantages:
    - Heat sources such as heating vents, and so on can cause false alarms.
    - Detector is least sensitive for persons moving toward the detector.
    - Detectors are useless if the ambient temperature approaches ambient body temperature.
  - Exploits:
    - Covering the intruder with a very heavy blanket, blocks the detection of infrared energy, and moving slowly may cause the detector to fail to detect intrusion.
    - Moving directly toward the detector.
- Dual-technology sensors
  - Description and application: Designed to address both the weaknesses and strengths of microwave and infrared detectors, dual-technology detectors use both technologies in one package. In order for detection to occur, both detectors must sense motion.
  - Advantages: These detectors are sensitive to motion both across and toward the detector, thus confirming detection internally and obviating the failure modes of both detection technologies.
  - Disadvantages: None.
  - Exploits: Virtually none.
- Ultrasonic sensors
  - Description and application: Ultrasonic detectors have fallen into disuse due to numerous false alarms and occasional failures to sense real security events. Two types exist (active and passive). Active detectors emit an ultrasonic frequency and listen for disruptions in its reflection. Passive systems listen for sounds in the ultrasonic range.

- Advantages: None.
- Disadvantages: Failure modes include keys jangling, vacuum cleaners, insects, and other noises, such as those from nearby airports, construction zones, and so on.
- Exploits: Many.
- Thermal imaging sensors
  - Description and application: Thermal imaging sensors detect the heat from bodies against the background.
  - Advantages: Very good detection, including imaging of the intruder.
  - Disadvantages: Very expensive.
  - Exploits: High ambient temperature.
- Point detection systems
  - Duress alarms:
    - Description and application: Unlike all other alarms already mentioned, which are unintentionally triggered by suspicious persons, duress alarms are switches that are intentionally triggered by authorized persons when they believe they need help. Most duress alarms are configured to be triggered discreetly, though there is also a class of duress alarms that are positioned for anyone to trigger, such as a call-security button by a security intercom on a train platform.
      - Two-finger switches: This type requires that two fingers press two adjacent pushbuttons to assure that no accidental duress alarm is sent.
      - Shroud switches: This type has a single pushbutton contained within a shroud to prevent false alarms.
      - Pull switches: This type requires the user to pull on a knob, usually contained within a shroud.
      - Footswitches: This type requires the user to place his or her foot under a bar and lift to trigger the alarm.
      - Bill traps: When the last bill in a cash drawer is removed, the alarm is automatically triggered.
    - Audio and video verification: All duress alarms should be used with both audio and video verification wherever possible.
    - Advantages: These alarms provide the user with the ability to call for help.
    - Disadvantages: Some types can be triggered accidentally or intentionally, creating false alarms.
    - Exploits:
      - The person confronting the duress alarm user will convince them not to trigger the alarm, usually by threat of force. Defeat the alarm communication media (telephone, etc.) so that even though the alarm has been triggered, it will not be reported to anyone who could respond.
  - Explosives detection systems
    - Description and application: Various types of explosives detection systems exist, including
      - X-ray
      - Millimeter wave scanner
      - Chemical residue detection systems
      - Dogs
      - Electronics

- Visual inspections systems
  - Hand inspection
  - Under-vehicle mirrors
  - Under-vehicle video detection systems
- Advantages:
  - X-ray: Comes in two types, transmission and backscatter x-ray systems. Can image the interior of packages and cargo including vehicles, trailers, and containers. Backscatter x-ray can scan individuals and identify objects concealed under clothing.
  - Millimeter wave scanner: Similar to backscatter x-ray in effect, this technology can scan persons from a distance and provides a visual image of the person scanned sans clothing, but displaying any objects concealed under the clothing. These are used with software that blurs the face and private areas; however, there is much discussion about whether they breach privacy expectations.
  - Dogs: Very efficient when properly trained and used; they also make good company, and in most parts of the world, people find the search of their articles and person by a dog to be unobtrusive and often welcome the interaction with the dog. This is not the case for persons carrying explosives.
  - Electronics: Electronic detection methods use mass-spectrometry or other means to "sniff" explosives residues. These do so with varying degrees of efficiency and efficacy. The best of these can detect minute traces of explosives on vehicle door handles, trunk latches, steering wheels, and radio knobs.
  - Visual inspections systems
    - Hand Inspection: Hand inspection is inexpensive and can be very thorough when x-ray machines are not available or for infrequent occasions.
    - Under-vehicle mirrors: These can detect unusual objects placed under vehicles that could be a threat to the vehicle occupants and anyone standing nearby. Note: Packages under vehicles rarely contain enough explosives to be a danger to buildings, but only to the vehicle occupants and persons nearby. Bombs under cars are usually placed there to assassinate the anticipated occupant.
    - Under-vehicle video detection systems: These systems can provide a complete under-vehicle view that is better than, and takes less time than, the use of a mirror.
- Disadvantages:
  - X-ray: Transmission x-ray machines can miss some organic substances, and the technician must be trained to properly read the images presented.
  - Backscatter x-ray machines do not penetrate objects as far as transmission x-ray systems do and illustrate only one side of the object. The best backscatter systems can only penetrate up to 30 cm (~12 in.) of solid steel. Backscatter x-ray used on individuals creates an image of the person without clothing, creating privacy concerns. Steps have been taken to blur private areas and to move the screener away from the person being screened to enhance privacy. However, privacy concerns remain unabated, especially in Arab and South Asian countries.

- Millimeter wave scanner: Similar concerns regarding privacy to back-scatter x-ray; also, millimeter wave scanners become inefficient as the ambient temperature rises to near body temperature and when clothes are wet, as when entering from a rainstorm.
- Dogs: Dogs are unacceptable in some Muslim countries due to religious beliefs. Dogs require frequent breaks, and thus many more dogs are needed than one might imagine for a single checkpoint. When used at many checkpoints, the quantity of dogs can become unmanageable. Trained dogs are costly and also require dedicated trained handlers and frequent scenario training to keep the dog's skills honed.
- Electronics: Many mass spectrometers require expensive supplies and must be constantly cleaned, thus reducing their effectiveness. The better systems are self-cleaning and require few supplies, but these are very costly compared to the less capable types.
- Visual inspections systems
  - Hand inspection: Exposes the inspector to possible bomb triggering.
  - A word about under-vehicle inspection: I am fascinated at the amount of effort put into under-vehicle inspection as a means of protecting facilities. There is no record of any bomb placed under a vehicle that has ever damaged any building's structure, nor is it ever likely to happen. Under-vehicle bombs are almost always placed for detonation to kill or maim the occupant(s) of the vehicle and not to damage property or kill large numbers of people. The use of under-vehicle inspection at a facility entry checkpoint is an indication of an ignorant security analyst and planner. This is yet another example of the placebo effect; that is, the attempt to appear to protect the public, while doing little to actually do so. These systems are most often used in an ineffective manner, thus compounding the problem by advertising to real threat actors that security measures are not only ill-conceived but also ineffective.
  - Under-vehicle mirrors: Often inspections using under-vehicle mirrors are cursory and ineffective, usually inspecting only the front or one side of a car.
  - Under-vehicle video detection systems: These systems represent an expensive solution in search of a problem. I have seen many of these in practice, and in no case could the operator identify any object that was not original to the car.
- Exploits:
  - X-ray: Placing objects in a manner to obscure their nature or function. For example, placing a gun against the side of a suitcase instead of placing it flat where its outline could be easily seen.
  - Millimeter wave scanner: Using rain, hot weather, or a heavy coat to render the system ineffective.
  - Dogs: Dogs are very hard to beat; maybe by offering the dog a steak, but then the handler might notice that.
  - Electronics: Also very hard to beat when used properly. These are a very potent deterrent.
  - Visual inspections systems:
    - Hand inspection of packages: Using accomplices to create a distraction.

- Under-vehicle mirrors and under-vehicle video detection systems: Generally pointless if their intended purpose is to protect the facility. That is unless it is you getting into the car.
- Video detection systems
  - Visible light cameras. These are the most common type, directing visible light into a lens and converting it through an imager into analog or digital signals that can be recorded and/or viewed on recorders, digital archivers, and video monitors.
    - Fixed video cameras (Figure 16.2)
      - Description and application:
        - These cameras have a constant unchanging field of view that is dependent upon the lens focal length.
        - Most cameras today also have automatic backlight compensation to prevent silhouetting, automatic gain control, automatic shutter speed and/or automatic iris to adjust for light levels, and digital image processing to help assure the best possible image under all light conditions.
        - Fixed cameras come either as an exposed camera on its own mount (often with an enclosure), or concealed within a dome for aesthetics and to conceal the direction that the camera may be viewing.
        - A third type is pinhole video cameras, which are discussed separately below.
        - Cameras are available in a broad variety of qualities.
      - Advantages: Least costly.
      - Disadvantages: Requires multiple cameras for multiple views.
      - Exploits:
        - Conduct crime outside the field of view of the fixed camera, which is more difficult with dome cameras as they often conceal which direction the camera is viewing.
        - Aim a laser at the imager to blind it.
        - Spray paint over the lens or enclosure glass.
    - PTZ video cameras

FIGURE 16.2   Video cameras.

- Description and application: PTZ cameras allow the viewing of multiple angles and zoom ratios, thus permitting a very versatile point of view for the camera. Most PTZ cameras are enclosed in domes and may be used indoors or outdoors. Multiple mounts are available depending on the configuration needed.
  - Advantages:
    - Multiple views and zoom ratios.
    - Dome PTZ cameras conceal the direction of the camera view.
  - Disadvantages:
    - Camera can only view one thing at a time. Other areas within its total hemisphere of view will not be seen.
    - Non-dome PTZ cameras are obvious as to their direction of view.
  - Exploits: Create a diversion to attract the attention of the guard viewing the camera, who will point the camera to the diversion, allowing crime to be committed outside the field of view of the PTZ camera.
- Pinhole video cameras
  - Description and application: Pinhole cameras are conventional cameras fitted with a pinhole lens, which is virtually impossible to detect. When mounted properly, only the tiny lens opening (2 mm) is exposed, thus appearing only as a fleck of dust on the wall.
  - Advantages:
    - Aesthetics are high, camera does not intrude into the visual environment.
    - Camera is discreet.
    - Threat actors would not know they are within a camera's field of view.
    - Pinhole cameras may provide a view inside hostage situations after all other cameras in the area have been disabled, allowing authorities to coordinate a response with the fewest possible casualties. As hostage terrorist attacks increase, this becomes an increasingly valid countermeasure.
  - Disadvantages:
    - Concealed cameras may not be acceptable in some areas due to policy or for cultural reasons.
    - Camera lens provides limited light, so bright light must be available within the scene view. Supplemental light can be provided by infrared illuminators configured as other normal types of fixtures.
  - Exploits: None.
- Day/night imagers
  - Description and application: Some cameras are available with day/night imagers, which allow the camera to convert from color (day) to black and white (night) operation when light levels fall.
  - Advantages: Better sensitivity with black and white imager at night.
  - Disadvantages: Unless light is very low, image may be more readable in color even in low light.
  - Exploits: As with other cameras.
- Analog cameras
  - Description and application: Analog cameras provide NTSC or PAL images compatible with older television standards.

- Advantages:
  - Comparatively inexpensive.
  - Single standard, easily converted to any digital standard.
  - Especially well suited to very small installations where an inexpensive digital video recorder with analog inputs is used to record and view cameras.
  - Analog cameras do not allow hacking into the security system network when used outdoors as might digital cameras. This can be an important feature when using digital systems and there are outdoor cameras to monitor and record.
  - Analog cameras arguably provide more reliable operation outdoors than digital cameras to date
- Disadvantages: Most analog cameras will have to be converted to digital before 2015. This can be done with the addition of a digital codec.
- Exploits: Same as other cameras.
- Digital cameras
  - Description and application: Digital cameras provide TCP/IP images in a variety of digital compression formats, including JPEG, Motion JPEG, MPEG1, 2, and 4, Wavelet, and H.264.
  - Advantages:
    - Inherently digital signal so that camera can easily be scaled into an enterprise system framework of long-distance archiving and monitoring of between hundreds and thousands of cameras.
    - Images can be processed for intelligent video algorithms.
    - Images can be enhanced.
    - Redundant archiving is possible.
    - Viewing across many sites and long distances is possible.
    - Megapixel digital cameras provide extreme detail.
  - Disadvantages:
    - For storage, large data files require large storage systems.
    - Multicast digital systems are required when camera count exceeds 50.
  - Exploits: Same as other cameras.
- Digital fish-eye PTZ cameras
  - Description and application: Digital fish-eye PTZ cameras are actually fixed megapixel cameras fitted with a 180° fish-eye lens. This allows the camera to view and record an entire hemisphere, such as a ceiling mounted camera viewing downward.
  - Advantages:
    - Cameras allow multiple PTZ views simultaneously.
    - Cameras allow PTZ viewing within archive video, impossible with analog PTZ cameras.
  - Disadvantages:
    - Special software is required to view footage as a normal image.
    - Megapixel cameras create very large digital files and thus require very large and expensive storage solutions.
  - Exploits: Virtually none.
- Thermal imaging cameras
  - Description and application: Thermal imaging cameras view heat signatures rather than visible light. They are especially useful for

viewing at night under very limited light and through smoke or fog (smoke and fog diminish performance).
  - Advantages: Can view in total darkness, especially well over long distances with cooled thermal cameras, less range with uncooled cameras.
  - Disadvantages:
    - Cost is high.
    - Extreme fog or fog over long distances can diminish the performance of the camera.
    - Maritime fog affects performance more than ground fog since maritime aerosols have in average greater particle radii than rural and urban aerosols.*
  - Exploits: Carry out attack in very foggy conditions and far from an infrared camera.
- Video analytics (intelligent video software)
  - Description and application: Video analytics software processes digital video images to help find useful information that implies possible unauthorized or criminal behavior. System alerts console operator to view camera to confirm unwanted behavior. Many algorithms exist including:
    - Line of crossing
    - Left article
    - Removed article
    - Unusual crowd behavior
    - Loitering
    - Unauthorized direction of movement
    - And many others
  - Advantages: Allows untended operation of between hundreds and thousands of cameras without missing relevant and important alerts to possible improper behavior.
  - Disadvantages: Expensive, but truly empowers large video systems.
  - Exploits: None, as no offender could know that there is analytic software operating, and criminals have been known to exploit the fact that most large video systems (such as transit systems) are not well watched.

Consoles and Management Offices

- Security command, control, and communications (C^3) consoles allow the viewing of multiple systems across campuses and great distances, including across state and national boundaries. This allows significant supervision over security monitoring and access control functions for an enterprise organization. C^3 consoles also help organizations uniformly apply corporate security, safety, and operations policies throughout the entire enterprise. C^3 consoles comprise two or more monitoring stations that monitor video, alarm and access control, and security voice communications throughout the enterprise. They are sometimes integrated with building engineering monitoring functions to provide a complete facility-wide view of a campus for security, fire, HVAC, safety, and elevators from a single location, thus enhancing the cost-effectiveness and coordination of operations across security and building engineering functions.

---

* FLIR Technical Note: *Seeing through fog and rain with a thermal imaging camera.*[2]

- Lobby consoles are the "face" of security to many public users. These consoles enable console offers to service the public by providing information, visitor accesscredentials, and authorizations for employees and visitors. The consoles often also provide a secondary alarm and video station for off-peak hours use (lobby consoles should not be used for monitoring video or access control assistance during peak business hours).
- Photo ID badging stations include
    - Camera(s)
    - Backdrop
    - Lighting
    - Mirror for readying photo session
    - Badging workstation with photo ID software
    - Badge printer(s)
- Security management offices should include
    - Office for the manager and *l*ead supervisor
    - Receptionist
    - Photo ID badging station
    - Interview room (for subjects of interest)
    - Toilets
    - Break room
    - Mustering room
    - Training center (often combined with mustering room)

Security System Archiving Technologies

- Description and application: There are two basic types of security archiving technologies:
    - Analog: Analog technologies use videotape to record analog video. These are rapidly falling into disuse and are being replaced by digital storage technologies.
    - Digital: There are two main types of digital storage technologies:
        - Digital video recorders (DVRs): DVRs are purpose-built computers that store video for a small number of cameras. Some of these can be networked together; however, none provide the flexibility of server-based archivers. These are most appropriate for small systems with limited budgets that will never see extensive system growth or other than very basic operational functionality.
        - Server-based archivers: Server-based archivers utilize the following types of devices to manage and store video:
            - Directory server: Manages where live images are directed (from which cameras to which workstations)
            - Archive servers: Manage the recording of between 32 and 70 cameras depending on the resolution and frame rate
            - Storage media:
                - Fiber channel disks: Very high throughput systems (most expensive).
                - SCSI-disk systems: Medium high throughput
                - SATA-disk systems: Lower throughput.
                - Tape storage: long-term storage on the shelf or in an automatic tape carousel.

- DVD storage: long-term storage on the shelf or in an automatic DVD carousel (Figure 16.3).
- Solid state disk storage: A large capacity memory chip solution, which is an emerging technology intended to replace disk types above.
- Storage systems: All of the above can be configured into the any of the following:
- Internal storage: storage within the archive server itself, local to the operating system.
- Network attached storage (NAS): A box of disks, DVDs, or tape storage designed to be attached to the server network. Files appear to be on the network rather than attached directly to the operating system.
- Storage area network (SAN): A network of storage boxes to which the server network itself attaches in such a way that the storage devices appear as though they are locally attached to the operating system.
- Digital storage solutions: advantages and disadvantages
  - DVRs are cost effective for very small applications but do not provide the flexibility to manage large systems for other than the most basic functions.
  - Internal storage is very inexpensive but lacks large capacity.
  - NAS offers higher capacity but slower throughput.
  - SANs offer the highest and most effective use of video digital data. Some SANs use creative file management to employ low-cost SATA drives for virtual very high throughput, which would otherwise not possible without fiber channel connections.
  - Fiber channel offers very high throughput but is most costly.
  - SCSI offers medium throughput but is most well suited to small applications or as extended short-term storage (from 2 to 30 days).
  - SATA offers lowest cost but also lowest throughput. Some SANs use creative file management to make SATAs "appear" to have high throughput by spreading files across multiple disks for simultaneous recording of segments rather than recording entire files onto a single disk. The SAN then pieces the file segments back together for viewing.

FIGURE 16.3 Digital video servers.

Security System Archiving Schemes

- Immediate and long-term archiving
  - Fiber channel: Fiber channel offers *immediate* access to very large amounts of video data. It is best used for large systems (over 70 cameras) with centralized storage for immediate access (up to 2 days). Its cost generally prohibits its use for longer term storage.
  - SCSI: SCSI disks offer immediate access to small systems and short-delay access (a few seconds to a minute delay) to larger systems.
  - SATA: SATA disks offer reasonable delay for their minimal cost on larger systems (several seconds to a minute depending on the system software).
  - Tape and DVD: Tape and DVD storage offer lower cost long-term retrieval of video archives without the cost of many multiple disk drives. Excess tapes and/or DVDs are stored on the shelf or cassette for retrieval when required. This retrieval process inserts a noticeable delay of up to several minutes while the system database locates and then retrieves and loads the video data for viewing.
  - Solid state storage: Solid state storage has great promise but is limited to experimental versions as of the date of this book.
- Description and application:
  - Small systems:
    - DVR
    - One archive server with internal disks and one tape drive
  - Medium systems:
    - A few archive servers and a small NAS or small SAN system
    - Long-term storage with one or more tape drives and/or a small tape carousel retrieval system
  - Large systems:
    - Many archive servers and a large SAN system using three types of data storage:
      - Very short-term storage: fiber channel disks on san switch and server (instant retrieval up to 2 days)
      - Short-term storage: SCSI or SATA SAN (near instant retrieval up to 2 weeks/1 month)
      - Long-term storage: Tape or DVD carousel on SAN
- Redundant archiving schemes: For business continuity, redundant archiving is recommended (to handle routine and emergency maintenance and loss of archivers due to accident, natural disaster, or intentional harm).
  - Basic redundancy: one spare archive server on location to handle emergencies or maintenance.
  - More adequate redundancy: two spare archive servers to handle emergency while maintenance is being conducted.
  - Full redundancy: Full replacement set of all primary archive servers and short-term and long-term storage off-site connected by multigigabit fiber connection.
- Advantages and disadvantages:
  - Basic redundancy: Least expensive option, very limited redundancy, but better than none at all
  - More adequate redundancy: Provides for on-site redundancy of up to two archive servers, reasonable cost
  - Full redundancy: Most preferred operationally, most expensive

Security System Infrastructures

Prior to 2003, security systems used three common types of infrastructures:

- Video: coaxial or analog fiber
- Intercom: two- or four-wire analog audio plus call/control
- Alarm/access control: RS-485 and minimal use of TCP/IP for interconnecting systems between buildings

There were rare exceptions to these, but the three types above were the most common. This all changed beginning in 2000, and by 2003 there was a substantial movement toward a total digital infrastructure for all but the smallest systems.

The security industry's move to digital infrastructure provided for the implementation of many functions not possible with analog and proprietary infrastructures. These included

- The ability to develop truly enterprise systems, operating as one across many cities and states and nations
- Truly scalable systems
- Centralized and remote redundant monitoring of many video, alarm/access control, and intercom systems
- Video analytics

Security digital infrastructures can take wired, fiber, and wireless forms.

- Wired
  - Wired infrastructures utilize CAT-5 or CAT-6 cable and digital switches and routers in a variety of configurations. The most common of these include
    - Small systems: Simple switch architecture, connected by a gigabit (GB) backbone. A tree architecture is common, though sometimes ring architectures are used. This will be a total CAT 5/6 network.
    - Medium systems: Hierarchical switch architecture, with branches segmented by virtual local area networks (VLANs). Either a tree or ring architecture may be used. Fiber switch backbone may be used. The network will comprise core and edge switches, where core switches connect together and also connect to servers, SANs, and routers. Edge switches connect to edge devices (cameras, access control controllers, intercoms, etc.) and to core switches. Workstations may reside on either core or edge switches, depending on preference.
    - Large systems: Redundant hierarchical switch architecture, using edge (access layer) switches to connect field devices and core switches to connect to servers and SANs; distribution layer switches may be used as the system becomes larger. All switches may be partially or fully redundant. All switches will connect by fiber using ever increasing capacity as one nears the core layer. For example:
      - 100 MB edge device
      - 1 GB edge switch to distribution layer switch
      - 10 GB distribution layer to core switch
      - 10 GB+ core layer

- Fiber-optic Cable
  - When to use fiber-optic cable: Fiber should be used whenever distances exceed ratings of CAT5 or CAT6 cables (90 m/270 ft),* or when capacities exceed the ratings of the CAT5 (100 MB)† or CAT6 (1 GB). For any speed above 1 GB or distance over 90 m, fiber should be used.
  - Types of fiber: There are two types of fiber: single-mode and multi-mode. Multi-mode fiber is the least expensive (usually plastic) and the transmitters and receivers are usually LED sources rather than lasers. Maximum distances vary, up to several miles. Single-mode fibers use glass cores instead of plastic, and their transmitters and receivers use lasers instead of LEDs. Single-mode fiber and its transmitters and receivers are thus more expensive and provide higher capacity and distance.
- Wireless
  - General:
    - All wireless options are less reliable and secure than wired or fiber-optic options regardless of any implications to the contrary by anyone.
    - Anyone thinking of using a wireless option should conduct a field radio-frequency survey to assure that the desired frequency is free and available and that the environment will support the operation of the system on the desired frequency.
  - Licensed versus unlicensed options:
    - Wireless solutions come in two broad variants: licensed and unlicensed options. The specific frequencies requiring licensing vary from country to country, so this book cannot provide uniform worldwide guidance on this topic. The designer should confirm that the solution selected is licensed if required.
  - Benefits of each:
    - Licensed options could provide more security in that fewer people are permitted to operate on the designated frequency. Licensed options assure that no one else will operate on the assigned frequency.
    - Unlicensed options do not have the cost or formalities burden of licensed options but provide no guarantee of continued clear operations, as anyone else could also begin using the same unlicensed frequency in the same space, thus diminishing its capacity in that environment. That is to say, one could set up an unlicensed wireless system only to discover that months later it will not support its desired operations due to the installation of a nearby wireless system on the same frequency.
  - 2.4 GHz: The most common unlicensed frequency worldwide is 2.4 GHz, which supports 802.11b/g/i/n operations. This frequency can support up to 3 simultaneous video channels in the same airspace. This frequency has the most amateur and commercial users, and thus the highest probability of interruption by adjacent users.
  - 5.8 GHz: 5.8 GHz supports 802.11a operations, which can support up to 10 simultaneous video channels in the same airspace. This frequency also

---

* Actual maximum engineered CAT 5/6 distances are 100 m or 300 ft, but it is best to provide some engineering factor for safety with digital video signals.
† CAT5 and CAT5e cables can run gigabit speeds, but are not certified for such.

has far fewer users and thus less likelihood of interruption by other users. 5.8 GHz may be licensed or unlicensed depending on the locale.

- 900 MHz: 900 MHz is the forgotten frequency, very seldom used. It supports short distances but can pass through trees, leaves, and so on better than the two frequencies already mentioned. 900 MHz may be licensed or unlicensed depending on the locale.
- WiMax: WiMax is an emerging technology that should support more reliable operations. WiMax is typically licensed depending on the locale.
- Microwave: Microwave communications are licensed in most areas and provide secure communications, with a line of sight of up to several miles depending on the equipment and frequency.
- Laser: Laser communications provide very secure transmissions over a line of sight of up to several miles.

- Antennas: Two types of antennas are available: directional and omnidirectional. Omnidirectional antennas should be used whenever signals from several cameras are being gathered together at a single access point. The omnidirectional antenna should only be used on the access point. For all outdoor remote cameras, directional antennas are best, and whenever possible, it is also best to use directional antennas at the access points as well, unless multiple cameras signals are collected from several directions. For a complete discussion on antennas, see my second book, *Integrated Security Systems Design*.[1]

Low-Tech Elements

Locks

- Electrified mortise locks are made from standard mortise locks that are fitted with a solenoid (to unlock the door) and can also be fitted with a request-to-exit switch on the handle (so that the request to exit is sent when the handle is turned, thus bypassing the normal door alarm). They can also be fitted with a door-closed switch and/or door-locked switch. Electrified mortise locks are very secure and require no special knowledge to use, and they comply with all known codes for non-fire-egress doors.
- Electrified panic hardware (EPH) is standard mechanical panic hardware (crash bars) that is fitted with a solenoid (to unlock the door) and can also be fitted with a request-to-exit switch in the push bar. EPH is available in mortise, rim, and concealed and exposed vertical rods. EPH fulfills the requirements for all known codes.
- Magnetic locks are fitted at the top of the door and supplement other door hardware with centrally controlled locks. Magnetic locks are often fitted to existing doors with existing locks to simplify the lock installation. Egress is from an infrared request-to-exit motion sensor above the door, by a switch in a panic bar, by a labeled pushbutton beside the door, by central command from the console, by a fire alarm interface, or by a special emergency unlock pull station (similar to a fire alarm pull station). Magnetic locks must receive code approval in most jurisdictions on a case-by-case basis, and special attention should be paid to the fire alarm interface and other safety measures to help assure that persons are not accidentally locked into the space, as has occurred many times due to bad design.
- Delayed egress hardware couples a magnetic lock with a crash bar, a countdown timer, and a local alarm. Signage advises the user to push and hold the push bar

for XX seconds (usually 15–30 s), after which the door will open. During that time, a countdown timer displays the countdown to zero and an alarm sounds to discourage casual use. Delayed egress hardware provides for high-security openings and a certain way of exiting no matter what.

- High-security electric locks. A few companies manufacture high-security hardware, which includes
  - Four- and six-point electrified deadbolts (for single or double doors)
  - Detention and housing authority quality door hardware are made to stand up to very heavy intentional abuse that would cause the immediate failure of normal locks.
  - Note: four- and six-point electrified deadbolts on robust doors are virtually impossible to breach with conventional tools, excluding only industrial diamond saws and certain very robust frame spreaders.
- Drop-bolt locks are out of favor due to door alignment problems, which cause lock jamming. However, they can be used on storeroom doors. They should never be used on occupied rooms. Generally, these have been replaced by magnetic locks. I do not recommend the use of drop-bolt locks on any door.
- Electrified cylinder locks: Very insecure conversions of mechanical cylinder locks. Avoid these always.
- Lock power/fire alarm supervision: Lock power should be centralized and backed up by a generator and uninterruptable power supply. The final power feed to the lock power supply should be serviced or interrupted by a relay that is supervised by the fire alarm system, thus assuring that all magnetic locks will permit passage during a fire alarm. The circuit should be equipped with a test switch that also sends an alarm to the alarm/access control system to log the test event.

Revolving Doors

Revolving doors and full-height mechanical turnstiles provide positive access control; that is, one card, one entry. This prohibits tailgating of unauthorized persons behind authorized users. When used at egress points, the revolving doors and turnstiles should be coupled with a conventional leaf door with a delayed egress hardware system.

Mechanical and Electronic Turnstiles

Mechanical (sports venue type) turnstiles and electronic turnstiles are becoming increasingly used due to the focus on assuring clearance of persons entering buildings. The user is granted access through the turnstile, usually with a visitor card. Employee cards are also valid at the turnstiles. Turnstile configurations include

- Tripod (sports venue type).
- Glass wing.
- Drop paddles.
- Swing-away paddles.
- No paddles (alarm only on violation); these have fallen into disfavor.

Electronic turnstiles help assure positive access control in a very aesthetic fashion. Throughput varies from one person per second up to one person every two to three seconds.

Vehicle Gates

Vehicle gates can be configured as lift-arm gates, swing fabric gates, and sliding fabric gates. Lift-arm gates provide the least security but deploy quickly. These should be used wherever the arm is manned and/or where security is lax, such as to a parking lot. Sliding and swing fabric gates (imagine chain link or estate fence) provide security also against pedestrians (which lift-arm gates do not) but deploy more slowly.

Deployable Barriers

- Vehicle barriers: Deployable vehicle barriers come in two types: high-security and low-security.
  - High-security barriers are capable of stopping vehicles traveling at speed with a payload in a very short distance, usually about one meter of over-travel. On most high-security barriers, destruction of the vehicle and death or serious injury to its occupants is a probability if the vehicle is traveling at speed and may occur even if the barrier deploys under a standing vehicle. Configuration of these types generally include:
    - Deployable bollards
    - Phalanx (rising wedge) barriers
    - Cable-beam barriers
  - Certain newer barriers can deploy without causing serious damage or injury by stopping the vehicle in a controlled fashion. Some of these also serve as mildly effective pedestrian barriers. These are typically configured as a rising web of aircraft landing capture cables and nylon webbed fabric.
  - Low-security barriers are usually configured as rising arms (parking control arms). These can also be configured with antipedestrian barriers.
- Pedestrian barriers: I have for many years advocated the use of deployable barriers inside public buildings to disrupt terrorist takeover attacks, such as occurred in the attacks of November 26, 2008, on hotels in Mumbai, India. The use of motorized operable walls, roll-down grilles, and deployable doors has the potential to save many lives when a hostage-oriented paramilitary attack occurs. These are appropriate for any public or commercial building where an attack by armed militants is a possibility. The use of deployable barriers requires close coordination with fire department authorities. Barriers should be placed mid-point between fire stairwell locations and where no sneak-paths are available. They are especially effective against "moving shooter" attacks such as the Mumbai attack, as they contain the shooter to a small segment of the building while allowing victims to exit nearby to safety. The shooter will not use the exit as he will be captured by armed police response forces. These should be used in cases where two exits are possible in each segment. My recommendation of these was long considered radical until their merits recently became obvious.

Lighting

Lighting can be used in four ways:

- To improve the safety of legitimate users: Lighting should be used on all natural vehicle and pedestrian pathways along with clear sight lines to help assure that offenders cannot easily approach legitimate users unsuspected.

- Lighting to indicate occupancy when buildings are occupied and imply occupancy when buildings are unoccupied: Lighting can be used to imply that a facility is occupied. For burglaries, indications of occupancy are the number one prevention technique. Studies have shown that burglars will nearly always avoid residential and commercial buildings they believe to be occupied.* Lighting should be scheduled and used with other indicators such as parked cars or sounds (radio station, etc.).
- Lighting to increase the risk of discovery upon entry or exit: For parking lots, lighting can be used to make the movements of burglars more obvious, especially around logical points of entry and the approaches to those areas.
- Lighting to disrupt a security event: Once a presence is detected, lighting can be used to disorient and disrupt the offender. The turning on of lights in response to motion sensed, especially inside the structure, makes the offender believe he has been detected and may cause him to abandon the attack. For very sensitive facilities, turning off lighting in an unoccupied building can help to disorient the attacker and allow the response force to follow the subject, especially where infrared enabled cameras are used indoors.

Signage

Two types of signage assist in the security program:

- *Way-finding signage* assists legitimate users in finding their way through a facility to their intended destination by "pointing the way." Well-designed way-finding signage has two distinct advantages: (1) assisting users and (2) reducing the time spent informing users of directions. The second of these helps improve the overall security program by allowing security personnel to focus on exceptions rather than on normal behavior. This is an elemental principle of security operations: that security personnel should focus on exceptions to the greatest extent possible and that all matters related to normal behavior should not require the intervention or interruption of security personnel from their normal duties. Good way-finding signage actually begins with good architectural and departmental planning. From the time a visitor or new employee enters the building, their attention is on finding their way to their intended destination. First-time visitors especially are generally unaware of any rules for visitors, such as signing in. So prominent signage guiding visitors to the reception desk is important. From there, either signage or map handouts are an effective way to guide visitors to their destination. For larger facilities, way-finding signage helps keep visitors on track. Sign colors can also help keep visitors guided more intuitively than language signs alone. Way-finding signs should be hierarchical in nature; that is, the signs will provide more detail as one progresses through the facility. For example, in the lobby, signage may indicate what floors certain departments are on, and room number ranges should be displayed just off elevator lobbies so that visitors are not wandering down the wrong halls looking for suites. Way-finding signage should also indicate where assistance and key services such as toilets are available. All signage should be readable from the distance intended.

---

* "90 percent of burglars we interviewed stated that they would not knowingly enter a residence where they knew someone was at home."[3]

For example, at 1500 ft, letters must be 2 ft high; however, in an elevator lobby, 1 in.-high letters are sufficient. Signage must also take into account the speed with which the reader may be traveling. For example, letters must be larger the faster a reader is traveling in order to facilitate time to read and the distance that will take.*

- *Security warning signage* helps guide employees and visitors as to the correct behavior by informing them of what is and is not considered acceptable. For example, at a liquefied natural gas (LNG) terminal, signage in large letters may warn watercraft not to approach closer to a vessel than 1500 ft and cite the federal regulation requiring that distance. Signage may also state possible penalties. For example, it is common to see signs at airports declaring what items may not be taken in carry-on baggage and warning of possible arrest for violation. Security warning signage both guides correct behavior and removes the excuse of ignorance. All security warning signage should be based on laws or on documented policies and procedures and should be stated simply and clearly and in a professional manner. Signage that is too wordy often does not get read and so fails in its intended purpose.

No-Tech Elements

Define the Deterrence Program

The primary goal of any security program is deterrence. If the program is successful in that goal, then it is completely successful. If it is unsuccessful in that goal, then it is very costly and dangerous to remedy that shortcoming. Remember, a good security program has two primary elements:

- A BSP
- Specific countermeasures to address specific vulnerabilities

The BSP comprises countermeasures that guide users to appropriate behavior through deterrence tactics and also help to detect, assess, respond to, and gather evidence of any inappropriate criminal behavior. No BSP is effective as anything other than a mild deterrent against terrorist behavior.

Specific countermeasures can be developed to address specific vulnerabilities, and these are intended to act as deterrents against terrorist behavior and reduce the likelihood of unique opportunities for criminal behavior.

For the BSP, the deterrence package includes security patrols and posts, CPTED Elements, a security awareness program, access control elements including both electronic and staffed, and a security investigations and intelligence program. The no-tech elements of these include patrols and posts, the security awareness program, and the security investigations and intelligence program.

- Security posts: The presence of security posts (also called fixed patrols) at property perimeter entries and exits and at building entries is a constant reminder that the organization is vigilant about security. The effectiveness of security

---

* Airmaster Letter Height Visibility Charts—20 mph/2 kph—4″/9 cm at 147 ft/45 m—65 mph/105 kph—12 ″/30 cm at 477 ft/145 m. www.airmastersales.com/hivisibility.html.

posts is entirely based on the professionalism of the officers and equipment at the post. This is especially true for antiterrorism checkpoints (bomb and weapons detection). It is at this point that professional offenders will judge whether the organization's security program is all for show or if it is a serious challenge to their criminal intentions.

Remember, appropriate users see a security post and immediately think that the facility is secure, while professional offenders see every vulnerability and imagine quickly how to exploit the holes in the procedures. Thus, effective policies and procedures, coupled with effective training and random scenario testing, help assure an effective deterrent.

- Patrols: Security patrols are one of the most effective deterrents because anyone on the premises with criminal intent is aware that they are at risk of being caught by a roving guard at any time. Patrols should not be predictable. That is, each time a guard patrols, he or she should vary the route and time so that the route is not predictable. This may include returning shortly to patrol check points that were just visited minutes or even seconds ago. This kind of unpredictability helps assure that no one with criminal intent will feel safe from observation by a patrol officer.
- Responses: Professional offenders will often "test" the organization's response to a security event. Thus, responses to "nonevents" are as important as responses to actual security events. The timing, manner, and actions of the responding officer(s) indicate to the offender how much of a challenge the security program will be to overcome. According to interviews with known terrorists and criminals, an effective response to a "nonevent" will nearly always deter an attack.
- Security awareness program: These have two objectives: (1) to help the organization's employees, contractors, and vendors to understand the organization's security policies as they relate to their own behavior and activities, and (2) to help create a safe and secure work environment by helping those constituents understand what behaviors are expected by the organization. Elements of a security awareness program often include
  - Security and way-finding signage: These help the public and visitors find their way and help assure that unauthorized people do not go into areas where they should not be.
  - Handouts.
    - Security rules: These help visitors, contractors, vendors, and new employees understand their behavioral obligations while on the property or while working on the organization's projects.
    - Security and safety guidances: These help the organization's constituents understand concerns and issues that could affect their security and safety and how to take steps to assure their own security and safety while on the organization's property and in their daily lives. These can also include such things as warnings about security and credit-card scams that could affect the organization's constituents. An organization's security and safety guidances are generally viewed by its employees as an added value to working with the organization.
  - Verbal guidance.
    - Security personnel should be trained to provide verbal guidance to persons having questions (way-finding, security questions, etc.).

- Security personnel should be trained to defer verbal guidance on subjects for which they are not qualified and direct the questioner to a better source (always to a manager).
- Security personnel should always carry a pocket guide for security policies to aid in answering any questions.
- Security personnel should be trained to escalate problems to supervisors or managers when they are confronted with a belligerent person.
- Security personnel who have contact with the public should be trained in basic conflict resolution.
- Newsletters, e-mails, and so on.
  - A security program periodical is a good way to transmit and focus the recipients on the organization's security mission.
- Security investigations program.
  - There are security problems in every organization. These problems can be internal, external, or external with internal collusion. Security problems can be either immediate or chronic. Security offense perpetrators may be obvious or concealed.
  - Security investigations programs help uncover the concealed offenders and assemble the evidence necessary to prosecute the offender and to put an end to the offenses, if chronic.
  - Immediate offenses leave evidence of the offense, which can be used to determine the methods and tactics of the offense; the asset used, taken, or destroyed; and the characteristics of the offender (time, method of entry and exit, concealment during the offense, etc.).
  - Chronic offenses also leave evidence (shortages, etc.). However, it may be difficult to tell when such shortages occurred and thus who suspects might be. Especially when organized crime is involved and when employees have been turned to be participants in or facilitators of the crime, investigations play a vital role in solving the problem.
- Security intelligence program.
  - Intelligence is information that is relevant to the protection of the organization from possible harm. Intelligence allows management to position the organization to avoid harm.
  - Both security and related risk management should receive intelligence reports.
  - Reports should be analyzed for urgency and importance upon receipt. Urgent and important intelligence requires immediate action. Important but not urgent intelligence requires planning and coordination rather than immediate action.
  - Common organization formal intelligence programs include
    - Contacts with law enforcement.
    - Commercial security intelligence service.
    - Selected news feeds.
    - Security blogs.
  - A word about commercial security intelligence services:
    - I recommend that you subscribe to at least one good commercial security intelligence service in order to keep up with intelligence agendas. However, do not place complete faith in these to keep you informed. I will cite an example. One of the sources that I use is a very comprehensive service. However, I was amazed to note that as I was writing

this book, its weekly intelligence guidance for February 8 featured only one line for February 12 on Lebanon. This was amazing to me because February 12, 2009, is the one-year anniversary of the assassination of Imad Mugniyah (the military strategist for Hezbullah, whose assassination was blamed on Israel by Hezbullah). Even though tensions were high between the two countries and Israel conducted mock air raids over Lebanon in the days before the anniversary, the intelligence service made only an anniversary mention of this event and ignored the fact that it had the potential to spawn a war between these two countries, and indeed that Israel expected an attack and had threatened war in response, all of which was published in its public press. At one time, this service had spot-on guidance on the region, but things can change as quality sources move into and out of regions. Missing an event such as this in intelligence guidance is very concerning and shows a lack of analysis expertise on a critical region.

- How to develop intelligence sources.
  - Commercial risk analysts only have open-source information sources available to them. So the challenge is to gather together as many sources as possible and filter them for relevance.
  - One good way to do this is to begin with Google® Alerts. Set a Google Alert on one or more key words that are relevant to your needs. These may include the names of countries or industries and security or terrorism. Google Alerts will feed relevant and irrelevant information to your mailbox daily. As you click on interesting articles, you can bookmark these sources and you will begin to build a wealth of credible open-source news sources. To filter these, you can also subscribe to Usenet Groups. For example, you can subscribe to Google Groups (one of the best) such as alt.security.terrorism and put in a keyword filter such as "Lebanon." On a typical day, this will return over 4000 relevant articles from all points of view.
- A few of the many other good sources include
  - The NEFA Foundation (http://www.trackingterrorism.org/resource/nefa-foundation-nefa-us).
  - The Investigative Project on Terrorism (Steve Emerson: www.investigativeproject.com).
  - Jane's World Insurgency and Terrorism Portal (https://www.ihs.com/products/janes-world-terrorism-insurgency-intelligence-centre.html): a subscription source.
  - www.Planet Data.net/sites/Intelligence/.
  - www.businessmonitor.com.
  - www.defensereview.com.
  - www.asisonline.org.
  - South Asia Terrorism Portal (www.satp.org).
  - You will soon develop many others.
- News connections.
  - One of the best is the World News Connection (WNC), which is a consolidation of up-to-date news from local news sources all over the world, all translated into English. The WNC is a commercial (for a fee) subscription service of the U.S. Government National Technical Information Service (NTIS) by the Open Source Center (OSC) and is a service of the Commerce Department. Though some consider it too expensive, I believe

that WNC may be the single most comprehensive open-source information source in the world.

- Emergency services liaison program.
  - An emergency services liaison program is essential to assure that when an emergency occurs, security personnel manage the scene to facilitate rapid and uninhibited response by emergency personnel and to manage curious onlookers.
  - The program should be planned in coordination with fire, paramedic, and police departments and should include the following essential elements:
    - Triage the scene to determine if emergency services are needed and which agency should be called.
    - Notify emergency responders and notify management of the call to emergency responders.
    - Manage the scene, including taking actions to protect anyone injured or ill, including life-preserving measures.
    - Secure the scene to protect the privacy of the victim(s) from curious onlookers and to protect evidence.
    - Mitigate any further damages, such as from fire, to the extent possible.
    - Facilitate emergency responders to rapidly locate the scene of the emergency.

Define the Response Program

- Communications: The most important element of any response is communications. Communications include
  - Communications between the console officer and responding patrol officers, providing them with information about the security situation, the event, and the suspects.
  - Communications between the console officer and security management or supervisors.
  - Communications between the console officer and any offenders within view of a video camera.
  - Communications between the console officer and anyone seeking assistance at an assistance phone or intercom.
  - Communications between security personnel and responding law enforcement.
  - Communication tools include security intercoms; telephones, including mobile phones; and two-way radios.
- Guards:
  - Guards or security officers are the security program's enforcement staff.
  - Guards should be well versed in all of the organization's security policies. No statement should be made by any guard regarding any security matter that is not based on security policy.
  - Guards have several basic duties, including posts, patrols, and office duties including reports, training, and photo ID badging.
  - Guards may be in house or contracted. Advantages of contracting guards include
    - Scalable staff: increase and decrease staffing on demand.

- Guards work for the guard company, not directly for the organization, so any improper guard action is mitigated to a varying extent by the guard company and their insurance. The primary role of a guard company is to provide trained and qualified guards. Any failure in that is the responsibility of the guard company.
  - Advantages of in-house guards include greater control over training. Some organizations utilize a mixture of contracted and in-house guards, with key staff in house and line staff contracted.
- Vehicles: Vehicles may include automobiles, trucks, motorcycles, bicycles, and golf carts, depending on the needs of the patrol. A vehicle's primary roles include patrols and response.
- Armed and unarmed: Guards may be armed or unarmed. Armed guards are appropriate only if they have excellent firearms training and especially training as to rules of engagement. Organizations should keep in mind that any accidental or improper shooting is on the organization's shoulders, with some mitigation by the guard company, if contracted.
- Response training requirements:
  - Security staff must be trained to respond properly to a variety of security and safety events. Training should include
    - Security and safety policies
    - Security laws, especially concerning laws regarding citizen's arrest
    - Security event identification, verification, and assessment, including what kind of response is most appropriate
    - Security staff position awareness (where all staff are at all times).
    - Response team selection and dispatching
    - Security event management, including observation and directions using CCTV and intercoms or radios
    - Suspect apprehension and citizen's arrest
    - Suspect holding for law enforcement
    - Evidence gathering and incident report generation, including note taking and report generation
    - Handing over suspect, evidence, and incident report to law enforcement
    - Testifying in court
- Security related medical emergencies:
  - Security staff is often the first responder to any emergency. Security staff should be trained in the types of emergencies and how to mitigate injuries or medical conditions, control the scene, and obtain help from emergency responders.
  - Security staff should be versed in all common types of medical emergencies, including
    - Common injuries
    - Heart attack and stroke
    - Carrying out cardiopulmonary resuscitation (CPR)
  - An automatic electronic defibrillator should be kept within minutes from every location on the facility, and all security staff should be trained in its use.
  - Scenario training is important as it points out how the security staff will interact with everyone in an emergency, including rendering aid, controlling the scene, and obtaining help from civic emergency responders.

Define the Evidence Gathering Program

- General: Every security event leaves its evidence, which could include witness statements, video, or forensic evidence. All evidence must be protected, noted, and preserved for law enforcement. Any activities by anyone including security staff could disturb evidence and reduce or eliminate its value. All security organizations should also maintain a supply of crime scene tape to protect evidence prior to the arrival of police investigators.
- Video and audio archiving elements:
  - All video and audio channels should be recorded and archived for a suitable period to determine if a security event has occurred. For most events this may be from two weeks to one month. For some types of events longer periods may be required.
  - Only archiving methods that are acceptable in court should be used.
- Crime scene security principles and evidence preservation:
  - Security staff should be trained in crime scene security principles, including how to secure a crime scene for law enforcement.
  - All possible evidence must be preserved.
- Witness statements:
  - All security staff should be trained in taking witness statements. This includes
    - Identifying possible witnesses
    - Separating witnesses from each other so that stories do not get mixed
    - Interviewing witnesses by asking non-leading questions, which should include
      - What did you see?
      - How did the event unfold?
      - Identification of suspects.
      - Witness contact information.
  - Witness statement reports: From the witness statement notes, develop reports that are unbiased, accurate (including any discrepancies in statements), and clearly written. The reports should agree completely with witness statement notes. Notes should be preserved.
- Follow-up investigations and training: For any security event that is not immediately handed over to law enforcement, a follow-up investigation will occur. Investigations should only be handled by qualified investigators.

SUMMARY

Introduction

Review: All security countermeasures have the goal of adjusting the behavior of potential threat actors so that they do not pose a threat to the organization.

This is done in three ways:

- Design an environment that encourages appropriate behavior and discourages inappropriate, criminal, or terroristic behavior

- Detect, assess, and respond to exceptions
- Design the program to mitigate any potential harm from hazards and threats

There are two primary types of countermeasure implementations, each having three elements. These are

- The baseline security program (BSP)
- Special countermeasures to address special vulnerabilities
- Each of these has high-tech, low-tech, and no-tech components.

Both the BSP and special countermeasures are necessary to cope with all the conditions that an organization may confront. The exact makeup of those programs is the result of recommendations from the risk analysis.

Baseline Security Program (BSP)

The BSP is the heart of the countermeasures. The BSP is designed to accommodate normal day-to-day operations and to allow for the identification of unwanted exceptions so that they can be handled. The BSP is not designed to cope with highly unusual conditions such as acts of terrorism. The BSP should include three elements:

- Design an environment that encourages appropriate behavior and discourages inappropriate, criminal, or terroristic behavior
- Detect, assess, and respond to exceptions
- Design the program to mitigate any potential harm from hazards and threats

Specific Countermeasures

During the course of the risk analysis, you may uncover certain threats that are not day-to-day threats but which the security program must be prepared to handle. These will require specific countermeasures over and above the BSP. Three common elements of specific countermeasures include

- Terrorism and major crimes deterrence program
- Emergency preparedness program
- Disaster recovery program

Countermeasure Selection Basics

Both the BSP and special countermeasures utilize high-tech, low-tech, and no-tech elements, including

- High-tech elements
  - Access control systems
  - Detection systems

- CCTV systems
- Two-way voice communications systems
- Consoles and management offices
- Security archiving technologies and schemes
- Security system infrastructures
- Low-tech elements
  - Locks
  - Revolving doors
  - Mechanical and electronic turnstiles
  - Vehicle gates
  - Deployable barriers including vehicle and pedestrian barriers
  - Lighting
  - Signage including way-finding and security warning signage
  - CPTED elements
- No-tech elements
  - Deterrence program
  - Security posts
  - Security patrols
  - Response program
  - Security awareness program
  - Security investigations program
  - Security intelligence program
  - Emergency agency liaison program
  - Evidence gathering program
  - Investigations
  - Training

REFERENCES

1. Norman, T. L. 2007. *Integrated Security Systems Design*. Butterworth Heinemann, Amsterdam.
2. FLIR Commercial Vision Systems. *Seeing Through Fog and Rain with a Thermal Imaging Camera*. FLIR Commercial Vision Systems, Breda. www.flir.com.
3. Cromwell, P. and J. N. Olson. 2004. *Breaking and Entering*. Wadsworth Publishing, Belmont, CA.

Q&A

Questions

Q1: All security countermeasures should have the goal of
   A. Adjusting the behavior of potential threat actors so that they do not pose a threat to the organization.
   B. Adjusting the behavior of the organization to effectively mitigate risks.
   C. Either or both of the above.
   D. Neither of the above.

Q2: The answer to Q1 above can be done in which way?
  A. Design an environment that encourages appropriate behavior and discourages inappropriate, criminal, or terroristic behavior
  B. Detect, assess, and respond to exceptions
  C. Design the program to mitigate any potential harm from hazards and threats
  D. All of the above

Q3: Primary countermeasure implementations include
  A. The baseline security program (BSP).
  B. Special countermeasures to address special threats.
  C. Neither of the above.
  D. Both of the above.

Q4: Each of the primary countermeasure implementations above has _____ components.
  A. High-tech
  B. Low-tech
  C. No-tech
  D. All of the above

Q5: The BSP is designed to
  A. Accommodate normal day-to-day operations.
  B. Allow for the identification of unwanted exceptions so that they can be handled.
  C. Neither of the above.
  D. Both of the above.

Q6: Which below are *not* included in the BSP?
  A. Design an environment that encourages appropriate behavior and discourages inappropriate, criminal, or terroristic behavior
  B. Control access to critical assets and detect, assess, and respond to exceptions
  C. Design the program to mitigate likely potential harm from hazards and threats
  D. Respond quickly to a terrorist attack

Q7: The specific countermeasures program should be designed to include which of the elements listed below?
  A. Terrorism and major crimes deterrence program
  B. Emergency preparedness program
  C. Disaster recovery program
  D. All of the above

Q8: All detection countermeasures should be used
  A. In layers or pairs.
  B. With audio or video assessment measures for independent verification of any alarm detection.
  C. Either or both of the above.
  D. Neither of the above.

Q9: High-tech elements include
   A. Detection/access control, video, and voice communications.
   B. Perimeter and interior detection systems.
   C. Video and voice communications systems.
   D. Access control systems.

Q10: Low-tech measures include
   A. Barriers, fences, gates, lighting, and signage.
   B. Fences, lighting, and signage.
   C. Gates, lighting, and signage.
   D. Dogs and guards.

Answers

Q1 – C, Q2 – D, Q3 – D, Q4 – D, Q5 – D, Q6 – D, Q7 – D, Q8 – C, Q9 – A, Q10 – A

CHAPTER 17

Countermeasure Selection and Budgeting Tools

INTRODUCTION

On completion of this chapter, you will understand what makes a security countermeasure effective or ineffective, the functions of security countermeasures, infiltration and attack scenarios, attack objectives, criminal offender types, criminal offender countermeasures, how to develop countermeasure effectiveness metrics, and how to develop a Decision Matrix to help decision makers reach consensus on a specific countermeasure when there are many points of view to consider.

THE CHALLENGE

Security organizations have historically been astoundingly poor at measuring their cost-effectiveness and even their effectiveness at securing the organization, for that matter.

Management is about metrics. The age-old management adage is "If you can't measure it, you can't manage it!"* But the security industry has been woefully inadequate not only in measuring its success in the execution of its program but also in the recommendation of countermeasures.

With the exception of national laboratories such as Sandia, most risk analysts have paid little attention to any measure of the effectiveness of their countermeasure recommendations. At best, risk analysts scale their program recommendations with "good, better, best" or some such qualitative estimate, on which no calculations whatsoever have been conducted.

This is most unfortunate, as clients deserve to know how well spent the money being budgeted for security programs is, that is, how likely it is that the program will succeed in its mission. I think that most analysts have not addressed effectiveness and cost-effectiveness for two reasons. The first is that most major risk analysis methodologies have no countermeasure effectiveness metric (with the notable exception of the Sandia model). The second is that the metrics that do exist require exceptional depth of analysis as well as considerable amounts of time and money to carry out, which is beyond the budget and capabilities of most analysts and arguably of most commercial organizations.

But, like anything else, if you can conceptualize the problem, you can create a solution.

---

* Credited to W. Edwards Deming, Peter Drucker, Robert Kaplan, and others variously from different sources.

COUNTERMEASURE EFFECTIVENESS

First, in order to measure countermeasure effectiveness, we have to ask: Effective against what? Against what threat? Versus what purpose? Using what formula?

FUNCTIONS OF COUNTERMEASURES

Let us start by examining the functions of security countermeasures. There are only seven things that any security countermeasure can ever hope to do:

- Control access
- Deter an attack
- Detect an attack
- Help the security force assess the attack
- Delay the attack
- Respond to the attack
- Collect evidence of the attack

Various countermeasures do one or more of these things more or less well at greater or less cost. Some countermeasures are effective against some threat actions and not against others. So now we have four dimensions of comparison for countermeasures:

- How many functions does the countermeasure fulfill?
- How well does the countermeasure perform each function?
- What threat actions is this countermeasure useful against?
- How much does the countermeasure cost?

Examples

Tables 17.1 and 17.2 illustrate why the function of a specific countermeasure's effectiveness can only be measured based on the threat it is acting against. In the simplistic examples below, no scale is given as to effectiveness (it is shown as the binary effective/

TABLE 17.1   Criminal Threat Countermeasure Functions

Security Function	Alarm	Access Control	CCTV	Intercom	Barriers	Locks	Lighting	Landscaping
Access control		X			X	X		X
Deterrence	X	X	X		X	X	X	X
Detection	X	X	X					
Assessment		X	X	X			X	
Delay		X			X	X		X
Response		X	X	X			X	
Evidence	X	X	X					
Functions	3	6	5	2	2	2	3	2

TABLE 17.2   Terrorist Threat Countermeasure Functions

Security Function	Alarm	Access Control	CCTV	Intercom	Barriers	Locks	Lighting	Landscaping
Access control					X			X
Deterrence					X			X
Detection	X		X					
Assessment			X	X			X	
Delay		X			X	X		X
Response			X				X	
Evidence	X	X	X					
Functions	2	2	4	1	2	1	2	2

not effective) since specific countermeasures are not under review, only the category of countermeasures against generic criminal or terrorist threats.

Table 17.2 illustrates that countermeasures that are effective against criminal threats may be of little use against a terrorist threat.

The more specific the threat, the more specific the countermeasure that can be estimated. For example, coating glass with blast film may reduce both smash-and-grab crimes and reduce the loss of life in a minor explosion, but it will be of no use if the bomb in question is a truck bomb at the curb of the building.

Also, specific countermeasures in specific locations have varying degrees of effectiveness. A normal resolution CCTV camera with a wide-angle lens on a camera pole can help describe the subject in question in terms of height, weight, build, sex, clothing, armament, actions, and so on, but it should not be considered capable of identifying the specific individual by facial recognition.

Let me pause here to state one of the most important principles of security that any risk analyst must understand. That is, *except for identifying persons carrying weapons or explosives, for terrorist threats on commercial, government, and critical infrastructure facilities, the only effective countermeasures are physical countermeasures.* I will say that again. Forget alarms, forget access control systems, forget CCTV systems, and certainly forget intercom systems. Forget the security guard force. In most cases the latter will just become additional victims, typically among the first.

Electronics has little if any function except to identify weapons on pedestrians and vehicles and give eyes to special forces if the system is designed properly (i.e., deny the system to the terrorists and give it solely to special forces). Nothing but physical barriers and deployable barriers matters for terrorism. That means that for terrorist considerations, any system that can deny access to the site, such as deployable vehicle barriers and security landscaping and any system that can protect glass from shrapnel effects or structural elements from structural collapse, will be effective against terrorism.

Consider the November 2008 attacks on hotels in Mumbai, India. If the Taj Mahal Palace Hotel had had available bulkhead operable walls to segment the hotel, these would have contained the moving shooters and dramatically reduced the number of casualties and shortened the siege to hours instead of days. Understand physical barriers. Get them in your head. For antiterrorism, it is mostly about physical barriers.

In order to understand how to protect facilities, one must understand how facilities are attacked. Once an attack begins, it is too late to consider countersurveillance, intelligence, or any other method that would have been useful before that moment. During an attack, it is all up to the physical protective systems to protect lives. Let us look first at infiltration scenarios and then attack scenarios.

Infiltration Scenarios

- Insider infiltration
  - False identity
  - Clean operative
- Special mission tactics and techniques
  - Foot infiltration
  - Air infiltration
  - Vehicle infiltration
  - Sea infiltration
- Authorized access with valid identification
- Illegal access
  - Calm infiltration
  - Gate crash
  - Air infiltration
  - Vehicle infiltration
- Infiltration of marine facilities
  - Infiltration by sea
  - Infiltration by land
  - Infiltration by scuba diver or swimmer

Attack Scenarios

- Moving shooter: One of the best examples of a moving shooter attack are the November 2008 attacks on hotels in Mumbai, India. In a moving shooter attack, shooters move through a space, shooting while aggressing and retreating as well as doing lateral movements. Being a successful moving shooter requires much skill and rehearsal. Moving shooters must continually scan for hidden adversaries lurking in the background. Moving shooters are much more difficult to counter than stationary shooters. In the Mumbai attacks, the shooters moved around each floor and from floor to floor. The forces deployed to find them did not know where they were or where they would be next. Moving shooters have the advantage of surprise and endurance, as outside forces cannot easily contain them to a siege area. Countermeasure: Denial of access and containment.
- Stationary shooter: Stationary shooters take a position and fire on moving or stationary targets. Stationary shooters have advantages over anyone within their line of sight. A good stationary shooter can usually land his first shot every time. Stationary shooters are often vulnerable to snipers, excellent targeting, and overwhelming force. Countermeasure: Denial of access and overwhelming force.
- Sniper: Snipers are stationary shooters that shoot from distance under cover. Snipers are deadly. Although sniper attacks from terrorists are very rare in civilian settings, logic indicates that the tactic will be used again. Countermeasure: Cover and concealment, safe exit for noncombatants under cover, and the deployment of countersnipers. Countersnipers are awesomely deadly to snipers.
- Standoff weapons: Standoff weapons include Stinger missiles, rocket-propelled grenades (RPGs), and the like. These are rocket powered, shoulder launched

grenades. Standoff weapons are typically used against vehicles and structures, particularly armored vehicles and reinforced structures, although they are devastating against conventional vehicles and structures. They can also be fitted with fragmentation warheads for use against personnel. Countermeasure: For conventional vehicles, none. Buildings and structures can be fitted with a decorative screen covering that detonates the RPG before it reaches the structure itself. The covering should be at least 1 m away from the structure.

- Improvised explosive devices (IEDs): IEDs are package bombs that are left in a location for detonation when the target arrives or after the bomber has left the area. IEDs may be left by the roadside (roadside bomb), in an airport or other public location, or at a place of work (as with the Unabomber). Countermeasure: Weapons detection and explosives detection systems including dogs, millimeter wave technology, x-ray imaging, electromagnetic imaging in the infrared, and terahertz or microwave spectral range systems.
- Vehicle-borne improvised explosives devices (VBIEDs): The VBIED is the preferred method of terrorists around the world for delivering large explosive charges to damage or destroy buildings and structures. VBIEDs have been creatively constructed to deliver incendiaries, such as in the Marriott Hotel blast in Islamabad in 2008. That building was massively damaged more by the incendiaries than by the blast itself. VBIEDs do not need to get next to a building, though closer is better for the terrorist. Countermeasure: Standoff. Create standoff by creating a security checkpoint at least 100 m (300 ft) from the building. An absolute minimum of 30 m (100 ft) is required. The checkpoint and the surrounding perimeter should be capable of stopping a large truck at speed. This can be accomplished with deployable barriers (crash barriers) and security landscaping.
- Suicide bomber: A suicide bomber is a human IED delivery vehicle. Suicide bombers can get close to crowds of pedestrians and place bombs in precise locations for maximum casualties. Suicide bombers can deliver bombs inside buildings where a wedding or meeting of leaders is taking place, inside buses, in the midst of gatherings of people, or any other precise location. Countermeasures: Weapons detectors including dogs, millimeter wave technology, video (human gait analysis), x-ray imaging, electromagnetic imaging in the infrared, and terahertz or microwave spectral range systems. Pity the security officer they pick to intercept the person detected. Many heroes have died in this essential but dangerous role.
- Hijacking: Hijacking is the act of seizing control of a vehicle, whether an aircraft, truck, car, bus, or ship, for the purpose of carrying out a terrorist attack. The attack may use the commandeered vehicle either as a delivery mechanism or as a bomb or incendiary device itself, as was the case in the attacks on the World Trade Center and the Pentagon on September 11, 2001. Countermeasures: Weapons detectors. Do not let terrorists board a vehicle or vessel. Detect the weapons they would use to hijack the vehicle.
- Hostages: The taking of hostages is important to terrorists because of the empathy that the victims' community feels for the event and the compounding of the tragedy beyond mere structural damage. The longer terrorists can hold hostages attended by high levels of media coverage, the better for the terrorists.
- Aircraft: Aircraft have been used on several occasions as bombs. Plans to continue to do so have been repeatedly found in terrorist safe houses before and after the attacks of September 11, 2001. Some of those plans include using rented

planes to strike buildings, thus obviating the need to hijack a plane. Others include the use of chartered planes, which often do not require passengers to be security screened. Countermeasure: There is no suitable countermeasure that any specific facility can take to counter this threat.

- Vehicles: Vehicles have been used to deliver bombs (VBIEDs), to deliver terrorists, and as weapons. Countermeasure: Deployable barriers and screening checkpoint.
- Watercraft: Watercraft have been used to deliver terrorists (Taj Mahal Palace Hotel, Mumbai, 2008) and bombs (USS Cole, 2000) and have been hijacked by terrorists (MS Achille Lauro, 1985). Countermeasures for waterfront facilities: Waterfront barriers, short-range radar, active use of CCTV, response team.
- Grenades: Grenades are used by terrorists for distraction, for offense, and for defense. Grenades can create significant casualties among unprotected civilians as part of a complete suite of a single terrorist's weaponry, such as in Mumbai in 2008. Countermeasure: Weapons screening checkpoint and preattack intelligence. Subsequently, special forces, including snipers.
- Incendiaries: Incendiaries are used to burn structures and may be configured as Molotov cocktails within VBIEDs configured as an incendiary. Countermeasures: Standoff, deployable barriers, security landscaping, and security checkpoints.
- Small bombs under or in vehicles: These are low-impact terrorism tools and are also used for assassinations. Contrary to popular opinion, a bomb under a vehicle is not likely to damage a structure, but only the people inside the vehicle and persons standing nearby. Some may be injured by broken glass. The use of under-vehicle screening at a security checkpoint is usually cosmetic rather than meaningful because the threat is not to the structure but the people in the car itself. Most of these systems are also staffed by personnel who are not trained to recognize an explosive if one is placed under the car, as tests have shown. Countermeasure: Check under vehicle with mirror by skilled observer.

Attack Objective Parameters

General objectives of terrorism: Each terror strike has its own objectives, though common objectives exist. Common objectives include

- Change of government policy: Terrorist attacks aim to draw attention to a cause by creating suffering among the "silent majority" of the public. Formerly, terrorists made direct demands to release hostages. That is uncommon today. The current trend is to claim the act in the name of the terrorist organization and its cause.
- Demoralize the public: Destroy the feeling of security and make the public fear future terrorist acts.
- Reduce faith in government: Terrorists aim to reduce the faith of the public in their government.
- Change of government: One primary aim is to cause public pressure to change the government either to one more friendly to the terrorist's cause (effectively done in the train bombings in Madrid, Spain, in 2004) or to a government that is more likely to get on the course of war with its neighbors (India, 2008).

- Cause economic chaos: One of the stated goals of Al-Qaeda is to cause economic chaos in Western countries. This is primarily due to increased spending for security in the public and private sectors in order to defend against terrorism.

Specific Targeting Objectives

Each individual attack has its own targeting objectives, some of which are listed below.

- Terror: Simply to sow terror among the populace.
- Mass casualties: While low-intensity terrorist attacks involve only a small number of casualties, spectacular attacks strive to obtain large numbers.
- Destruction of iconic structures: High-intensity terrorism is almost always focused on an icon of the community's economic or cultural self-image.
- Media coverage: All terrorists crave media coverage. Any target that can be ideal for video coverage is also ideal for a terrorist attack.
- Time: Terrorists want the attack to last as long as possible; either the attack itself (as in Mumbai in 2008), the response (as in the Islamabad Marriott fire of 2008), or the repercussions (as in the still reverberating attacks of September 11, 2001).
- Assassination: Many terrorist attacks are targeted against strategic individuals. (On January 2, 2009, a suicide bomber killed 24 Iraqi tribal leaders who were discussing national reconciliation at house of a Sunni sheik.) Many car bombs were detonated in Lebanon following the assassination of former Prime Minister Rafic al Hariri in 2005. Those bombs uniquely targeted outspoken critics of Syria.

Criminal Violent Offender Types

Criminal violent offenders fall into two main groups: Those who are mentally unstable and those who use violence as a means to an end or as an end in itself.

Mentally Unstable Offenders

Mentally unstable offenders often appear unexpectedly and behave erratically. They may or may not have any connection to the organization and may range from highly agitated to completely irrational, having no sense of reality whatsoever. Countermeasure: Depending on the extent of the mental instability, the weapons being used, and the offender's ability and intent to harm others, countermeasures may range from talking the subject down to a swarming attack aimed at disarming the offender.

Focused criminals who use violence intentionally fall into two groups: Those who use violence to an end, and those who use violence for its own purpose. Criminal violence objectives include:

- Intimidation in order to establish and maintain control: Criminals often use violence as a means to establish and maintain control over their crime victims. Intimidation may include
  - Brandishing a weapon
  - Using a weapon against property
  - Using a weapon against a person or persons to intimidate that person or others
  - Rape to intimidate that person or others

- Murder to intimidate others
- Assault, rape, or murder
  - Criminals may use assault to target a specific individual, with violence against that person being the objective of the attack itself and not a means to an end.
  - Criminals may also rape or murder a victim with no other crime in mind.

Economic Criminal Types

- Economic criminals fall into two main groups: internal and external.
  - Internal criminals have much greater access to the organization's assets, resources, and proprietary information, in particular the full nature of the organization's security measures. For the well-prepared criminal, internal access is golden. With time to surveil, plan, test, and then execute, internal criminals can be very difficult to counter. Internal criminals can *come to the well* again and again and can even place clues to implicate other employees, contractors, or even outsiders.
  - External criminals do not have the access of insiders, but they do have surprise and anonymity. Most external economic criminals execute their crimes once rather than repeatedly. Most do not know their victims.
- Most economic criminals of both types prefer to remain completely anonymous and escape undetected.

Economic Criminal Objectives

- Embezzlement: Internal theft, usually by those with access to cash or cash-like instruments (checks, purchase orders, etc.) Most embezzlement is conducted by a single trusted person in a relatively small business and almost always where there are poor accounting controls (only one person controlling expenses and income reports). Countermeasure: Accounting controls by two or more people.
- Robbery: Robbery is a direct *in your face* crime, usually involving intimidation and force. Robbery is common in convenience stores and other small establishments. Most robbers escape with only a few dollars. Some victims do not escape with their lives. Home-invasion robberies are more common than robberies at convenience stores or banks. These can also be quite violent. Countermeasures: Physical protection for employees such as bullet-resistant glass cash enclosures and the presence of multiple employees in the store at all times. Few robbers want to try to control multiple employees. An exception to this are bank robbers, who are willing to take on an entire bank full of employees and customers; in such cases, physical protection for the cashiers is usually an effective countermeasure, reducing the likelihood of the success of the robbery and thus serving as a strong deterrent.
- Burglary: Burglary is a faceless crime where the criminal makes entry, usually through breaking and entering, for the purpose of removing assets. Countermeasures: Robust physical security on the property and for interesting assets, alarm system, CCTV system, dogs, and patrols.

- Theft of information: Most theft of information today is via networks and the Internet. However, information is sometimes also taken via audio interception (phone, microphone, or acoustic). Document theft is also a concern. Countermeasures: Information technology countermeasures, office technical countermeasures (bug) sweeps, clean desk policies, secure file management, and a security awareness program focused on creating understanding about eavesdropping in public places.
- Shrinkage: Shrinkage is reduction in retail inventory caused by shoplifting and internal theft. Countermeasures for shoplifting: vigilant employees, shop layout to deter shoplifting, and actively watched CCTV. Countermeasures for internal theft: internal investigators, secret shoppers, and internal controls.
- Diversion: Diversion of assets often occurs by collusion between internal and external criminals. This often takes place in the shipping/receiving departments. Countermeasures: CCTV, internal investigations, document controls, law enforcement liaison.

Criminal Offender Countermeasures

For all the criminal offender objectives stated above, a baseline security program is essential. The purpose of the baseline security program is to address through a uniform and comprehensive approach a whole range of statistically anticipated criminal behaviors and policy violations. Without treating the protective systems in a systematic and comprehensive way, offenders can and will find the weaknesses in individual countermeasures, which can be exploited for their own purposes. The basic elements of a baseline security program are shown below. All these countermeasures below are discussed in detail in Chapter 16.

- Baseline security program
  - Security policies and procedures
  - Use of space definitions and alarm/access control systems
    - Define access levels
    - Control access to the access levels
      - Physical barriers
      - Authorization granting
      - Access portals
    - Perimeter and access level penetration detection
  - Use of video
    - Perimeter video
    - Entry point video
    - Circulation node video
    - Surveillance
    - Video patrol
    - Video pursuit
    - Video archiving
  - Use of voice communications
  - Use of guards
    - Posts
    - Patrols
    - Random applications of countermeasures

- Security awareness program
- Security training program
- Emergency services liaison program
- Security investigations program
- Special countermeasures to address unique vulnerabilities

COUNTERMEASURE EFFECTIVENESS METRICS: FUNCTIONAL EFFECTIVENESS

The first measure of the effectiveness of a countermeasure is its functional effectiveness. As each countermeasure has one or more functions as outlined below, one can estimate its ability to perform each function on a scale of 0 to 10, with 10 being absolute effectiveness and 0 being no function.

The functions again include

- Access control
- Deterrence
- Detection
- Assessment
- Delay
- Response
- Evidence

Take the list of vulnerabilities that you created from the vulnerability assessment and create a spreadsheet with those vulnerabilities listed as rows on the left and possible countermeasures listed in columns above. I array the vulnerabilities, grouped by asset classifications (i.e., people, property [sub-categorized], information, and reputation), and array the countermeasures by functions (access control, detection, assessment, delay, response, and evidence measures).

For example, under the property category, I may have the perimeter with subcategories of north, east, south, and west perimeters; then the main building (with subcategories of entrances and also of each entrance); then the ground floor (subcategories of lobby, etc.); and so forth.

For countermeasures, the categories are access control, detection, assessment, delay, response and evidence gathering, with subcategories of high-tech, low-tech, and no-tech countermeasures, each itemized under the category above. We might see evidence subcategories such as video, patrols, witness statements, sniffer dogs, and so on.

If multiple countermeasures apply to a particular vulnerability, duplicate those rows so that only one countermeasure is assessed for each row. Thus we might have four rows for the same countermeasure, with two rows considering existing countermeasures and two rows considering new countermeasures.

For each countermeasure related to each vulnerability, estimate its ability to deter, detect, assess, delay, and assist in a response or to gather evidence. Estimate each from 0 to 1, with 1 being complete effectiveness and 0 being none. This process identifies the effectiveness of each countermeasure for its purpose.

HELPING DECISION MAKERS REACH CONSENSUS ON COUNTERMEASURE ALTERNATIVES

Sometimes when you present several alternative solutions to a committee, you will find that the committee cannot reach a consensus. Each stakeholder has a different agenda or takes a position, and people become entrenched. Some people want the lowest cost, while others want the most effective countermeasure, and still others want the solution that is the most convenient to use or the most aesthetic. For such cases, I help the committee reach consensus by using a Decision Matrix. This is a simple spreadsheet tool that helps decision makers reach consensus by laying out the goals, risks, costs, and other factors. It scores each countermeasure by its ability to achieve the goals and mitigate the threats, and it considers other factors, including costs. Just as importantly, the Decision Matrix shows what risks the organization is accepting if a given countermeasure is selected. When I have used the Decision Matrix, the committee's decision after reviewing it has often been unanimous in favor of one single countermeasure, which is often not the least costly. An example of a Decision Matrix is shown in Table 17.3.

TABLE 17.3   Decision Matrix for Our Lady of Perpetual Funding Medical Center Security Landscaping and Fencing

Goals	Description
1	To deny access to nonauthorized persons to parking areas
2	To create a pleasant and visually pleasing environment
3	Cost-effectiveness based on goals and threats mitigated or eliminated
4	Convenience for employees
5	Conformance to business culture
6	Conformance to aesthetic values

Risks	Description
A	Harmless unvetted visitor—No criminal intent
B	Unauthorized visitor having no business with BMC—Possible criminal actor based on crimes of opportunity
C	Property criminal: Nonviolent criminal intent directed at property crimes only
D	Personal or sexual attack criminal: Non-victim-specific violent crime with intent to compel property or induce victim to comply with sexual demands
E	Workplace violence visitor: Victim-specific violent crime, which sometimes escalates to include violent attacks against innocent coworkers and law enforcement

The Decision Matrix begins by listing the goals of the countermeasure, numbered 1 through N. This is followed by a listing of the possible risks for the countermeasure to mitigate, lettered A through X. The matrix continues by listing the countermeasure methods in rows and then has sections for goals achieved, risks mitigated, score, rank, risks accepted, estimated cost, effectiveness, and convenience. This is followed by notes that help the reader understand the matrix.

SUMMARY

Introduction

Security organizations have historically been poor at measuring their cost-effectiveness and even their effectiveness at securing the organization, for that matter.

Management is about metrics. The age-old management adage is "If you can't measure it, you can't manage it!"

Countermeasure Effectiveness

First, in order to measure countermeasure effectiveness, we have to ask: Effective against what? Against what threat? Versus what purpose? Using what formula?

Functions of Countermeasures

Let us start by examining the functions of security countermeasures. There are only six things that any security countermeasure can ever hope to do:

- Deter an attack
- Detect an attack
- Help the security force assess the attack
- Delay the attack
- Respond to the attack
- Collect evidence of the attack

Various countermeasures do one or more of these things more or less well at greater or less cost.

Except for identifying persons carrying weapons or explosives, for terrorist threats on commercial, government, and critical infrastructure facilities, the only effective countermeasures are physical countermeasures.

Security attacks involve two protective considerations: infiltration and attack.

Infiltration Scenarios

- Insider infiltration
  - False identity
  - Clean operative

- Special mission tactics and techniques
  - Foot infiltration
  - Air infiltration
  - Vehicle infiltration
  - Sea infiltration
- Authorized access with valid identification
- Illegal access
  - Calm infiltration
  - Gate crash
  - Air infiltration
  - Vehicle infiltration
- Infiltration of marine facilities
  - Infiltration by sea
  - Infiltration by land
  - Infiltration by scuba diver or swimmer

Attack Scenarios

- Moving shooter
- Stationary shooter
- Sniper
- Standoff weapons
- Improvised explosive devices (IEDs)
- Vehicle-borne improvised explosive devices (VBIEDs)
- Suicide bomber
- Hijacking
- Hostage
- Aircraft
- Vehicles
- Watercraft
- Grenades
- Incendiaries
- Small bombs under/in vehicles

Attack Objective Parameters

General Objectives of Terrorism

- Change of government policy
- Demoralize the public
- Reduce faith in government
- Change of government
- Cause economic chaos

Specific Targeting Objectives

- Terror
- Mass casualties

- Media coverage
- Destruction of iconic structures
- Extend the time duration of the attack
- Assassination

Offender Types

Criminal Violent Offender Types

Criminal violent offenders fall into two main groups: those who are mentally unstable and those who use violence as a means to an end or as an end itself.

Rational criminals who use violence intentionally fall into two groups: those who use violence to an end and those who use violence for its own purpose. Criminal violence objectives include

- Intimidation to establish and maintain control
- Assault, rape, or murder

Economic Criminal Types

- Economic criminals fall into two main groups: Internal and external.

Economic Criminal Objectives

- Embezzlement
- Robbery
- Burglary
- Theft of Information
- Shrinkage
- Diversion

Criminal Offender Countermeasures

For all the criminal offender objectives stated above, a baseline security program is essential. The purpose of the baseline security program is to address through a uniform and comprehensive approach a whole range of statistically anticipated criminal behaviors and policy violations. Without treating the protective systems in a systematic and comprehensive way, offenders can and will find the weaknesses in individual countermeasures, which can be exploited for their own purposes.

Countermeasure Effectiveness Metrics

Functional Effectiveness

The first measure of the effectiveness of a countermeasure is its functional effectiveness. As each countermeasure has one or more functions as outlined below, one can estimate its ability to perform each function on a scale of 0 to 1, with 1 being absolute effectiveness and 0 being no function.

Helping Decision Makers Reach Consensus on Countermeasure Alternatives

When a committee cannot reach a consensus, the Decision Matrix is a valuable tool to help decision makers find common ground.

Q&A

Questions

Q1: Clients deserve to know
  A. How well the money being budgeted for security programs is likely to be rewarded in bonuses.
  B. How well the money being budgeted for security programs is likely to succeed in its mission.
  C. Both of the above.
  D. Neither of the above.

Q2: Which below are *not* things that a security countermeasure can ever hope to do?
  A. Control access
  B. Detect an attack
  C. Respond to an attack
  D. Encourage good hygiene

Q3: Are the four dimensions of comparison for countermeasures below accurate or not?
  • How many functions does the countermeasure fill?
  • How well does the countermeasure perform each function?
  • What threat actions is this countermeasure useful against?
  • How much does the countermeasure cost?
  A. Yes
  B. No
  C. Maybe
  D. None of the above

Q4: Except for_____, for terrorist threats on commercial, government, and critical infrastructure facilities, the only effective countermeasures are physical countermeasures.
  A. Deterring attacks
  B. Identifying persons carrying weapons or explosives identifying persons carrying weapons or explosives
  C. Stopping a terrorist attack
  D. Being vigilant

Q5: Security attacks involve two protective considerations:
  A. Infiltration and defense
  B. Defense and response
  C. Infiltration and attack
  D. Response and attack

Q6: Which below is *not* a terrorist attack scenario?
- A. Moving shooter
- B. VBIED
- C. Suicide bomber
- D. Smash and grab

Q7: Without treating the protective systems in a systematic comprehensive way, offenders can and will find the _____, which can be exploited for their own purposes.
- A. Weaknesses in individual countermeasures
- B. Resources for management
- C. Management resources
- D. Management

Q8: For all the criminal offender objectives stated above, a _____ is essential.
- A. Dog security program
- B. Baseline security program
- C. Antiterrorism program
- D. Theft prevention program

Q9: The first measure of effectiveness of a countermeasure is its
- A. Practical deployment.
- B. Effective deployment.
- C. Functional effectiveness.
- D. None of the above.

Q10: When a committee cannot reach a consensus, a _____ is a valuable tool to help decision makers find common ground.
- A. Decision tree
- B. Decision Matrix
- C. Decision branch
- D. Decision from management

Answers

Q1 – B, Q2 – D, Q3 – A, Q4 – B, Q5 – C, Q6 – D, Q7 – A, Q8 – B, Q9 – C, Q10 – B

CHAPTER 18

Security Effectiveness Metrics

INTRODUCTION

On completion of this chapter, you will understand the elements of security effectiveness and learn how to develop a useful Security Effectiveness Model suitable for every project not involving extremely high national security.

THEORY

One of the most difficult challenges of security management is the challenge of estimating the effectiveness of security countermeasures in their role of preventing crime and terrorism. By its very nature, crime and terrorism that has been deterred cannot easily be measured.

However, as we have seen from previous chapters, many things about security can be measured or estimated with a reasonable degree of accuracy. So too can the effectiveness of countermeasures to detect, assess, delay, assist in a response, and capture evidence. All these can assist in deterrence. So while deterrence itself cannot be accurately assessed, all other factors can, and these all contribute to enhancing the difficulty of a successful attack or, looking at it another way, reducing the probability of success of an attack. Then a reasonable person would assume that as the difficulty level increases, deterrence does also. So difficulty could be construed as a surrogate for deterrence for most crimes and also for terrorism.

Security effectiveness is also a primary contributor to cost-effectiveness. The basic goal of cost-effectiveness is lower cost and higher effectiveness. So first we must measure or estimate effectiveness in order to determine cost-effectiveness (Chapter 19).

SANDIA MODEL

Absolutely the best metrics for countermeasure effectiveness are contained within the Sandia Vulnerability Assessment Model. The Sandia Model was developed to address mission-critical military and nuclear facilities (and other highly critical facilities for which security is a core mission). Weapons storage facilities, nuclear power plants and storage facilities, and such are all proper for application of the Sandia Model, and most of these mandate the use of the Sandia Model. The Sandia Model measures the performance of each aspect of the security countermeasures program with great precision through firm scientific process.

I strongly recommend that all readers of this book also obtain a copy of Mary Lynn Garcia's book titled *Vulnerability Assessment of Physical Protection Systems*.[1] No better book has ever been written on vulnerability assessment. The Sandia Model applies great precision to measuring every aspect of both vulnerability and the effectiveness of existing and proposed protective systems.

However, the Sandia Model is so intricate and precise that the cost to fully apply it puts it beyond the reach of many organizations' security budgets. Commercial enterprises and many second- and third-tier critical infrastructure facilities can be estimated with less costly tools. In recognition of this fact, the U.S. Department of Homeland Security does not require this level of precision for most critical infrastructure facilities.

Quoting from Mary Lynn Garcia's book:[1]

> The Sandia Model expresses system effectiveness as a probability, P_E. P_E is determined using two terms: the probability of interruption (P_I) and the probability of neutralization (P_N). Performance-based analysis techniques use adversary paths, which assume that a sequence of adversary actions is required to complete an attack on an asset. ... It is important to note that PE varies with the threat. As the threat capability increases, performance of individual security elements or the system as a whole can decrease. (p. 255)

The two types of analysis are compliance-based and performance-based analysis. Compliance-based analysis compares the system to specified mandates (codes, regulations, policies, and procedures) and assures that required elements are in place. Conformance-based analysis evaluates how the various components of the protection systems might perform against estimated threat scenarios. Each individual element can be analyzed or estimated against threat scenarios, and its contributions to overall system effectiveness can be determined.

The Sandia Model utilizes six steps:

1. ASD: Create an Adversary Sequence Diagram for each asset location.
2. P_I: Conduct a path analysis. This provides P_I. Interruption is the arrival of responders to interrupt adversary progress.
3. SA: Perform a scenario analysis.
4. P_N: Complete a neutralization analysis where appropriate. This provides P_N. Neutralization is the defeat of the adversaries by direct engagement.
5. P_E: Determine system effectiveness, P_E.
6. RMU: Risk mitigation upgrade. If system effectiveness (or risk) is not acceptable, develop and analyze proposed upgrades.

For the Sandia Model, $P_E = P_I * P_N$. These are the factors:

- For adversaries that are likely to give up when confronted by a responder, P_N is not a factor.
- If no immediate response is possible, P_N is not a factor. In these cases, $P_E = P_I$.
- For the system to be considered effective, it must detect an attack while there is time to respond (before the critical detection point [CPD]).
- Provide a rapid assessment of alarms so that only valid alarms yield a response.
- Communicate the detection to an adequate response force in a timely manner.
- Collect evidence.
- Ensure that detection occurs before delay and delay the adversary long enough to process the detection, perform assessment, communicate to a response force, and get that force to the delay point (succeed at interruption).

- Use protection in depth (multiple layers) to assure that there are multiple opportunities to detect and delay an offender.
- Balance protection. That is, assure that all paths to assets have roughly the same probability of interruption (P_I).
- Engage and neutralize the offender with adequate and appropriate force.
- Conduct a full analysis of adversary paths and system effectiveness (interruption and neutralization) as the overall performance metric. Analysis must occur along all credible paths.

The Sandia Model is the pinnacle of vulnerability and risk analysis. The security industry high-security facilities throughout the world owe a debt of gratitude to Mary Lynn Garcia and the entire Sandia team for their excellent work.

Although the Sandia Model is undoubtedly the best model in terms of quantifying every aspect of protection system effectiveness, it achieves this result at great cost in terms of the number of hours of research and computation to achieve the analysis results. Accordingly, the full Sandia Model is almost totally unused for commercial facilities. The Sandia Model should always be used for projects such as nuclear power plants, weapons storage facilities, military bases, hydroelectric dams, and other projects where the loss of the asset would represent completely unacceptable consequences.

However, for most commercial projects, save only a few, the cost of the Sandia Model has historically made any deep analysis of system effectiveness less likely to occur. Over the years, several other approaches have been developed by various individuals to provide some metrics to system effectiveness without the cost of the Sandia Model. Many of these have been less than helpful with respect to determining actual effectiveness of security programs, systems, and system elements.

What has been needed is a method that is both easy enough for a single qualified analyst to use and which results in metrics that are meaningful in terms of helping budget decision makers to decide on which portions of a security program to fund in which order. What follows is just such a model.

A USEFUL COMMERCIAL MODEL

Before we look at the model itself, let us review the needs. Security program effectiveness metrics are needed by two classes of users:

- Security program managers
- Security budget decision makers

What is needed by each user:

- Security program managers need to know which program portions are the most critical and effective, which portions need improvement, and the priority in which they should be improved (cost to render effective and the importance of that program element in the overall security program [priority]).
- Security budget decision makers need to know which portions of the program are most critical and effective based on the available budget and which elements can be funded.

- Both users need to know the impact on security effectiveness of unfunded portions. That is, what assets are left exposed by unmitigated vulnerabilities, and what consequences could result if those vulnerabilities are exploited?
- Both users need to know what risks they are accepting by not mitigating the remaining vulnerabilities.

To achieve the above results, the model needs to do the following:

- For new projects: Identify what types of countermeasures could be effective to mitigate each listed vulnerability
- For existing programs: Identify which existing countermeasures are effective to mitigate each listed vulnerability
- Identify the effectiveness of each countermeasure in terms of
  - Entry control
  - Intrusion detection
  - Assessment
  - Delay
  - Response
  - Evidence gathering

It is a common mistake to try to evaluate security programs in terms of "intrusion events interrupted or defeated." There is a very small category of facilities for which this criterion is the chief criterion for consideration and even in those, it would be a mistake to use it as a key or chief criterion, because one cannot know what has been deterred. But virtually every metric ever developed focuses on detecting and interrupting intrusions (including the Sandia model).

One must consider what kind of security events one wants to control. Let us look at the universe of offenders again:

- Terrorists
- Economic criminals
- Violent criminals
- Subversives
- Petty criminals

In my opinion, any effectiveness metric that evaluates only one factor (intrusion) completely misses the point. What is the range of offenses?

- Intrusions by unauthorized persons
- Destruction/damage/theft of assets (including people, property, and intellectual assets)
- Subversion of the business environment to fulfill personal agendas
- Damage to business reputation arising from one of the above

Let us look at a few classic cases and what the victim organizations could have done to prevent the attacks:

- Terrorism
  - 9/11: Absolutely nothing that the Port Authority of New York and New Jersey could have done could have prevented these attacks. The attacks were

carried out by subverting the business processes of airports and airlines to carry out the agendas of the attackers. Once the terrorists got past the airport security checkpoints and into the cockpits, the World Trade Center towers and everyone on the upper floors were doomed.

- Marriott Hotel, Islamabad, Pakistan, September 20, 2008, suicide truck bomb attack: A large truck rammed the crash-resistant gate to the hotel, then there was a small explosion in the truck, followed by a massive explosion. A massive fire erupted, fed by a gas line that was ruptured when the powerful explosion blew off the front of the building.* This set off fires on the fourth and fifth floors, fueled by the gas line, reaching temperatures of 400°C according to the *Guardian*, overwhelming the sprinkler system and fire services. The fire was further fueled by the addition of aluminum powder† to the bomb, which adhered to everything it struck, maintaining a flame and causing that surface to burn. Aluminum powder is a component in thermobaric bombs, including the 15,000-pound BLU-82 (daisy cutter) and the 21,000-pound MOAB (Mother of All Bombs). In both cases, aluminum powder is used to increase their destructive force.‡ Aluminum powder creates a longer blast pulse that is far more damaging to buildings. This also extends the "reach" of the blast, damaging structures farther away than a conventional explosive and creating more destruction to the façade and structure. It is not a good idea to have gas lines that do not shut off automatically when ruptured. It would have been better if the checkpoint was more than 60 ft (20 m) from the front door. Otherwise, it was a good checkpoint design, having a sharp turn with no direct line of approach. A more thorough approach to risk analysis including utilities studies would have uncovered the gas line vulnerability before the bomb did. Moving the checkpoint out to 30 m (100 ft) would have reduced damage from both the bomb blast and the flaming aluminum powder and might well have prevented the attack altogether.
- Economic criminals
  - Burglaries
    - Unsophisticated burglars can be easily deterred, detected and, denied by conventional security programs with good response characteristics.
    - Sophisticated burglars are the economic equivalent of terrorists in that they spend considerable time selecting targets, planning, and testing before carrying out an attack. These burglars often bypass alarm and closed-circuit television (CCTV) systems. Sophisticated burglars target extreme valuables (jewels, etc.), large vaults of cash ($100,000+), and proprietary information. Professional burglars spend considerable time planning their burglaries. Countersurveillance programs are most helpful, as most professional burglars will abandon an attack if they are intercepted during the target selection, planning, and testing phase.
  - Insider crimes
    - Insiders have time, access, and special knowledge of the facility and its assets working for them. However, most insiders do not have the skill

---

* http://lessakele.over-blog.fr/article-22995764.html; http://terrorwonk.blogspot.com/2008/09/islamabad-bombing-i-brute-force-tactics.html.

† http://terrorwonk.blogspot.com/2008/09/islamabad-bombing-i-brute-force-tactics.html.

‡ http://www.nationalterroralert.com/updates/2008/09/29/thermobaric-bombs-al-qaedas-new-weapon-of-terror/.

and patience to leverage these advantages. Often investigation of insider crimes must go beyond conventional security systems, which many insiders circumvent or simply conduct their crime while at work when these systems are off or in areas where cameras do not monitor.

- Violent criminals in the workplace
  - Outsiders
    - Economic crimes using violence to control the victims. Most outsider violent crimes occur as opportunistic crimes (such as convenience store robberies), though some are planned (such as bank robberies).
    - Outsiders who may be related to workers or the organization in some way (spouse/lover/ex-worker). If ex-employees continue to contact other employees or management with grievances or harassment, this should be taken as a sign of possible future violence.
  - Insiders
    - Workers being disciplined are the most common form of insider violent crime. Workplace violence can be minimized by proper human resources policy and a coordinated security program of workplace violence prevention. Other insider violent crimes include mentally ill students of high schools and universities. These crimes should be acted on with great immediacy as time delays may lead to more victims. Programs to identify possible students at risk of severe mental defect may also be helpful.
- Subversives
  - Outsiders: Activist groups are the most common types of subversives that organizations have to deal with. These typically involve intrusions and harassment actions. Security elements that detect, assess, respond to, and collect solid identification evidence are most helpful in deterring these crimes.
  - Insiders: Insider subversives include chronic rule breakers and those who misuse the organization's assets for their own use. Improper Internet use, persistent rule-breaking, agitating, and sexual harassment all can affect the productivity and profitability of an organization. Insider subversive actions should be defined in employee policy manuals.
  - Subversives and saboteurs include
    - Cause-oriented subversives: These may include activist groups with an agenda opposed to a government, religion, cause, or industry. This includes groups such as the Animal Liberation Front (ALF), the Environmental Liberation Front (ELF), and others.
    - Nonaligned subversives: Other subversive acts can include civil disorder events that are related to protests or civil riots. For example, the city of Los Angeles, California, was gripped by civil disorder and riots in 1992 following the trial of Rodney King, a black motorist who was beaten by Los Angeles Police Department officers. His beating was caught on camera and played on local television news stations.[2] Many businesses were damaged in the riots that followed.
    - Political and industrial spies: Increasingly, organizations are being targeted by political and industrial spies. One article noted that industrial spies play a very big role behind the scenes at World Trade Organization talks.[3] There have been many cases of industrial and political spies prying into the secrets of large and small organizations alike.

- Hackers: Hackers may deface websites, damage networks, and act as spies to extract important information. In one recent case, hackers stole highly sensitive data on the U.S. Pentagon's newest fighter jet, the Joint Strike Fighter, from the military contractor's computers that were connected to the Internet.
- Invasion of privacy threat actors: Paparazzi and celebrity stalkers are the bane of celebrities for their invasion of privacy. Businesses that cater to the wealthy and celebrities are often confronted with aggressive celebrity seekers, photographers, and autograph seekers who interrupt the private moments of their clientele and subvert the purpose of a commercial enterprise for their own purposes.
- Persistent rule violators: These are individuals who frequent the organization's facilities either as employees or as visitors and who act as though the organization's assets are their own to use or abuse as they wish. Though warned of rules of conduct, they persist in violating the rules. These individuals create problems for the organization in several ways:
  - They set a bad example of behavior for others.
  - They often require special attention to accommodate their demands or actions.
  - They often create safety or code of conduct preconditions that could lead to either injuries or conduct problems on a larger scale (when one person acts out, it is common to see others follow their example).
  - They disrupt a normally orderly environment.
  - Their behavior may be illegal or affect the good business reputation of the organization, in some cases putting the organization itself at risk of prosecution for not abating the behavior, such as in racial or sexual misconduct cases; for example, where a manager is abusing his or her power over an employee.
  - Persons who abuse parking privileges, cut in line, demand special treatment, or act abusively toward employees—all these are subversive influences.

  While organizations do not like to have to deal with these individuals, they are a special class. These are individuals who, through their own narcissism and belligerence, become a law unto themselves and demand that the world accommodate their perspective. These people are threat actors.
- Petty criminals
  - Petty crimes are offenses that are less than felonies and are usually punishable by a fine, a penalty, forfeiture of property, or imprisonment in a jail facility rather than in a penitentiary (misdemeanors).
  - Vandals: Vandals destroy a property's value by defacing it. Vandals have caused millions of dollars in damage to property and have damaged the business opportunities of entire communities.[4]
  - Pickpockets: Pickpockets ply their trade in many public places including hotels, restaurants, retail malls, parking lots and parking structures, and elevator lobbies—literally anywhere two or more people come into contact and especially where one of those people may be distracted. Businesses that provide these environments can be harmed by the damage to their reputation as a safe environment to frequent.

- Prostitutes, pimps, and panderers: Prostitution can affect hotels, retail malls, and other public spaces and can damage the reputation of the business.
- Other petty crimes include disturbing the peace, public nuisance, and drunkenness in public.
- Business reputation crimes
  - Outsiders: In 1982, an unknown criminal laced Tylenol capsules with cyanide and placed the contaminated packages back onto store shelves where they were sold and taken by unsuspecting consumers. Johnson & Johnson, whose market share dropped from 35% to 8% after the incident, responded with very aggressive action including removing the product entirely from the marketplace, developing triple seals, and aggressive product pricing. Within a year, Tylenol had recaptured its place in the market.
  - Insiders: Enron lost its entire business as a result of the improper accounting actions of some of its key management. Organizations should focus on their mission. Periodic oversight by shareholders or owners should audit the organization's actions against its mission, lawful actions, codes, and regulations.

The above information is not meant to discourage analysts from metrics-based effectiveness studies, but rather to indicate that there is a limit to what they can achieve. Much of security has to do with human resources policy development and enforcement and management ethics enforcement. More importantly, this is to point out that intrusion-based metrics will not result in a valuable tool to reduce security incidents, as many security incidents do not involve intrusions. Having said all that, it is better to evaluate security programs on the basis of being able to identify and respond to all types of security incidents, not simply security intrusions.

WHAT KIND OF INFORMATION DO WE NEED TO EVALUATE TO DETERMINE SECURITY PROGRAM EFFECTIVENESS?

Security managers need to know

- Asset locations
  - People
  - Property
  - Proprietary information
- Vulnerabilities
  - Intrusions
    - Where intrusions are possible
    - Where intruders are likely to travel where they can be delayed or interrupted
    - Where intruders can be detected along the way to valuable assets
  - Direct attacks: Where direct attacks from the perimeter can be conducted
  - Removals/misappropriations: Where assets are readily available that can be stolen or misused
- Countermeasures
  - Locations and types of countermeasures
    - Entry control points
    - Detection systems

- – Assessment systems
- – Delaying systems
- – Response systems
  - – Technologies
  - – Communications systems
  - – Guards
  - – Transportation
  - – Weapons
  - – Tactics
  - – Functions
  - – Detect intrusion
  - – Verify intrusion
  - – Assess intentions
  - – Delay intrusion
  - – Intervene
  - – Defeat aggression
  - – Identify intruder
- – Evidence-gathering systems
- • Vulnerabilities they can address (a matrix of vulnerabilities and countermeasures)
- • Probable effectiveness of countermeasures in addressing the type of vulnerability
  - – Detection
  - – Assessment
  - – Delaying
  - – Responding
    - – Deterrence (e.g., patrols and intercom response)
    - – Denial (delaying systems and respond and defeat force)
    - – Containment (prevent the adversary from leaving with the asset)
    - – Recovery (after the loss of the asset)
    - – Observe and report
    - – Respond and defeat
  - – Evidence gathering
- • Remaining vulnerabilities
  - • Remaining percentage of vulnerabilities addressed inadequately by existing countermeasures

WHAT KIND OF METRICS CAN HELP US ANALYZE SECURITY PROGRAM EFFECTIVENESS?

There are several possible metrics to use. Each metric evaluates a different factor in security program effectiveness. These can be used in combination to achieve a complete picture of overall system effectiveness. Some metrics are useful for both new and existing security facilities, and others are only applicable to existing facilities.

- • Metrics usable for proposed security programs:
  - • Vulnerability/Countermeasure Matrix
  - • Adversary Sequence Diagrams
- • Metrics usable for existing security programs:
  - • Adversary Sequence Diagrams

- Vulnerability/Countermeasure Matrix
- Security event logs
- Patrol logs (vulnerabilities spotting/violations spotting)
- Annual risk analysis

Each of these is explained in the following subsections.

Adversary Sequence Diagrams

Adversary Sequence Diagrams relate to a specific type of threat actor: those who use intrusion to gain access to their target asset. The most valuable assets of organizations are not located at their front gate at street side. In order for an intruder to get to their target, they must make their way from outside the property through various gates, doors, and corridors and then finally to their target. This is true whether the attacker is a terrorist, criminally violent threat actor, or economic or intellectual property criminal. It is true for all burglars, attackers using force, or subversives. Whether the threat actor is breaking in, breaking down doors, or secretly making his way to an office during working hours to steal money or information, they all have one thing in common: each attacker must make entry, make their way through passages and barriers, and arrive at their target. For most attackers, the plan is also to make their way back out again, without detection if possible.

Intrusion attackers come in three types:

- Those using overwhelming force to make entry
- Those using stealth to make entry
- Those using the organization's normal business operations to make entry

Obviously, each of these types presents different requirements for detection, assessment, and response. These three types also present themselves as two main types when encountering a response force:

- Those who will surrender peacefully or try to flee (mostly economic criminals, petty criminals, and some violent criminals)
- Those who will resist:
  - Those who will resist with moderate force (any threat actor except terrorists)
  - Those who will resist with overwhelming force (all terrorists and some violent criminals; only a few economic or petty criminals)

Intrusion threat actors are further categorized into two broad groups:

- Sophisticated criminals following an organized plan
- Opportunistic criminals mostly following their instincts (spontaneous planning)

Sophisticated criminals present special challenges for the following reasons:

- Intrusions are generally well planned.
- Sophisticated criminals know their target (its value, its location, the paths to the target, protective measures they will encounter on their way in and out).
- Sophisticated criminals know your facility, including its daily operations.

- They know your detection capabilities.
- They know the quality, size, training, capabilities, and weaknesses of your security force.
- They can generally predict what your security response will be.
- Except for terrorism, from an evidence standpoint, sophisticated criminals usually leave little evidence.

Unsophisticated criminals also present special challenges.

- Unsophisticated criminals exhibit little or no preplanning, usually responding to opportunities without knowing much about their target, its detection capabilities, its occupants, and its response capabilities.
- Poor planning means they may not act predictably in terms of what direction they go.
- Poor planning also means they may not act predictably in terms of how they will respond when encountered by a response officer.
- Unsophisticated criminals rarely make a prolonged entry for fear of detection and response.
- From an evidence standpoint, unsophisticated criminals often leave a chaotic crime scene.

The key to dealing with intrusion threat actors is to detect them as early as possible and intercept them with a superior response before they can make their way to their intended target. Failing that, you can detect them and present a superior response on their exit.

This is where the design basis threat becomes relevant again. The quality of detection, assessment, and response should be proportionate to the level of threat actor and their worst-case scenario. Countermeasure selection must be appropriate to the sophistication and force of the design basis threat.

The Adversary Sequence Diagram is used to evaluate the possible points of entry and the paths that a threat actor could take to their target and then to their exit. This of course will result in multiple Adversary Sequence Diagrams, one for each entry/target combination (Figure 18.1).

The next type of metric is the Vulnerability/Countermeasures Matrix.

Vulnerability/Countermeasure Matrix

The Vulnerability/Countermeasure Matrix is a spreadsheet of vulnerabilities (rows) and various types of countermeasures (columns). Ideally, every vulnerability that was identified should be listed in its own row. The vulnerabilities can be categorized by major asset groups, buildings, areas, and so on. At intersection points between a vulnerabilities and countermeasures, place a percentage of probable mitigation (1 being 100%).

For example, for detection systems, if detection of an exploiter of this vulnerability is assured, that gets a 1. For assessment, if there is a camera that can verify the alarm, that gets a 1.

For response, if a response can be mounted that can intervene before the subject reaches his target, that gets a 1. This could, for example, be a security intercom that allows the console officer to intervene and interrogate the subject remotely, while a patrol

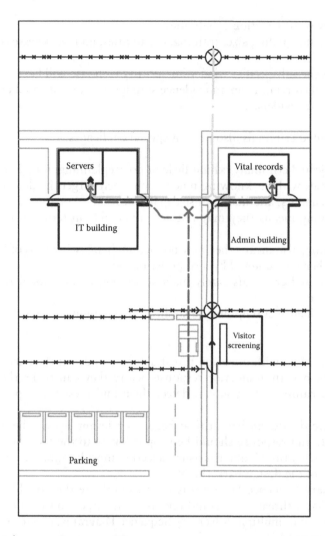

FIGURE 18.1   Adversary Sequence Diagram.

officer is being sent. The subject's response will dictate further action. If the subject continues after being intercepted by an intercom call, that defines intent. Then three other options exist. These include denial, containment, and recovery.

For facilities where the acquisition of the asset itself could cause unacceptable consequences, such as chemical plants and nuclear power plants, denial is required. This requires a robust security force with excellent training.

For facilities where the mere acquisition of the asset itself is not a consequence, only its loss would be, containment is a possibility. This allows the security force time to plan a response including staging a recovery on the aggressor's exit.

For sites where a robust response force is not financially feasible, recovery may be a legitimate option. For this, excellent evidence is required, including vehicle ID including the license plate. A clear photo of intruders (face and clothes, height, weight, gender, etc.) is required, as is evidence of the crime itself and evidence of the removal and getaway. Few commercial security systems can accomplish this, though all should.

For evidence, if there is a camera that can get a good identification, that would receive a 1. For a camera that can read gender, clothing description, and so on, but not facial identification, that might be a 0.5. For a camera that can see form and movement but cannot identify gender, that might be a 0.2.

It may be useful to assemble columns in the spreadsheet into groups. I have done this two ways but have finally settled on the second. The first grouping included hi-tech, lo-tech, and no-tech countermeasures. The second grouping included access control, detection, assessment, delay, response, and evidence. I now use the second group because it explains the function of each countermeasure more clearly. Some countermeasures can serve multiple functions, which is not evident in the first categorization. For example, a video camera can detect and assess. Arguably, it could even be considered a response if a pan/tilt camera is seen to move from one position to follow a subject. This would be observable by the subject and thus constitute a response that could be a deterrent.

You will notice that there is no category for deterrence. That is because deterrence cannot be easily measured or estimated. Deterrence is purely a subjective phenomenon completely reliant on the subject in question. Factors involved in deterrence include

- The subject's motivation
- The subject's determination
- The subject's concern for detection and capture (This is a key reason why terrorism is so difficult, because many terrorists do not care if they die in the attack, so they certainly expect to be detected and responded to. Thus, none of the usual factors comprise deterrence for a terrorist, except any response factors that could compromise the fulfillment of their mission.)

Thus, if a subject wishes to elude detection, the deterrence value of alarms, dogs, cameras, lights, and so on may be high. But if a subject has little concern for detection or response (terrorists, workplace violence threats, mental health threats, activist action groups, etc.), deterrent value of the same countermeasures may be low. Thus, one cannot estimate deterrence from the existence of countermeasures, and I do not recommend that you even consider it as a factor.

This same principle should guide the design of response countermeasures. The degree of response should be directly correlated to the consequences of a threat action. If the consequences of a threat action are acceptable and can be mitigated after the loss, then the response can be unarmed and muted, such as in a normal office or commercial environment. However, if the consequences of the loss are wholly intolerable, such as at a nuclear power plant, nuclear weapons storage facility, or phosgene (CG) chemical production plant, then the response capability should be superior to the severest possible threat action.

For any very severe consequence that could affect community welfare (chemical plant, etc.), I recommend the Sandia Risk Assessment Model and very robust countermeasures. Sadly, this is most often not the case for facilities in the commercial sector that are not subject to strict government security regulations. In my opinion, the government should mandate stricter risk assessment and countermeasure programs at many more types of facilities than they do now, because many facilities with relatively relaxed risk assessment and countermeasure requirements constitute a grave risk to society.

So back to the categorizations: By categorizing countermeasures by their functions, one can get a picture of the overall effectiveness of the countermeasures that relate to a specific vulnerability. Within the categories of entry control, you might include access control reader, vehicle checkpoint, and so on. For detection, you might have door position switch (DPS), motion detector, motion video detector, fence line detector, buried perimeter detector, left-behind article detection, patrol detection, dog, and so on. For assessment, you might include video camera, intercom, and patrol officer. For delay, you might include deployable barriers, burglar bars, and so on. For response, you might include patrols, dispatch, intercom, and so on. For evidence, you might include video archiving, audio intercom archiving, telephone and 911 logging recorder, and so on. For a given security program, there may be dozens of types of countermeasures.

Different countermeasures will be applicable to different types of vulnerabilities; for example, if a glass façade is vulnerable to blast and intrusion. Countermeasures could include glass break detectors, blast film CCTV cameras, crime prevention through environmental design (CPTED) measures providing blast standoff, and so on. Because certain vulnerabilities may apply to multiple threat actions, the range of possible countermeasures are not universally applicable. However, each countermeasure does have an effectiveness factor against each threat. Glass break detectors are of no help to a blast threat, but they are helpful against burglary. It is appropriate to list all possible countermeasures and rate them each for effectiveness against the types of threats that they can mitigate. This provides an overall view of effectiveness. It may also be useful for high-consequence vulnerabilities to add a remarks field to the right of all columns to note the highest consequence; this may be taken into consideration when preparing the qualitative report. Apply an effectiveness estimate to every applicable countermeasure. The value of layering countermeasures will begin to display itself as the value of each of the countermeasures begins to add to a value of 1.

Do this for every vulnerability listed in the vulnerability analysis until all applicable countermeasures for all vulnerabilities have been estimated. You will note that certain countermeasures are capable of mitigating multiple vulnerabilities and most vulnerabilities require multiple countermeasures to fully mitigate. Also keep in mind the design basis threat. If the design basis threat is violent crime, countermeasures that will mitigate violence may be of little use to economic threats. For economic crime, countermeasures that could mitigate terrorism may be of little use. For complex projects, I have actually developed Vulnerability/Countermeasure Matrixes for several types of threat actions. This is not usually done for every vulnerability in the facility, but only for key assets (for violence, you may do this for people, but not for office equipment vulnerabilities).

The Vulnerability/Countermeasures Matrix should be prepared *after* the Adversary Sequence Diagrams, which will help to point out vulnerabilities that cannot be noticed without performing them (Figure 18.2).

Having explained this process to classes and individual consultants, a step-by-step explanation is required to help them fully understand it.

Step 1: Create a spreadsheet of every vulnerability in the project. This spreadsheet will also serve as the basis for the risk register, if the project requires it (see Chapter 10). For the purposes of illustration, we will look at two. Each vulnerability will reside in its own row, separated by asset class or area of facility.

Step 2: Add columns for risk number, probability score vulnerability score, consequences score, and risk score $R = (P + V + C)/3$. Add a column for recommended countermeasure and estimated cost.

Step 3: Create columns for each type of countermeasure, grouped by functions. Function classes include

Vulnerability	Risk	Countermeasure	Access	Deterent	Detection	Assess	Delay	Response	Evidence	Total	Critical	Medium
		Baseline Security Program										
Outdated Post Orders	Critical	Develop new Post Orders	14%	14%	14%	14%	14%	14%	14%	98%	1	
Similar Day/Evening Methods	Critical	Develop Different Day/Evening Procedures	14%	14%	14%	14%	14%	14%	14%	98%	1	
Access Control on Policies	Critical	Limit Access of Critical Policies	14%	14%						28%	1	
Security force is inadequate	Critical	Review competency of all officers for possible reassignment	20%							20%	1	
Posts & Patrols may be inappropriate	Critical	Audit Posts and Patrol Positions	20%							20%	1	
Security force is inadequate	Critical	Reassign poorly performing officers	20%							20%	1	
Unable to hire new security staff	Critical	Consider Contracting Security Staff	20%							20%	1	
Smuggling	Critical	Periodic Forensic Audits/Undercover Investigations		20%	20%			20%	20%	80%	1	
Unvetted Visitors	Critical	Institute full security checks on non-VIPs	10%	10%	10%	10%	10%	10%	10%	70%	1	
No ID Badges for Employees	Critical	Implement Photo ID Badges	10%	10%		14%	7%		5%	46%	1	
No BOH Visitor Badges	Critical	Implement BOH Visitor Badges	20%	20%						40%	1	
Civil Disorder Events	Critical	Additional Training in Civil Disorder Events		30%						30%	1	
Civil Disorder Events	Critical	Develop Rapid Response Plan		30%				30%		60%	1	
No Business Recovery Plan	Critical	Develop Business Recovery Program								0%	1	
Current CCTV Room inadequate	Medium	Establish a proper Security CCTV Room								0%		1
No radio coordination with ISF	Critical	Radio Link to ISF						14%		14%	1	
Forced Entry & Pedestrian Safety	Medium	Speed Bumps at Hairpin Turn	7%	14%		4%	7%		14%	46%		1
Forced Entry	Critical	Camera outside Stage Door/Monitor within	14%	14%	14%	14%	14%		14%	84%	1	
Weapons/Explosives Screening	Critical	Consider an Architectural Study for Security Area								0%	1	
Package Bombs	Critical	X-Ray Machine for Package Screening	14%	14%	14%	14%	14%		14%	84%	1	
Package Bombs	Critical	Consider screening packages off-site or move room								0%	1	
Package Bombs	Critical	Negative pressure HVAC in Mail Room					14%			14%	1	
Moneylenders in Casino	Critical	Cameras at Casino Entrances-Facial Recognition		7%	14%	14%	7%	14%	14%	70%	1	
Moneylenders in Casino	Critical	Cameras at Upper Main Road-Facial Recognition		7%	14%	14%	7%	14%	14%	70%	1	
Moneylenders in Casino	Critical	Camera outside each Toilet-Facial Recognition		7%	14%	14%	7%	14%	14%	70%	1	
Main Doors subject to confusion	Medium	RH Doors In/LH Doors Out	14%	7%	14%	14%	7%	14%	14%	84%		1
All exterior openings no alarm	Medium	Alarm on all exterior openings		14%	14%			14%	14%	56%		1
Many exterior doors left open	Medium	Access Control on most exterior doors	14%	14%	14%	14%	14%	14%	14%	98%		1
Banned Persons hard to recognize	Medium	Facial Recognition Software		7%	14%	14%	7%	14%	14%	70%		1
		Anti-Terrorism Measures										
In the Dark about Developing Problems	Critical	Subscribe to Intelligence Briefing				12%				12%	1	
Vulnerable to Vehicle Intrusion	Critical	Upper Drive In/Lower Drive Out (2 Lanes in Upper Drive)	14%	14%		14%	14%		14%	70%	1	
Forced Vehicle Entry	Critical	Reinforce Main Gates (2 In)	14%	14%		14%	14%		14%	70%	1	
Explosives in Vehicle	Critical	Utilize highly effective explosives detector	14%	14%	14%	14%	14%		14%	84%	1	
Explosives in Vehicle	Critical	Consider using Blast Containment Vessel										

FIGURE 18.2 Countermeasure Effectiveness Matrix.

- Entry control
- Detection
- Assessment
- Delay
- Response
- Evidence

To the left of each function, include a column marked "Countermeasure Effectiveness Estimate (or CEE)." To the right of all columns, add an additional column titled "Total Mitigation Estimate (or TME)."

Step 4: For each vulnerability, place an X under each countermeasure that applies. Then, for each function, place an estimate from 0 to 1, where 1 is total mitigation for that function, and 0 is no mitigation for that function.

For example, for detection, countermeasures might include door position switch, glass break detector, guard dog, patrol, and so on. For each of these that are applicable for this vulnerability, place an X under the countermeasure. Then, estimate the total mitigation for that vulnerability for the detection function. If detection is assured, place a 1 in the Estimate column. If detection is not likely to occur, place a 0 in the column. If detection is nearly always likely, place a number lower than 1 and more than 0.5 in the column. Do this for each vulnerability and for each functional group. This provides the mitigation score for each function for each vulnerability.

Then place a weighting on the functional estimates. Since we have six functions, a balanced weighting would be 16.6% for each function.

The formula for total mitigation is simple and straightforward: Total Mitigation = (Entry Control*Weighted Score{WS}Entry Control) + (Detection*WS Detection) + (Assessment* WS Assessment) + (Delay*WS Delay) + (Response*WS Response) + (Evidence*WS Evidence).

Security Event Logs

Security event logs are also a very good way to determine overall security program effectiveness. Across a period of 1 year, security logs will display trends and identify unresolved vulnerabilities. We are interested in both, but especially the unresolved vulnerabilities.

Since it is unlikely that every last vulnerability will be identified in any risk assessment, you can be certain that offenders will notice any unresolved vulnerabilities and try to exploit them. These will often be found by minor offenders or the guard staff itself. These minor exploits will show up as security events in the logs and are a valuable source for tightening up those unresolved vulnerabilities that would otherwise go unnoticed.

I recommend that whatever logging method you use to keep track of security events should have a column to track whether each security event was related to an unresolved vulnerability; an additional column could identify the unresolved vulnerability. This allows the security director to relate security events to either misbehavior that was handled in accordance with policy or an event that should spark reconsideration of security countermeasures.

Over the course of a year, any unresolved vulnerabilities that develop into security events will draw management's attention to the needs for those vulnerabilities to be mitigated with appropriate countermeasures. Adding the column to identify the security event as related to an unresolved vulnerability and describing that vulnerability allows the security director to quickly identify any unresolved vulnerabilities and also note which vulnerabilities are related to recurring security events.

The goal of ongoing risk assessments is to continuously uncover unresolved vulnerabilities and emerging threats and to make accommodations for them. Security event logs are one of the very best tools an analyst can use to achieve this goal.

In the event that there is no column to identify if each security event is related to an unresolved vulnerability, all is not lost. An analyst can import the logs to a spreadsheet program and add the columns. If the analyst is familiar with the facility, he/she will likely think of the vulnerabilities that could relate to the security event. If not, he/she can assemble the related security events and then discuss these events with staff to uncover any unresolved vulnerabilities.

The spreadsheet acts as a metric, listing both incidents related to vulnerabilities and those that are not. The percentage of incidents related to vulnerabilities is a useful metric to determine whether the security program is minimizing risk.

Patrol Logs (Vulnerabilities Spotting/Violations Spotting)

In the same manner that security incident reports can uncover unresolved vulnerabilities, so to can patrol logs. Quality security program directors train their patrol officers to understand vulnerabilities and to spot them when they see them. I always find it interesting when performing risk analysis surveys that interviews with both post and patrol officers *always and without exception* uncover unresolved vulnerabilities.

There is a wealth of information among the officers "on the ground" regarding the weaknesses in security countermeasures. It is very common after a major security incident to hear one or many officers say "Yeah, I knew that was going to happen someday." So why didn't they report it? Usually, it is because management does not emphasize focusing on vulnerabilities and reporting them to management.

By training security officers to observe, and not just to see, management can find those vulnerabilities that are missed by risk analysts and management alike due to their lack of intimate familiarity with the facility and its operations. Security officers, who spend hours every day interacting with the business operations and every corner of the facility, know every vulnerability well. But in most cases, they are not trained to see them as vulnerabilities that should be addressed and reported to management.

The patrol logs spreadsheet acts as a metric, listing both patrol notes that are related to vulnerabilities and those that are not. The percentage of patrol notes related to vulnerabilities is a useful metric to determine whether the security program is minimizing risk.

Annual Risk Analysis

Finally, the risk analysis should be updated annually. This presents an opportunity once each year to compare overall risk progression year over year. The delta between this year and previous years serves as a useful metric to determine risk progression.

SUMMARY

Introduction

One of the most difficult challenges of security management is the challenge of estimating the effectiveness of security countermeasures in their role of preventing crime and terrorism. By their very nature, crime and terrorism deterred cannot be measured.

However, as we have seen from previous chapters, many things about security can be measured or estimated with a reasonable degree of accuracy. So too can the effectiveness of countermeasures to detect, assess, delay, assist in a response, and capture evidence. All these can assist in deterrence. So while deterrence itself cannot be accurately assessed, all other factors can, and these all contribute to enhancing the difficulty of a successful attack or, looking at it another way, reducing the probability of success of an attack. Then a reasonable person would assume that as the difficulty level increases, deterrence does also. So difficulty could be construed as a surrogate for deterrence for most crimes and also for terrorism.

Security effectiveness is also a primary contributor to cost-effectiveness. The basic goal of cost-effectiveness is lower cost and more effectiveness. So first we must measure or estimate effectiveness in order to determine cost-effectiveness (Chapter 19).

Sandia Model

Absolutely the best metrics for countermeasure effectiveness are contained within the Sandia Vulnerability Assessment Model. The Sandia Model measures the performance of each aspect of the security countermeasures program with great precision through firm scientific process.

However, the Sandia Model is so intricate and precise that the cost to fully apply it puts it beyond the reach of many organizations' security budgets. Commercial enterprises and many second- and third-tier critical infrastructure facilities can be estimated with less costly tools. In recognition of this fact, the U.S. Department of Homeland Security does not require this level of precision for most critical infrastructure facilities.

For the Sandia Model, $P_E = P_I * P_N$
Factors:

- For adversaries that are likely to give up when confronted by a responder, P_N is not a factor.
- If no immediate response is possible, P_N is not a factor. In these cases, $P_E = P_I$.
- For the system to be considered effective, it must detect an attack while there is time to respond (before the CPD).
- Provide a rapid assessment of alarms, so that only valid alarms yield a response.
- Communicate the detection to an adequate response force in a timely manner.
- Collect evidence.
- Ensure that detection occurs before delay and delay the adversary long enough to process the detection, perform assessment, communicate to a response force, and get that force to the delay point (succeed at interruption).
- Use protection in depth (multiple layers) to assure that there are multiple opportunities to detect and delay an offender.
- Balance protection; that is, assure that all paths to assets have roughly the same probability of interruption (P_I).
- Engage and neutralize the offender with adequate and appropriate force.
- Conduct a full analysis of adversary paths and system effectiveness (interruption and neutralization) as the overall performance metric. Analysis must occur along all credible paths.

A Useful Commercial Model

Before we look at the model itself, let us review the needs. Security program effectiveness metrics are needed by two classes of users:

- Security program managers
- Security budget decision makers

To achieve the above results, the model needs to do the following:

- For new projects: Identify what types of countermeasures could be effective to mitigate each listed vulnerability
- For existing programs: Identify which existing countermeasures are effective to mitigate each listed vulnerability and which countermeasures can best address any gaps in coverage that are found in the risk analysis
- Identify the effectiveness of each countermeasure in terms of
  - Entry control
  - Intrusion detection
  - Assessment
  - Delay
  - Response
  - Evidence gathering

It is a common mistake to try to evaluate security programs in terms of "intrusion events interrupted or defeated." There is a very small category of facilities for which this criterion is the chief criteria for consideration, and even in those it would be a mistake to use it as a key or chief criteria. But virtually every metric ever developed focuses on detecting and interrupting intrusions (including the Sandia model).

In my opinion, any effectiveness metric that evaluates only one factor (intrusion) completely misses the point. What are the range of offenses?

- Intrusions by unauthorized persons
- Destruction/damage/theft of assets (including people, property, and intellectual assets)
- Subversion of the business environment to fulfill personal agendas
- Damage to business reputation arising from one of the above

What Kind of Metrics Can Help Us Analyze Security Program Effectiveness?

There are several possible metrics to use. Each metric evaluates a different factor in security program effectiveness. These can be used in combination to achieve a complete picture of overall system effectiveness. Some metrics are useful for both new and existing security facilities, and others are only applicable to existing facilities.

- Metrics usable for existing security programs:
  - Vulnerability/Countermeasure Matrix
  - Adversary Sequence Diagrams
  - Security event logs
  - Patrol logs (vulnerabilities spotting/violations spotting)
  - Annual risk analysis
- Metrics usable for proposed security programs:
  - Vulnerability/Countermeasure Matrix
  - Adversary Sequence Diagrams

The Adversary Sequence Diagram is used to evaluate the possible points of entry and the paths that a threat actor could take to their target and then to their exit. This of course will result in multiple Adversary Sequence Diagrams, one for each entry/target combination.

Security Event Logs
Security event logs are also a very good way to determine overall security program effectiveness. Over 1 year, security logs will display trends and identify unresolved vulnerabilities. We are interested in both, but especially the unresolved vulnerabilities.

Patrol Logs (Vulnerabilities Spotting/Violations Spotting)
In the same manner that security incident reports can uncover unresolved vulnerabilities, so to can patrol logs. Quality security program directors train their patrol officers to understand vulnerabilities and to spot them when they see them. I always find it interesting when performing risk analysis surveys that interviews with both post and patrol officers *always and without exception* uncover unresolved vulnerabilities.

The patrol logs spreadsheet acts as a metric, listing both patrol notes that are related to vulnerabilities and those that are not. The percentage of patrol notes related to vulnerabilities is a useful metric to determine whether the security program is minimizing risk.

Annual Risk Analysis

Finally, the risk analysis should be updated annually and on the occurrence of any major security event, which might change a variable in the risk analysis. This presents an opportunity once each year to compare overall risk progression year over year. The delta between this year and previous years serves as a useful metric to determine risk progression.

REFERENCES

1. Garcia, M. L. 2006. *Vulnerability Assessment of Physical Protection Systems.* Butterworth-Heinemann, Amsterdam.
2. Cannon, L. 1999. *Official Negligence: How Rodney King and the Riots Changed Los Angeles and the LAPD.* Basic Books, New York.
3. Blumenthal, L. and Doyle, M. 1999. Spies bring trade secrets to the table at WTO talks. *Star Tribune* (Minneapolis, MN), November 27.
4. Rivera, J. 2008. *Vandal Squad: Inside the New York City Transit Police Dept, 1984–2004.* Miss Rosen Editions, New York.

Q&A

Questions

Q1: One of the most difficult challenges of security management is the challenge of
    A. Estimating the effectiveness of security guards and dogs.
    B. Estimating the effectiveness of security countermeasures in their role of preventing crime and terrorism.
    C. Both of the above.
    D. Neither of the above.

Q2: Security effectiveness is also a primary contributor to
    A. Cost-effectiveness.
    B. Security management.
    C. Business management.
    D. None of the above.

Q3: For the Sandia Model,
    A. $P_E = P_I * P$.
    B. $P = P_I * P_N$.
    C. $P_E = P_I * P_N$.
    D. $P_N = P * P_N$.

Q4: It is a common mistake to try to evaluate security programs in terms of
    A. Intrusion events interrupted or defeated.
    B. Intrusion events.
    C. Terrorism events deterred.
    D. None of the above.

Q5: For existing projects,
  A. Identify what types of countermeasures could be effective to mitigate each listed vulnerability.
  B. Identify which existing countermeasures are effective to mitigate each listed vulnerability and which countermeasures can best address any gaps in coverage that are found in the risk analysis.
  C. Neither of the above.
  D. Both of the above.

Q6: Security program effectiveness metrics are needed by two classes of users:
  A. Security program managers
  B. Security budget decision makers
  C. Neither of the above
  D. Both of the above

Q7: Which below *cannot* provide usable metrics for existing security programs:
  A. Vulnerability/Countermeasure Matrix and annual risk analysis
  B. Adversary Sequence Diagrams
  C. Dogs
  D. Security event logs and patrol logs

Q8: The _____ is used to evaluate the possible points of entry and the paths that a threat actor could take to their target and then to their exit.
  A. Adversary Sequence Diagram
  B. Patrol log
  C. Security event log
  D. None of the above

Q9: Security event logs and _____ are also a very good way to determine overall security program effectiveness.
  A. Post comments
  B. Patrol logs
  C. Street video archives
  D. None of the above

Q10: The risk analysis should be updated
  A. Annually.
  B. On the occurrence of any major security event, which might change a variable in the risk analysis.
  C. Annually and on the occurrence of any major security event, which might change a variable in the risk analysis.
  D. None of the above.

Answers

Q1 – B, Q2 – A, Q3 – C, Q4 – A, Q5 – B, Q6 – D, Q7 – C, Q8 – A, Q9 – B, Q10 – C

CHAPTER 19

Cost-Effectiveness Metrics

INTRODUCTION

One of the most difficult questions for the management of any organization is how much to spend on different organization programs. Each organization has two types of programs: revenue-producing and overhead programs. Even nonprofit organizations have revenue-producing programs. These are usually fund-raising or something similar, which is used to raise funds to support the mission of the organization. For for-profit organizations, it is much more clear cut; the mission of the organization includes the selling of goods or services, which is to result in the organization making a profit. If it does not make a profit, it has not fulfilled its mission.

Programs like human resources, accounting, facilities, and security are all administrative programs, the purpose of which is to support the primary mission of the organization through the provision of resources and the protection of those resources from risk.

For most administrative programs, the cost formula is clear cut. How much does it cost for this program to provide the services needed by the programs that directly support the mission of the organization? That, then, is the budget.

For the security program, the answer is not so clear cut. The security program must be funded adequately so that it can protect the assets of the organization from harm. But in any given year, little harm may occur naturally, and then suddenly in one year great harm can occur. Security programs must be effective at preventing both *chronic* security problems and the *one-off* events that get everyone's attention.

But in a year when there is no one-off event, it can easily appear that security's budget is too much. And, unlike any other program, quite ironically, the better the job that the security program is doing, the less it seems that security is needed at all! No other program suffers like security from its own success.

It could probably be accurately said that most organizations' security programs suffer from a lack of effective management metrics. And the lack of management metrics in any program is a certain cause of program inefficiencies and possible mission failure.

The presence of useful management metrics not only helps assure the success of the mission of the program, but also helps the security program director justify and explain the legitimate need for the program to upper management so that they can make informed financial decisions that are in the best interest of the organization. Cost-effectiveness metrics are at the heart of this approach.

WHAT ARE THE LIMITATIONS OF COST-EFFECTIVENESS METRICS?

The challenge of cost-effectiveness metrics is effectiveness. Cost-effectiveness has only two components: cost and effectiveness. As we have seen from the last chapter, it is possible to measure effectiveness, and the measurement of cost is straightforward. But how do we derive cost-effectiveness?

There are many possible ways, most of which are either too complicated or conclude in meaningless results. For example, in order to determine overall program cost-effectiveness, we could apply a formula such as security budget/security events. While such a formula will result in a dollar value per security event, it is not a meaningful formula. For example, if we were able to achieve such effectiveness that only one event occurred and our organization had a $500,000 annual budget, then we would have a result of $500,000 per security event. This is not only absolutely meaningless because it does not take into account security events that were deterred (an unknowable number), but it is also very alarming to budget makers; so context is everything.

But to create a useful result, one must constrain the arguments in order to get reasonable results. It is often helpful to reduce arguments to the ridiculous in order to understand the principles. Let us look at just such a simplistic but illustrative example.

If I want to protect my house and all of its occupants and belongings from harm, there is a wide array of options, which include the reasonable and the ridiculous. Let us look at a comparison of cost-effectiveness between just two extremes. In this competition for best cost-effectiveness, the contenders are my dog Spot! (that is his name, Spot!) versus the U.S. Navy.

In this corner: my dog Spot!

- Countermeasures include
  - Detection sensors
    - Very good ears
    - Very good nose
    - Eyes (fur is in the way so these are not so good)
  - Assessment
    - Any person with food: good
    - Known person friendly to owner: good
    - Mailman: bad
    - Unknown person without food: bad
  - Delay
    - Spot!'s responses can act as a useful barrier to an intruder
  - Response
    - Spot! is quick on his feet and can reposition quickly to counter any movement by an intruder
    - Spot! barks
    - Spot! growls
    - Spot! bares his pointy teeth
    - Spot! will chase intruder up a tree or over a fence
  - Evidence-gathering tools
    - Pointy teeth
- Effectiveness factors
  - Deterrence: Depends on the type of offender: unknowable

- Detection: Spot! is pretty good at detecting unknown intruders (and the mailman); let us say Spot! is 80% effective at detection.
- Assessment: Spot! is weak here (he thinks the mailman is fast food). His IFF (Identify Friend and Foe) circuit is weak; let us say Spot! is 20% effective at assessment.
- Delay: Spot! can be pretty good at delaying intrusion; let us say he is 50% effective at delay.
- Response: Spot! will definitely respond, both audibly running to engage the intruder and with his clashing pointy teeth. Only highly determined intruders will get past him; Spot! is 80% effective at response.
- Evidence: This is not Spot!'s strong suit. He may bring back a shred of pants cuff, but not much more. Spot! is 1% effective at evidence.
- Overall, Spot! is 49.2% effective.
- Cost factors
  - Capital cost
    - Original purchase price: $25 at the animal shelter, including first set of shots
  - Operating costs
    - Food: $250/year
    - Vet visits: $100/year
    - Dog license: $10/year
    - Upgrade to home insurance: $40/year
    - Total annual operating cost: $400/year

And in this corner: the U.S. Navy.

- Countermeasures include
  - Detection
    - Thousands of underwater, airborne, and satellite sensors; human intelligence feeds from CIA and NSA; airborne visual sensors (unmanned and manned aerial vehicles); law enforcement liaison (local, state, and federal); and the Naval Criminal Investigative Service (NCIS)
  - Assessment
    - Hundreds of millions of dollars budget for analysts
  - Delay
    - Delay through response and liaison with U.S. State Department and law enforcement liaison
  - Response
    - 11 aircraft carriers
    - 14 ballistic missile submarines
    - 4 guided missile submarines
    - 97 surface combatants
    - 53 nuclear attack submarines
    - 33 amphibious warfare ships
    - 32 combat logistics ships
    - 29 support/mine warfare ships
    - 9 active reserves
    - Unknown number of strategic sealift vessels
    - The U.S. Navy can strike almost any target anywhere when assisted by aerial refueling planes.

- Evidence-gathering tools
  - Video footage from aircraft and naval vessels
  - Ship and airborne radar
  - Human intelligence
  - Law enforcement liaison
- Effectiveness factors
  - Deterrence: pretty good deterrence, but still unknowable, although probably higher than for Spot!
  - Detection: 99% effective
  - Assessment: 99% effective
  - Delay: 90% effective
  - Response: 99.5% effective
  - Evidence: 60% effective
  - Overall, the U.S. Navy is 90.5% effective (the U.S. Navy loses points for evidence, which is not its strong suit).
- Cost factors:
  - Annual budget: 2008 budget = $159.8 billion* U.S. dollars

Clearly, the U.S. Navy wins the effectiveness argument hands down. While Spot! is only 49.2% effective, the U.S. Navy is 90.5% effective. However, Spot! wins the cost argument equally handily. While the U.S. Navy's annual budget is $159.8 billion, Spot!'s annual budget is only $400.00. So then the question becomes how much is too much? How much is too much cost and, equally, how much is too much effectiveness?

So how do we determine which is more cost effective? Perhaps we should consider the value of the assets under protection. Let us say that my home is worth $150,000 and property assets are worth another $100,000, including cars, furniture, tools, jewelry, and so on. So with a total of $250,000 in assets to protect, Spot! is beginning to look like a bargain and the U.S. Navy is starting to look like massive cost-effectiveness overkill. But wait, there's more! I forgot the value of my family. While personal assets are replaceable, family members are not. If one of the threats includes home-invasion robberies, which can be traumatic and sometimes fatal, I would do well to consider more protection than Spot! can provide.

While I could stand to lose $250,000 in assets, the consequences of a home-invasion robbery are actually much, much higher. They could include lengthy hospitalization or a funeral for myself or a loved one. Now, these are considered unacceptable consequences.

So, it is not really the asset value that we are protecting, it is in fact the consequences that we are protecting against. This is a most important principle that must be understood.

While I cannot afford to employ the U.S. Navy, and Spot! is a wonderful budget fit, I would like more protection and more effectiveness than Spot! alone can offer. When we combine Spot! with other protective measures, we can achieve a much higher level of effectiveness and still keep the budget within reasonable bounds.

Perhaps I should consider a complete home security program to include Spot! and a complement of burglar bars, reinforced doors and locks, an alarm system with central station monitoring, motion-activated automated lighting, CCTV system, and a private patrol and response force. All this will be complemented by a set of home security policies and procedures to help make sure that the family is security aware. The capital budget for all this is $5000 and the annual operating budget rises from $400 for Spot! alone to $1600. So if I have valuables and a high probability of intrusion, this is still quite a

---

* http://www.finance.hq.navy.mil/FMB/08PRES/HIGHBOOK/08PRESs_Brief.pdf.

reasonable sum to spend to protect my family, home, and valuables, which are certainly worth their asset value and, with the addition of casualty considerations, in fact are worth much, much more. And Spot! can take a day off occasionally.

Looking at the third option, the complete home security program:

- Countermeasures
  - Detection sensors
    - Spot!
    - Alarm system
    - CCTV system programmed with motion detection
    - Private patrol
  - Assessment
    - Spot!: not so good
    - Alarm system with central station monitoring: good
    - CCTV system with central station monitoring: very good
  - Delay
    - Spot!: good
    - Burglar bars: good
    - Reinforced doors and locks: good
  - Response
    - Spot!: good
    - Private response force: good
    - Automated lighting: good
  - Evidence-gathering tools
    - Spot!: not so good
    - Alarm system: good
    - CCTV with central station monitoring: very good
    - Private response force: very good
- Effectiveness factors
  - Deterrence: depends on the type of offender: unknowable
  - Detection: 95%
  - Assessment: 95%
  - Delay: 90%
  - Response: 90%
  - Evidence: 95%
  - Overall, the complete home security program is 93% effective
- Cost factors
  - Capital cost: $5000
  - Operating cost
  - Spot!: $400/year
  - Complete home security program: $1600/year
  - Total annual cost: $2000/year

So it is really all about reasonable ratios to achieve reasonable security goals. We want the highest possible effectiveness for an affordable budget. So then three questions present themselves:

- What is the value of the possible consequences? (baseline for consideration)
- What is an affordable budget to mitigate these consequences? (reasonable cost)

- What is the highest effectiveness we can achieve within this budget? (highest effectiveness)

Research that I have conducted personally throughout my long career indicates that well-prepared security programs for nonstrategic facilities usually have a capital budget range of between 1% and 2% of the cost of the facility alone, excluding fixtures, furnishings, and equipment (FF&E), and can go higher if the FF&E values are high (such as for expensive medical equipment like MRIs, etc.). This budget estimate is appropriate for commercial, noncommercial, and critical infrastructure facilities alike. Exceptions include those facilities that house assets, the loss of which could constitute great harm to the community, such as chemical plants, nuclear power plants, nuclear weapons storage facilities, central banks, presidential palaces, and the like. For these types of facilities, the capital and operating costs of the program should be entirely driven by the consequences.

Let me cite an example. While I might want to buy a family car that is likely to protect my family in a serious crash (kudos to Volvo), I do not have an imminent need for an armored limousine. However, if I were the founding president of what had grown from a small business into a national critical petrochemical company, located in an area of the world where there is a history of kidnappings of corporate CEOs and their families, I would be foolhardy not to own an armored limousine and a proper security program for my home, office, and family. In such a case, deciding on an annual security budget of $1600 would be foolhardy. *Consequences drive the budget!*

In such a case, it is not only the consequences of the loss of the president or his family member that drives the decision, but also the consequences of the loss of this person to the corporation and indeed the country. This is why presidents and prime ministers are so well protected. But this is not always the case. In February 2009, the new prime minister of Zimbabwe, Morgan Tsvangirai, and his wife were driving in a SUV on a two-lane highway in Zimbabwe, going home to their ancestral village. They were accompanied only by their driver and an aide. There were no escort cars ahead or behind. On this very bad road, they had a head-on collision with a large truck, causing the Tsvangirais' SUV to roll over three times, killing Mr. Tsvangirai's beloved wife of 30 years and mother to his six children, whom most also considered a mother to their nation. The country mourned the loss of Mr. Tsangirai's wife and closest confidant. Zimbabwe's president Robert Mugabi allegedly had considered the cost of executive protection for Mr. Tsvangirai, his political rival, to be too high, though he reserved such for himself. *Consequences drive the budget!*

For a nuclear power plant, the annual cost of security can be many times the cost of that for a nonnuclear power facility. *Consequences drive the budget!*

WHAT METRICS CAN BE USED TO DETERMINE COST-EFFECTIVENESS?

Remembering that we have found a way to estimate effectiveness, and that cost is self-evident, how then do we comprise a formula to estimate cost-effectiveness? If we are comparing systems that all have the same cost and different effectiveness, this is quite simple. This table shows an example. As costs stay the same, the difference in cost-effectiveness is the difference only in effectiveness.

The answers in this table are the result of multiplying each cost by each effectiveness, factored to 1. That is, we assume that since all costs are the same, they are all equal to a factor of 1.

	System 1	System 2	System 3
Cost	1,000,000	1,000,000	1,000,000
Effectiveness (%)	60	75	90
Cost/Effectiveness (%)	60	70	80

(Cost1 * Effectiveness1), (Cost2 * Effectiveness2) and (Cost3 * Effectiveness3)

And the comparison is equally easy when the prices differ but the effectiveness is the same:

	System 4	System 5	System 6
Cost	1,000,000	1,100,000	1,200,000
Effectiveness (%)	60	60	60
Cost/Effectiveness (%)	60	54.5	50

As the costs of each system rise, the difference in cost-effectiveness becomes the reduced value of effectiveness versus increasing costs.

The answers in above are also the result of multiplying each cost by each effectiveness, with costs again factored to multiples of 1. We achieve this by dividing the baseline cost (in this case $1,000,000) by the cost under consideration. The result is $1,000,000=1, $1,100,000=0.909 and $1,200,000=0.833. Therefore the results above derive from factoring all costs to multiples of 1: ([Cost1 = 1] * Effectiveness1), ([Cost2 = 0.909] * Effectiveness2), and ([Cost3 = 0.833] * Effectiveness3).

This method works equally well for differing costs and differing effectiveness:

	System 7	System 8	System 9
Cost	1,000,000	1,100,000	1,200,000
Effectiveness (%)	60	75	90
Cost/Effectiveness (%)	60	68	75

The answers above are also the result of multiplying each cost by each effectiveness with costs again factored to multiples of 1. That is, $1,000,000=1, so $1,100,000=0.909 and $1,200,000=0.833. Therefore the results in the table above derive from factoring all costs to multiples of 1: ((Cost1 = 1) * Effectiveness1), ((Cost2 = 0.909) * Effectiveness2), and ((Cost3 = 0.833) * Effectiveness3).

The complexities of changing costs and changing effectiveness are resolved by factoring all costs against a baseline of 1 for the lowest cost. This assures that all ratios result from a single point of comparison. All costs are compared to the lowest cost and all effectiveness numbers are compared to the ratio of the system cost under comparison to the baseline cost. Therefore, all results are relational.

This formula is simple:

- (SystemCost1/SystemCost1) * Effectiveness1
- (SystemCost1/SystemCost2) * Effectiveness2
- (SystemCost1/SystemCost3) * Effectiveness3

The baseline cost is always divided by the cost under consideration so that all costs reduce the value of effectiveness by the factor of the increase of the cost over the baseline cost.

Let us go back to our first example to test this formula to the extreme. Here is the same formula being applied to the protection of my home, where the alternatives are (1) my dog Spot!, (2) complete home security program, and (3) the U.S. Navy. This example factors in capital costs plus first year annual costs:

	Spot!	Complete Program	U.S. Navy
Cost	$425	$7,000	$159,800,000,000
Effectiveness (%)	49.2	93	90.5
Cost/Effectiveness (%)	49.2	5.6	0.0000002407

Although Spot! is very cost effective, his overall effectiveness is below 70%. As a rule of thumb, I do not consider any packages of countermeasure solutions that fall below 70%. So if we throw out Spot! and consider only the complete program versus the U.S. Navy, we get the following numbers:

	~~Spot!~~	Complete Program	U.S. Navy
Cost	~~$425~~	$7,000	$159,800,000,000
Effectiveness (%)	~~49.2~~	93	90.5
Cost/Effectiveness (%)		93	0.0000039643

And the hands-down winner is the complete home security program. If you doubt these results, consider that it actually does not matter whether we use the least cost, middle cost, or most cost as the baseline reference. Revising the numbers to use the U.S. Navy as the baseline, we get the following numbers:

	U.S. Navy	Complete Program
Cost	$159,800,000,000	$7,000
Effectiveness (%)	90.5	93
Cost/Effectiveness (%)	90.5	2,123,057,142.9

Are these the same ratios? Yes, they are:

- From the second table on this page: $93/.0000039643 = 23459374.9$
- From the third table on this page: $2,123,057,142.9/90.5 = 23459194.9$

As it is messy to have any ratios above 1 (100%), I always use the lowest system that achieves a minimum of 70 as the baseline number for calculation.

Let us see how this works when we compare all three results again:

	Complete Program	Spot!	U.S. Navy
Cost	$7,000	$425	$159,800,000,000
Effectiveness (%)	93	49.2	90.5
Cost/Effectiveness (%)	93	871.3	0.0000039643

And when comparing our reasonably similar systems, just to last and finally check the validity of the numbers, let us throw out the system that is below 70% effective and use the 75% effective system as the baseline number for calculation:

	System 4	System 5	System 6
Cost	1,000,000	1,100,000	1,200,000
Effectiveness (%)	60	75	90
Cost/Effectiveness (%)	66	75	82.5

Although the numbers shift, their relationships stay the same. Remember the cost number used as the baseline will always result in the cost/effectiveness ratio being the same as the effectiveness number. All other system numbers will line up relative to the baseline number.

Are they the same ratios? Yes they are, as we can see below:

- From the first comparison where system 4 was used as the baseline number, the ratios between system 4, system 5, and system 6 were 60%, 68.2%, and 75%. These relate to the following ratios between these three percentages: 60% = 1, 68.2% = 0.88 and 75% = 0.8.
- From the second comparison where system 5 was used as the baseline number, the ratios between system 4, system 5, and system 6 were 66%, 75%, and 82.5%. These relate to the following ratios between these three percentages: 66% = 1, 75% = 0.88 and 82.5% = 0.8.
- The ratios are always the same.

If I am going over this formula to the point of nausea, it is because it is highly important to understand it completely. Many mistakes are made by analysts who think they understand cost-effectiveness but in fact do not.

This formula may be used to compare capital costs, operating costs, or system component costs and their effectiveness ratios. This is a reliable formula.

COMMUNICATING PRIORITIES EFFECTIVELY

Making the Case

Virtually every organization is facing financial challenges. Understanding that many program directors are vying for the same budget dollars, it is necessary for the security program manager to make a clear case for security program budget dollars.

I often say that accounting and security programs have much in common. They both are required to comply with codes and regulations and limit the organization's exposure to risks (in one case financial risk and in the other, security risks).

But accounting organizations make a far better case for their needs and successes than do most security organizations. We can change that. The very process of developing a comprehensive risk analysis will go a long way to making the case. Though many may read no more than the executive summary, it should include a summary paragraph of each section and graphics illustrating the risk summary. The proposed countermeasure budget should be based on a comprehensive solution with a caveat that it can be adjusted to accommodate implementation phasing.

Developing the Arguments

- Determine the priorities of management: This simple but often overlooked item is essential to targeting management's interests in budgeting arguments. Priorities can be determined from annual statements, memos issued by management to employees, and by directly asking executive management to outline their priorities for the next fiscal year in an e-mail. They will appreciate your interest.
- Identify the points of view of stakeholders and acknowledge them. In order for the security program to get its own share of the overall budget, you will have to contend with other organization stakeholders who have their own priorities and agendas. By understanding these, you can make the case for security program countermeasures in the context of all these other competing agendas. By preparing the argument in this context and acknowledging the points of view, all of which need executive management's attention, you are more likely to succeed than if the argument is made in the absence of this information. This helps executive management to place the security program in the context of the overall organization's needs. This is one of the most important elements of a successful presentation.
- Provide a list of consequences: The only reason to have a security program at all is to prevent the unwanted consequences of not having a security program. This is what risk analysis is all about. By identifying all risks and consequences, executive management can develop the priorities of its budget. It is useful to create a comprehensive list of consequences and to ask executive management which of the consequences would be acceptable losses. This is not a rhetorical question, and it is not intended to provoke management. It is a logical question directly related to prioritizing budgets. Remember, all risks can be dealt with in one of several ways:

  - You can accept the loss.
  - You can duplicate the asset.
  - You can insure the asset.
  - You can protect the asset.

  Executive management needs to make these decisions about all assets, and this list gives them the tools to do so.
- Provide a tiered plan presenting countermeasure budgets versus solutions. Chapters 17, 18, and 19 (17: Countermeasures Selection; 18: Budgeting Tools, Security Effectiveness Metrics; and 19: Cost-Effectiveness Metrics) will assist in preparing a workable tiered plan. The tiered plan should present achievable goals versus budgets and explain clearly what cannot be achieved (what risks will be accepted) for deferred budgets. Chapter 18: Security Effectiveness Metrics includes a spreadsheet tool (the Decision Matrix) that helps present what can and cannot be achieved with various budget options. Management needs to

understand what risks they are accepting for budgets that they defer or program elements they decide not to budget for.
- Use a Decision Matrix to help committees reach a consensus when there is no agreement on the choice of a particular approach. Chapter 17 explains and illustrates the use of the Decision Matrix.

Presenting the Case

Now it is time to present your case. Good budget presentations are formed as an argument.

Basis of Argument

I recommend the following approach (get agreement at each step):

- Explain that the overall role of security is to protect the mission of the organization against individuals who would attack or misuse its assets for their own purposes.
- Explain the four kinds of assets every organization has
  - People
  - Property
  - Proprietary information
  - Business reputation
- Explain the three types of users
  - Those who share the mission of the organization
  - Those who oppose the mission of the organization
  - Those who mostly share and sometimes work in opposition to the mission of the organization (those involved in crimes, misuse of organization assets for personal purposes, creating security risks to people, property, information, and reputation by their behaviors).
- Explain types of threat actors
  - Terrorists
  - Economic criminals
  - Violent criminals
  - Petty criminals
  - Subversives (including persistent policy offenders)
- Explain the overall vulnerabilities and potential consequences of threat actions against those vulnerabilities.
- Explain types of countermeasures available to address the threats and vulnerabilities
  - High-tech
  - Low-tech
  - No-tech
  - Baseline security program (comprising all three types above)
  - Special countermeasures to address unique vulnerabilities
- Explain that for a security program to be effective, it must include all three elements (high-tech, low-tech, and no-tech; and both a baseline security program to address policy, criminal, and terrorism threats and special countermeasures to address criminal and terrorism threats).

- Present the threats and consequences.
- Present the baseline security program elements and their benefits and risks.
- Present the proposed security program and budget.
- Identify each budget item with a vulnerability or vulnerabilities and its potential consequences.
- As you go through this list, ask management to check off which consequences are acceptable losses, which they can duplicate, which they can insure, and which they would like to protect.
- Let management draw their own conclusions. Their conclusions may not be entirely what you want as the program manager, but this approach, when used repeatedly, plants the seeds of an understanding of priorities. Also, when asked to check off what consequences are acceptable early in the discussion, there is a higher likelihood that management will find the resources to meet the need to protect against unacceptable consequences.
- Ask them what conclusions they reach resulting from these considerations and if they need further assistance with any elements. It is a good idea to either gain consensus step by step or to stop at key points and gain consensus. As management agrees with each individual element of the presentation, it is more likely that they will also agree with the need to fund the programs that can avoid the unwanted consequences. After saying yes so many times along the way to the argument's conclusions, it is less likely that they will say no to funding critical elements.

Countering Arguments

Management may bring up questions or objections to programs. In all cases, it is best to refer back to authority, so preparation is essential. The best authority is always the formation documents of the organization itself, its mission statement, its core policies and procedures or its codes and regulations.

Other authorities include crime statistics (to support threat claims, particularly relating to violent crimes), and industry or community crime trends.

Credible data presented in an unemotional way ("Just the facts, ma'am!")* are always more forceful than emotional pleas. Never let ego enter the equation, not yours and not theirs. Defer to egotistical arguments with a statement like "I know you will decide what is best for the organization when you have time to examine the data." This kind of response helps management defer potentially bad decisions till after they have time to collect their thoughts.

It is at this point that security program managers fully understand the power of personal relationships in an organization. Time spent with key decision makers, influencers, and stakeholders can help you build a chorus of support during presentations when you need it most. Make sure you understand what your supporters and opposing stakeholders need so that you can provide legitimate support at key times. Make sure that they understand that you are a supporter of their own department's cause in management discussions.

Always refer back to potential consequences and their relationship to programs. Remind management that you are not driving toward a particular solution, but that

---

* Catchphrase of Joe Friday, a character on the *Dragnet* TV series.

you want them to have the information necessary for them to make the best possible decisions.

COMPLETE COST-EFFECTIVENESS MATRIX

Those readers who are not interested in building their own matrixes may skip the balance of this chapter. Following are instructions for building the Cost-Effectiveness Matrix.

In Chapter 18: Countermeasure Effectiveness, we studied how to build a matrix to evaluate the effectiveness of various aspects of the security program and indeed the entire program. In this chapter, we will review how to build the Cost-Effectiveness Matrix.

The Cost-Effectiveness Matrix is by far the most complex and complicated matrix you can build. It is not for the faint of heart and can take many hours to build. However, if you have built the Security Program Effectiveness Matrix from Chapter 18, you are already about halfway done building the Cost-Effectiveness Matrix. So congratulate yourself. Before you begin the instructions, you are already halfway finished!

Figure 19.1 illustrates the Complete Cost-Effectiveness Matrix for a small project. The Complete Cost-Effectiveness Matrix also serves to illustrate and support the recommendations both for the baseline security program and for the antiterrorism measures.

It is obvious from this illustration that the Complete Cost-Effectiveness Matrix is a very large and complicated spreadsheet. However, it is not beyond your ability. We will break the spreadsheet down into its constituent elements in the next several illustrations and it will become obvious how the spreadsheet is assembled. The Complete Cost-Effectiveness Matrix for a very small project is illustrated in Figure 19.1. As you can see, it is a very large and complicated worksheet.

COMPLETE COST-EFFECTIVENESS MATRIX ELEMENTS

Although the Complete Cost-Effectiveness Matrix is large and complex, it is comprised of a relatively small number of elements that we will break down in sufficient detail, illustrating each element separately for understanding. Together, these will comprise the Complete Cost Effectiveness Matrix.

These include:

- Title
- Security program recommendations summary board
- Vertical elements
  - Headers
  - Risk items
  - Divisions of risk items by category (baseline security program and antiterrorism measures)
  - Column totals
  - Column totals (broken down into baseline security program and antiterrorism measures)
- Horizontal elements
  - Risk descriptions

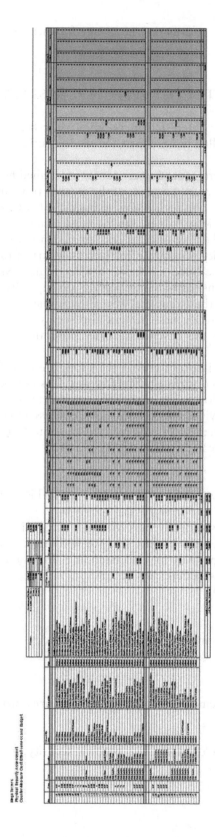

FIGURE 19.1 Complete Cost-Effectiveness Matrix.

- – Item number
- – Page reference in the risk analysis report
- – Area
- – Location
- – Vulnerability class
- – Vulnerability description
- – Risk level
- Countermeasure options
- Cost elements
  - – CCTV
  - – Alarm/access control
  - – Physical security
  - – Operations
  - – IT/communications
- Mitigation value
  - – Access
  - – Deterrent estimate
  - – Detection
  - – Assessment
  - – Delay
  - – Response
  - – Evidence
- Risks by rankings
  - – High
  - – Medium
  - – Low
- Budgets by risk rankings
  - – High
  - – Medium
  - – Low
- Phase recommendations
  - – Immediate action items
  - – Phase 1
  - – Phase 2
  - – Phase 3
- Budgets by phase recommendations
  - – Immediate action items
  - – Phase 1
  - – Phase 2
  - – Phase 3
- Budget breakdowns by phases and consequences
  - – Immediate action items
    - – High
    - – Medium
    - – Low
    - – Phase 1 items
      - – High
      - – Medium
      - – Low

     – Phase 2 items
       – High
       – Medium
       – Low
     – Phase 3 items
       – High
       – Medium
       – Low

Security Program Recommendations Summary Board

Perhaps the most interesting part of the spreadsheet for consultants and decision makers is the security program recommendations summary board, shown in Figure 19.2. The security program recommendations summary board illustrates the recommendation budgets by consequence rankings and by implementation recommendations. It also provides breakdowns and totals in both dimensions.

Vertical and Horizontal Elements

The spreadsheet is broken into vertical and horizontal elements. The key vertical elements include the Column Headers, Section Breakdowns (Baseline Security Program vs. Antiterrorism Measures), the List of Vulnerabilities, and Column Totals.

Vertical Elements

For the purposes of illustration, Figure 19.3 hides several columns so that you can easily see the big picture. Figure 19.3 illustrates the major vertical elements. A few vulnerabilities are also illustrated in this Figure for context. Note: Most of the figures hide irrelevant or redundant columns or rows so that the principle is more simply illustrated to facilitate understanding.

Horizontal Elements

Horizontal elements include Risk Descriptions, Countermeasure Options, Cost Elements, Mitigation Values, Risk Rankings, and Budgets (by Risk Rankings and

Security program recommendations: Summary board					
	Risk rankings>	High	Medium	Low	Totals
Phases>	Immediate action items	518,400	1,000	0	519,400
	Phase 1	428,000	435,000	0	863,000
	Phase 2	28,000	0	0	28,000
	Phase 3	0	0	0	0
		974,400	436,000	0	1,410,400

FIGURE 19.2   Summary board.

	A	F	G	H	I	J	K
1	Mega towers						
2		Physical security assessment					
3		Countermeasure cost-effectiveness and budget					
11							
12					Cost elements		Physical
13	Item	Vulnerability	Risk	Countermeasure	CCTV	AACS	Physical
14							
15				Baseline security program			
16	1.01	Security program development	Medium	Develop a security steering committee			
17	1.02	Security policy enforcement	Medium	Consider an inspections department			
18	1.03	Outdated security policies	High	Develop new security policies			
19	1.04	Outdated security procedures	High	Develop new security procedures			
20	1.05	Outdated post orders	High	Develop new post orders			
46	1.31	All exterior openings no alarm	Medium	Alarm on all exterior openings		40,000	
47	1.32	Many exterior doors left open	Medium	Access control on most exterior doors		40,000	
48	1.33	Banned persons hard to recognize	Medium	Facial recognition software	25,000		
49							
50				Anti-Terrorism Measures			
51	1.34	In the dark about developing problems	High	Subscribe to commercial intelligence briefing service			
52	1.35	Vulnerable to vehicle intrusion	High	East drive in/west drive out			
53	1.36	Forced vehicle entry	High	Reinforce main gates (2 in)			160,0
64	1.45	Forced vehicle entry	High	Fixed crash-resistant bollards @ main entry			12,0
65	1.46	Forced entry	High	Burglar bars on rear windows <4 meters			1,0
66	1.47	Forced vehicle entry	High	K-12 barrier at property entrance			75,0
67	1.48	Forced entry	High	Reinforce stage door			4,0
68	1.49	Explosives in vehicle	High	Explosive sniffing dogs			
69							
70					54,000	98,000	811,0
71							
72				Baseline security program	54,000	80,000	99,0
73				Antiterrorism measures	0	18,000	712,0

FIGURE 19.3 Vertical elements.

Phase Recommendations) and finally Phase Recommendations and Budgets by Phase Recommendations with Budgets Breakdowns both by Phases and Risk Rankings.

Risk Descriptions

The left-most columns horizontally define the Risks in the following manners (Figure 19.4):

- What is the vulnerability item number? (This should also align with item numbers in the risk analysis report)
- On what page in the report can this vulnerability description be found?
- What general area of the facility does this vulnerability concern?
- What specific location does the vulnerability concern?
- What class of offender does this vulnerability concern?
- The vulnerability description (brief descriptor).
- The risk ranking.

Countermeasure Options and Cost Elements

The next set of columns defines the countermeasures and their rough-order magnitude budget estimates. These are broken out by the types of countermeasure technologies that they fall into. Figure 19.5 illustrates a simplified example.

Countermeasure Mitigation Values

Refer back to Chapter 18 for instructions on how to prepare the Security Countermeasure Effectiveness table. As you can see, it serves well as the basis for the complete Cost Effectiveness Matrix, simply by inserting the additional required rows and columns that are needed to complete the Cost-Effectiveness Matrix (Figure 19.6).

Risk Rankings and Budgets

The next section horizontally breaks out the budgets by Risk Rankings. You will note that I have used three columns corresponding to the Risk Rankings (High, Medium, and Low). This is to more simply total the vulnerabilities of each ranking and to facilitate budget extrapolation from the Countermeasure Cost Estimates in cells to the left. The budgets are taken by multiplying the Risk Ranking cell (*always a value of 1 to serve for calculation purposes to follow*) times the Cost total Row "N" (from Figure 19.5, above). Figure 19.7 illustrates the Risk Rankings and Budgets by Risk Ranking. This set of columns gives us the Risk Dimension costing for the Security Program Summary Board at the top of the sheet (See Figure 19.2).

Phase Recommendations and Phasing Budgets

The next dimension is provided by planning the work into phasing recommendations. Few clients will approach the entire set of security program recommendations in one

	A	B	C	D	E	F	G
1	Mega towers						
2		Physical security assessment					
3			Countermeasure cost-effectiveness and budget				
11							
12					Vulnerability		
13	Item	Page	Area	Location	Class	Vulnerability	Risk
14							
15							
16	1.01	5,67	All	All	Every class	Security program development	Medium
17	1.02	5	All	All	Every class	Security policy enforcement	Medium
18	1.03	5,66	All	All	Every class	Outdated security policies	High
19	1.04	5,66	All	All	Every class	Outdated security procedures	High
20	1.05	5,66	All	All	Every class	Outdated post orders	High
46	1.31	5,67	Main floor	Main doors	Every class	All exterior openings no alarm	Medium
47	1.32	5,67	Main floor	Main doors	Every class	Many exterior doors left open	Medium
48	1.33	5,67	Main floor	Main doors	Economic & violence	Banned persons hard to recognize	Medium
49							
50							
51	1.34		Main floor	All	Terrorism	In the dark about developing problems	High
52	1.35	5,67	Site	Site	Terrorism	Vulnerable to vehicle intrusion	High
53	1.36		Site	East drive	Terrorism	Forced vehicle entry	High
64	1.45		Main floor	East drive	Terrorism	Forced vehicle entry	High
65	1.46		Main floor	Rear of building	Terrorism & economic	Froced entry	High
66	1.47		Site	Property entrance	Terrorism	Forced vehicle entry	High
67	1.48		Main floor	Stage door	Terrorism	Froced entry	High
68	1.49		Site	Vehicle screening	Terrorism	Explosives in vehicle	High
69							

FIGURE 19.4 Risk descriptions.

Mega towers

Physical security assessment

Countermeasure cost-effectiveness and budget

| Item | Vulnerability | Risk | Countermeasure | Cost elements | | | | | |
				CCTV	AACS	Physical	Operations	IT/Common	Totals
			Baseline security program						
1.01	Security program development	Medium	Develop a security steering committee						0
1.02	Security policy enforcement	Medium	Consider an inspections department						0
1.03	Outdated security policies	High	Develop new security policies				20,000		20,000
1.04	Outdated security procedures	High	Develop new security procedures				20,000		20,000
1.05	Outdated post orders	High	Develop new post orders				10,000		10,000
1.31	All exterior openings no alarm	Medium	Alarm on all exterior openings		40,000				40,000
1.32	Many exterior doors left open	Medium	Access control on most exterior doors		40,000				40,000
1.33	Banned persons hard to recognize	Medium	Facial recognition software	25,000					25,000
			Anti-terrorism measures						
1.34	In the dark about developing problems	High	Subscribe to commercial intelligence briefing service				400		400
1.35	Vulnerable to vehicle intrusion	High	East drive in/west drive out						0
1.36	Forced vehicle entry	High	Reinforce main gates (2 in)			160,000			160,000
1.45	Forced vehicle entry	High	Fixed crash-resistant bollards @ main entry			12,000			12,000
1.46	Forced entry	High	Burglar bars on rear windows <4 meters			1,000			1,000
1.47	Forced vehicle entry	High	K-12 barrier at property entrance			75,000			75,000
1.48	Forced entry	High	Reinforce stage door			4,000			4,000
1.49	Explosives in vehicle	High	Explosive sniffing dogs				200,000		200,000
				54,000	98,000	811,000	434,400	13,000	1,410,400
			Baseline security program	54,000	80,000	99,000	184,000	12,000	429,000
			Anti-terrorism measures	0	18,000	712,000	250,400	1,000	981,400

FIGURE 19.5   Countermeasure options and cost elements.

	Item	Countermeasure	Access	Deterent	Detection	Assess	Delay	Response	Evidence	Total
Mega towers										
Physical security assessment										
Countermeasure cost-effectiveness and budget										
							Mitigation value			
	Baseline security program									
	1.01	Develop a security steering committee								0%
	1.02	Consider an inspections department								0%
	1.03	Develop new security policies								0%
	1.04	Develop new security procedures								0%
	1.05	Develop new post orders	14%	14%	14%	14%	14%	14%	14%	98%
	1.31	Alarm on all exterior openings		14%	14%			14%	14%	56%
	1.32	Access control on most exterior doors	14%	14%	14%	14%	14%	14%	14%	98%
	1.33	Facial recognition software	7%	7%	14%	14%	7%	14%	14%	70%
	Antiterrorism measures									
	1.34	Subscribe to Commercial Intelligence Briefing Service				12%				12%
	1.35	East drive in/west drive out	14%	14%		14%	14%		14%	70%
	1.36	Reinforce main gates (2 in)	14%	14%		14%	14%		14%	70%
	1.45	Fixed crash-resistant bollards @ main entry	14%	14%			14%			42%
	1.46	Burglar bars on rear windows <4 meters	14%	14%			14%			42%
	1.47	K-12 barrier at property entrance	14%	14%			14%	14%		56%
	1.48	Reinforce stage door	14%	14%	14%	14%	14%	14%	14%	98%
	1.49	Explosive sniffing dogs	14%	14%	14%	14%	14%	14%	14%	98%
										0%

FIGURE 19.6 Countermeasure mitigation values.

	A	F	G	H	W	X	Y	Z	AA	AB
1	Mega towers									
2	Physical security assessment									
3	Countermeasure cost-effectiveness and budget									
11										
12					Risk			Budget		
13	Item	Vulnerability	Risk	Countermeasure	High	Medium	Low	High	High	Low
14										
15				Baseline security program						
16	1.01	Security program development	Medium	Develop a security steering committee		1		0	0	0
17	1.02	Security policy enforcement	Medium	Consider an inspections department		1		0	0	0
18	1.03	Outdated security policies	High	Develop new security policies	1			20000	0	0
19	1.04	Outdated security procedures	High	Develop new security procedures	1			20000	0	0
20	1.05	Outdated post orders	High	Develop new post orders	1			10000	0	0
46	1.31	All exterior openings no alarm	Medium	Alarm on all exterior openings		1		0	40000	0
47	1.32	Many exterior doors left open	Medium	Access control on most exterior doors		1		0	40000	0
48	1.33	Banned persons hard to recognize	Medium	Facial recognition software		1		0	25000	0
49										
50				Anti-terrorism measures						
51	1.34	In the dark about developing problems	High	Subscribe to commercial intelligence briefing service	1			400	0	0
52	1.35	Vulnerable to vehicle intrusion	High	East drive in/west drive out	1			0	0	0
53	1.36	Forced vehicle entry	High	Reinforce main gates (2 in)	1			160000	0	0
64	1.45	Forced vehicle entry	High	Fixed crash-resistant bollards @ main entry	1			12000	0	0
65	1.46	Forced entry	High	Burglar bars on rear windows <4 meters	1			1000	0	0
66	1.47	Forced vehicle entry	High	K-12 barrier at property entrance	1			75000	0	0
67	1.48	Forced entry	High	Reinforce stage door	1			4000	0	0
68	1.49	Explosives in vehicle	High	Explosive sniffing dogs	1			20000	0	0
69								0	0	0
70					42	7	0	974,400	436,000	0
71										1,410,400

FIGURE 19.7   Risk rankings and budgets.

single effort. The consultant who breaks down his or her recommendation into recommended phases usually gets a much warmer reception. Rather than leaving it to the client to figure out how to phase the project, it is useful to make a recommendation for phasing. While the actual phasing may vary as the details of each phasing plan are evaluated by the client, this approach helps assure that the program succeeds in reaching the phasing evaluation effort.

In Figure 19.8, please note that the values for the phases are calculated based upon the budgets in columns to the left times the "1" in the Phasing cells (AC ~ AF) shown in Figure 19.8.

Budget Breakdowns by Phases and Risks

The final set of columns is used entirely to populate the Security Program Summary Board at the top of the page (See Figure 19.2). These are divided into four sets of columns as follows:

- Immediate action items
  - With subcolumns for
    - High risk
    - Medium risk
    - Low risk
- Phase 1
  - With subcolumns for
    - High risk
    - Medium risk
    - Low risk
- Phase 2
  - With subcolumns for
    - High risk
    - Medium risk
    - Low risk
- Phase 3
  - With subcolumns for
    - High risk
    - Medium risk
    - Low risk

These breakdowns array the individual budget numbers into information that can directly populate the cells in the Security Program Summary Board at the top of the complete Cost-Effectiveness Matrix.

For Figure 19.9, please note that the values shown in the Phasing columns are separated by Risk based upon a multiple of the values in the Phasing columns from Figure 19.8 and Risk column from Figure 19.7. For example, the values in column AK (Figure 19.9) are derived from the values of column AG (Figure 19.8) and the values in column W (Figure 19.7).

For simplification and so that this illustration can be readable in the space available in a book figure, only the Immediate Action Items and Phase 1 are shown; however, as is obvious, columns are also created for Phase 2 and Phase 3, if applicable.

	A	H	AC	AD	AE	AF	AG	AH	AI	AJ
1	**Mega towers**									
2	**Physical security assessment**									
3	**Countermeasure cost-effectiveness and budget**									
11										
12			**Phase elements**				**Budgets**			
13	Item	Countermeasure	Immediate	Phase 1	Phase 2	Phase 3	Immed items	Phase 1	Phase 2	Phase 3
14										
15		**Baseline security program**								
16	1.01	Develop a security steering committee	1				0	0	0	0
17	1.02	Consider an inspections department	1				0	0	0	0
18	1.03	Develop new security policies	1				20000	0	0	0
19	1.04	Develop new security procedures	1				20000	0	0	0
20	1.05	Develop new post orders	1				10000	0	0	0
46	1.31	Alarm on all exterior openings		1			0	40,000	0	0
47	1.32	Access control on most exterior doors		1			0	40,000	0	0
48	1.33	Facial recognition software		1			0	25,000	0	0
49										
50		**Antiterrorism measures**								
51	1.34	Subscribe to commercial intelligence briefing service	1				400	0	0	0
52	1.35	East drive in/west drive out	1				0	0	0	0
53	1.36	Reinforce main gates (2 in)	1				160000	0	0	0
64	1.45	Fixed crash-resistant bollards @ main entry	1				12000	0	0	0
65	1.46	Burglar bars on rear windows <4 meters	1				1000	0	0	0
66	1.47	K-12 barrier at property entrance	1				75000	0	0	0
67	1.48	Reinforce stage door	1				4000	0	0	0
68	1.49	Explosive sniffing dogs		1			0	200,000	0	0
69										
70			27	20	2	0	519,400	863,000	28,000	0
71										1,410,400

FIGURE 19.8 Phasing and phased budgets.

	A	H	AK	AL	AM	AN	AO	AP
1	Mega towers							
2	Physical security assessment							
3	Countermeasure cost-effectiveness and budget							
11								
12			Immediate action items			Phase 1		
13	Item	Countermeasure	High	High	Low	High	High	Low
14								
15		Baseline security program						
16	1.01	Develop a security steering committee	0	0	0	0	0	0
17	1.02	Consider an inspections department	0	0	0	0	0	0
18	1.03	Develop new security policies	20,000	0	0	0	0	0
19	1.04	Develop new security procedures	20,000	0	0	0	0	0
20	1.05	Develop new post orders	10,000	0	0	0	0	0
46	1.31	Alarm on all exterior openings	0	0	0	0	40,000	0
47	1.32	Access control on most exterior doors	0	0	0	0	40,000	0
48	1.33	Facial recognition software	0	0	0	0	25,000	0
49								
50		Antiterrorism measures						
51	1.34	Subscribe to commercial intelligence briefing service	400	0	0	0	0	0
52	1.35	East drive in/west drive out	0	0	0	0	0	0
53	1.36	Reinforce main gates (2 in)	160,000	0	0	0	0	0
64	1.45	Fixed crash-resistant bollards @ main entry	12,000	0	0	0	0	0
65	1.46	Burglar bars on rear windows <4 meters	1,000	0	0	0	0	0
66	1.47	K-12 barrier at property entrance	75,000	0	0	0	0	0
67	1.48	Reinforce stage door	4,000	0	0	200,000	0	0
68	1.49	Explosive sniffing dogs	0	0	0	0	0	0
69			0	0	0	0	0	0
70			518,400	1,000	519,400	428,000	435,000	863,000
71								

FIGURE 19.9 Budget breakdowns.

SUMMARY

Introduction

The security program must be funded adequately so that it can protect the assets of the organization from harm.

Most organizations' security programs suffer from a lack of effective management metrics. And the lack of management metrics in any program is a certain source for program inefficiencies and possible mission failure.

The presence of useful management metrics not only helps assure the success of the mission of the program, but also helps the security program director justify and explain the legitimate needs for the program to upper management so that they can make informed financial decisions that are in the best interest of the organization. Cost-effectiveness metrics are at the heart of this approach.

What Are the Limitations of Cost-Effectiveness Metrics?

The challenge of cost-effectiveness metrics is effectiveness. Cost-effectiveness has only two components: cost and effectiveness. As we have seen from the last chapter, it is possible to measure effectiveness, and the measurement of cost is straightforward. But how do we derive cost-effectiveness?

Cost-effectiveness is all about reasonable ratios to achieve reasonable security goals. We want the highest possible effectiveness for an affordable budget. So then three questions present themselves:

- What is the value of the possible consequences? (baseline for consideration)
- What is an affordable budget to mitigate these consequences? (reasonable cost)
- What is the highest effectiveness we can achieve within this budget? (highest effectiveness)

Research that I have conducted personally throughout my decades-long career indicates that well-prepared security programs for nonstrategic facilities usually have a capital budget range of between 1% and 2% of the cost of the facility alone, excluding fixtures, furnishings and equipment (FF&E), and can go higher if the FF&E values are high (such as for expensive medical equipment like MRIs, etc.). This budget estimate is appropriate for commercial, noncommercial, and critical infrastructure facilities alike. Exceptions include those facilities that house assets the loss of which could constitute great harm to the community, such as chemical plants, nuclear power plants, nuclear weapons storage facilities, central banks, presidential palaces, and the like. For these types of facilities, the capital and operating costs of the program should be entirely driven by the consequences.

For a nuclear power plant, the annual cost of security can be many times the cost of that for a nonnuclear power facility. *Consequences drive the budget!*

What Metrics Can Be Used to Determine Cost-Effectiveness?

Remembering that we have found a way to estimate effectiveness and that cost is self-evident, how then do we comprise a formula to estimate cost/effectiveness? If we are comparing systems that all have the same cost and different effectiveness, this is quite simple. As costs stay the same, the difference in cost/effectiveness is the difference only in effectiveness.

The answers above are the result of multiplying each cost by each effectiveness, factored to 1. That is, we assume since all costs are the same, they are all equal to a factor of 1. (Cost1 * Effectiveness1), (Cost2 * Effectiveness2), and (Cost3 * Effectiveness3).

And the comparison is equally easy when the prices differ but the effectiveness is the same. As costs of each system rise, the difference in cost/effectiveness becomes the reduced value of effectiveness versus increasing costs.

The answers thus calculated are the result of multiplying each cost by each effectiveness, with costs again factored to multiples of 1. We achieve this by dividing the baseline cost (in this case $1,000,000) by the cost under consideration. The result is $1,000,000=1$, $1,100,000=0.909$, and $1,200,000=0.833$. Therefore the results derive from factoring all costs to multiples of 1: ([Cost1 = 1] * Effectiveness1), ([Cost2 = 0.909] * Effectiveness2) and ([Cost3 = 0.833] * Effectiveness3).

The answers above are also the result of multiplying each cost by each effectiveness, with costs again factored to multiples of 1. That is, $1,000,000=1$, so $1,100,000=0.909$ and $1,200,000=0.833$. Therefore the results in the table above derive from factoring all costs to multiples of 1: ((Cost1 = 1) * Effectiveness1), ((Cost2 = 0.909) * Effectiveness2) and ((Cost3 = 0.833) * Effectiveness3).

The complexities of changing costs and changing effectiveness are resolved by factoring all costs against a baseline of 1 for the lowest cost. This assures that all ratios result from a single point of comparison. All costs are compared to the lowest cost and all effectiveness numbers are compared to the ratio of the system cost under comparison, to the baseline cost. Therefore, all results are relational.

This formula is simple:

- (SystemCost1/SystemCost1) * Effectiveness1
- (SystemCost1/SystemCost2) * Effectiveness2
- (SystemCost1/SystemCost3) * Effectiveness3

The baseline cost is always divided by the cost under consideration so that all costs reduce the value of effectiveness by the factor of the increase of the cost over the baseline cost.

Communicating Priorities Effectively

Making the Case

Virtually every organization is facing financial challenges. Understanding that many program directors are vying for the same budget dollars, it is necessary for the security program manager to make a clear case for security program budget dollars.

- Develop the arguments.
  - Determine the priorities of management.
  - Identify the points of view of stakeholders and acknowledge them.
  - Provide a list of consequences.
  - Remember, all risks can be dealt with in one of several ways
    - You can accept the loss.

 – You can duplicate the asset.
 – You can insure the asset.
 – You can protect the asset.
    Executive management needs to make these decisions about all assets and this list gives them to tools to do so.
  • Provide a tiered plan presenting countermeasure budgets versus solutions.
  • Use a Decision Matrix to help committees reach a consensus when there is no agreement on the choice of a particular approach.
 • Presenting the case: Good budget presentations are formed as an argument.

Q&A

Questions

Q1: Each organization has two types of programs, including _____.
  A. Revenue-producing programs.
  B. Overhead programs.
  C. Both of the above.
  D. Neither of the above.

Q2: The better the job that the security program is doing,
  A. The more obvious it is that the security program is working.
  B. The less it seems that security is needed at all.
  C. Both of the above.
  D. Neither of the above.

Q3: The lack of management metrics in any program is
  A. Certain mission failure.
  B. A source of possible program inefficiencies.
  C. A possible source for program inefficiencies and certain mission failure.
  D. A certain source for program inefficiencies and possible mission failure.

Q4: Cost-effectiveness has two components:
  A. Cost and effectiveness
  B. Effectiveness and administration
  C. Administration and cost
  D. None of the above.

Q5: Cost-effectiveness is all about
  A. Exactly 1% of total capital value.
  B. Exactly 2% of total capital value.
  C. Reasonable ratios to achieve reasonable security goals.
  D. None of the above.

Q6: The challenge of cost-effectiveness metrics is
  A. Cost.
  B. Effectiveness.

C. Cost-effectiveness.
D. None of the above.

Q7: Which below is the formula for cost-effectiveness?
  A. (SystemCost1/SystemCost1) * Effectiveness1
  B. (SystemCost1/SystemCost2) * Effectiveness2
  C. (SystemCost1/SystemCost3) * Effectiveness3
  D. All of the above

Q8: Which below is *not* a question related to evaluating cost-effectiveness?
  A. What is the value of the possible consequences (baseline for consideration)?
  B. What is an affordable budget to mitigate these consequences (reasonable cost)?
  C. What is the highest effectiveness we can achieve within this budget (highest effectiveness)?
  D. What is the highest cost-effectiveness possible within 12% of total capital asset value?

Q9: All risks can be dealt with in one of several ways. Which below is *not* one of the ways?
  A. Accept the loss or duplicate the asset
  B. Insure the asset
  C. Replace all employees
  D. Protect the asset

Q10: Cost-effectiveness answers are the result of
  A. Multiplying each cost by each effectiveness, with costs factored to multiples of 1.
  B. Multiplying each cost by each effectiveness, with costs factored to multiples of 2.
  C. Multiplying each cost by each effectiveness, with costs factored to multiples of 4.
  D. Multiplying each cost by each effectiveness, with costs factored to multiples of 8.

Answers

Q1 – C, Q2 – B, Q3 – D, Q4 – A, Q5 – C, Q6 – C, Q7 – D, Q8 – D, Q9 – C, Q10 – A

CHAPTER 20

Writing Effective Reports

INTRODUCTION

On completion of this chapter, you will understand how to write effective reports, including the four main documents that a presentation should include, the elements of a well-received report, report supplements, and the elements of a good boardroom screen presentation.

Up to now, we have been discussing all of the tools necessary to create a good risk analysis report. The risk analysis report is the only thing decision makers will see, and thus it is the only element of the work that they will care about; so despite all the hard work, research, and analysis that the analyst has done, if the report is flawed in any way, that will be all the decision makers will notice. The form and content should be complete, easy to read, digestible, and comprehensive.

Reports typically comprise four main documents:

- The *comprehensive report*, including an executive summary: The comprehensive report is the heart of the presentation (hereinafter we will call this the report). Except for the budgets and the executive summary, the other documents may be viewed only briefly and superficially. The report presents all the data in two forms: the executive summary and detailed sections. The executive summary should contain all the essential points of the detailed sections but in a form that is brief and easy to interpret. The detailed sections will contain the "meat" of the report and will provide the support for the conclusions, recommendations, and all statements in the summary section.
- *Countermeasure budgets* are also presented in two versions: summary and detailed spreadsheets. The summary section contains the totaled results from the detailed sections. Ideally, the detailed sections should be broken down into high-tech, low-tech, and no-tech programs and may be further broken down from those broad areas. Microsoft Excel® allows for related spreadsheets to be viewed as individual pages of the same workbook. Using this method, one can create a summary sheet that totals the results of all other sheets for inclusion in the executive summary of the report.
- A *Microsoft PowerPoint® presentation* is useful when presenting the risk analysis report to a group or to a high executive. PowerPoint presentations allow condensed information to be presented in a manner that is easy to digest, and they can be highly graphic. They also guide the presentation and help recipients stay on point in their comments.
- *Handouts* echo the PowerPoint presentation and allow the recipients to follow along and make notes to facilitate their own memory or for later discussion.

These documents together comprise the total report, and these alone make the case for security program needs. If the report fails in any way, the security program will not be supported or funded properly to achieve its goals. Failures can occur in several ways:

- Flawed presentation
- Flawed analysis (obvious bias, unsupported conclusions, etc.)
- Budgets that exceed the appropriate in the context of the overall project

Presentation

The client's report committee will most likely want a formal report presentation. Two types of readers review the risk analysis report: readers who skim the document and readers who read and study the detail in the document. The comprehensive report must speak to both.

Key presentation elements for success include

- Presentation should review project purposes and objectives
- Presentation should follow a predictable outline (handouts help here)
- Stay on logical key points and not stray to irrelevant minutia
- Make the case for any interventions (countermeasures) proposed
- Show a budget, ideally phased by priorities
- Answer all questions about consequences and budgets

Graphics

Graphics are most helpful in explaining concepts and making points. Common useful graphics include

- Risk analysis process map: a graphic showing the steps of analysis (Figure 20.1)
- Assets map: a list of assets by categories/criticalities
- Threat actor map: a list of threat actors, ranked
- Vulnerabilities map: a list of vulnerabilities, sorted by assets
- Risk map: V^2 graphics
- Countermeasure examples: photos of implementations and products
- Budget summary: colored graphic of budgets/phased
- Optionally, a risk register: a table outlining all the above

Preparation for a Successful Presentation

The risk analyst should prepare and present the report in a manner that will be well received by the intended recipients. This requires research into two main areas: business culture and personal biases.

- Business culture: The business culture of client organizations may vary significantly from one organization to the next. Some organizations want a focus on numbers and validation, while others are more interested in the effect of

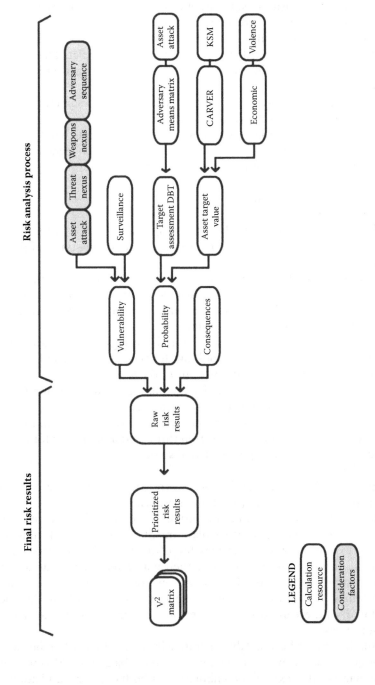

FIGURE 20.1 Risk analysis process map.

countermeasures on their business operations. The analyst should research and understand such factors while preparing the report and the presentation. Tips as to the business culture can be gathered from the organization's mission statement and from observing how management discusses and relates to its employees, contractors, vendors, customers, the public, activist groups, and the media. The following types of business cultures are common:

- Top-down: Top-down cultures are those that impose business behaviors from top management downward and impose behaviors by edict. These organizations are common in militaries and highly structured organizations that are rules driven.
- Lateral: Lateral cultures are more democratic and sometimes chaotic. Objectives are set and achieved by consensus.
- Personal biases: Similarly, the personal biases of key recipients will largely affect the acceptance of the presentation and conclusions. Each person inherently brings at least three biases with them to a project:
  - Their industry's agenda
  - Their organization's agenda
  - Their personal agenda
- Personal biases vary as substantially as the recipients. The more information one can gather about the key recipients, the better. The following types of personalities are common:
  - General biases: Different people have different ways of seeing things. Some are cautious, while others are aggressive. Some are deliberate, while others rush to decisions. Some are consensus builders, while others are forceful and opinionated and still others are timid.
  - Industry biases: Each project participant also brings their industry biases to the project. They will naturally look out for the best interests of their building system or industry in all discussions of the work.
  - Organizational biases: Each participant may also keep in mind the best interests of the organization they work for, constantly looking to protect and defend their organization's reputation and project position, looking for opportunities to improve their position through opportunities for additional services, self-directed compliments, and so on.
  - Personal biases:
    - Executive biases: Executive biases are focused on the organization's purpose and objectives (including business culture objectives) and budget. As these are sometimes in conflict with each other, executive biases can be confounding to other team members as they try to understand why executives will sometimes focus on the project's purpose, objectives, and business culture and then may later shift focus to budget, sometimes apparently abandoning purpose and objectives. Also it is common for business culture objectives to be poorly understood or stated, as these are often assumptions that are not well translated into objectives.
    - Administrative biases: Administrative biases are focused on business and project process over project purpose and objectives. (Effective project managers often exhibit a combination of both executive and administrative biases.)
    - Technical biases:

- Tactical biases: Tactical technical biases are focused on the tactical technical details of how to achieve the project objectives (e.g., which products, types of cables, lenses, etc.). It is common for technical personnel to become distracted by minutia to the detriment of project purposes and objectives. However, technical personnel who maintain focus on project purposes and objects are extremely valuable.
    - Analytical biases: Analytical technical biases are usually focused more on project purposes and objectives and on how to use technical tools to achieve those. Personnel with these biases are highly valuable to the project process as they are able to discuss technical details in a way that maintains the focus and achieves the support of other project team members. They are also especially valuable in coordination efforts.
  - Egocentric biases: Egocentric personalities can overlay any of the others. Every project member has some ego. More productive project members set aside their own personal biases for the betterment of the project and organization. Lesser individuals view everything through the lens of their own perception and always in the best short-term interest of themselves and their allies.
- Understanding the industry, organization, and personal biases of each project participant is of great value in being able to prepare and present the report in a manner that will be well received by every key project stakeholder.
  - Executive and administrative personalities usually prefer presentations that focus on the project purpose and objectives and how the findings fit those objectives, and by extension what interventions are necessary to assure that the organization's programs are not disrupted by security events. Executive and administrative personalities are also highly concerned about the cost of any interventions, and executive personalities are more interested on the impact of such interventions on their business culture.
  - Technical personalities are more interested on how such interventions will be implemented.
  - Each participant also filters the presentation by their industry, organization, and personal biases and by how it affects their position in the group.
  - Virtually all stakeholders are concerned about the security budget or operations infringing on their own budget or operations.
  - Sensitivity to these issues will help result in better analysis, better conclusions, and better acceptance.

COMPREHENSIVE RISK ANALYSIS REPORT

Executive Summary

The executive summary provides the essential delivery of all of the data of the report. The executive summary will be read by everyone who sees the report, and thus it must be complete, highly readable, and convincing.

The executive summary should

- Provide a document outline, identifying the sections and their general contents
- State the project purpose and objectives

- Identify the key assets
- Identify the key threats
- Identify the key vulnerabilities
- Identify the key risks
- Identify the key countermeasure program interventions
- Present budgets
- Make recommendations

Introduction

The introduction frames the readers' understanding of the rest of the document. This is done by providing the background information the reader needs to put the balance of the report into perspective. The introduction should include

- Project authorization: a statement including who authorized the report and for whom the report is being prepared (usually, but not always, the same person or organizational unit).
- Background statement on the project, including
  - Its location(s)
  - Project attributes (how many buildings, what types, usages, etc.)
  - Goals of the security program
- Assessment team qualifications

Assessment Process

The assessment process section can be included in the introduction or it may be separate. On smaller projects, I usually combine these. This section should include

- The methodology selected
- Reasons for selecting this particular methodology (why it best fits the project: budget, completeness, appropriateness to the industry, U.S. Department of Homeland Security (DHS) mandates, etc.)
- Methodology process map
- Assessment process planning

Facility Characterization

The facility characterization section is sometimes also called the asset characterization section. This section itemizes and categorizes all of the assets of the organization related to the project.

Each of the assets in question will comprise a system, asset, component, or critical node. Systems are whole functional organisms that are often crucial to the mission of the organization. Assets are individual facilities, buildings, business units, people, property, proprietary information, or the organization's business reputation. Components are individual elements of assets and systems. Critical nodes are elements that are critical to the operation of an entire system. If a critical node is lost, so will be an entire system.

Then list all of the facility assets by the following categories:

- People
  - Key executives
  - Managers and employees
  - Contractors, vendors, visitors, and the public
- Property
  - Individual areas
  - Categorized by facilities and major areas of facilities
- Proprietary information
  - Information technology system
  - Special servers and mass storage
  - Paper files
  - Special information systems (building management system/security, etc.)
- Business reputation

Threat Assessment

The key elements of the threat assessment section include identification of the threat actors and the selection of a particular class of threat actor as the design basis threat.

There are five types of threat actors. It is useful to explain each of these in detail.

- Terrorists
  - Class I terrorists: (state sponsored)
  - Class II terrorists: (religious extremist professional terrorists)
  - Class III terrorists: (radical revolutionaries or quasi-religious extremists)
  - Class IV terrorists: (guerrilla/mercenary soldiers)
  - Class V terrorists: (lone wolves)
- Economic criminals
  - Transnational criminal organizations
  - Organized criminals
  - Sophisticated economic criminals
  - Unsophisticated economic criminals
  - Street criminals
  - Lone wolves
- Nonterrorist violent criminals
  - Domestic crime violent criminals
  - Disgruntled employee or ex-employee
  - Deranged persons
- Subversives
  - Cause-oriented subversives
  - Nonaligned subversives
  - Invasion of privacy threat actors
  - Persistent rule violators
- Petty criminals
  - Vandals
  - Pickpockets
  - Prostitutes, pimps, and panderers

The design basis threat is that class of threat actor that the proposed security program is designed to effectively counter.

Although terrorism is the most potent threat, it may not be relevant to the organization or facility in question. If there is no history of terrorism against this type of organization or facility and if it does not meet many or most of the criteria of the terrorism asset target value profiles, it may not need to be considered as a valid threat. Ultimately, the client must make the decision whether or not to consider terrorist threat actors.

It may be good to discuss the relevant considerations in detail. While the threat matrixes identify all these factors, the matrix does not explain them. The two threat matrixes are the Asset/Attack Matrix and the Adversary/Means Matrix. Both of these identify threat scenarios, while the Adversary/Means Matrix also identifies information about the threat actors' characteristics, including their motivation, capabilities, and history. While these are estimated in the matrix, they can be explained in the threat assessment section of the report.

The analyst should explain in detail each column of the threat matrixes so that the reader understands the context of the estimates.

Additionally, I recommend that the analyst should conduct research into each class of threat actor listed for which any serious consideration is recommended by the analyst and provide references and evidence as to why each of these are relevant to the project. For example, if a particular terrorist group is relevant to the project, cite examples that illustrate this relevance.

The threat assessment section should conclude with a section on the design basis threat. Make a case for the choice of class of threat actor and why this is the most relevant. Also list the type of entry methods and weapons most used by the design basis threat. It will be these entry methods and weapons that the countermeasure program must be designed to counter.

Vulnerability Assessment

Vulnerability assessment involves the following steps:

- Define scenarios and evaluate specific consequences
- Evaluate effectiveness of any existing security measures
- Identify vulnerabilities and estimate the degree of vulnerability

These steps are carried out by utilizing the following steps:

- Utilize an Asset/Attack Matrix, which identifies which attack scenarios are most effective against each asset
- Utilize a threat/target nexus location, which identifies which areas are most likely to be used by threat actors
- Utilize a weapon/target nexus location, which identifies which types of weapons are most likely to be used at each threat/target nexus location
- Review surveillance opportunities for each major asset under consideration
- Review vulnerabilities for each asset under consideration
- Identify whether or not the vulnerability will be addressed by a baseline security program
- Especially for those assets for which vulnerabilities are not addressed adequately by a Baseline Security Program, list the criticality of each of those assets

- For the purposes of the Executive Summary, prioritize assets by the following criteria as described in Chapter 11

The analyst should consider and report which assets are subject to which types of attack scenarios. Regardless of which analytical tool is used (commercial software or spreadsheet templates), this step must be accomplished for the vulnerability report to have meaning.

Most commercial software has a tool that evaluates each asset against each type of applicable threat scenario. The Asset/Attack Matrix is the template used to do this in the software template tools in this book, but any such tool will work as long as it considers each asset and each applicable threat scenario.

Vulnerability includes the following constituent components:

- Surveillance opportunities
- Accessibility
- Intrinsic vulnerability

The following factors mitigate intrinsic vulnerability:

- Existing and natural countermeasures
- Electronic countermeasures
- Physical countermeasures
- Operational countermeasures

The result of the first three factors minus the last four equals vulnerability.

Asset/Attack Matrix

The Asset/Attack Matrix or its equivalent should be included in this section to support the vulnerability findings. Each aspect of the Asset/Attack Matrix should be explained in detail.

The analyst should explain the applicable threat scenarios in detail in the vulnerability section of the report and then show the evaluation of each asset for each scenario. This is the most basic vulnerability assessment and most assessment tools do not go beyond this first step. The Excel templates in this book also provide for three other vulnerability evaluations.

Threat/Target Nexus Matrix

The threat/target nexus evaluates circulation path nexus points that could be crossing points between especially vulnerable people (celebrities, C-level executives, female students, etc.) and potential threat actors. The Threat/Target Nexus Matrix helps the analyst identify areas of the facility where personal attacks could occur.

Weapon/Target Nexus Matrix

Similar to the threat/target nexus, the weapon/target nexus evaluates circulation path nexus points between especially vulnerable people and the types of weapons that could be used at those locations. For example, a vehicle drop-off area is exposed to a much wider range of possible weapons than an executive elevator lobby. The Weapons/Target Nexus Matrix helps the analyst understand what types of weapons the victim might encounter at the circulation nexus points.

Surveillance Opportunities

Surveillance is a function of vulnerability. In order to carry out any type of attack (terrorism, economic crime, violent crime, subversive act, or petty crime), the perpetrator must know something about the facility and organization they plan to attack. This requires surveillance. If surveillance is necessary for the attacker, then it is useful to understand that any threat actor that is performing surveillance is themselves vulnerable to detection by an organization that has the skills to detect surveillance. This fact alone can reduce vulnerability.

Surveillance can be conducted several ways:

- Fixed visual surveillance
- Mobile surveillance
- Acoustic eavesdropping
- Electronic surveillance (wiretaps, electronic bugs, etc.)
- Information technology system surveillance
- Document/information interception

Minimizing the opportunities for surveillance and/or implementing a surveillance detection program can reduce the potential for all types of terrorism and criminal attacks.

The analyst should identify the types of surveillance possible and, using the Surveillance Matrix or a similar tool, can identify those assets that are at most risk of surveillance.

Beware of risk analysis software tools that estimate vulnerability using only one cell labeled "Vulnerability". This will almost always produce ineffective results. Vulnerability has many factors, and without considering each one individually, it is very easy to miss a factor that can raise the overall vulnerability of an asset while thinking only of another factor. For example, an analyst who only considers accessibility in vulnerability would likely rank a bank vault with low vulnerability if they were thinking about outside threat actors, but if embezzlement was not considered, that would be a false ranking.

Likelihood (Probability) Calculation

Chapter 9 focuses on the estimation of probability.

$$\text{Likelihood} = (\text{Vulnerability} * \text{Threat}) \text{ or } (\text{Vulnerability} \pm \text{Threat}) / 2.$$

By performing this calculation, one can determine how likely a threat is to occur. For some risk analysis approaches use the formula Risk = Likelihood * Consequences. This is a valid risk formula.

Risk Calculation

Risk = (Probability * Vulnerability * Consequences) or ((Probability + Vulnerability + Consequences)/3). There are numerous ways to calculate risk using a variety of tools. All such methods that take these three factors into consideration will result in a useful calculation.

By performing this calculation on all the assets under consideration, the analyst can reach individual risk calculations for all the assets. These can then be ranked for severity.

Let us pause here to talk again about the difference between quantitative and qualitative analysis methods and how they relate to risk calculations. Qualitative analysis methods typically review many assets and then discard most after some initial consideration, leaving relatively few assets for the final risk analysis.

I have seen qualitative reports that considered less than a dozen assets for a multi-hundred-million dollar project. In my opinion, this is a woefully inadequate analysis.

On one such project, where the owner hired two consultants just to be sure, I found a critical node that if attacked would have disabled all operations for the organization for up to two years while the critical node was being repaired. This attack scenario on a minor building system would have left the key facilities intact but completely unusable until repairs were made, which were estimated to take between one and two years. This critical node was completely missed by the other consultant who had discarded as irrelevant the asset that had the critical node. Let me say that I also would have missed the critical node if I had not performed the full analysis, since it was not obvious until the analysis was complete. I have seen similar results on many projects. This is why I am a believer in a combination of quantitative and qualitative analysis. The combination of both qualitative and quantitative analysis is far better than either one alone.

Countermeasures

There are three main factors to selecting countermeasures:

- All vulnerabilities should be addressed to some extent by a comprehensive baseline security program.
- Identify key assets that should receive special attention by reviewing countermeasure options, including
  - High-tech options
  - Low-tech options
  - No-tech options
- Costs should be estimated for:
  - The baseline security program
  - Countermeasures to address key assets not adequately mitigated by the baseline security program

Baseline Security Program

Every facility requires a baseline security program. The baseline security program should include all of the elements covered in detail in Chapter 15: Goals of Countermeasures. The key elements that should be discussed in some detail include

- Security program mission statement
- Policies and procedures
- Security management and supervision
- High-tech elements:
  - Alarm/access control system
  - Parking control system
  - Security video system
  - Security communications system
  - Command/control elements
- Low-tech elements:
  - Locks
  - Pedestrian and roadway barriers
  - Lighting
  - Signage

- CPTED* elements
  - Security landscaping
  - Security architectural elements
- No-tech elements:
  - Security management elements
  - Security guard program
    - Posts
    - Patrols
    - Security guard training program
  - VIP handling program
  - Security awareness program
  - Physical security program
  - Security intelligence program
  - Countersurveillance program
  - Emergency preparedness and response program
  - Civil disorder preparedness and response program
  - Law enforcement liaison program
  - Security management metrics

Identifying Key Assets for Special Consideration

- Identify key vulnerabilities that are not adequately addressed by the baseline security program
- Rank each of those vulnerabilities by:
  - Mitigated/not mitigated by the baseline security program (sort 1)
  - Above assets most vulnerable (sort 2)
  - Above assets (sort 1 and 2) that are the highest asset target value (sort 3)
  - Above assets (sort 1 through 3) that have the highest consequences (sort 4)
- For the above filtered assets (those with special vulnerabilities), focus on key countermeasures that exceed the baseline security program and that could mitigate the vulnerabilities (See more about this in Chapter 16: Types of Countermeasures. The essentials include
  - Can the asset be easily replaced, duplicated, or insured?
  - Consider each special vulnerability as to access (What is the asset? What is the threat scenario? Who is the likely threat actor? What access is available to attack the asset?)
    - How can access be limited or denied to unauthorized persons?
    - What about unauthorized access using force?
    - What about access by insiders, contractors, vendors, and so on?
    - Can the vulnerability be mitigated by limiting access?
    - How could access be limited (safe, bullet-resistant/blast-resistant glass, guard, barriers, delaying technologies, etc.)?
  - What other types of countermeasures could
    - Control access
    - Deter

---

* CPTED = Crime prevention through environmental design: A scientifically proven architectural discipline that helps reduce criminal behavior by creating spaces that encourage appropriate behavior while reducing the likelihood of criminal activity.

- Detect
- Help assess the threat act
- Help respond to and delay a successful attack
- Gather evidence

- Could countersurveillance reduce the possibility of an attack?
- What is the relative effectiveness of each of the possible countermeasures?
- Are multiple countermeasures required to mitigate the threat?
- What are the cost estimates of these countermeasures?
- If multiple options are available, what are their overall effectiveness ratings and relative costs?
- What are the cost-effectiveness rankings of the multiple options?
- What are your recommendations?
- What consequences for organizational operations (productivity, convenience, and business culture) will result from using the recommended countermeasures?

Develop Countermeasure Budgets

Use the countermeasure budgeting tool or a similar tool to develop countermeasure budgets. Provide separate budgets for the baseline security program and for the special countermeasures.

Provide a budget summary sheet that identifies the key budget elements and recommended phasing.

Provide a detailed budget analysis for each the baseline security program and for the special vulnerabilities.

Provide recommended countermeasure interventions (high-tech, low-tech, and no-tech) for the baseline security program and for the special vulnerabilities. Provide justification for each recommendation in terms of

- Criticality of the assets protected
- Probability of a loss
- Consequences of the loss
- Probable effectiveness of mitigation using recommended countermeasures
- Cost of countermeasure recommended
- Consequences on organizational operations (productivity, convenience, and business culture)

Provide a Decision Matrix if multiple options are presented. See Chapter 19: Countermeasure Selection and Budgeting Tools.

Countermeasure Implementation Recommendations

Provide a recommended countermeasure implementation phasing plan. There are two separate types of phasing programs for construction oriented projects and non-construction-oriented programs.

Construction oriented programs: For any programs that are focused on the construction of new facilities or major renovations of facilities, the countermeasure phasing program can be coordinated with the construction program. This typically follows a schedule such as

- Schematic (planning) phase: The security program planning should occur during this phase.

- Design development phase: policy development and security systems device placements planning should occur during this phase.
- Construction (bid) documents development phase: Procedures development, program development, and staff planning should occur during this phase.
- Bidding phase: Bids for systems and guard services can go out at this time.
- Construction phase: The construction of the security systems and physical security elements as well as guard staffing and training can occur during this phase.
- Project completion: Acceptance testing for systems and guard scenario training will occur during this phase.

Non-construction-oriented programs: Non-construction-oriented programs will follow the same steps, but they will be independent of coordination with a construction cycle. They will, however, need to be coordinated with ongoing operations.

Report Supplements

Risk Register

A risk register is a table that includes columns for

- Risk category
- Risk name
- Risk number
- Probability (1–3)
- Vulnerability (1–3)
- Consequences (1–3)
- Risk score ($P * V * C$) or (($P + V + C$)/3)
- Mitigation recommendation
- Contingency
- Action by
- Action when

A risk register can most easily be assembled from the data in the Vulnerability/Countermeasure Matrix (Table 20.1).

Footnotes

Reports that use ample footnotes are better received than reports that are unsupported. Footnotes give the analyst the opportunity to provide source references for statements made that might not be common public knowledge. Footnotes can also be used to define terms as they are introduced or to expand by opinion or example on a point made in the text.

Tables

The following tables are very helpful in any sizable report:

- Table of contents, including chapter numbers and chapter names, major headings, and page numbers
- Table of figures

TABLE 20.1 Risk Register

Mega LNG Terminal Risk Register

Risk Number	Risk Category	Risk Name	Probability	Vulnerability	Consequences	Risk Score	Mitigation Recommendation	Contingency	Action By	Mitigation Action When	Contingency Action When
1.1	Perimeter	Civil disorder	1	3	2	6	Coordinate with police	Close down facility	Security mgr.	Now	On appropriate intelligence
1.2	Perimeter	Car/truck bomb	1	3	3	9	K-12 security barriers & procedures	Mitigation plan	Capital projects	Phase 1	On event
1.3	Perimeter	Waterside bomb	1	3	3	9	Waterfront barrier	Patrol boats	Security committee	Immediate	Immediate
2.1	LNG Tanks	Airplane attack	1	3	3	9	Radar warning system	Mitigation plan	Capital projects	Immediate	On event
2.2	Lobby	Swarming attack	1	3	2	6	Access control system	Full height counters	Capital projects	Immediate	Immediate

Index and Glossary

Following the report text, it is useful to provide an index and glossary.

Index: Better word processors have index functions that make creating an index relatively easy. Generally, the analyst can assemble the document into a single file (if not already formatted as such) and then scan the file for key words the analyst would like to include in the index. Then, using the index function in the word processor, that word will be marked for indexing and the index function will automatically reference everywhere in the document that the word is used. Finally, the index function will alphabetize the index and add page numbers.

Glossary: It is good to define any unfamiliar or industry-specific terms used throughout the report as the term is introduced. This can be done either in the text or in footnotes, and unfamiliar terms can also be assembled in a single place in the glossary. The glossary defines key terms used in the report in a single location. The index and footnotes are also the keys to building the glossary. The glossary can be built by opening a separate word processing document named glossary and then scanning the footnotes and index for key words that you want to place in the glossary. Then go back and define each term in the glossary, using footnote references if necessary.

Attachments

I also recommend the use of supporting attachments, which could include such documents as

- Terrorism risk determination variables
- Bomb threat standoff distances
- Chemical, biological, or radiological agent threats
- Reports on any relevant terrorist or organized crime organizations
- Countermeasure budgets

Countermeasure Budget Presentation

The summary and comprehensive budgets should be presented as attachments. See Chapter 19: Countermeasure Selection and Budgeting Tools for information on how to prepare countermeasure budgets. Then insert the budget as an attachment to the report.

Microsoft PowerPoint Presentation

It is useful in most cases to prepare a PowerPoint presentation as a talking tool when presenting the risk analysis and countermeasure recommendations and budgets. When preparing the presentation, stay on the key points of the executive summary and follow that summary exactly.

Use illustrations of assets, threat actors, vulnerabilities, and risk analysis conclusions. Present an initial overview of the contents of the presentation, followed by sections and pages with each slide showing the section and the page relative to the overall contents. This helps the viewers maintain focus on the progress of the presentation.

Conclude with a questions and answers slide. Slides that help viewers maintain focus are usually of light background colors, sans-serif fonts, and coordinated colors for the headers and subject fonts. The master slide should also include page numbers (page X of XX), and it helps to have a set of section names at the bottom that change color as you move through the section, such that sections already reviewed are shown on the left and are of a lighter color, the section currently being viewed is more prominent, and sections remaining to be viewed are a lighter color to the right.

For certain clients, having your name and contact coordinates in the footer also helps them to get back to you for further comment or questions. This is especially helpful if some viewers are mid-level managers who have lots to contribute but might feel intimidated in the midst of high-level executives. Their comments can be conveyed in a supplemental report later. If you have any known disruptive attendees, supplemental comments could be unwanted.

Handouts for the Presentation

Microsoft PowerPoint has a handouts print function that provides handouts in several formats. I have found that the "three slides per page with notes beside format" is most useful as the viewer can follow along and take notes for the questions and answers section. Handouts are always best when given in color.

SUMMARY

Reports typically comprise four main documents:

- The comprehensive report
- Countermeasure budgets
- A Microsoft PowerPoint presentation
- Handouts for the presentation

Comprehensive Report

The comprehensive report is the heart of the presentation. Except for the budgets, the other documents may be viewed only briefly and superficially. The report presents all the data in two forms: summary and detailed sections. The summary should contain all the essential points of the detailed sections but in a form that is brief and easy to interpret. The detailed sections will contain the "meat" of the report and will provide the support for the conclusions, recommendations, and all statements in the summary section.

Countermeasure Budgets

Countermeasure budgets are also presented in two versions: summary and detailed spreadsheets. The summary section contains the totaled results from the detailed sections. Ideally, the detailed sections should be broken out by high-tech, low-tech, and no-tech programs and may be further broken down from those broad areas.

PowerPoint Presentation

A PowerPoint presentation is useful when presenting the risk analysis report to a group or to a high executive. PowerPoint presentations allow condensed information to be presented in a manner that is easy to digest, and they can be highly graphic. They also guide the presentation and help recipients stay on point in their comments.

Handouts for Presentation

Handouts echo the PowerPoint presentation and allow the recipients to follow along and make notes to facilitate their own memory or for later discussion.

Presentation

The client's report committee will most likely want a formal report presentation. Two types of readers review the risk analysis report: readers who skim the document and readers who read and study the detail in the document. The comprehensive report must speak to both.

Key presentation elements for success include

- Presentation should review project purposes and objectives.
- Presentation should follow a predictable outline (handouts help here).
- Stay on logical key points and not stray to irrelevant minutia.
- Make the case for any interventions (countermeasures) proposed.
- Show a budget, ideally phased by priorities.
- Answer all questions about consequences and budgets.

Graphics

Graphics are most helpful in explaining concepts and making points. Common useful graphics include

- Risk analysis process map: a graphic showing the steps of analysis
- Assets map: a list of assets by categories/criticalities
- Threat actor map: a list of threat actors, ranked
- Vulnerabilities map: a list of vulnerabilities, sorted by assets
- Risk map: V^2 graphics
- Countermeasures examples: photos of implementations and products
- Budget summary: colored graphic of budgets/phased

Preparation for a Successful Presentation

The risk analyst should prepare and present the report in a manner that will be well received by the intended recipients. This requires research into two main areas: business culture and personal biases.

- Business culture: The following types of business cultures are common:
  - Top-down: Top-down cultures are those that impose business behaviors from top management downward and impose behaviors by edict. These organizations are common in militaries and highly structured organizations that are rules driven.
  - Lateral: Lateral cultures are more democratic and sometimes chaotic. Objectives are set and achieved by consensus.

- Personal biases: Similarly, the personal biases of key recipients will largely affect the acceptance of the presentation and conclusions. Each person inherently brings three biases with them to a project:
  - Their industry's agenda
  - Their organization's agenda
  - Their personal agenda

Comprehensive Risk Analysis Report

Executive Summary

The executive summary should

- Provide a document outline, identifying the sections and their general contents
- State the project purpose and objectives
- Identify the key assets
- Identify the key threats
- Identify the key vulnerabilities
- Identify the key risks
- Identify the key countermeasure program interventions
- Present budgets
- Make recommendations

Introduction

The introduction should include:

- Project authorization
- Background statement on the project including:
  - Its location(s)
  - Project attributes (how many buildings, what types, usages, etc.)
  - Goals of the security program
- Assessment team qualifications

Assessment Process

The assessment process section can be included in the introduction or may be separate. On smaller projects, I usually combine these. This section should include

- The methodology selected
- Reasons for selecting this particular methodology (why it best fits the project: budget, completeness, appropriateness to the industry, etc.)
- Methodology process map
- Assessment process planning

Facility Characterization

Then list all of the facility assets by the following categories:

- People
  - Key executives
  - Managers and employees

- Contractors, vendors, visitors, and the public
- Property
  - Individual areas
  - Categorized by facilities and major areas of facilities
- Proprietary information
  - Information technology system
  - Special servers and mass storage
  - Paper files
  - Special information systems (building management system/security, etc.)
- Business reputation

Threat Assessment

The key elements of the threat assessment section include identification of the threat actors and the selection of a particular class of threat actor as the design basis threat.

There are five types of threat actors:

- Terrorists
- Economic criminals
- Nonterrorist violent criminals
- Subversives
- Petty criminals

The design basis threat is that class of threat actor that the proposed security program is designed to effectively counter.

Vulnerability Assessment

Vulnerability assessment involves the following steps:

- Define scenarios and evaluate specific consequences
- Evaluate effectiveness of any existing security measures
- Identify vulnerabilities and estimate the degree of vulnerability

Risk Calculation

Risk = (Probability * Vulnerability * Consequences) or ((Probability + Vulnerability + Consequences)/3). There are numerous ways to calculate risk using a variety of tools. All such methods that take these three factors into consideration will result in a useful calculation.

By performing this calculation on all the assets under consideration, the analyst can reach individual risk calculations for all those assets. These can then be ranked for severity.

Countermeasures

There are three main factors to selecting countermeasures:

- All vulnerabilities should be addressed to some extent by a comprehensive baseline security program
- Identify key assets that should receive special attention by reviewing countermeasure options, including

- High-tech options
- Low-tech options
- No-tech options
- Costs should be estimated for:
  - The baseline security program
  - Countermeasures to address key assets not adequately mitigated by the baseline security program

Countermeasure Budgets

Use the countermeasure budgeting tool or a similar tool to develop countermeasure budgets. Provide separate budgets for the baseline security program and for the special countermeasures.

Provide a budget summary sheet that identifies the key budget elements and recommended phasing.

Provide a detailed budget analysis for the baseline security program and for the special vulnerabilities.

Provide recommended countermeasure interventions (high-tech, low-tech, and no-tech) for the baseline security program and for the special vulnerabilities. Provide justification for each recommendation in terms of:

- Criticality of the assets protected
- Probability of a loss
- Consequences of the loss
- Probable effectiveness of mitigation using recommended countermeasures
- Cost of countermeasure recommended
- Consequences for organizational operations (productivity, convenience, and business culture)

Provide a Decision Matrix if multiple options are presented. See Chapter 19: Countermeasure Selection and Budgeting Tools.

Countermeasure Implementation Recommendations

Provide a recommended countermeasure implementation phasing plan. There are two separate types of phasing programs for construction oriented projects and non-construction-oriented programs.

Report Supplements

- Footnotes: Reports that use ample footnotes are better received than reports that are unsupported. Footnotes give the analyst the opportunity to provide source references for statements made that might not be common public knowledge. Footnotes can also be used to define terms as they are introduced or to expand by opinion or example on a point made in the text.
- Tables: The following tables are very helpful in any sizable report:
  - Table of contents including chapter numbers and chapter names, major headings, and page numbers
  - Table of figures
- Index and glossary

- Attachments
- Countermeasure budget presentation: The summary and comprehensive budgets should be presented as attachments. See Chapter 19: Countermeasure Selection and Budgeting Tools for information on how to prepare countermeasure budgets.
- A Microsoft PowerPoint presentation: When preparing the presentation, stay on the key points of the executive summary and follow that summary exactly. Use illustrations of assets, threat actors, vulnerabilities, and risk analysis conclusions. Conclude with a questions and answers slide.
- Handouts for the presentation: "Three slides per page with notes beside format" is most useful as the viewer can follow along and take notes for the questions and answers section.

Q&A

Questions

Q1: Which below is part of a successful risk analysis presentation?
   A. The comprehensive report, including an executive summary
   B. Countermeasure budgets
   C. A PowerPoint presentation and handouts for the presentation
   D. All of the above

Q2: Common failures in presentations include
   A. A flawed presentation.
   B. A flawed analysis.
   C. Budgets that exceed the appropriate in the context of the overall project.
   D. All of the above.

Q3: Elements of a risk analysis report *do not* include
   A. An executive summary.
   B. An introduction.
   C. An assessment process.
   D. A presentation assessment.

Q4: Elements of a risk analysis report *do not* include
   A. Facility characterization.
   B. Threat assessment.
   C. Executive compensation assessment.
   D. Vulnerability assessment.

Q5: A common Risk Assessment formula is
   A. Risk = (Likelihood * Consequences) or Risk = (Likelihood + Consequences)/2.
   B. Risk = (Probability * Vulnerability * Consequences) or ((Probability + Vulnerability + Consequences)/3).
   C. Both of the above.
   D. Neither of the above.

Q6: Qualitative analysis methods typically review many assets and then
  A. Discard most after some initial consideration, leaving relatively few assets for the final risk analysis.
  B. Discard all after some initial consideration, leaving relatively few assets for the final risk analysis.
  C. Discard none after some initial considerations.
  D. None of the above.

Q7: The combination of _____ is far better than either one alone.
  A. Both qualitative and exotative analysis
  B. Both qualitative and quantitative analysis
  C. Both qualitative and introvative analysis
  D. None of the above

Q8: Factors for selecting countermeasures include
  A. All vulnerabilities should be addressed to some extent by a comprehensive baseline security program.
  B. Identify key assets that should receive special attention by reviewing counter-measure options.
  C. Costs should be estimated for the baseline security program and countermea-sures to address key assets are adequately mitigated by the baseline security program.
  D. All of the above.

Q9: Provide a budget summary sheet that identifies
  A. The key budget elements.
  B. Recommended phasing.
  C. The key budget elements and recommended phasing.
  D. None of the above.

Q10: Provide recommended countermeasure interventions including _____ for the baseline security program and for the special vulnerabilities.
  A. High-tech
  B. Low-tech
  C. No-tech
  D. All of the above

Answers

Q1 – D, Q2 – D, Q3 – D, Q4 – C, Q5 – C, Q6 – A, Q7 – B, Q8 – D, Q9 – C, Q10 – D

Index

A

Access cards, 305
  active, 306
  bar coded, 307
  contactless smart, 307
  key fobs, 306
  magnetic stripe, 305–306
  proximity, 306
  radio frequency devices, 306–307
  TWIC, 307
  Wiegand wire cards, 306
Access control
  after-hours, 254
  card technologies, 305–306
  credential reader technologies, 306–311
  goals, 280
  and impediments to business, 291–292
  modes, 282
  policies for, 254
  program, 253–254
  restricted space, 254
  strategies, 282
  systems, 244
  types, 282
Accessibility
  posts, 255
  in vulnerability evaluation, 167, 169
Accidents, 123
Active cards, 306
AcuTech Consulting Services, 61
Administrative biases, 414
Advanced searches, 52–53
Adversary/Means Matrix, 63–64, 136,
    139, 142
  attributes, 137–138
  example, 138
  functions, 137
  objectives, 137
  purpose, 137
Adversary Sequence Diagram (ASD), 31, 64,
    66, 164, 165, 203, 367, 368–369
Aircraft, 347

Alarms
  duress, 285, 286
  false, 305, 312, 313, 314
  hold-up, 285
  nuisance, 286
  silent, 286
  systems, 245
All-hazard risk analysis
  economic criminals, 125–126
    lone criminals, 129
    organized criminal enterprises, 128
    sophisticated, 128–129
    street criminals, 129
    street gangs, 129
    transnational criminal organization, 128
    unsophisticated, 129
  nonterrorist violent workplace criminals,
    129–131
    angry visitors, 130
    deranged persons, 131
    disgruntled employee, 130
    domestic violence criminals, 129–130
    muggings/parking lot violence, 130
    robberies, 130
    sexual criminals, 130
    stalkers, 131
  petty criminals, 132
  subversives, 131–132
    cause-oriented, 131
    hackers, 131
    nonaligned, 131
    persistent rule violators, 131–132
    political and industrial spies, 131
    threat actors, invasion of privacy, 131
  terrorists, 125, 126–128
    amateur, 127
    antiterrorism reference, 128
    government-trained professional,
      126–127
    guerrilla/mercenary soldiers, 127
    radical revolutionary, 127
    religious extremist, 127

Al-Qaeda, 65, 127, 136, 140, 157, 185, 186
Amazon, 51
American Bankers Association stripe,
        305–306
Analog cameras, 320–321, 323
Analysis phase, 42
Analytic system and software for
        evaluating safeguards and security
        (ASSESS), 32
Analytical technical biases, 415
Angry visitors, 130
Animal Liberation Front, 364
Annual risk analysis, 375
Antennas, 328
Antiterrorism
    checkpoints, 333
    expenditures, 180
    reference guide, 128
API/NPRA (American Petroleum Institute/
        National Petrochemical and Refiners
        Association)
    Sandia model versus, 24, 195–198
Archiving
    immediate and long-term, 325
    redundant systems, 325
    schemes, 325
    technologies, 323–324
    video and audio, 338
ASD, see Adversary Sequence Diagram (ASD)
ASIS International's Protection of Assets
        Manual®, 57
ASIS International's Security Industry Buyers
        Guide®, 56
ASIS International's Seminar and Exhibits
        Final Program and Exhibits Guide,
        56
ASME-ITI tools, 30
ASME RAMCAP, 11
ASME RA-S, 31, 33
Assassinations, 348, 349
ASSESS, see Analytic system and software for
        evaluating safeguards and security
        (ASSESS)
Asset/Attack Matrix, 66, 136, 419
    objectives of, 137
    for vulnerability assessment, 158–159, 160
Asset Target Value Matrices, 64–66, 136,
        203–205
    Carver+Shock Matrix, 64
    Economic Crimes Asset Target Value
        Matrix, 65
    KSM Matrix, 64–65
    Petty Crimes Matrix, 66
    Subversives Matrix, 65–66

Terrorism Asset Target Value Matrixes,
        64–65
    Violent Crimes Asset Target Value
        Matrix, 65
Assets; see also Surveys
    categorization of, 29, 54
        business reputation, 48, 93
        people, 46, 92
        property, 46, 92
        proprietary information, 47, 93
    control policies, 254–255
    criticality factors of, 55–56
    diversion of, 351
    identification tools, 63
    interviews, 93–95
    list, 91–92
        facility and, 95–97
    research, 97
    in risk analysis report, 416–417
    surveys, 97–103
    theory, 91
    tools, 103–105
Attacks
    Columbine High School, 164
    cyber, 169
    detection, 285–286
    Mumbai, 157, 183, 186, 243, 330
    9/11 attacks, 184, 362–363
    objective parameters, 348–349
    scenarios, 346–348

B
Barcode cards, 307
Barcode readers, 309
Barriers, 245
    deployable, 330
    pedestrian, 330
    vehicle, 330
Baseline security program, 138, 216, 421–422
    countermeasures, 301–302
    deterrence package, 332–336
    elements, 301–303
Bedford/St. Martin's, 51
Best practices, 231
Bhutto, Benazir, 169
Bibliography building, 56
Biometric reader technologies, 310
    advantages, 311
    applications of, 310–311
    description and application, 310
    disadvantages, 311
    exploits, 311
Bistatic microwave detection systems, 312–313
Black September, 126, 182

Bookmarking, 56
Border security, 269
Budget, 423; *see also* Cost-effectiveness
    decisions, 218–219
    phases, 398, 403
    risk rankings and, 398, 402
Burglary, 350, 363
Business culture
    complying with, 290–291
    and policy development, 235
    and presentations, 412, 414
Business organizations
    functional organization chart, 46, 99
    hours of operation, 99, 101, 254
    impediments to operation, 291–292
    mission statement, 45, 46, 94
    productivity, 235
Business reputation, 93
    characterizing, 48, 391
    crimes against, 366

C
Cameras, *see* Video detection systems
CAP Index Inc.®, 187, 202
Capacitance detection systems, 311–312
CARVER+Shock, 31, 33, 64, 184–185
Castro, Fidel, 78
Casualties, 208
CAT 5/6 network, 326
Cause-oriented subversives, 131, 364
CCTV, *see* Closed-circuit television (CCTV)
CEE, *see* Countermeasure Effectiveness
        Estimate (CEE), 373
CFATS, *see* Chemical Facility Anti-Terrorism
        Standards (CFATS)
Chemical Facility Anti-Terrorism Standards
        (CFATS), 33–34, 270
Chemical security assessment tool (CSAT), 34
Chemical security, 270
Chemical weapons, 251
CIKT, *see* Critical infrastructure and key
        resources (CIKR)
Circulation Path/Threat Nexus Matrix, 66,
        203, 207
Circulation Path/Weapons Nexus Matrix, 66,
        203, 207
Civil disorder, 364
Closed, structured response interview, 49
Closed-circuit television (CCTV), 345, 351,
        363, 372, 385
Columbine High School attack, 164
Commercial security intelligence services,
        334–335
Commercial software programs, 26

Communications systems, 244, 287–288, 302
Community versus facility methodologies, 32
Complete Cost-Effectiveness Matrix, 393
    budget breakdowns by phases and risks,
        402, 403–405
    countermeasure costs, 398, 400
    countermeasure mitigation values, 398, 401
    elements, 393–396
    horizontal elements, 393, 395, 396, 398
    phase recommendations and budgets,
        398, 403
    risk descriptions, 398, 399
    risk ranking and budgets, 398, 402
    summary board, 393, 396
    vertical elements, 393, 396, 397
Consequence
    and budgeting, 384
    components, 208
    criticality and, 109–118
    definition, 109
    and degree of response, 371
    and risk prioritization, 216, 217
    variables, 27
    visualization, 111–112
Consequence analysis, 14, 28, 29, 112, 113
    criticality and, 109–118
Consequence Matrix, 113, 142
Consoles and management offices, 322–323
Construction oriented programs, 423–424
Contactless smart card readers, 307,
        308–309
Contractors, 46, 99
    background checks, 253–254
    vetting of, 100
Control points, 236
Cost-benefit analysis, 60
Cost-effectiveness; *see also* Complete Cost-
        Effectiveness Matrix
    basis of argument, 391–392
    calculation methods, 386–389
    countering arguments, 392–393
    developing arguments, 390–391
    limitations of metrics, 382–386
    making the case, 389–391
    metric limitations, 382
    recommendations summary board, 396
Costs
    of asset replacement, 112
    and risk prioritization, 217–218
    of software programs, 8, 41
    training, 24
Countermeasure budgets, 411
Countermeasure Decision Matrix, 16,
        353–354

Countermeasure Effectiveness Estimate
    (CEE), 373
Countermeasure Effectiveness Matrix,
    372–373
Countermeasure Matrix, 369–373
Countermeasure mitigation values, 398, 401
Countermeasure options analysis tool, 16
Countermeasure selection, 305
    for assessment of threat, 286–287
    consensus of decision makers, 353–354
    cost-benefit analysis, 60
    for criminal offenders, 351–352
    for deterrence, 283–284
    elements of protection, 60
    and exploits, 305
    threat action response, 288–289
    types, 59
Countermeasures, 3–4; see also Access control;
    Countermeasure selection; Detection
    baseline, 301–302
    complaints about, 233–234
    criminal threat, 344
    defining, 232–233
    effectiveness metrics, 344, 352
    functions of, 344–346, 281
    goals of, 244, 249–250, 280
    hierarchy, 248
    hi-tech elements, 244–245
    implementation objectives, 280
    legal challenges to, 233
    low-tech elements, 244, 245
    no-tech elements, 244, 245–247
    research, 56–57
    in risk analysis report, 421–424
        baseline security program, 421–422
        budgets, developing, 423
        implementation recommendations,
            423–424
        key assets, 422–423
    role of, 244–247
    special, 246, 251–252
    supporting policies, 232–233, 247–248
    terrorist threat, 345
Countersurveillance program, 251, 253
CPTED, see Crime prevention through
    environmental design (CPTED)
    program
Credential readers, types of, 307–308
Crime
    economic, 363–364
    incident likelihood estimates, 186–189
    investigations, 253
    organized, 183
    prevention policies, 252–253

Crime prevention through environmental
    design (CPTED) program, 59, 244,
    245, 292, 297, 372
Criminals
    domestic violent, 129–130
    economic, 125–126, 128–129, 183–184,
        350–351
    information technology, 184
    lone, 129
    nonterrorist violent workplace criminals,
        126, 129–131
    organized, 128
    petty, 126, 365–366
    sexual, 130
    sophisticated, 128–129, 368–369
    street, 129
    unsophisticated, 129, 369
    violent offender types, 349–350
Crisis management policy, 271, 272
Critical infrastructure and key resources
    (CIKR), 23, 24
Critical Infrastructure Information Act, 268
Critical thinking, 5
    analysis requires, 73–74
    applying, to risk analysis, 83–84
        analysis process, 85
        inductive versus deductive reasoning,
            84–85
    concepts and goals of, 76
    economic, 363–364
    elements of, 75–76, 77–81
        concepts, 75, 81
        gather assumptions, 75, 79
        gather information, 75, 79–80
        implications and consequences, 75,
            80–81
        interpretation and inference, 75, 81
        point of view, 75, 78–79
        purpose, 75, 77
        question at issue, 75, 78
    importance of, 71–73, 82–83
    intellectual traits for, 82
    overview of, 71
    principles of, 76–77
    pseudocritical thinking, 82
    root of problems, 85–86
    website, 85
Criticalities And Consequence Matrix,
    55–56, 63
    building your own, 113
    instructions, 113–117
Criticality
    analysis, 28, 29
    consequence versus, 109–110

definition, 109
intrinsic, 111
measures of, 110–111, 112
to operations, 111
and risk prioritization, 216–217
scale for, 112
to sustainability, 111
visualization, 111–112
CSAT, *see* Chemical security assessment tool
(CSAT)

D

Data crunching, 58
Data gathering, 6, 44–48
assets by classification, 46–48
existing countermeasures, 48
interviews, 45
organization's mission statement, 45–46
organization's programs, 46
types of data required, 45
Data mining, 58
Day/night imagers, 320
DBT, *see* Design basis threat (DBT)
Decision Matrix, 9, 219, 354
Deductive versus inductive reasoning, 84–85,
147
deductive reasoning, 147
inductive context, 148
inductive reasoning, 147–148
predictive threat analysis, 148
Deliveries, 255
Department of Homeland Security (DHS), 5,
10, 21–22, 24, 41, 191, 195, 268
on information sharing, 269
on preparedness, 270
on prevention, 269
risk assessment methodologies, 30–32
regulations from, 268–270
tools, 30, 31
Deployable vehicle barriers, 330
Deranged persons, 131
Descriptive statistics, 123
Design basis threat (DBT), 64, 132–133
Detection; *see also* Detectors; Video detection
systems
assessment of threat, 286–287
building perimeter, 313–314
capacitance systems, 311–312
confirmation, 286
door position switches, 313–314
goals, 284–285
interior space, 314–315
intrusion, 285
property perimeter, 311–312

seismic systems, 312
surveillance, 285
Detectors
factors, 371
fibre optic, 312
ground-based radar, 312
infrared, 313, 314, 315
laser light beams, 313
microwave, 312–313
photoelectric beam, 314
pneumatic underground, 313
Deterrence
goals, 284–285
program, 332
strategies, 285–286
Digital cameras, 321
Digital fish-eye PTZ cameras, 321
Digital storage solutions, 324
Digital video recorders, 323
Digital video servers, 324
Directional antennas, 328
Disaster recovery program, 102
Disgruntled employee, 130
Diversion, 351
Document theft, 351
Domestic violent criminals, 129–130
Door position switches, 313–314
Drop-bolt locks, 329
Dual-technology sensors, 315
Duress alarms, 316
Dyadem International Ltd, 61

E

Economic crime, 363–364
Economic Crimes Asset Target Value Matrix,
65, 187, 191
Economic Crimes Matrix, 205
Economic criminals, 125–126, 128–129,
183–184, 350–351
Egocentric biases, 415
Electrified cylinder locks, 329
Electrified mortise locks, 328
Electrified panic hardware (EPH), 328
Electronic turnstiles, 329
Elements, of critical thinking
concepts, 75, 81
gather assumptions, 75, 79
gather information, 75, 79–80
implications and consequences, 75,
80–81
interpretation and inference, 75, 81
point of view, 75, 78–79
purpose, 75, 77
question at issue, 75, 78

Embezzlement, 350
Emergency management program, 102
Emergency security plans, 256–257
Emergency services liaison program, 336
Emotional suffering, 85–86
Employees
    background checks, 253–254
    business reputation characterization, 48
    disgruntled, 130
Employment regulations, 270
Enron, 366
Entry methods, 140–141
Environment
    context of surveys, 97–98
    safe and secure, 292, 297
    security hazards, 122
Environmental Liberation Front, 364
EPH, *see* Electrified panic hardware
        (EPH), 328
Equipment
    control policies, 254
    security hardware, 254
Escort systems, 252
Evidence gathering; *see also* Research and
        evidence gathering
    goals, 289
    program, 338
    for prosecution, 383
    strategies, 289–290
    tools for, 383
Executive biases, 414
Existing security measures, evaluating,
        170–171
    electronic countermeasures, 170
    operational countermeasures, 171
    physical countermeasures, 170
Explosive detection, 316
    advantages, 317
    description and application, 316–317
    disadvantages, 317–318
    exploits, 318–319
    screening, 251
    under vehicle inspection, 348
    visual inspection systems, 318

F
Facility characterization, 416–417, 429–430
False alarms, 312, 313, 314, 315, 316
FEMA 386-7, 30
FEMA-426, 30
FEMA-452, 30, 31
Fiber channel, 325
Fiber-optic cable, 327
Fiber-optic detection systems, 312

5.8 GHz, 327–328
Firefox, 56
Fixed video cameras, 319
Force Protection Exhibition and
        Demonstration (FPED), 128
FPED, *see* Force Protection Exhibition and
        Demonstration (FPED)
Full-scale Sandia process, 32–33

G
Gangs, 129
Garcia, Mary Lynn, 359
Glass break detectors, 314
Google, 51, 52, 56
Goslin, Charles, 146
Graphics, 412
Grenades, 347, 348
Guards, 255–256, 336–337
Guided interview, 49
Gunaratna, Rohan, 157

H
Hackers, 131, 365
Hand inspection, 317, 318
Harris, Eric David, 164
Hazards, 121
    safety, 122
    security, 122
    threat versus, 121
Health Insurance Portability and
        Accountability Act (HIPPA), 268
Hearst, Patricia, 127
Highbeam Research, 51, 52, 53
High-security electric locks, 329
High-tech (electronic) countermeasures, 59
Hijacking, 347
HIPPA, *see* Health Insurance Portability and
        Accountability Act (HIPPA)
Home security program, 385
Homeland Security Act of 2002, 23
Hostages, 347

I
IEDs (improvised explosive devices), 347
Incendiaries, 348
Incident reporting, 253
Inductive context, 148
Inductive versus deductive reasoning,
        84–85, 145
    deductive reasoning, 147
    inductive context, 148
    inductive reasoning, 147–148
    predictive threat analysis, 148
Infiltration and attack vulnerabilities, 162

Infiltration scenarios, 346
Informal, conversational interview, 49
Information security, policy protection and, 254
Information sharing, 269
Information technology
    criminals, 184
    proprietary information and, 43
    security programs, 244
Information theft, 351
Infrared and laser detection system, 313
Infrared detection sensors, 315
Insider crimes, 363–364
Integrated Security Systems Design (Norman), 289, 328
Intellectual traits, for critical thinking, 82
Intelligence
    analysis, 72, 84, 102
    news connections, 335–336
    program, 102, 253
    sources, 335
International Association for Counterterrorism and Security Professionals, 128
Internet research, 51–53
Interviews
    conducting, 48, 50
    follow-up, 50–51
    for organization's assets, 93–95
    preparation for, 49
    question types, 49
    sequence of questions, 50
    types of, 49
    wording of question, 50
Intrinsic criticality, 111
Intrinsic vulnerabilities, 169
Intrusion threat actors, 368–369
Invasion of privacy, 365
Investigations, 253
    follow-up, 249, 338
    program, 102, 253, 334
Investigative Project on Terrorism, 202, 335
ISO 31000, 25, 38, 179, 201

J
Jane's World Insurgency and Terrorism Portal, 335
JCATS, *see* Joint combat and tactical simulation (JCATS)
Johnson & Johnson, 366
Joint combat and tactical simulation (JCATS), 32

K
Kennedy, Robert, 78, 162
Keypad readers, 309

Khalid Sheikh Mohammed (KSM)-Asset Target Value for Terrorism Matrix, 135–136
Khrushchev, Nikita, 78
KSM Matrix, 64–65
KSM-Asset Target Value Model, 185–186
Ku Klux Klan, 127

L
Laser communications, 328
Lashkar-e-Taiba, 157
Law enforcement liaison program, 102, 253
Lexis/Nexis, 51
Licensed versus unlicensed options, 327
Lighting, 245, 330–331
Likelihood (probability), 179
    assessment, 28, 240
    calculation, 420
Likelihood variables, 27
Loading docks, 254
Locks, 245
    delayed egress, 328–329
    drop-bolt, 329
    electrified cylinder, 329
    electrified mortise, 328
    electrified panic hardware, 328
    high-security electric, 329
    and key control, 254
    magnetic, 328
    power/fire alarm supervision, 329
Lone criminals, 129
Long-range card readers, 309
Los Angeles Police Department, 364
Losses
    by asset, 208
    severity ranking, 28
Low-tech countermeasures solutions, 59
Low-tech elements, 328–332
    deployable barriers, 330
    lighting, 330–331
    locks, 328–329
    mechanical and electronic turnstiles, 329
    revolving doors, 329
    signage, 331–332
    vehicle gates, 330

M
Magnetic locks, 328
Magnetic stripe cards, 305–306, 308
Mail recipients, 255
Mail rooms, 100, 254
Management
    business reputation violations, 253
    policy backing, 234

priorities, 218
priority of security program, 102–103
senior, 48, 94, 95, 112
Maritime Transportation Security Act
    (MTSA), 307
Marriot Hotel, Pakistan, 363
McAfee®, 51
McVeigh, Timothy, 127
Mechanical turnstiles, 329
Mentally unstable offenders, 349–350
Microsoft Excel, 8, 62, 63, 41, 42, 61,
    158–159, 165
Microwave communications, 328
Microwave detection systems, 314–315
*Military Studies in the Jihad against the
    Tyrants*, 156
Millimeter wave scanner, 317, 318
Mission statements, 45–46
MOM, *see* Motive, Opportunity and Means
    (MOM)
Monostatic microwave detection systems, 312
Moore, David A., 61
Moore, David T., 78
Mossad, Israeli, 127
Motive, Opportunity and Means (MOM), 135
Moving shooters, 345, 346
MTSA, *see* Maritime Transportation Security
    Act (MTSA)
Muggings/parking lot violence, 130
Multi-mode fiber, 327

N
Nance, Malcolm W., 128, 134, 135, 136
NAS, *see* Network attached storage (NAS)
National Environmental Policy Act
    (NEPA), 268
National Fire Protection Association
    (NFPA), 62
National Infrastructure Protection Plan
    (NIPP), 23–24, 268
National Technical Information Service
    (NTIS), 335
Natural countermeasures, 169–170
Natural hazards, 122, 123
NEFA Foundation, 335
NEPA, *see* National Environmental Policy Act
    (NEPA)
Network attached storage (NAS), 324
NFPA, *see* National Fire Protection
    Association (NFPA)
900 MHz, 328
NIPP, *see* National Infrastructure Protection
    Plan (NIPP)
NIST 780 methodology, 24, 25, 33

NIST 780—SVA-Pro (Dyadem), 31
Nonaligned subversives, 131, 364
Non-construction-oriented programs, 424
Nonterrorist violent workplace criminals, 126,
    129–131
No-tech countermeasures solutions, 59
No-tech elements, 332–338
NTIS, *see* National Technical Information
    Service (NTIS)
Nuclear facilities, 359

O
Occupational Safety and Health Act (OSHA)
    Section 1910, 31
Offender characteristics, 134
Omnidirectional antennas, 328
Open Source Center (OSC), 335
Open-ended interview, 49
Organizational context, of surveys, 99–100
    functional organization chart, 99
    organizational elements, 99–100
Organization's mission statement, 44,
    45–46, 414
Organized criminal enterprises, 128
OSC, *see* Open Source Center (OSC)
OSHA, *see* Occupational Safety and Health
    Act (OSHA) Section 1910
Oswald, Lee Harvey, 162
Outdoor passive infrared detectors, 314

P
Pakistan suicide attack, 363
Palestinian Al-Fatah organization, 126
Palestinian Liberation Organization Black
    September movement, 126
Parking
    access control, 254
    lighting, 100
    lot violence, 130
Path analysis, 164
Patrol logs, 374–375
Patrols, 252, 255
Pedestrian barriers, 330
Persistent rule violators, 131–132, 365
Personal biases, presentations and, 414–415
Petty Crimes Matrix, 66
Petty criminals, 126, 365–366
Photo ID badging, 306, 311, 323
Photoelectric beam detectors, 314
Pinhole video cameras, 320
Pneumatic underground detection
    systems, 313
Point detection systems, 316
Policies, 229; *see also* Policy development

access control, 254
asset protection, 254–255
for authorities and responsibilities,
    250–251
benefits of having, 234–235
and business culture, 235
and business productivity, 235
circumvention, 235
compliance, 230, 234
control factors, 235–236
crime prevention, 252–253
emergency security plans, 256–257
enforceability, 234, 235
goals of, 248–249
individual responsibilities, 255
maintenance, 251
and procedures, 230–231
for protection of life, 251
role of, 243
in support of countermeasures, 232–234,
    247–248
theory, 241–243
violations, 253
for VIPs, 256
Policy development
basic policies, 266–267
change triggers, 263–264
impact statements, 264–265
implementation guidelines, 267–268
nonregulatory-driven, 270–272
process steps, 265–266
regulatory-driven, 268–270
request review, 264
requirements, 266
review process, 264
Political and industrial spies, 131, 364
Position paper, 232
Posts, 101, 255, 267, 332–333
Potential threat actors, 125–126, 133, 279,
    280, 283
PowerPoint presentations, 411, 426–427
Predictive risk example, 148
Predictive threat analysis, 148
Predictive threat assessment, 145–147
Preparedness, 248, 270
Presentations, 426–427
and business culture, 412, 414
handouts, 411–412, 427
key elements, 412
and personal biases, 414–415
preparation, 412, 414–415
Probability, 26, 27, 179–189
of criminal incidents, 186–189
criminal threat actors, 183–184

economic crime, 187
factors, 199–200, 201
likelihood, 179–181
nonterrorism violent crime, 187–188
petty crimes, 188–189
range of threat actors, 181–184
terrorism estimates, 181, 184–186
terrorist threat actors, 181–183
using criminal statistics, 186–187
Probability Summary Matrix, 205, 206
Problem solving
critical thinking and, 76, 77, 78
and policies, 230
Procedures, 230, 231–232
changes in, 264
Procedures for Handling Protected Critical
    Infrastructure Information Act, 268
Process-driven cost prioritization, 218
Professionalism, 140
Property
building type, 98
context of surveys, 98
control policies, 255
lost and found policy, 255
Property perimeter detection systems, 311–313
Proximity cards, 306
Pseudocritical thinking, 82
PTZ video cameras, 319–320
Purdue University's CORE, 51

Q
Qualitative analysis, 58–59, 171–172
converting quantitative data into, 59
quantitative analysis versus, 5–8
vulnerability assessment, 171–172
Quantitative analysis, 57–58, 168
converting qualitative data into, 59
qualitative analysis versus, 5–8
Questia, 51
Questions
sequence of, 50
types of, 49
wording of, 50

R
Radio frequency devices, 306–307
Rafic Al Hariri, 162
RAM (Risk Assessment Methodology), 24,
    25, 30
API/NPRA versus, 195–198
security effectiveness, 359–361
RAMCAP framework, 33
RAMCAP™, 30
RAMCAP Plus—ASME software tool, 31

RAMCAP Plus®, 62
Rand Research, 51
REAPS technologies, 289
Records research, 53
Redundant archiving schemes, 325
Reports; *see also* Presentations; Risk analysis
        report
    comprehensive, 411
    documents of, 411–412
    graphics, 412
    incident, 248–249
    post and patrol, 252–253
    writing, 5, 7, 44, 60, 140
Research and evidence gathering, 48
    for asset characterization, 97
    asset classifications, 54
    bibliography building, 56
    countermeasures research, 56–57
    criticalities and consequences assessment,
        55–56
    historical data relating to security
        events, 54
    Internet research, 51–53
    interviews, 48–51
    for prosecution, 386
    records research, 53
    surveys, 53–54
    telephone research, 53
Response
    and consequences, 371
    degree of, 371
    goals, 288
    program, 336–337
    regulations, 270
    strategies, 288–289
    training requirements, 337
Revolving doors, 329
Riots, 364
Risk
    analyzing, 13
    calculation, 208–209, 420–421
    definition, 12
    degree of, 27
    descriptions, 398, 399
    eliminating, 13
    factors, 28
    mitigating, 13
    organizations care about, 13
    types of, 12
Risk analysis, 3, 10
    annual, 375
    basics, 26–27
    for facilities and structures, 22–23
    methodologies, 10–11, 27

qualitative versus quantitative analysis, 5–6
    required skills, 6–8, 18
    tools, 8
    principles, 10
    process, 199–203, 413
    report, 14
    tools, 15–16, 26, 18, 41
Risk analysis report, 411; *see also*
        Presentations
    assessment process, 416
    attachments, 426
    countermeasure budget presentation, 426
    countermeasures, 421–424
    executive summary, 415–416
    facility characterization, 416–417
    footnotes, 424
    glossary, 426
    index, 426
    introduction, 416
    PowerPoint presentation, 426–427
    risk register, 424, 425
    tables, 424
    threat assessment, 417–418
    vulnerability assessment, 418–421
    writing, 5–6
Risk assessment, 4, 14, 28
    codes and standards, 30–32
    checklists, 14–15
    deliverables, 42–43
    objectives, 195–199
    phases, 42–43
    practice, 13–15
    programs, 24
    science of, 4
    steps involved in, 28–32
    theory, 12–13
    tools, 8, 15–16, 18, 41
Risk assessment methodologies, 13–14,
        22–23, 24
    ASME RA-S, 33
    CARVER+Shock, 33
    CFATS information, 33–34
    community versus facility, 32
    CSAT Security Vulnerability
        Assessment, 35
    CSAT top screen, 34–35
    Full-scale Sandia process, 32–33
    NIST 780, 33
    RAMCAP framework, 33
    strengths and weaknesses of, 32–34
Risk formula, 26, 30
    basic, 179
    calculation steps, 208–209
    displaying results, 196–198

mathematical result versus
relationship, 195
sorted results, 220
unranked results, 209
used by Homeland Security, 179
Risk management, 14, 29
Risk mitigation programs, 11
Risk prioritization, 14, 29
best practices, 219–221
and communication, 218–219
by consequences, 216–217
by cost, 217–218
criteria, 215
by criticality, 217
by formula, 216
natural prioritization, 216
by probability, 217
Risk register, 424, 425
RiskWatch software, 62
Robbery, 130, 350
Rockefeller, John D., 111
Ruby, Jack, 162
Rudolph, Eric Robert, 127

S
Saboteurs, 364–365
Safe and secure environment, 297
SAFETY Act, *see* Support Anti-Terrorism
by Fostering Effective Technologies
(SAFETY Act)
Safety hazards, 122
SAN, *see* Storage area network (SAN)
Sandia model, 30, 31, 359–361
Sandia National Laboratories, 24, 25, 30, 33
Sarbanes-Oxley (SOX) Act of 2002, 269
SATA, 324, 325
SAVI, *see* Systematic analysis of vulnerability
to intrusion (SAVI)
Scramble keypad readers, 309–310
SCSI, 324, 325
Security
archiving technologies, 323–324
awareness program, 102, 252, 333
budget decision makers, 361
checkpoints, 234, 283
context, of surveys
lighting levels, 100
physical security vulnerabilities, 100
security organization, 101–103
security zones, 100–101
digital infrastructures, 326
hazards, 122
safety guidances and, 333
way-finding signage and, 333

Security command, control, and
communications (C^3), 322
Security controls
policies, 235
technical versus staff, 235–236
Security effectiveness
commercial model, 361–362
information needed,366–367
metrics for, 367–375
theory, 359
users of metrics, 361–362
using Sandia model, 359–361
Security events
assessing, 249
detect, 249
evidence of, 250
historical data relating to, 54
logs, 374
reporting and follow-up, 249
response to, 250
Security Industry Buyer's Guide, 56
Security intelligence program, 253, 334
Security investigations program, 334
Security management, 234, 266
offices, 323
qualification, 101
responsibilities, 250
training, 101, 102
Security officers
arming, 249
challenges by users, 233–234
counseling role, 249
performance evaluation, 235
policies for, 255
professionalism, 248
training, 235
Security patrols, 255, 333
Security posts, 255, 332–333
Security programs
auditing, 248
awareness, 102
charter, 250
development, 229
disaster recovery, 102
emergency management, 102
information technology, 103
intelligence, 102
investigations, 102
law enforcement liaison, 102
managers, 361
metrics, 234
patrols, 101
photo ID badging, 102
posts, 101

priority to upper management, 102–103
recommendations summary board, 396
role of policies, 243
surveys, 97–103
Security risk analysis
    skills
        countermeasures selection, 44, 59–60
        critical thinking, 43, 57
        data gathering, 43, 44–48
        qualitative analysis, 43–44, 58–59
        quantitative analysis, 43, 57–58
        report writing, 44, 60
        research and evidence gathering, 43,
            48–57
    tools, 44, 61–67
Security risk management, 4, 125
Security staff, 337
Security system
    antennas, 328
    archiving schemes, 325
    archiving technologies, 323–324
    infrastructures, 326–328
    licensed versus unlicensed options, 327
Security unit chief, 250, 265–266
Security warning signage, 332
Seismic detection systems, 312
Server-based archivers, 323
Sexual criminals, 130
Shipping/receiving docks, 255
Shooters, 346
Shoplifting, 351
Shrinkage, 351
Signage, 245, 331–332
Simple cost prioritization, 217
Single-mode fiber, 327
Snipers, 346
Software, 5, 33, 151
    commercially available tools, 26, 36
    DHS approved, 21
    economical, 61
    for report writing, 60–67
    Sandia, 31–32
Solid state storage, 325
Sophisticated criminals, 128–129, 368–369
Sorted Risk Matrix, 67
SOX Act of 2002, see Sarbanes-Oxley (SOX)
    Act of 2002
Stakeholders, 218, 390
Stalkers, 131
Standard Oil Company, 111
Standard proximity readers, 308
Standoff weapons, 346–347
Stationary shooters, 346
Statistics

crime, 186–187, 202
descriptive, 123
of historical data, 64, 123, 202
Storage area network (SAN), 324
Storage media, 323–324
Street criminals, 129
Street gangs, 129
Subject matter expert analysis, 257, 265–266
Subversives, 126, 364–365
Subversives and Petty Crimes Matrix, 205
Subversives Matrix, 65–66
Suicide bombers, 347
Support Anti-Terrorism by Fostering Effective
    Technologies (SAFETY Act), 268
Surveillance
    detection, 285
    opportunities, 207, 420
Surveillance Matrix, 66, 207
Surveillance Opportunities Matrix, 164–167
Survey points, 168
Surveys, 53–54
    day and night, 54, 55
    deliverables, 42
    environmental context, 97–98
    files, 54
    notes, 53–54
    organizational context, 99–100
    photos/video, 54
    property context, 98
    security context, 100–103
    for vulnerability, 168
SVA-Pro, 61–62, 137, 159, 164
Symbionese Liberation Army, 126
Systematic analysis of vulnerability to
    intrusion (SAVI), 31

T
Tactical technical biases, 415
Tape and DVD storage, 325
Target selection
    and area of operation, 201
    CARVER method, 184–185
    information, 201
    KSM-Asset Target Value Model, 185–186
    terrorism, 201–202
    tool for Special Forces, 184–185
    variables, 27
Technical biases, 414–415
Telephone research, 53
Terrorism, 157, 304, 335; see also Target
    selection
    antiterrorism reference guides and
        resources, 128
    and asset target value estimates, 184–186

attack scenarios, 141, 202, 362–363
objectives, 348–349
probability estimates, 181
threat actors, 181–183
Terrorism Asset Target Value Matrixes, 64–65
Terrorism Awareness and Education as a Prevention Strategy for First Responders, 134
Terrorist, 125
amateur, 127, 182
classes of, 126–127
government-trained, 125, 126–127, 181–182
guerrilla/mercenary soldier, 127, 182
radical revolutionary, 125, 127, 182
religious extremists, 127, 182
targeteering, 135
Terrorist Recognition Handbook, 128, 134, 136
Theft
of information, 351
internal, 350
risk, 180
Thermal imaging cameras, 321–322
Thermal imaging sensors, 316
Threat, 26, 125
access to types of weapons, 140
accidents, 123
all-hazard risk analysis (*see* All-hazard risk analysis)
analysis, 121, 148
assessing, 133–136
and countermeasure functions, 344
entry methods, 140–141
hazards versus, 121
inductive versus deductive reasoning, 147–148
matrix set up, 141–142
natural hazards, 122–123
predictive risk example, 148
predictive threat assessment, 145–147
professionalism, 140
safety hazards, 122
security analysts, 123–124
threat scenarios, 141
tools, 136–138
variables, 27
Threat action, accessibility as key to, 169
Threat actors, 12–13, 125–126, 155
design programs to mitigate, 297
invasion of privacy, 131, 365
range of, 181–184
surveilling, 165
types, 181–184, 417–418

Threat assessment, 14, 17, 29, 74, 417–418
Threat identification, 14, 28, 29, 201
Threat/Target Nexus Matrix, 159, 161, 162, 419
TME, *see* Total Mitigation Estimate (TME)
Tools
for asset characterization and identification, 103–105
assets and consequences, 63
asset list, 63
criticalities and consequence matrix, 63
probability (likelihood) assessment, 63–66
Adversary/Means Matrix, 63–64
adversary sequence diagram, 64
Asset Target Value Matrixes, 64–66
for risk analysis reports, 8, 44, 61–67
affordable tools examples, 62–67
commercially available software tools, 61–62
lesser software tools, 62
vulnerability assessment, 66–67, 207–208
Adversary Sequence Diagram, 66
Asset/Attack Matrix, 66
Circulation Path/Threat Nexus, 66
Circulation Path/Weapons Nexus, 66
Surveillance Matrix, 66
Vulnerability Matrix, 66–67
Total Mitigation Estimate (TME), 373
Training
continuing education, 101
costs, 24
department managers, 103
in intelligence analysis, 102
in investigations, 102
need for, 26
and policies, 235
security management, 101
security officers, 234, 255
Transnational criminal organizations, 128
Transportation Worker Identification Credential (TWIC) cards, 307
Travel security, 269–270
Turnstiles, 329
TWIC, *see* Transportation Worker Identification Credential (TWIC) cards
2.4 GHz, 327
Tylenol tampering, 366

U
Ultrasonic sensors, 315–316
Under-vehicle mirrors, 317, 318
Under-vehicle video detection systems, 317, 318

University of California, Irvine: Criminology, Law and Society, 51
Unranked risk results, 209
Unsophisticated criminals, 129, 369
Unsorted risk matrix, 67
U.S. Coast Guard, 24
U.S. Department of Health and Human Services, 268
U.S. Department of Homeland Security (DHS), *see* Department of Homeland Security (DHS)

V
Vandals, 365
VBIEDs (Vehicle-Borne Improvised Explosive Devices), 347, 348
Vehicles
  gates, 330
  parking control, 254
Verbal guidance, 333–334
Veteran security analysts, 15–16
Video analytics software, 322
Video and audio archiving elements, 338
Video detection systems, 319–322
  analog cameras, 320–321
  day/night imagers, 320
  digital cameras, 321
  digital fish-eye PTZ cameras, 321
  fixed video cameras, 319
  pinhole video cameras, 320
  PTZ video cameras, 319–320
  thermal imaging cameras, 321–322
  video analytics, 322
  visible light cameras, 319
Video surveillance, 244, 285, 294
Violations
  categorizing, 253
  handling of, 266
  safety, 122, 253
  spotting, 374–375
Violent crime
  probability, 187–188
  in workplace, 129–131
Violent Crimes Asset Target Value Matrix, 65
Violent Crimes Matrix, 205
VIP protection
  circulation paths, 162
  policies, 256
Virtual local area networks (VLANs), 326
Visible light cameras, 319
Visualization, 111–112
VLANs, *see* Virtual local area networks (VLANs)
V² Matrix, 67, 198, 220, 221

Vulnerability, 26
  analysis, 14, 28, 29
  calculation spreadsheet, 171
  definition, 155
  detail matrix, 173
  detail spreadsheet, 173
  evaluation, 167
  listing, 176
  matrix, 172
  spotting, 374–375
  survey, 167–168
  variables, 27, 29
Vulnerability assessment, 155, 205–209
  antiterrorism, 158
  components, 205–207
  effective process of, 158–159
  evaluating, 167
    determine accessibility, 169
    existing security measures, effectiveness of, 170–171
    intrinsic vulnerabilities, 169
    natural countermeasures, 169–170
    qualitative analysis section, 171–173
    quantitative analysis matrixes, 168
    survey points, 168
    vulnerability calculation spreadsheet, 171
    vulnerability detail matrix, 173
    vulnerability detail spreadsheet, 173
  model, 156
  in risk analysis report, 418–421
  scenarios and evaluate specific consequences, 156
    adversary sequence diagrams and path analysis, 164
    Asset/Attack Matrix, 159
    Surveillance Opportunities Matrix, 164–167
    Threat/Target Nexus Matrix, 159–162
    Weapons/Target Nexus Matrix, 162–164
  tools, 207–208
    adversary sequence diagram, 66
    Asset/Attack Matrix, 66
    Circulation Path/Threat Nexus, 66
    Circulation Path/Weapons Nexus, 66
    quantitative analysis, 207
    Surveillance Matrix, 66
    Vulnerability Matrix, 66–67
Vulnerability Assessment of Physical Protection Systems (Garcia), 359
Vulnerability/Countermeasure Matrix, 369–373
Vulnerability Detail Matrix, 173
Vulnerability Matrix, 66–67, 207–208

W

Watercraft, 348
Way-finding signage, 331–332
Weapons
  access to types of, 140
  policies, 251, 255
  screening, 251
  standoff, 346
  in workplace, 251, 255
Weapons/Target Nexus Matrix, 162–164, 419
Welch, Alicia L., 134, 135
Wiegand swipe readers, 308
Wiegand wire cards, 306
WiMax, 328

Wired infrastructures, 326
Wireless options, 327
Witness statements, 338
WNC, *see* World News Connection (WNC)
Workplace
  illegal substances, 255
  personal security, 255
  screening, 251
  violence, 364
  violence threat actors, 129–130
  weapons in, 251, 255
World News Connection (WNC), 335
World Trade Center, 363
World Trade Organization, 131, 364